F 1435 .M44 G73 2002
Graham, Ian, 1923-
Alfred Maudslay and the Maya
a biography / Ian Graham.

Alfred Maudslay and the Maya

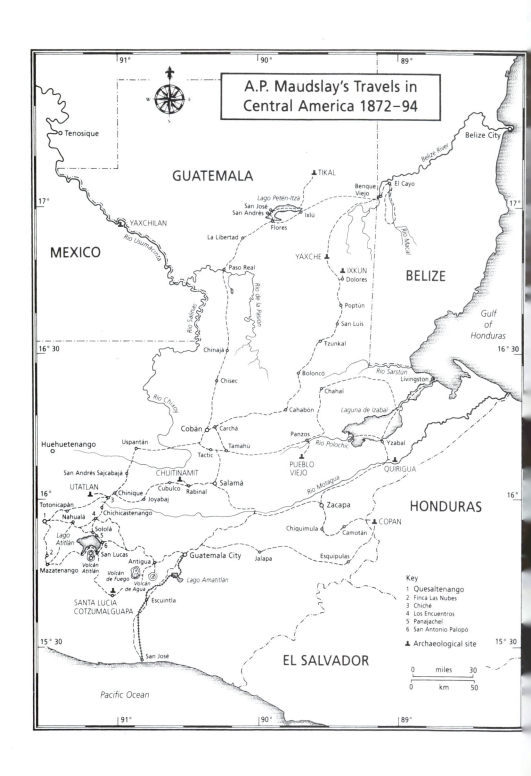

A.P. Maudslay's Travels in
Central America 1872-94

91° 90° 89°

Tenosique

Belize City

GUATEMALA

TIKAL

Benque
Viejo

El Cayo

17° 17°

Lago Petén-Itzá

San José
San Andrés

Ixlú

YAXCHILAN

Flores

Río Macal

Río Usumacinta

La Libertad

MEXICO

Paso Real

YAXCHE

IXKUN
Dolores

BELIZE

Río de la Pasión

Río Salinas

Poptún

San Luis

Gulf
of
Honduras

16° 30 16° 30

Chinajá

Tzunkal

Chisec

Boloncó

Río Sarstún

Livingston

Chahal

Río Chixoy

Cahabón

Laguna de Izabal

Cobán Carchá

Panzos

Río Polochic

Yzabal

Huehuetenango

Uspantán

Tamahú

Tactic

San Andrés Sajcabajá

CHUITINAMIT

PUEBLO
VIEJO

QUIRIGUA

UTATLAN

Cubulco

Salamá

Río Motagua

16° 16°

Totonicapán

Chinique
3

Rabinal

HONDURAS

Joyabaj

Zacapa

1

Nahualá

4

Chichicastenango

Chiquimula

COPAN

Lago
Atitlán

Sololá
5

Camotán

2

6

Esquipulas

San Lucas

Antigua

Guatemala City

Jalapa

Key

Mazatenango

Volcán
Atitlán

Volcán
de Fuego

Volcán
de Agua

Lago Amatitlán

1 Quesaltenango
2 Finca Las Nubes
3 Chiché
4 Los Encuentros
5 Panajachel
6 San Antonio Palopó

SANTA LUCIA
COTZUMALGUAPA

Escuintla

15° 30 15° 30

Archaeological site

San José

0   miles   30

0   km   50

EL SALVADOR

Pacific Ocean

91° 90° 89°

Alfred Maudslay and the Maya

A Biography

Ian Graham

THE BRITISH MUSEUM PRESS

© 2002 Ian Graham

Ian Graham has asserted his moral right to be identified as
the author of this work

First published in 2002 by The British Museum Press
A division of The British Museum Company Ltd
46 Bloomsbury Street, London WC1B 3QQ

A catalogue record for this book is available from the British Library

ISBN 0 7141 2561 X

Map by John Gilkes

Designed and typeset in Palatino by Behram Kapadia

Printed in England by The Bath Press

Contents

Preface

Anyone acquainted with the pre-Columbian cultures of Mesoamerica who has had access to the original edition of Alfred Maudslay's great work *Archaeology* is likely to remember the experience of opening those weighty volumes for the first time. For the fact that such a vast collection of superb photographs accompanied by minutely detailed drawings could have been published more than a century ago is a cause for astonishment.

Maudslay's intention in making this great effort, which took him the best part of twenty years, was simply this: to record with the greatest possible precision as much as he could of a body of sculpture of the highest importance for scholarly and educational purposes before it could suffer further weathering or other damage. Much of that sculpture had previously been quite unknown to scholars, and all of it then lay abandoned in the ruined cities of Mesoamerica.

(If Maudslay's work causes astonishment on first acquaintance, then another little surprise awaits the newly introduced reader: that of finding that these impressive volumes were published simply as an appendix to a much vaster illustrated compendium on the birds, beetles, fishes, and other forms of wildlife of southern Mexico and Central America, hence the confusing title given his work: *Biologia Centrali-Americana: 'Archaeology'.)*

In any case, speaking for myself, I have never forgotten the moment when the attendant in the old Reading Room of the British Museum Library deposited with a thump those five *Archaeology* volumes on the pale-blue leather desk I was seated at in that hallowed and much lamented temple of the printed word.

Then a novice in this field, I didn't at first appreciate to the full the magnitude of the achievement embodied in those volumes, nor their historical importance. But as soon as I'd gained more experience of the Maya area, I began to wonder about the author of this great work, and his life.

I looked him up in *Who's Who*, only to find a very brief and unsatisfying entry. The great *Dictionary of National Biography* overlooked him entirely; as did (and still does) the *Encyclopaedia Britannica*, despite a generous allotment of space to those Old World archaeologists who were contemporaries of his and of equivalent importance, such as Heinrich Schliemann, Sir Arthur Evans, Sir Flinders Petrie and Augustus Pitt-Rivers.

Nearly fifteen years would pass before it occurred to me that perhaps I myself might venture to fill this gap in the history of Mesoamerican archaeology. It seemed an audacious plan, but by the greatest of fortune my very first move was rewarded with success. I had started hunting for any Maudslays who might be listed in British telephone directories, and at almost the first attempt found a Mrs Maudslay living in Dorset.

When I reached her by telephone and explained my interest, she revealed that indeed she was related to Alfred Maudslay: doubly so in fact, since by blood she was his first-cousin-once-removed, and then she had married his favourite nephew, Cyril. She expressed delight that someone was interested in her revered uncle, and immediately invited me to pay a visit.

In fact Dorothy Maudslay, or Dolly as I learnt to call her, encouraged me to return twice more for weekend visits, and then, only two years after I'd met her, she died. Owing to the fact that Alfred Maudslay and his wife had married late in life and thus had no children to inherit memorabilia, an assortment of scrapbooks, photographs, letters, and other material not covered by his will had been removed from his house to that of Cyril, his principal executor. Then, in her library, I found some items containing useful information and showed them to Dolly, whereupon she encouraged me to rummage about in odd corners of the house, and on finding something useful for my purposes to keep it. And when, after her death, her niece Mrs Margaret Whittingdale came across a few more useful items, she also kindly set these aside for me. (One was Maudslay's own set of *Archaeology* volumes, rather badly bound in red morocco; but I drew the line at accepting these.)

All this material, which otherwise would have been dispersed, has been immensely valuable. But for many years the claims of my proper employment, both at the desk and in the field, allowed of little progress in writing the text, although in 1977 I did, at the request of Ms Elizabeth Carmichael of the British Museum's Department of Ethnography, contribute a short article about Maudslay in the second issue of a new but short-lived annual published by the Museum.

In 1995, however, I was fortunate enough to be granted a month's residency at the Rockfeller Foundation's Study Center at Bellagio, on the shores of Lake Como, Italy, and the writing momentum generated there under such ideal circumstances has carried the work fitfully to its conclusion.

Among those to whom I owed an early debt of gratitude was Ann Miller for her able transcription of a substantial portion of Maudslay's field notes, preserved in the British Museum, for the producer of a BBC-TV film in the 'Footsteps' series. Another early and valued contribution was that of Nikki Smith, of Guatemala, who transcribed documents in the archives of the Victoria and Albert Museum while working as an intern in the Textile department; subsequently these data were augmented through the kindness of Jennifer Wearden, the Curator of Textiles. Much appreciated also was the kindness of Mr Ronald Raymond-Cox in providing a photocopy of the translation of Bishop Landa's *Relación* that Maudslay had begun and Charles Fenton, his grandfather, had attempted to finish.

To Dr Colin McEwan, Assistant Keeper, Central and South America, in the Department of Ethnography at the British Museum, and Ms Clara Bezanilla, also of that department, I render especial thanks for their help in various ways, not least for securing permission for me to make prints from Maudslay's glass plates. (Here, I may mention my hope of producing a book of freshly and carefully made prints from those plates, to be reproduced at full scale by the best available reproduction technique.)

Lastly, because most recently, I pay tribute to Nina Shandloff of the British Museum Press, for her patience with an often careless and muddle-prone author.

Chapter 1

Introduction

On 9 September 1872 the SS *Guatemala*, a one-thousand-ton vessel of the Panama Rail Road Company, dropped anchor off San José, then the principal port of Guatemala on its Pacific coast. But as no natural harbour existed anywhere along that coast, ships were obliged to anchor offshore on an open roadstead, and passengers and freight alike had to be ferried between ship and shore in lighters – boats resembling large lifeboats, worked with oars. The ceaseless and often very heavy ocean swell made those landings disagreeable to say the least, and often dangerous.[1]

Most of the passengers on this ship would have been Latin-Americans, since travellers heading for California from Panama used a more direct service of the same line, calling at fewer Mexican and Central American ports; so one may imagine that two tall and well-dressed young Englishmen preparing to land at San José that day may have felt a little conspicuous.[2]

They were brothers, Charles and Alfred Maudslay. Alfred, the younger of the two, probably attracted more attention, with his round head and broad forehead, blond hair parted near the middle and tending to curl at the sides, and his look of concentrated attention. Charles had darker hair, a narrower head, and a mouth and jaw that might be judged as showing less determination.

As the steamer lay at anchor, rolling and pitching in the swell, the passengers had time to admire the scene while awaiting the arrival of lighters to take them off – and what a scene that was! The coast there runs perfectly straight, east and west, as far as the eye can see. The ocean swell, breaking on the beach, continually throws up sheets of white spray, in stark contrast with the jet-black volcanic sand of the beach itself. Behind the beach stands a fringe of coconut and other palms, then broken only by the Customs shed, a rickety wooden pier and a few shacks; behind that, a natural canal runs parallel with the beach, although this might not be visible from the boat. Beyond these features nothing but treetops could have been seen, for a vast uninhabited rain-forest then covered the entire piedmont plain up to foothills 30 miles away to the north.

And in the far distance, 45 miles away, two great volcanoes majesti-cally reared their heads, both of them likely to have been capped by little cotton-wool clouds. With silhouettes that show up silvery-blue on fine days against the clear blue of the sky, those volcanoes dominate the entire panorama.

While waiting to be taken ashore, Alfred had been reading *Les Misérables* in a large-format paperback edition in French. Raising his eyes, perhaps, to look again at that glorious view, he took the opportunity to make a quick pencil sketch of it on the unprinted inside of the book's back cover – and later, when the opportunity arose, took out his ink-pot and pen, and went over this drawing in ink, signing and dating it.

By extraordinarily good fortune, this unpretentious sketch has survived as a memento of Alfred Maudslay's first glimpse at Guatemala – or at any part of Mesoamerica, for that matter. No one could then have dreamt, least of all Alfred himself, that he would one day become the pio-neer of scientific exploration of ruined cities which had lain abandoned for a thousand years in similar jungles far away beyond those volcanoes.[3] At that stage in his life, the only career he had in mind was medicine, while his avowed motive for making this long journey to Guatemala had simply been to study tropical birds in their natural habitat. There is no suggestion that he had any intention of visiting ruins, in spite of a friend's having previously shown him photographs (as he is known to have done) of the great ruins at Copán and Quiriguá.

What then might Alfred Maudslay have known about Guatemala when he and Charles landed at San José? With the enquiring mind he would prove to have, he is unlikely to have arrived completely ignorant of the country's past, but as he knew no Spanish the sources he could read were limited. It is safe to assume that he had read the two best-known works by John Lloyd Stephens, *Incidents of Travel in Central America, Chiapas and Yucatan,* and its sequel, *Incidents of Travel in Yucatan*. These were pub-lished in 1841 and 1843 respectively, both of them brilliantly illustrated by his friend and travelling companion, Frederick Catherwood, and they do also contain descriptions of the contemporary political scene. Stephens wrote well, had an urbane wit, and showed good sense in judg-ing contemporary theories about the ancient ruins and their builders.[4]

Catherwood, for his part, was an architect and first-rate draughts-man, already renowned for his renderings of Roman and Egyptian ruins. In addition, he came equipped on these travels with a 'camera lucida', a simple device consisting of a prism of special form attached to the draw-ing board by an adjustable arm. Applying his eye to the prism, he would have been able to see, as if projected on to his sheet of paper, a ghostly image of the object being drawn, allowing him to trace its outlines accurately in pencil. Catherwood's illustrations are therefore as accurate as any could be until, more than thirty years later, it became possible to illustrate books photographically.

There are some other books Maudslay may possibly have read, or dipped into, before setting out for Guatemala. Whether or not he had as an undergraduate any interest in antiquities is unknown; but if he did, and happened to open the pages of a book well-regarded by scholars at Cambridge, William Robertson's weighty *History of America*, written in 1777, he might have found a statement (really a second-hand opinion) that there did not exist in Spanish America 'any monument or vestige of any building more ancient than the Conquest'. Catherwood's illustrations of Maya ruins, of course, would soon have demonstrated that statement to be false (and for Robertson this was a rare lapse, since he made great efforts to obtain copies of documents needed for his work, and in his preface complains that 'Spain, with an excess of caution, has uniformly drawn a veil over her transactions with America').[5]

In his book of reminiscences, *Life in the Pacific Fifty Years Ago*, Maudslay devotes a few paragraphs to the reverend dean of his Cambridge college, a notably shy and eccentric man, but an adventurer too, for he took his summer vacation one year in Mexico. So this dean may well have planted in Maudslay the first seeds of curiosity about that country, and may well have introduced him to a very readable and informative book, William Bullock's *Six Month's Residence and Travels in Mexico.*

In 1822 Bullock, who had built a museum in Piccadilly, London, for the display of curiosities of all kinds – stuffed animals, historical relics and so forth – lost no time when the long-standing law prohibiting the entry of Protestant visitors to Mexico was rescinded. He and his son promptly departed for that mysterious country, intent on collecting material, both natural and cultural, for his museum. Just one of his ambitious operations may be mentioned: he decided to make moulds of the great Aztec Calendar Stone, the Stone of Tizoc and the Coatlícue, but as the two last-named had been buried, he had first to have them dug out (Coatlícue, he tells us, had been buried in the courtyard of the university for fear that its terrifying aspect might frighten the Indians!). The exhibitions on 'Ancient and Modern Mexico' that Bullock mounted soon after his return were a great success.

Another book that Maudslay could have brought with him for reading during the voyage is William H. Prescott's classic, *The Conquest of Mexico.* But when it came to information about Guatemala, rather than Mexico, either in English or French (which, on the evidence already cited, he must have been able to read quite well), that was more difficult to find. One book with a promising title was E. G. Squier's *The States of Central America* (Squier 1858). This has a useful section devoted to Guatemala, but virtually all of it is based on the reports of others. Since Squier's interest in Central America was centred upon his promotion of an inter-oceanic railway to be built within the borders of Honduras, the area he knew best was its southern portion.

A principal source of Squier's chapters on Guatemala was Arthur Morelet's account of his own travels, *Voyage dans l'Amérique Centrale, Cuba et le Yucatan*, published in 1857, an English translation of which appeared in 1871, just in time for Maudslay to obtain it before embarking for Guatemala. Morelet had no interest in railways, nor unfortunately in antiquities – natural history was his hobby, but he provides a lively account of the experiences he had while travelling from the port of Sisal (in Yucatán) overland to the mouth of the Usumacinta, then up that river to Tenosique, from there across a considerable expanse of uninhabited forest to Flores. Then he headed south via Poptún, Boloncó, Cahabón, Cobán – a route that Maudslay would follow forty years later – to reach Guatemala City at last. After a side trip to Antigua and Lake Amatitlán, Morelet made his way to Yzabal, passing by the recently discovered ruins of Quiriguá, but not visiting them because he had 'neither the time nor any desire to see them'. From Yzabal he embarked for Belize and then Cuba.

All of the information in these books had been collected before Maudslay was six years old, a circumstance easy to explain, in that only a few years after Stephens and Catherwood, Morelet, and a few others had braved the hardships and deprivations of travel in Yucatán and Central America, political disturbances and military conflict in those parts of Mesoamerica began to add danger to the normal discomforts of travel. Years passed therefore before observant travellers were once again able to gather information and illustrative material able to cast light upon the origins of the 'mysterious' people responsible for building those impressive ruins. So, for another decade or two the conventional explanation of their origin had to reside in a long-past Golden Age, as suggested by Prescott.

Chapter 2

Background and schooling

A nyone familiar with the ways of the world who happened to
meet the young Maudslays during their trip to Guatemala
would have recognized them at once as coming from a prosperous family. Just the quality of their clothes and luggage would have
made this obvious, while the astonishing fact of their having travelled
thousands of miles simply to enjoy an unusual vacation watching birds
eliminated any other possible conclusion. And indeed their family was
extremely prosperous, although they'd enjoyed this condition for no
more than about fifty years.

The paternal great-grandfather of Charles and Alfred, Henry
Maudsley (for so he usually wrote his name), had occupied a distinctly
modest station in life. A native of Yorkshire, he had joined the Royal
Artillery as a young man, and rose to the rank of sergeant-wheelwright.
Dispatched to the West Indies, he suffered an injury there and was sent
back to the regimental headquarters at Woolwich. He then married, and
obtained work in the Arsenal, later becoming a store-keeper in the
Dockyard. He and his wife had settled into one of a pair of tiny semi-
detached dwellings at the rear of the Salutation Inn in Beresford Square;
these were dwellings so decrepit that in the 1860s they were condemned,
and soon collapsed.[1]

It was in this house that the fifth of their seven children was born in
1771. He was named Henry after his father, and at twelve years of age
began work in the dockyard as a powder monkey, making and filling
cartridges. But quite soon he was spotted as a promising lad, and was
transferred, first to the carpenters' shop and then to the smithy.

So rapidly, in fact, did his skill as a mechanic develop and become recognized that by the age of eighteen he had been taken on by Joseph
Bramah, an engineer still remembered for two important inventions: one
was the hydraulic ram or jack, such as those used to raise the shovels of
bulldozers, or to do the same for one's car; the other, his 'unpickable'
lock, was the forerunner of the 'Yale-type' door-lock. But it seems that in
the manufacture of both these products practical difficulties arose, and it

was young Maudslay, according to some accounts, who helped solve them.

From these beginnings Henry Maudslay's life and work advanced rapidly, and were so remarkable that his grandson, Alfred, can hardly have failed to be influenced by his heritage. Thus, a more than passing reference to his family background may help us understand some facets of both his character and his circumstances.

At Bramah's Henry Maudslay was soon promoted to be in charge of the workshop, and it is known that while there he was experimenting with slide-rests for lathes. Soon, though, he left, and it was probably the encouraging trend of these experiments that led him to take the bold step of setting up his own business in London.[2]

The slide-rest may be described as a tool-holder firmly fixed to the lathe-bed, yet movable at will both lengthways and in-and-out by means of hand-wheels. While it is possible (although difficult) to turn a soft metal such as brass with a hand-held tool, in the manner of wood-turners, this isn't feasible with metal pieces of any size. The tool has to be held more firmly, hence the need for a rigid but movable tool-holder, or slide-rest. The concept of this was not new, for the germ of the idea had occurred to Leonardo da Vinci, but it was Maudslay's achievement to produce in 1798 a metal-turning lathe widely regarded as the first satisfactory machine tool of the industrial age.

Next, he went on to produce a screw-cutting lathe, a device that would make an enormous contribution to precision in engineering. Previously, brass nuts and bolts such as were used in assembling clocks first had to have their threads squeezed into them, after which it was necessary to chase them by hand to fit individual nuts. Each paired nut and bolt had therefore to be marked as belonging to one another, and accurate repetition work was impossible. The iron bolts needed for attaching one piece of machinery to another could certainly have threads cut in them by primitive dies and taps, but they conformed to no standard, and thus were unsuitable for well-made machinery. Again, no technique then existed for making the accurately and evenly threaded rods that were required for measuring instruments, or for controlling the movement of large astronomical instruments.

The problem of forming a bolt by *cutting* threads in a cylindrical blank turned in a lathe was really of the 'chicken or egg: which came first?' variety, since, to cut a thread on a bar, an accurate lead-screw was needed to move the slide-rest with its cutting tool smoothly along the lathe-bed while the bar to be threaded was rotating; but how was such a lead-screw to be made in the first place without the benefit of a screw-cutting lathe, which of course had to incorporate a lead-screw?

Maudslay was not the first to tackle this problem, for a reasonably good lead-screw of huge size had already been made in Birmingham by a complicated and clumsy method. Maudslay's approach was far simpler and gave superior results. Having conceived a simple screw-generating device that would inscribe the helix on a bar, he laboriously and carefully cut the thread by hand, thus producing a lead-screw that can be regarded as the direct progenitor of all modern threaded rods and bolts.[3]

Next, Maudslay took an important step towards standardization by developing a thread profile for all sizes of nuts and bolts, known as the Maudslay thread.[1] Then, in 1800, he completed an improved lathe with a lead-screw cut with fifty threads per inch and paired with a foot-long nut (which thus contained six hundred turns) for actuating the tool. Such a long nut would move more uniformly along the lead-screw, since the effects of any small, local imperfections in the thread would be evened out. On this lathe Maudslay made a triple-start threaded rod required by the Royal Observatory for use in a telescope mounting. But then, finding that it failed to match the specified figure of turns per foot by 0.05 per cent, Maudslay devised an ingenious mechanism which allowed him to eliminate this error from a second threaded rod that he made. In recognition of the contribution this would make to the accuracy of astronomical measurements, the government awarded him a prize of £1000 – then a vast sum.

Having mastered the production of accurately cut threaded rods, Henry Maudslay was now in a position to make a really accurate micrometer, or instrument for determining dimensions, the heart of it being a calibrated screw thread of fine pitch. This he referred to jokingly as the workshop's Court of Final Appeal, or Lord Chancellor, since it delivered the final judgment on disputed dimensions. This historic micrometer is now preserved in the Science Museum, London, where, when tested in 1918, it proved to have remained accurate to within about two ten-thousandths of an inch.

This, and the surface plate made by him (a dressed steel plate used as a standard of flatness, and as a base on which to place objects to be measured), earned him the title, still generally recognized, as the father of precision in engineering. With such instruments at hand, Maudslay could now draw all the components of a machine, and have them manufactured to dimensions closely specified in the drawings. From then on, in the best workshops, the services of fitters were less in demand, their job having been to file and otherwise adjust components until they could be fitted together. Naturally Maudslay also demanded engineering drawings of the highest quality.

In about 1801, Maudslay was consulted by Marc Brunel about the design and construction of certain machines. Brunel had been living in New York as a refugee from the French Revolution, and had come to London in the hope of exploiting an idea that had struck him. At

Alexander Hamilton's dinner table in New York one evening he had heard another guest tell of the difficulties besetting the Admiralty in its efforts to build up the Royal Navy to meet the growing menace of Napoleon. The problem was a bottleneck caused by inadequate production of pulley-blocks, a vast number of which, in several sizes and with one, two, or three sheaves or pulley wheels, were needed for each man-of-war – and they were still being made largely by hand.

Brunel's idea was to break down the manufacture into a number of relatively simple operations, each of which could be performed by a single machine-tool designed for the purpose. Then, having arrived at preliminary designs for these machines, and taken out patents on the more elaborate ones, he started looking for an engineer with a good workshop and the ability to transform these designs into practical machines.[5]

In this he was fortunate. He had a friend whose curiosity about a lead-screw displayed in Maudslay's shop-window had drawn him into conversation with its maker. This man put Brunel in touch with him, and in due course Maudslay accomplished what was asked of him with resounding success. The first set of machines, installed at Portsmouth dockyard between 1802 and 1808, worked perfectly from the start, and became a wonder of the age, attracting visitors as diverse as the novelist Maria Edgeworth and the Tsar of Russia. They came with good reason, for, although this was not quite the first production line in the world (Eli Whitney's flintlock factory, built a few years earlier, holds that title), that at Portsmouth consisted of more numerous and much more sophisticated machine-tools. Indeed, so well made were they that two of them remained in use at Portsmouth until after the Second World War.[6]

Maudslay's reputation was now firmly established as a designer and constructor of machines – one who showed, as a contemporary expressed it, 'the most scrupulous attention to accuracy and durability, at the same time preserving an elegant proportion to their form which is very agreeable to the eye'.

When new workshops were needed, they were built in Lambeth on the south bank of the Thames, upon a site where, a century later, the London County Council offices were to rise. The most striking of the various buildings was the Front Erecting Shop, the hall where machines were assembled from their component parts. To provide a large area unencumbered with pillars, Maudslay gave the building a roof supported on cast-iron trusses – probably the first of its kind.

Before long, ambitious young engineers began coming to these works in the hope of obtaining employment, or of being taken on as apprentices. Among the latter were several, such as Nasmyth, Roberts, Clement, and Whitworth, who would in time make great names for themselves. And just as one can identify among the violin and piano virtuosi of the nineteenth century several 'genealogies' of masters and pupils through whom recognizable traditions of playing were transmitted, so too can a few similar lines of descent be traced for engineers in the same period, one of them stemming from Henry Maudslay, who in turn owed part of his heritage to Joseph Bramah. Among Nasmyth's achievements was the invention of the steam-operated drop hammer, a vital tool for forging crankshafts and other large items, while Clement was chosen by Charles Babbage to construct his Universal Calculating Engine, doing so with such precision that frictional losses in bearings and gears were kept low enough to make it workable.

During the little more than twenty years of life remaining to Henry Maudslay – for he was only fifty-nine when he died – the principal activity at his factory was the production of steam engines. The best-known product was his Table Engine, or Maudslay's Vertical, a particularly successful design of small engine for factories because, as its designer stated in his patent application of 1807,

> My said improvements consist in reducing the number of parts in the common steam engine and so arranging them as to render it more compact and portable, every part being fixed to a strong frame . . . detached from the walls of the building, and therefore less expensive in fixing, and not liable to get out of order by sinking of foundations, etc.

This self-contained engine remained in production for forty years.

In time Henry Maudslay brought in Joshua Field as a partner, and later his two surviving sons as well, whereupon the company was renamed 'Maudslay, Sons and Field'. After about 1820 the firm began to specialize in marine engines, although the general engineering side of the business was never given up.

Near the end of his life Henry Maudslay became interested in astronomy as the result of a visit to Berlin, and decided to construct an observatory with a 24-inch reflecting telescope. Having searched for a site with a clear atmosphere, his choice fell on Knight's Hill, in Norwood, on the southern edge of London, and there he bought a house.[7] But in February, 1831, before construction of the observatory had begun, his life was cut short, apparently by pneumonia.[8]

Henry Maudslay was described by his contemporaries as a genial and good-natured man. He was 6 feet 2 inches tall, with a large, round head and a wide forehead. His workmen apparently revered him, and he paid them well, for in 1807 his best men were receiving the very high wage of 60 shillings a week. As an engineer Maudslay's guiding principles were simplicity of design, rigidity of framework, and accuracy of manufacture; other important goals were elegance of design and perfection of finish. James Nasmyth recorded that, when as a young man he was taken on by Maudslay, the latter took the opportunity to deliver one of his favourite maxims: 'Keep a sharp look-out upon your materials; get rid of every pound of material you can do without; put to yourself the question, "What business has it to be there?"; avoid complexities, and make everything as simple as possible.' This tradition was to persist at the Maudslay works, the products of which always had a high reputation for reliability.[9]

Maudslay was buried in the churchyard at Woolwich. The monument erected to him, his parents, and his children, with inscriptions on all four sides, was probably unique for being constructed of cast iron. The inscription ran as follows:

> To the memory of Henry Maudslay. Born in this parish in 1771. Died at Lambeth, February 15th, 1831. A zealous promoter of the Arts and Sciences. Eminently distinguished as an engineer for Mathematical Accuracy and Beauty of Construction; as a Man for Industry and Perseverance; as a Friend for a kind and benevolent heart.

It is painful to relate that in 1966 the Rector (a Mr Stacey), together with the church council, decided to tidy up the churchyard and turn it into a nice lawn. The Maudslay memorial appears to have been sent for scrap, while the other tombstones and monuments were set up round the edge of the lawn. Just one monument was left untouched, this being a marble lion commemorating a prize-fighter. It seems that here, in the eyes of the Rector and his colleagues, was a son of Woolwich so justly renowned that the memory of him could not be allowed to fade . . . .

Of the two sons who succeeded Henry Maudslay in the business, his second surviving son, Joseph, was the more distinguished as an engineer. Among his many inventions was a propeller for sailing ships equipped with auxiliary engines. This could be feathered to reduce drag when the vessel was under sail alone, and today many cruising yachts are fitted with improved versions of the same. So it is delightful to report that Thomas Barker, comically dubbed the Poet Laureate of Steam, was quick to celebrate in verse the triumph of Maudslay's design over competing models.[10]

Joseph Maudslay's ingenuity is also apparent in the various configurations of engines designed by him for vessels of different kinds. Then, once the relative efficiency of paddle-wheel and screw had been settled by the famous tug-of-war between the *Rattler* and the *Alecto*, he was the first to understand, and demonstrate, that propellers are best driven by direct coupling to relatively high-speed engines.

In the 1830s and 1840s orders for marine engines and boilers began coming in at such a pace that the work-force at Maudslay, Sons and Field grew to a thousand. Peak activity came during the Crimean War, when the process of manufacture began to resemble mass-production. Sixty-two naval vessels active in that war were engined by Maudslays, against a total of 150 by four other manufacturers.

Naturally Joseph and his elder brother Thomas Henry, the two family partners, prospered exceedingly. Both now lived in Norwood, then still in open country, although it would soon be engulfed in suburbia. Joseph had bought Norwood Lodge, a large, rambling, single-storeyed house in Crown Lane (demolished, some decades later, and the British Home for Incurables built on its site). There, on 18 March 1850, the seventh of their eight surviving children was born to Anna Maria Stamp Maudslay and her husband, Joseph, and named Alfred Percival (their first-born had died in infancy). But soon afterwards the new baby's father was felled by an aneurism which left him unable to walk for the remaining eleven years of his life. Nevertheless he continued to be active at the works, visiting the various workshops in his Bath chair. Three more patents were taken out by him in 1858, and even within a year of his death in 1861 he built himself a new 110-ton steam yacht.[11]

Only one of his six sons, Walter, became a full-time engineer. But inventiveness had not died out altogether in this family, although it was applied to less weighty purposes than boilers and marine engines. The eldest son, Herbert Charles, was briefly a partner in the family firm before becoming involved with railways and the construction of lock-gates. Much of his time, however, was devoted to fox-hunting and yachting, and it was in this latter field that he could claim to have invented (or at least co-invented) something still in widespread use, the spinnaker sail.[12]

A more prolific inventor in the family was Athol, the third son. He is said to have been brilliant but rather mad, and – unlike others in this family – cursed with a terrible temper. Athol's first patent was for a calendar ring for the finger, which was actually manufactured and put on the market. Encouraged by this success he applied, over the years, for a dozen patents in respect of improvements to such things as tents, sleeping-bags, dog kennels, and the rigging of small boats. As the subjects suggest, Athol was an outdoorsman, but also the author of several books, none of them at all interesting.[13]

No other Maudslays of that generation, save their cousin Henry, applied for patents. The next brother, Charles, who had been Alfred's companion on that first trip to Guatemala, joined his brother Herbert in business for a time, but then retired to live quietly with his unmarried sister Isabel, known familiarly as Bella, and by Alfred as 'Bob'. The youngest of the family, Eustace, seems to have been rather ineffectual and immature. His lack of judgment was displayed to full effect when, as a young officer in the 16th Lancers, he chose to have an affair with his Colonel's wife, on whom he fathered a child. Naturally, his career in the

Lancers came to an abrupt end.[14] The other sister, Clara Rose, married Joshua Field, son of the Joshua who had been Henry Maudslay's original partner, and himself later a partner with Walter in the firm.

The mother of Alfred and his siblings, Anna Maria Maudslay, remains unfortunately a shadowy figure. Anna Maria Stamp Johnston was born in 1810, and had two brothers, both of whom became surgeons. The elder, Henry Charles (1809–63), became Professor of Surgery at St George's Hospital, London, while the younger, Edmund Charles (1821–95), was best known for his work on behalf of the blind. For many years he was companion of the blind Viscount Cranborne, heir to the Marquis of Salisbury, and together they made extensive journeys through Europe visiting schools for the blind. One journey, before the days of railways, took them across Russia, from St Petersburg to Odessa. Edmund Johnston encouraged the use of Braille, which he may have introduced into Britain, and of the Typograph, a very early typewriter with embossed letters on the keys.

The impression of Anna Maria that can be gleaned from sparse surviving correspondence is of a mother much loved by her children, and to her must go some of the credit for the family remaining so close-knit all their lives. Their unity is exemplified by the way they continued for decades after her death to gather each year at one or another's house, or at a Scottish castle such as Armadale, Dunvegan, or Uppat which some family member, usually Charles, had taken for a shooting and fishing season. Anna Maria died in 1878, when Alfred was twenty-eight.

Alfred was born on 18 March 1850 in Norwood, then a semi-rural area south of London, where his chilhood was uneventful until, at ten years of age, he was packed off to a boarding school in Tunbridge Wells. In *Life in the Pacific Fifty Years Ago*, a charming book of reminiscences of his life up to the age of thirty (but written near the end of it), Maudslay describes this school as living on its past reputation. It was run by the Reverend George Allfrey, the good-natured but indolent son of the founder, assisted by his wife, who drank. There, the boys learnt practically nothing (as Maudslay recollected), but happily he was able to study wildlife in the surrounding meadows. Four years later he went on to Harrow, where the teaching was only a little more satisfactory.

Like other ancient boarding schools founded for the benefit of poor scholars, but later to become 'public schools', Harrow remained very small until fee-paying boarders were admitted early in the nineteenth century. At none of them can the expansion have been so rapid as at Harrow, where the number of boys, which had fallen to sixty-eight, rose to 460 in the course of just fifteen years, this growth having ended a couple of years before Alfred's arrival there. The strain on the school administration imposed by such a rapid expansion can be imagined.[15]

One result of the reorganization during this period was that the school ceased to admit small boys of seven to ten, with the consequent elimination of the First and Second Forms. So it came about that the Third Form into which Alfred was initially placed was actually the bottom form. In his reminiscences Maudslay modestly declares: 'At the entrance examination I was placed last but one, for strange to say there was found one boy who knew less than I did.' In this instance his recollection, after the passage of nearly seventy years, wasn't quite accurate, for in fact he was placed fifth from the top of the form, and at mid-term was promoted to the form above.[16]

Still, it is true that his scholastic career never sparkled. In end-of-term exams he generally came about three-quarters of the way down the form, and, since a boy's promotion from one form, or division, to the next depended on exam results, Alfred never rose higher than the lowest of four subdivisions of the Fifth Form. And the Fifth was not even the top form; above it, remote and unattainable, lay the Sixth.

The conclusion of his schooldays brought Alfred further discouragement, for in final exams he was placed bottom of his form. One is reminded of other boys who conspicuously failed to show promise at Harrow. One was Anthony Trollope. Not only was Trollope avoided by other boys for being incredibly dirty and untidy, but a contemporary of his declared that he 'gave no sign of promise whatsoever, was always in the lowest part of the form, and was regarded by the masters and by the boys as an incorrigible dunce'. Between them, they lend some substance to Hazlitt's remark that anyone who has passed through the regular gradations of a classical education, and is not made a fool by it, may consider himself as having had a very narrow escape.

Fairly consistently Alfred scored his best results in mathematics, and his worst in modern languages, with classics in between. But it was classics that caused him most despair, at least in retrospect.

> Most of one's time was taken up in writing nonsense Latin verses. . . . I seldom or never had a set of Latin verses passed, even with the help which was often afforded me by my school-fellows; but I did perpetrate eight or ten lines of an invocation to the muse, which was useful on several occasions, with suitable intervals of time between, and suited to any subject. . . . As I got slowly up the school, the form I was in was always far ahead of me in classics, and I practically left them alone and scraped together a few marks in other subjects. But these subjects were very few; there was no English history, no geography, and very little time devoted to Roman or Greek history, and I remember that if one was half asleep in class, and a question was put to you, it was safest to take a shot and answer, 'A river in Asia Minor', or 'An island in the Aegean Sea'.

One of his form-masters comes in for criticism because he had pet good boys and pet bad boys.

> I was one of the latter, and he used to tap me on the head with his long pointing rod and call me 'a barren tree' and 'an arid desert,' with plentiful rolling of r's. Yet this same master at about this time gave a lecture at the Royal Institution in which he criticized the prevalent system of education, and spoke of the ordinary intelligent boy who gained little by it.

Afterwards he told Alfred's mother it was her son that he had in mind.

Saturday was Alfred's busy day, for the evening exercise was a map. This did not mean any instruction in map-drawing,

> it only meant that we had a map to copy out of the school atlas, and one bought a twopenny bit of cardboard and a paintbrush and a couple of paints. If the subject was given out early enough, I generally got my map done the day before. Then it would be 'Be a good fellow and put in my outsiders and lats. and longs'. Then another would want his mountains put in, and I drew caterpillars across the card more or less in position. Another would want his tints put on, or his rivers inked, and as I did not make them run uphill they were quite satisfactory. So I was generally kept busy all evening.
>
> In the lower school, if any particularly good exercise was sent in to a form master the author was 'sent up' with it to the headmaster. I only twice had this honour conferred upon me, once for an English epitaph on Socrates, which I cannot say anything about, and the other time for a map of Harrow to be done out of our own heads, and we were put on our honour not to look at any printed map or plan. I believe mine was really quite a creditable performance.

A tempting thing to do, because it was strictly prohibited, was to go to the Harrow Races, which were held a mile or two from the foot of the hill upon which the school stands. 'This, however', as Maudslay related,

> I was determined to do, and with two boys from another house arranged our plans. I hired a little rough pony-cart, which was to meet us at the bottom of the hill. We were to be disguised as three local raga-muffins, and were to send our coats and hats, etc. to the care of the owner of the pony-trap. When we changed our clothes in a shed, it was decided that my coat was too respectable, so I borrowed the coat from the boy who had brought the trap. One watch was taken with no chain, and this watch Stephenson put loose in his trousers pocket.
>
> We got to the course all right, and as we all knew the native lingo [cockney], there was little chance of detection. I got some coppers from a schoolfellow for holding his horse. He was got up with a false moustache and swagger clothes and was driving a dog-cart, and he

never recognized me. After a time I noticed we were followed by the police, and finally were all three arrested on a charge of stealing a watch. Then they searched us, and the loose watch was found in Stephenson's pocket, and he could neither tell the name of the maker nor the number on the watch, when asked. I had not dared put my hands into the pockets of the coat I had borrowed, but when they were turned out they produced several curious articles which I could not account for. So I was led off with Bobby's hand on my collar. For a time we kept up our disguise, but when I saw that the matter was serious, for the owner of the lost watch was insistent that we had taken it, I asked to see the Superintendant, and told him we were three Harrow boys out on a spree. He first of all told me 'that wouldn't do,' but after I had talked to him in my natural voice and answered questions about whose house I was in, he began to have doubts; but it was some time before I could convince him, and then he sent us back in charge of a mounted policeman. . . .

There was a draggletail old charwoman who came to clean out our rooms once or twice a week, and I used to make love to her, because she would bring me flowers from her cottage garden. When next the old girl . . . came, she nodded her head mysteriously and whispered 'I know all about it. I know where you've been. My son's a policeman, and 'twas him as arrested you.'

Alfred's health was never very sound, as he frequently caught heavy colds and had a chronic cough, which going out to school unfed on winter mornings did nothing to alleviate, so he was sent to the doctor for examination. The doctor banned football and cricket for him, and ordained a glass of rum and milk for him every morning before he went out for early school. The rum and milk was put by his bedside every night, and Maudslay pays tribute to his schoolfellows for never once playing tricks with the drink, which he regarded as his salvation.

The house he was in, The Grove, was notorious as the roughest in the school, but, though his health might be delicate, Alfred was quite strong and well able to look after himself in the rough and tumble of school life – if necessary with his fists. Aesthetically, the house itself may have seemed preferable to the other cheaply built modern houses, as John Addington Symonds scornfully described them. It was an old house, originally a manor, and built largely of wood. Since it was common practice for boys to read in bed after lights-out by using pen-nibs as nails with which to fasten candles on the wooden siding of their beds, Maudslay thought it a wonder the house had never gone up in flames.

It was not long before the boarding houses at Harrow were improved, and the curriculum changed to bring in the teaching of science and history. Maudslay naturally approved, but in retrospect avowed that he didn't for a moment regret his own experience there, although he acquired little book learning, and passed through some hard times in the house.

Chapter 3

Cambridge and Guatemala

I n October 1868 Alfred went up to Trinity Hall, Cambridge University, as a freshman. In reminiscences written late in life he had little to say of his time there, and that need not surprise us, for in those days there was little for undergraduates to do when not attending lectures and tutorials. Some cricket was played, but no football or hockey, and it has been said that, when a complete beginner at golf wandered on to Coldham Common swinging a club, he was promptly recruited for the Varsity team![1] There were rackets courts, but lawn tennis was unknown, and a few more years would have to pass before the invention of pneumatic tyres would make bicycling all the rage. Thus, piety may not have been entirely responsible for the packed attendance at Sunday services in Chapel (in such numbers, reportedly, that sometimes many undergraduates were reduced to sitting on the floor), for in those days there were few rival attractions for the ungodly.

In Maudslay's words,

> there is really not much to record, except that I had a delightful time, belonged to the Athenaeum and the Pitt [clubs] and the A.D.C. [Amateur Dramatic Club], where I used to play women's parts, and was a good deal at Newmarket [races]. Times were good, money fairly plentiful and champagne flowed freely. I won the Freshmen's Hurdle Race, but the following winter, my brother having given me a mount for a day's hunting in the Vale of Aylesbury, on a very windy day, a gate broke away and gave me a compound fractured leg, and I was taken back to London and laid up in my brother's house for five or six weeks. When I was well enough, I went with him on a trip in his cutter yacht the *Volante* to Ireland, racing at Belfast and elsewhere.[2]

In his last year at Cambridge, Alfred was Secretary of the ADC,[3] and family tradition has it that the dresses required for those female roles were made by his mother's dressmaker in Paris.[4]

The only remaining evidence of the many friendships he must have formed with fellow students is supplied by a photograph showing him posed with two of them. Their names, Forster and Knight, are inscribed on it, the latter being Edward F. Knight, two years younger than

Maudslay and at Caius College, close to Trinity Hall. His adventurous nature could scarcely have failed to influence Maudslay, because even before going up to Cambridge, and while living with his family in France, Knight had found his way to Algiers, walked to the edge of the desert, made friends with a mixed lot of French soldiers unaccompanied by officers, marched south with them for 250 miles to the last French outpost on the caravan route to Timbuctoo, gone off alone through Khabyle country, had his first of several experiences of being arrested, and at last made his way home. (After graduation, he was to embark on daring voyages in small sailing vessels, one of them in search of treasure on an extremely inhospitable island in the South Atlantic.)[5]

Cambridge at that time had recently undergone long-overdue reform. As at Harrow, the curriculum had been restricted to classics and mathematics. In natural sciences, for example, only those subjects amenable to mathematical analysis – that is, mechanics and optics – were taught, while in mathematics itself the more problematical fields that threatened to disturb the vision of a simple, orderly universe were eschewed. Since the highest purpose of the university had, in effect, been to train men for the clergy, it was sometimes referred to disparagingly as 'a vast theological seminary'.

Much of the credit for reform, when it came, belongs to Prince Albert, who to considerable astonishment had agreed to be a candidate for election as chancellor of the university. Conservatives were confident that he would act as a shield against any reformist measures that Russell's Liberal government might instigate; they were therefore outraged that when elected he took the initiative in lobbying for the introduction of history and natural science as new Bachelor degree subjects – and this while holding a position that was supposed to be largely ceremonial![6]

The Natural Science Tripos, instituted in 1851, contained five divisions: chemistry, mineralogy, geology, botany, and comparative anatomy (including zoology). Physics was not recognized until 1870. At the end of his first year Maudslay failed his exams, but passed them at the second attempt. He was then free to specialize, and chose botany and comparative anatomy as special subjects. 'The student of the present day', he wrote,

> would smile at the botanical instruction in those times. Professor Babington's lectures were dreadfully dull, and I made arrangements with Mr Mud, the head of the Botanical Gardens, to take me in hand. He was an illiterate Scotchman who smoked very strong tobacco and smelt strongly of whisky, but he knew his classification and grounded me in 'Natural Orders,' and he used to supply me with specimens to dissect and describe. We would wander round the garden for an hour examining plants and talking botany, but if I ventured to say, 'But Mr Mud, Darwin says so and so,' he used to

glare at me and say, 'Mr. Mudslay' (as he called me), 'that man Darwin will go to hell.' I was luckier in my other studies, for I had already made friends with J. W. Clark, who was Curator of the Museum of Comparative Anatomy and gave me the run of the museum and helped me in every way.

He eventually got a Second Class degree in the Tripos, which in those days the university conferred upon 'Those to whom the Examiners have only not refused their Certificate of Approval'!

Of all the people Maudslay came to know while at Cambridge, John Willis Clark (known to his friends as 'JW', or 'J') was to have the most enduring influence on him. Clark's interests ranged widely, for he was a naturalist, an historian, a University administrator adept at raising funds, a librarian, and an archaeologist – indeed, in 1887 a candidate for the Disney Professorship in Archaeology. A remark (quoted later in this chapter) made by Maudslay in a letter to his mother two years after graduation reveals that she, too, had become acquainted with Clark, Maudslay having perhaps brought him to their house in Hyde Park Square, London. We may safely assume, then, that, when Maudslay first showed a glimmer of interest in archaeology, Clark would have encouraged it. It is possible that Maudslay's engagement in ADC productions also owed something to Clark, for he was the club's staunchest supporter, and would later be elected its Perpetual Vice-President. In any case, the two men remained friends, and before long would become collaborators.[7]

After graduation Alfred registered as a medical student, then set out on a Long Vacation visit to America. 'My great desire now', he wrote, 'was to see a tropical forest, so in June, 1872, I persuaded my brother Charlie to come with me to the West Indies. We sailed on the 17th . . . touched at Barbados . . . reaching Jamaica on the 31st.' There they travelled about, finding people most hospitable. After a stay of three weeks, they left for Colon, the Caribbean port of Panama, crossed the isthmus by the new railway, and soon after arrival at Panama City boarded the SS *Guatemala* for San José, reaching their destination on 6 August.[8]

Landing at San José was always a frightening ordeal, but as Maudslay left no description of his arrival in 1872, and the landing procedure was changed at about that time, it is unclear which kind of ordeal he and Charles had to go through. More than twenty years later he was to land there for the third time in his life, on that occasion accompanied by his wife. Her description of the alarming experience of being lowered from the steamer into a lighter bobbing alongside will be quoted later; as also the process of scrambling out of the lighter and into an iron cage hanging from a crane, which then winched it up to deposit its distraught occupants on the pier.

But after describing this experience Mrs Maudslay went on to concede that at least it was 'preferable to that of the older method when the lighter was dragged through the surf, and the unfortunate passengers landed, soaked and terrified, even if they were lucky enough to escape a capsize and the teeth of hungry sharks'.

She is likely to have owed her knowledge of that earlier procedure to her husband's recollection of the ordeal he and Charles had endured on that earlier visit. Some idea of the technique can be gathered from photographs taken by Eadweard Muybridge three years later at Champerico, a roadstead landing place resembling San José topographically (for the Maudslays, it would have been the next stop, sailing in the same direction). From his photographs it appears that a long cable was permanently laid from shore, out to a pulley-block moored to an anchor or heavy sinker at some distance out to sea. This made possible a system of hauling boats in or out through the surf by mule-power.[9]

'San José de Guatemala is even now a miserable place', Maudslay wrote half a century later.

> In those days it consisted of the custom-house and a few shanties. We had great difficulty engaging mules to take us inland, and we did not get off until noon the next day. After leaving the swamp the track led through dense forest, and my chief remembrance is of the marvellous profusion of butterflies of all sizes and colouring, showing like a tessellated pavement on the damp patches in the track, and rising like a bouquet of bright flowers on our approach.
>
> As we started so late on such wretched animals, and had forty-four miles to ride to Escuintla, of course we were benighted, and did not reach our destination until ten o'clock. I well remember the last part of the ride. We were in a strange country about which we had been told hair-raising tales of the dangers of travelling; we could not speak or understand the language, and it was a very dark night.
>
> Our half-caste guide rode a white horse, and I could just manage to keep a white blur in front of me; so I kept a loaded revolver handy in my pocket in case of accidents. Of course it was quite safe, and the wild stories one had heard at Panama were mostly inventions. From Escuintla we travelled in the diligence to the capital, where we put up at the Globe Hotel.
>
> My friend Osbert Salvin, who had passed some years collecting birds and studying the natural history of Guatemala, had given me letters to Mr Nelson, a coffee planter, and he and his agent, Mr Whitney, were most helpful in making arrangements for our trip through the Altos [highlands]. We had arrived at the time of the great Jocotenango fair, which gave us a chance of seeing the city at its best, and the Indians who crowded into the city in their native costume. We were hospitably entertained by Mr Corbet, the English Chargé d'Affaires, Mr Magee and others, but the dinner I remember best was

given us about three o'clock in the afternoon by a Guatemalteco fellow-passenger at a little restaurant kept by a Frenchman, who spoke delightful broken English, and cooked and served the dinner himself. It was a most excellent dinner, and as we had had nothing decent to eat for many days we did justice to it. When I thought it was all over, imagine my horror when the Frenchman came into the room bearing a huge plum-pudding on fire! 'This,' he cried, beaming with pride, 'is what the Englishman always eats,' and he proceeded to pile my plate with it. This, after a good dinner, with the thermometer over 80! But I struggled on manfully, and then followed the inevitable bottle of sweet champagne.

After a week in the city we started on a trip for a fortnight through the Altos, Antigua and Quetzaltenago, down . . . to Las Nubes, Mr. Nelson's coffee finca [above Mazatenango], and back by the Lake of Atitlan. It was a very enjoyable trip. . . . After a few days in Guatemala City we rode to the port, and on the way met Mr Sarg, and stayed with him for the night or two we had to remain at San José. Thus commenced a friendship which endured until his death in 1920.

From San José, Alfred and Charles sailed on to Acapulco, and thence to San Francisco, California.

After a few days in San Francisco we left for the big trees and the Yosemite Valley. The railway then went only as far as Merced, and the next morning we were to take the coach. The landlord said to me, 'Well, I guess you boys will have a good time, as there is a party of ladies from the East going on with you.' To which I replied, 'Then I think we will wait for the coach next day.' But he replied, 'Then you won't see Yosemite, for this is the last coach going towards the valley this year.'

'So I met my fate!' added Maudslay, for among the party of ladies from the East were Mrs Gouverneur Morris and her two daughters, one of whom many years later he was to marry.

After a trip with the Morrises to the geysers, the brothers went on to Salt Lake City, where they called on Brigham Young. It seems that he, as the head of a reconstituted Old Testament Hebrew kingdom and of a family of twenty-four wives, had become something of a tourist attraction. But unluckily he was away.

In Salt Lake City the Morrises and their friends caught up with them. As both these families were involved with railroads they were travelling in a private car on the newly completed transcontinental railroad, and they invited the Maudslay brothers to travel with them in this car as far as Niagara. Along the way they were particularly impressed by the herds of buffalo and antelope visible from the train, and by the devastation caused by the great fire in Chicago. Then after visits to Boston and New York, they sailed for England, landing in Liverpool on 8 December.

For Long Vacation in the following year, Maudslay planned another adventurous trip, this time with his younger brother Eustace, who had gone up to Cambridge the previous autumn. Their destination was to be Iceland – an unusual choice, but here again the influence of J. W. Clark may be suspected, since he had visited that island in 1860. There, they made their way round the great mass of the Vatna Jokul where the glaciers come close to the seashore, sending broad streams of icy water flowing out over quicksands.

Several times their ponies began to sink, and nearly disappeared from view, but each time with some assistance they gamely struggled out. Maudslay was glad that his experience of mule travel in Guatemala had prompted him to bring from England pack-saddles, spare girths, halters, and so on. Instead of using halters, it appears, the Icelandic practice was to tie a rope round the pony's lower jaw, and in consequence they frequently found a pony's tongue badly cut, sometimes almost cut in two.

Another kind of emergency arose when Eustace developed an abscessed tooth. The only remedy would be extraction, but the one instrument they had was the pincers used for drawing nails from the ponies' shoes, and these were too big to get into Eustace's mouth. A messenger was sent running back to the wife of a doctor who was known to be away. She sent a bundle of instruments, luckily including a good pair of forceps, and Alfred, the medical student, performed his first operation with success.

That autumn Maudslay returned to Cambridge, but was so much troubled with coughs and catarrh that he gave up his medical studies and decided to flee to the tropics. In January 1874, then, he sailed for the West Indies with the intention of growing tobacco in Jamaica. Evidently he had heard that in Jamaica there were a number of refugees from Havana who understood the cultivation of tobacco and were seeking employment. But on reaching Barbados he heard that a strict quarantine had been imposed in Jamaica because of yellow fever. This fever, Maudslay was told, often came on at the end of the rainy season – but would die out again. Not wanting to languish in quarantine, he was persuaded by fellow-passengers to go on with them to Trinidad, and wait there until the quarantine was lifted.

In Trinidad he visited sugar and cacao plantations. The latter he found were often badly managed, although there seemed to be nothing very difficult about the cultivation or the harvesting of the bean, and the crop appeared less affected than sugar by the vagaries of the weather. Maudslay now began thinking seriously of cultivating cacao instead of tobacco. In addition to the commercial possibilities, he was favourably impressed by the year-round calm and quiet as opposed to the seasonal bustle and noise of a sugar plantation, and by the beauty of the plantations. Alternating with rows of cacao trees were rows of *bois immortel* planted to shade them, these being handsome trees bearing red flowers. V. S. Naipaul has described mature cacao woods as being 'like the woods of fairy tales, dark and shadowed and cool. The cacao pods, hanging by thick short stems, were like wax fruit in brilliant green and yellow and red and crimson and purple.'[10]

A fresh turn of events, however, soon caused Maudslay to shelve or discard his tentative and half-formed plan. Having gone back to Barbados with a friend to look at sugar refineries, he found on the return journey to Trinidad that among the passengers on the steamer was the newly appointed governor of the island, William Cairns, who was coming directly from his last appointment as Governor of British Honduras. The day before arriving in Trinidad, Cairns offered Maudslay the post of Private Secretary, warning him that the post might be only temporary, as he was expecting someone out from England. 'Thinking it would be an interesting experience, I accepted, and much to the amusement of my Trinidad friends, I stepped ashore as His Excellency's Private Secretary.' As Maudslay wrote to his mother, 'a private secretaryship to a "first class" government is considered much the most respectable way of entering the Colonial Service – and one is quite sure of promotion if you want it – but I don't think that will ever be my case – a couple of years will teach me all I need to know.'

Cairns he describes as a bachelor of about forty-four, tall and not good-looking, and terribly particular about his food. He told his mother, 'The more I see of the Governor the more I think that he must be an unknown brother of J. W. Clark's, steadied and toned down by the cares of office.' Cairns had brought no servants with him, and Maudslay, in addition to other work, found himself in entire charge of the house, and thus had plenty to do. There were also a great number of letters to write 'which is rather trying to one's spelling' (Maudslay was never a strong speller).[11]

The former Governor's house had burnt down, and the new one was not quite finished, so they were living in a small house known as The Cottage. There the supply of plates and dishes was so meagre that they had to borrow some from the Colonial Secretary, and this very much upset the Governor, who soon applied for leave of absence, and was granted it, as he'd had none since taking up his post in Belize. For the next six weeks Maudslay had an easy time, and much enjoyed having the run of the excellent Botanical Garden, in the midst of which The Cottage stood.[12]

Then he received a letter from Cairns, writing from England, to tell him he would not be returning to Trinidad. In his reminiscences

Maudslay writes that, having been left in the lurch, he thought it best to return to England. Apparently, those earlier plans to grow tobacco or cacao were now abandoned.

Home then he came, and soon went on to France with the intention of learning French, accompanied by his brother Eustace. But while there he heard again from Cairns, who now wrote to tell him he had been appointed Governor of Queensland, and was hoping Maudslay would accept the post of Private Secretary, at a higher salary than in Trinidad. (In retrospect it seems surprising that Cairns accepted a post so close to the Equator, since he had resigned from the governorship of Trinidad for health reasons, and indeed his decision would prove unwise.)

Maudslay accepted Cairns's offer, and in November 1874 met up with him and his ADC (aide-de-camp, or right-hand man to a general or a governor) in Venice to begin their voyage to Australia aboard a succession of P & O Line steamers. At Suez they joined the heavily laden SS *Pekin*. Just before reaching Ceylon, a heavy sea poured water through the open port-holes on the port side, leaving three inches of water in most cabins. 'Much feeble swearing and cursing of fate', reported Maudslay, whom fate had blessed, his cabin being on the not so 'posh' starboard side.[13]

At Galle, Ceylon, they transferred to the SS *Pera*, an old and poorly maintained steamer. So much cargo had been put aboard that coal had to be piled up on deck abaft the mainmast, so that coal-dust often blew over them; and the ship lay so low in the water (those were pre-Plimsoll load-line days) that the portholes could not be opened at all. Their passage through the tropics was exceedingly unpleasant, and Maudslay's was made no easier by the behaviour of Captain MacCarthy, Cairns's ADC, who had recently returned from the Ashanti campaign and was still suffering occasionally from fever. The rats, which were plentiful in the cabin they shared, drove McCarthy wild; but when he took to trying to spit them with his sword Maudslay thought it time to make up a bed on a table outside.

Within a week of taking up his post with Cairns in Trinidad, Maudslay had written home: 'The only thing I am afraid of is that he will require me to be too much with him . . . I have scarcely been out of his company.' And now, even before reaching Brisbane, he was beginning to have doubts whether the position he held was an endurable one. As he wrote later,

Mr Cairns, or Sir William as he had become, was a very odd man. Many years of what I expect was a rather lonely life in Ceylon [an earlier posting] had not made him more sociable. He could be very pleasant at times but his moods were fitful; and his digestion was not good. He considered himself a gourmet, but I cannot say he showed any knowledge of good cooking. I once heard him talking to an acquaintance and discussing a third party, and he wound up his description by saying, 'I tell you what he is like; he is the sort of man who eats marmalade for breakfast.' I asked him afterwards what he considered to be a perfect breakfast, and he replied, 'A bottle of fresh strawberries and a pint of champagne.'

Towards the end of January 1875, they reached Brisbane at last, arriving from Melbourne aboard HMS *Barracouta*, an ancient and sluggish paddle-steamer. Government House proved to be quite a good building, adjoining the Botanical Gardens (to Maudslay's pleasure), but there were less encouraging aspects to their life. The servants engaged by Cairns – inexperienced youths brought out from England, a cook lured away from the Café Anglais in Paris, two stewards picked up by Cairns on the SS *Pera* – were all either incompetent or drunken; the groom and carriage-horses were impossible too.

The fears expressed by Maudslay proved to be only too well grounded.

As MacCarthy and I are the Governor's only companions, and he hates being alone when not in his office, we have plenty of his society, and it is not of the liveliest description. When he is in a good temper he can be pleasant enough, but one never knows how long it will last, and our meals are often too dismal. I used to force the conversation at first, but he was such a wet blanket that I have given it up, and eat too much in consequence. . . . We dine at eight, and afterwards go into the drawing-room, where Cairns will sometimes play a little on the piano, or we play dummy whist or dominoes for about an hour – when H.E. usually falls asleep, and as soon after ten as he happens to awake we all go to bed. Altogether not a very interesting day.

At some point Maudslay had a 'regular bust-up' with Cairns, and before long wrote formally, asking him to look for someone to take his place, as he found life there unsuitable.

Shortly after this letter was written, news came that the new Governor of Fiji, with his family and staff, would soon be arriving from England and would be spending a night in Brisbane on their way to Fiji. Naturally they would have to be invited to stay in Government House, and entertained. The Prime Minister, the Speaker, and other dignitaries were therefore asked to dinner to meet them. Unfortunately, just then the usual chaotic state of the household suddenly became more acute as most of the servants went on strike. Maudslay took upon himself some of their work, and heard afterwards that the visiting Governor's steward reported to his ADC: 'This is a rum Government House, Sir. I have just seen the Private Secretary laying the table for dinner.' Just before dinner Maudslay managed to persuade some of the servants to resume work, and the dinner was fairly well served.

During their stay, Maudslay confided to the visiting ADC and Private Secretary (who were dossed down for the night in his own bedroom, as Cairns hadn't extended to them an official invitation to spend the night) that he had decided to leave Brisbane and might pass through Fiji on his way home. This information must have been passed on to their chief, Sir Arthur Gordon, because on reaching Sydney Gordon wrote to Cairns suggesting that if he could spare Maudslay's services, they would be useful to him in Fiji, where he would be very short-handed. It seems that Sir Arthur, too, during his short stay in Brisbane, had been impressed by Maudslay's resourcefulness and good nature. Cairns agreed to gazette Maudslay as going on special duty to Fiji, thus avoiding, as Maudslay comments, any need to explain why he was leaving.

By the end of July he had left. And Cairns himself was soon to leave Brisbane. With his delicate appearance, lack of skill as a horseman and inhospitable ways, he was never popular with the rather rough settlers, one of whom wrote of him: 'he looks like a Mute at a funeral, and does not seem a very convivial individual.' His transfer to South Australia, however, was stated to be out of regard for his health, which it was thought might benefit by his removal to a cooler climate. That hope would not be realized, for after only eight weeks in Adelaide he resigned on account of insomnia and 'the effects of long tropical residence upon the nervous system'.[14]

Chapter 4

Fiji

T he new Governor of Fiji owed the creation of his post to problems that arose in the South Pacific soon after white traders became active there in the early 1800s. Abuses of the native people, as well as by them, had reached such a level by mid-century that many people felt that efforts to control them were urgently needed. Though cannibalism was no longer rampant, abduction and slavery had taken its place as an evil, and lack of jurisdiction usually made punishment of the offenders impossible. Another problem was that the introduction of firearms had led to warfare between chiefdoms becoming almost endemic.[1]

The task facing Sir Arthur Gordon and his newly recruited administration cannot be understood without a little knowledge of Fiji's circumstances earlier in the century. Before 1800 many South Sea islands had received fleeting visits from European explorers without suffering serious disturbance of their traditional way of life, but inevitably more disruptive visitors would arrive, initially involved in frenetic episodes of trading. First it was sandalwood they sought, and, when that became exhausted, it was sea-slugs, or 'bêches de mer', for the China trade (used in preparation of a culinary delicacy, *trepang*). One of the undesirable consequences of their visits was the diseases they introduced; another was the arrangement made by some traders for part of their payment for sandalwood to consist of help in attacking the Fijian vendor's neighbours.

Worse was to follow. In 1808 a sailor who survived the wreck of a sandalwood trading vessel was rescued by the crew of a canoe, who presented him to the *vunivalu* or war-chief of Mbau, to be 'the *vunivalu*'s white man'. This man organized the rescue of a cargo of muskets from that ship, and, as a result, Mbau soon gained ascendancy over other small chiefdoms, many of which consisted of a just a few miles of coastline with perhaps a village perched on a high rock. With larger stakes, warfare soon increased in violence, villages were burnt, and captives eaten, frequently roasted alive.[2]

But astonishingly, the problem of cannibalism had been solved by the 1850s. Neither political pressure nor armed intervention had been necessary, for, simply by courageous and tactful persuasion, Wesleyan

Methodist missionaries succeeded in converting most of the chiefs, and thus put an end to cannibalism with the loss of just one of their brethren.[3]

Even before the end of the eighteenth century, a growing sense of Christian obligation towards coloured peoples was stirring in Britain, exemplified most notably by the foundation in 1787 of Freetown, Sierra Leone, as a colony for freed slaves, and by the anti-slavery campaign of Samuel Wilberforce. In the Pacific area, Tahiti became the first target of the missionaries, and by 1825 two native Tahitian converts had been sent on from there as missionaries to Fiji.

The many and widely scattered islands that constitute Fiji amount to a land area roughly equivalent to that of Wales or Massachusetts, the largest of these being Viti Levu, or Great Fiji, with about half of the total terrain ('Fiji', the Tongan version of Viti, entered into English usage because that was the version eighteenth-century mariners had first heard in Tonga). Much of Viti Levu is hilly, with a peak of over four thousand feet, and before the importation of European tools the land had been mantled with forests of giant *kauri* pines and other useful trees such as *casuarina* (ironwood, the wood of choice for war-clubs). The soil is rich – mostly old volcanic lavas – so that at the eastern end of the island, where rain falls most abundantly, there is vegetation of truly tropical lushness.

The warm reception the missionaries received owed a good deal to the fact that they were accompanied by an envoy of George Tupou, king of two of the three Tongan islands (Vava'u and Ha'apai), who since 1831 had been a Christian. At baptism the former Taufa'ahau and his queen had taken the names George ('Jiaoji' in Tongan spelling) and Charlotte (Salote) in honour of King George III and his queen. From 1845 they were to reign over a united Tonga – as their descendants still do.

In 1837 one of the missionaries, William Cross, sailed from his base on Lau, a Fijian island with a large Tongan population, to Mbau, an island of only about 20 acres, and so close to Viti Levu that one can wade from one to the other. The acquisition of firearms had enabled the *vunivalu* of this tiny island to become one of the most powerful in the archipelago, and now, following various coups, its ruler was Seru, an ambitious man who thereupon called himself Thakombau, literally 'the Disturber of Mbau'. Thakombau received Cross, but explained that he could not attend to his teaching just then as he was engaged in war.[4]

So Cross established his mission at Rewa, a neighbouring petty kingdom at the southeastern corner of Viti Levu, between Mbau and Suva, the site of the modern capital of Fiji. There he set up a small printing press, for experience had shown that the best technique of proselytizing was to teach the Fijians to read and write, and then give them printed copies of such portions of the scriptures as they had translated.

Another attempt by Cross to approach Thakombau was rebuffed; and yet the tide was turning. In one historian's view, however unwilling the chiefs might have been to acknowledge it, the missionaries exercised a restraint over their actions. . . . Superstition also played its part in extending missionary influence. Among the survivors [of a shipwreck] had been one or two men . . . dressed in black, presumably passengers. These men were killed and probably eaten; and the disastrous epidemic that appeared shortly afterwards was thought to have been due to the wrath of these black-coated strangers' gods. Now, when black-coated missionaries came among them, the Fijians associated them with those earlier visitors.

At last, in 1854, Thakombau made his profession of Christianity and was baptized as Ebenezer (a name seldom if ever used, it seems). Several factors influenced his decision, but among them were the urgings of King George of Tonga, made in person a few months earlier, and repeated in a letter that reached Thakombau not long before he made that decision. The ovens on Mbau were demolished, and there followed a landslide of conversions in western Fiji.

Though cannibalism was nearly extinguished, peace had yet to spread across the land. Before long, Thakombau's fortunes were in decline, and his dream of being a real *Tui Viti* (king of Fiji) evaporating. At this point, having received a hint of help from King George, he offered him his treasured 102-foot double canoe as a gift. Early next year the Tongan fleet duly arrived, and Thakombau's enemies at Rewa were defeated in a terrible battle.

International disputes were also arising from the activities of white settlers in Fiji. Thakombau's worst trouble was instigated by the US Commercial Agent, John B. Williams. This man, a native of Salem, had established his office on a small island off the Rewa delta, and there in 1849 he was firing cannon to celebrate the Fourth of July when one of his cannons burst at the touch-hole and set fire to his house. Among Fijians a fire was always an occasion for legitimate plunder, and the onlookers didn't miss the opportunity. Clearly, the local Rewans were responsible, but at that time they were helpless before the onslaughts of Mbau, so Williams held Thakombau liable for his losses. In a second incident, for which Thakombau was equally innocent, both the mission house and another belonging to Williams were destroyed.[5]

Previous incidents of this kind had had no great repercussions, but Williams's position as US Commercial Agent enabled him to press his claims for compensation with greater force. When an American warship paid a visit, Williams asked the Captain to obtain redress from Thakombau, his claim in the second case resting solely on the grounds that Thakombau was then nominal king of the area. The Captain, all too willing to impose punitive damages, never questioned the grossly inflated figures for damages; $30,000 was demanded at the first hearing, when $5000 might have been more realistic, and somehow at a second hearing the figure rose to $43,531. The Captain told Thakombau that unless he paid within a year he would be transported to the United States. This threat terrified him, and threw him into depression.

Thakombau could see only one solution: to cede his kingdom to the British crown, for by doing so he would also thwart the designs he knew the Tongans of Lau had on his dominions. He therefore asked the newly appointed British Consul, William Pritchard, the first occupant of that post, to prepare a formal deed of cession to the British crown, which would assume responsibility for settling the American claim. The document was drawn up, he signed it, and Pritchard, who seems to have been unaware that Thakombau was ceding lands that had never belonged to him, immediately left with it for London.

In response to this approach, the British government dispatched two men: a Colonel Smythe to report on the political and commercial aspects of the situation, also the possibility of suppressing inhuman practices, and a distinguished botanist, Berthold Seemann, who was to assess the agricultural possibilities. The latter's encouraging report on the possibilities of growing cotton resulted in an influx of would-be farmers from Australia, although the colonel, a pompous man with a preference for full-dress uniform and plumes in the bush, recommended against cession.[6]

The new settlers soon established cotton plantations and sheep stations, and sugar production began. Land disputes inevitably arose, yet no one had authority to make laws or settle them. So, in an attempt to supply this authority, a confederacy of the seven principal chiefdoms was created in 1865, and a code of laws promulgated. For two successive years Thakombau was elected president, but, when his old Tongan rival from Lau jockeyed for this place of honour, he was so greatly distrusted by the other chiefs that they withdrew and the confederacy collapsed.

Concerning his debts to the USA and the threat of transportation, Thakombau had probably ceased to worry, since ten years had passed without hearing more about the matter. In fact the cause of this respite was the more urgent need for US naval vessels to play their part in the Civil War. By 1867, however, a warship could be spared to enforce settlement of those claims. It anchored at Levuka, the chief port, and under threat of bombardment, Thakombau agreed to pay the first instalment within a year, and pledged three islands as security.

When news of his plight became known in Melbourne, a group of adventurers formed a company – the Polynesia Company – for the purpose of buying 200,000 acres from Thakombau in return for payment of his debt and provision of an annuity for him; they would also assume authority to make laws, establish courts, etc. The principals of this company then sailed to Fiji, and took Thakombau on board, where they treated him to a champagne breakfast, after which, in the opinion of the

British consul who saw him that afternoon, he was unfit for business of any description. But he did sign the agreement.

Once again, he had sold land and transferred powers that he had never possessed. The Company immediately ran into opposition from the rightful owners of the land, as well as from the British authorities. It did, however, pay Thakombau's American debt before collapsing.

With cotton fetching a high price owing to the blockade imposed on the American south during the Civil War, there had been a land boom, and cotton plantations sprang up along the Rewa River, and soon were spreading west along the coast. Labour then became scarce, because Fijians were unaccustomed to working as hired hands, so plantation owners began to look outside Fiji for labour. At first, the men imported from Vanuatu, west of Fiji, were well looked after, and duly returned when their term of service ended. But by 1869 concern was already being expressed in the Foreign Office 'that a slave trade with the South Seas was gradually being established by British speculators for the benefit of British settlers . . . in the Fiji Islands'. Voices in favour of annexation were heard in London, but the Colonial Secretary opposed it.

Under existing laws, naval officers had limited powers. This became clear when the notorious small schooner *Daphne* arrived in Fiji, and was then boarded by Captain Palmer of the Royal Navy, and 'found to be carrying a hundred men, and fitted up precisely like an African slaver minus the irons'. The men were stark naked, without even a mat to lie on; there were no bunks or partitions, merely shelves. Yet when Palmer had the ship taken to Sydney under a prize crew as a suspected slaver, the case was dismissed for lack of evidence that force had been used to get or detain the labourers on board.

At last, in 1872, the 'Kidnapping Act', or Polynesian Islanders Protection Act, was passed 'to deal with criminal outrages by British subjects upon natives of islands in the Pacific Ocean not being in Her Majesty's domains nor within the jurisdiction of any civilized power'. This helped, but it was not the end of the story.[7]

One consequence of the activities of the Polynesia Company had been a large influx of settlers. By 1870 the white population had reached about 2500, of whom 600 had squeezed into the narrow coastal strip of Levuka, by then the principal port of Fiji and its commercial capital. On the map Levuka does not look promising as a harbour, but in fact it is protected by reefs, and the prevailing wind favoured the arrival and departure of sailing ships. It stands on the east coast of Ovalau, a volcanic island about 8 miles by 6, which lies some 20 miles northeast of Mbau. Strung out along the narrow strip between foot hills and sea were warehouses, stores, a hotel, mission-station, ramshackle wooden houses, grog-shops, and so on. Along the beach there were rootling pigs, garbage, and empty gin bottles by the hundred. The upland portions of the island, including the fertile bottom of its ancient crater, were inhabited by a wild and hostile tribe, the Lovoni.

Sea Island cotton from Fiji had found a good market in France, but with the outbreak of the Franco-Prussian War in 1870 the price dropped abruptly. The resulting hardship provided one stimulus to the formation in the following year of a single government of Fiji, headed by Thakombau but largely run by Europeans. At last he was king of Fiji! But finding the money needed to form the government was still a problem.

Unexpectedly, it was the Lovoni people on Ovalau who furnished part of it. They had refused to pay a tax imposed by Thakombau, and had then raided villages down on the coast. Thakombau responded with all-out war, and two months later the half-starved Lovoni surrendered. The survivors were sold to plantation owners, as were their confiscated lands, to replenish the *vunivalu*'s treasury. An additional sum came from the sale of two Lovoni warriors and a dwarf pagan priest equipped with the pickled arm of a slain chief, to Barnum, Coup and Costello's Great American Railroad Circus.

Thakombau's government began badly, with the British still withholding recognition, then for a while it found its feet and introduced several elements of good government, but by March 1874 it was foundering again, entirely out of money and wracked by dissension on the question of voting rights for the Fijians. Cession was perhaps the only solution, and there were signs the British might be willing to accept it. The hope it offered of controlling the traffic in labour would certainly be a factor, as would disgust at Thakombau's treatment of the Lovoni.

Two commissioners were appointed to report on the question, Commodore Goodenough, Commander of the Navy's Australia Station, and E. L. Layard (a brother of the famous archaeologist), who as a Colonial Office official had recently made a study of tribal rights and land tenure in New Zealand. Their conclusion was, 'We see no prospect for these Islands should Her Majesty's Government decline to accept the offer of cession, but ruin to the English planters and confusion in the native Government, but as a Crown Colony, we think that Fiji would certainly become a prosperous settlement.' The government then instructed Sir Hercules Robinson, the Governor of New South Wales, to visit Levuka and restate the whole case to the chiefs and the white population. When told that cession would now be accepted, Thakombau replied that, if matters remained as they were, Fiji would become like a piece of driftwood in the sea, and be picked up by the first passer-by. The whites who had come to Fiji, he said, were a bad lot; they were mere beachcombers, or cormorants who would swallow them.

Thakombau and four ruling chiefs signed the deed of cession, and the official ceremony took place on the tenth of October. In a graceful gesture, Thakombau relinquished his old and favourite war-club – 'the former, and until lately, the only known law of Fiji'. Sixty years later, the club was returned to Fiji, now embellished with silver emblems, for use as the mace of the Legislative Council.

Robinson set up a provisional government under Layard, and two months later Thakombau went off to Sydney with two of his sons, for the first vacation of his life. They came as guests of the Robinsons, who arranged for stalls resembling the sleeping spaces in traditional Fijian houses to be rigged up for them in the ballroom of Government House. Thakombau was particularly delighted when Sir Hercules's golden-haired little granddaughter climbed on to his knee, whispering 'You won't eat me, will you?'

Their stay was spoilt by Thakombau's sons' both getting the measles. By the time of their return in mid-January 1875 they were already convalescent, but alas! they were still infectious, and the contagion spread throughout the country. Having no immunity against this new disease, about a quarter of the population perished. Its ravages were diminishing by the time Goodenough returned in June, bringing with him the new Governor, Sir Arthur Gordon, but the remaining population of the island was in a state of shock and depression.

Early in September Maudslay, now in Sydney, joined Lady Gordon, her two children, and several members of Gordon's staff in boarding a steamship bound for Fiji. If the original plan had been for Commodore Goodenough to transport them, then that plan had to be changed, for in August the Commodore, who had gone to Santa Cruz Island 'to open friendly discourse with the natives', was hit by two poisoned arrows, and died a week later.

A new Government House had been built at Nasova, some three-quarters of a mile south of Levuka and almost out of the sight of it, thanks to a small intervening point of land. It was large, with a verandah running all the way round, and constructed of reeds tied together with palm-fibre and fixed to a wooden framework. At first, Maudslay's status in the household was that of a guest, but he leant a hand wherever he could, chiefly in helping Lady Gordon get the house straight. Early in their acquaintance she noted these impressions of him in letters home:

> he is a good photographer and is bringing out a large camera [in fact, he even came equipped with a 'magic lantern']. . . . Mr. Maudslay is very fond of children [the Gordons had two] . . . [he] is working very hard at the language . . . [and] is most handy and useful at contriving all sorts of things, and always arranges the flowers, for which he has a special gift. He is a very clever fellow, and he seems to have plenty of money.[8]

But the Private Secretary, Arthur Gordon[9] (a distant cousin of the Governor's), disliked the work he was expected to do, and, as he was often away travelling on the main island, Viti Levu, Maudslay found himself doing most of it. As he wrote,

> The Governor had an uncomfortable habit of jotting down para-graphs of dispatches or other business memoranda on the backs of old envelopes or any other scraps of paper he could put his hands on, and this made the copying of dispatches, etc., often tedious work, and his table was usually heaped with documents. I was told by the others that it was as much as my life was worth to touch the Governor's papers; but the first time he went away for a few days I thoroughly cleared up his room, put all the papers in order, destroyed all envelopes and scraps of paper, and placed half-sheets tied together at the corner with a conspicuous red silk ribbon on his office table . . . and when he returned not a word of complaint was raised.

Initially Maudslay had no official position, but in December 1875 he was gazetted as Private Secretary and made a member of the commission for settling pre-annexation debts, but without salary.

His new chief, Sir Arthur Hamilton Gordon, was fourth son of the Earl of Aberdeen, Prime Minister of Great Britain from 1852 to 1855, and a man whose conscience made him miserable when political forces beyond his control drew Great Britain into the Crimean War during his premiership. Sir Arthur, already a seasoned governor of colonies (among them Trinidad, before Cairns), was now coming into full development of his powers. Later he was to be Governor General of New Zealand and then of Ceylon.

In a letter to his sister, Maudslay gave a vivid description of him, which is worth quoting almost in full for the light it reflects on the writer as a judge of character:

> A short man, dark, not good-looking, careless of his appearance, short-sighted. As a boy and young man he was his father's greatest friend and companion, and was his Private Secretary when he was Prime Minister. I believe his father never went anywhere, never did anything without him. He was brought up at Haddo, the Scotch coun-try seat (I believe an awfully dull place), was never sent to school, but took a degree at Cambridge. . . . Nowhere has he been popular, since he has a very bad manner with strangers, and he is perfectly aware of it and regrets it much. He is very determined, and puts aside all oppo-sition when his mind is made up, but with people with whom he is in sympathy, though not agreeing, he is perfectly open, and even diffi-dent with subordinates. His personal staff have always been strongly attached to him; with them he is always on the most perfectly easy terms, and not in the least exacting. He is a high Churchman with strong religious opinions which he does not air. He professes to be a thorough liberal, but his aristocratic leanings come out insensibly. He

is very large-minded, and in some things almost an enthusiast. Well-read, particularly in history and in some curiously odd subjects. Very fond of nature and scenery, he has a very artistic appreciation of light and colour. Active, a good walker, utterly careless of what he eats or drinks – or rather, I don't believe he ever knows what he eats or drinks. Often preoccupied when there are difficult matters to settle or schemes to devise, he has a dreadful habit of putting off all writing until the last minute.

The latter was particularly vexing for a Private Secretary!

Upon graduating from Cambridge, Gordon had begun to study for Holy Orders before it came clear to him that he also had a yearning to exert political power for public good. These two tendencies seem to have combined to give him a feeling of divinely inspired mission in the world. Another significant factor in his life had been to serve as liaison between his father as Prime Minister and Bishop Wilberforce.

Initially, Gordon's chief preoccupations were the general depression and discontent in the colony, and the problem of revenues that fell far short of meeting necessary expenditures. As he wrote,

the white settlers had apparently imagined that by some magical process, the assumption of power by Great Britain was to be followed by an immediate change from poverty to wealth . . . and that their claims to supremacy over the natives . . . would at once be acknowledged. They were therefore bitterly disappointed. The natives were cowed and disheartened by the pestilence, which they believed to have been introduced purposely to destroy them [and] perplexed by reiterated assurances from the whites that . . . their own laws and customs had been abolished . . . and their lands had become property of the Crown.

In fact, Gordon's policies were exactly the opposite, for he was determined to preserve as much as possible of the existing social and administrative structures. By placing former chiefs in positions of responsibility in their old territories, he hoped to avoid the creation of a dangerous class of unemployed and disaffected men who still commanded traditional loyalties; and by not employing British district commissioners, magistrates, and so on, money would be saved.

His policies were, in any case, underlain by a basic opposition to the doctrine that the powerful peoples might rightfully exploit the less advantaged. In these views he was echoing his father, who as Foreign Secretary many years earlier had stated that:

the object of Her Majesty's Government in increasing their connexion with the Chiefs ought to be rather to strengthen those authorities and to give them a sense of their own independence, by leaving the administration of justice in their own hands, than to make them feel their dependence on foreign powers.

In Fiji the system worked remarkably well, and was to become a landmark in British colonial history. Gordon's Chief Medical Officer in Fiji, William MacGregor (later knighted), followed in his footsteps when he was appointed Governor of British New Guinea (Papua), and much later the famous system of indirect rule applied by Lugard in Nigeria would owe a considerable debt to his practice.

Gordon's policies in Fiji have naturally been the subject of considerable later discussion. An historian, Peter France, saw them as espousing 'evolutionary biology and insisting . . . that mankind has progressed on uniform lines all over the globe through a series of identifiable stages from barbarism through savagery to civilization' – in other words, Lewis Morgan's theory of unilinear evolution.[10] Gordon was indeed interested in the nascent discipline of anthropology, and approved of the work of Sir Henry Maine, who stated that

> the usages which a particular community is found to have adopted in its infancy . . . are generally those which are on the whole best suited to promote its physical and moral well being; and if they are retained in their integrity until new social wants have taught them new practices, upward march of society is almost certain.

But Maine had unequivocally dissented from Morgan's theory, and, as Ian Heath has shown, Gordon's writings show him to have known nothing of Morgan's terminology or theories.[11]

Gordon's belief that by appointing former chiefs to new responsibilities they would embrace new loyalties was soon to be tested. In the central mountainous regions of Viti Levu there were living about seven thousand mountain people, or Kai Tholo, who had kept themselves apart, beyond the reach of ambitious chiefs in former times, and were still untouched by Christian teaching. They had caused trouble five years earlier, but after Walter Carew, the government agent who knew them best, had brought them news of cession, and explained that they would be exempted from ordinary laws, he was able to persuade ten of the village chiefs to come down to Levuka and meet the Governor. This was Maudslay's first encounter with the Kai Tholo, 'wild-looking creatures', as he described them:

> one or two of the younger ones stark naked and the others with the scantiest loin-cloth, but all with huge heads of hair. The Governor made a good speech to them, and they appeared to be impressed. In the evening they gave us a war dance. The coconut grove where they danced was illuminated with bonfires, and it was a most weird and striking scene.

Maudslay may not have known that the big heads of hair, up to 5 feet in circumference (sometimes, though, these were wigs), were also a symbol of independence. But unfortunately, all of them caught the measles in Levuka, and naturally they attributed the outbreak to poison, or the anger of heathen gods at their reception of Christianity.

Carew, now Resident Commissioner at Nasauthoko, half-way up the Singatoka River, sent down discouraging reports, one of them declaring, 'I cannot see how one can govern mountaineers who constantly have double-cocked guns in their hands.' Soon, indeed, they 'threw off the cloth', that is, by returning to total nakedness they expressed their defiance of the government; then in April 1876 they attacked and burnt some Christian villages on the coast, taking several lives. Gordon was now faced with a problem: the British troops at his disposal were too few to be used alone, and, if reinforcements were sent for, further raids and killings could be expected before they arrived. His decision was to use Fijian irregulars commanded by officers of his staff, so a call was sent out to the local chiefs, asking each of them to provide thirty men. In the event, double or treble the numbers asked for were sent, and the Governor's theory was confirmed.

Gordon, accompanied by Maudslay and an interpreter, then sailed from Levuka round the north coast to a town on the Nandi River, at the western extremity of the island. From there the Governor proposed to walk up to Nasauthoko, or at least to a village half-way up, to meet Captain Knollys, who was in command of the native troops. In preparing for this expedition, Maudslay examined and tested the ancient muskets of their armed guard (half of them refused to go off the first time), and since the men were wearing *sulus*, native kilts without pockets, he set about making ammunition pouches out of canvas, which he sewed up with bureaucratic red tape from his dispatch box.

A long walk next morning took them across the coastal plain, then up a ridge and along it, reaching Wai Wai before dark. This was a fortified settlement, protected by a fighting ditch backed by a bamboo fence. Maudslay stood guard on the middle watch of a cold and rainy night, and early next morning Knollys arrived with his troops.

> A very barbaric-looking force they were – faces painted black and red, streamers, sashes and turbans of white or smoke-browned masi [bark-cloth], white or scarlet sulus, or long black bead-strung likus [fringed kilts of glossy seaweed, or of pandanus leaves] and big fighting fans in the hands of every chief. Each dress seemed more fantastic than the last ones I had looked at, and many of my old acquaintances were so disguised that I could not recognize them.

They then set off for Nasauthoko in single file, with a young chief running ahead, quivering his big war fan. A walk of some miles brought them in sight of Nasauthoko, two camps or villages with double defensive walls, some two thousand feet below.

Ever since leaving Nandi, Maudslay had suffered a sore foot, and, because the descent to Nasauthoko had made it worse, he stayed behind when the Governor set off on the return journey to Nandi. Two days later, when the expected instructions from him had not arrived, and as food supplies were running low, Knollys thought it time to make a raid on the enemy's plantations. As Maudslay noted,

> He did not like to leave camp himself, expecting that [Arthur] Gordon might arrive, so sent sixty of his police under Tevita and [others] under Neamani. It was such a lovely morning and my foot was so much better that I could not resist the temptation to go with them. Our hunting grounds were to be the river flats of the Singatoka. . . . Tevita and Neamani seemed determined to take good care of me; they impressed the [Nandi] parson (who was of course armed himself) into my service to carry my rifle and ammunition, and one or other of them insisted on carrying me over the many brooks.
>
> [At the top of a hill,] Tevita called a halt . . . and the men grouped themselves on a [hillock] facing us. Then Tevita rose and made a long speech, urging them to act like brave men . . . asking, 'Could they fight? What deed would they have to boast of when the war was over?' Then, as the name of the land was called out, the *sotias* [soldiers] from that place rushed out like wild men from the crowd, dancing frantically in front of us, and shaking their guns in our faces, made the boast of what they would do. . . .
>
> When the men from each district had made their '*bole*' (boast), Tevita wound up his oration with a warning I had hardly expected of him, telling them that they were no longer making war Vaka Viti, but Vaka Piritania (British fashion); that should any fighting occur that day they were not to rush forward to club fallen men for the honour of securing their bodies.

Their scavenging produced only meagre returns in yams and taros, and they saw but two of the enemy. Maudslay's account of this episode ends there because his leg became so bad that he had to be sent back to the coast on the only horse in the island. His native guard called it '*na paca levu*' (the big pig) and kept feeling its ribs and asking if it was good to eat.

By early July his leg had recovered, and by the end of the month the little war was over. A few of those responsible for the worst atrocities were executed, and by October the Governor was able to issue a proclamation of free pardon to all Kai Tholo. Two only recently Christianized chiefs were given gold rings for their conspicuous gallantry in removing kegs of gunpowder from a burning house.

There was good news also for Maudslay, for, in consequence of the Colonial Secretary's leaving Fiji for a new posting, he was now appointed Acting Colonial Secretary and Receiver General, with salary. But Maudslay knew that J. B. Thurston would later be given the post of Colonial Secretary, although time would have to pass before antipathy to him felt by the white settlers would abate, this being due to his refusal, while a member of Thakombau's government, to allow them to take complete control of it.

Jocularly, Maudslay wrote to his sister:

> after the Chief Justice and the Officer commanding the troops, I am the biggest swell in the colony, and the whole of the administrative work is done through me. Of course I know that the appointment is not likely to be permanent, but I think I have every chance of holding it for a year, and by that time I hope to get something I should like under the High Commission [for the Western Pacific]. The Governor thanked me very heartily for the work I had already done for him, and told me that without flattery he must say that he did not know what it was to have a good Private Secretary until I had come to him. I sigh when I think that I shall have to give up my scheme of six months ruralizing among the natives, but of course this is far too good a chance to let slip in favour of schemes of my own.

'Ruralizing' – an intriguing expression, but what did Maudslay mean by it? Perhaps he was hoping to spend time wandering at leisure through Fiji, and perhaps other islands; he would stay in villages making friends and improving his grasp of Fijian dialects; he would study the people, add to his ethnographic collections; and of course study birds. From boyhood ornithology had been the subject closest to Maudslay's heart; it had been birds of the tropical rain-forest that had lured him to Guatemala on graduating from Cambridge; in the Caribbean and Australia they had absorbed his attention; but now in Fiji they began to take a back seat to ethnographic objects.

By chance a note of Maudslay's that confirms his changing interests has survived. It was preserved only because the other side of the sheet of paper on which it was jotted down (and later cancelled) was used by him for setting down a legend from Rotuma Island. The paragraph of twenty-two lines is apparently a draft entry for a catalogue of his collection, and in it he discusses the use of hafted adzes in building dug-out canoes: whereas latterly such adzes had been used mainly for opening *ivi* nuts, in 1875 he had learnt from an old canoe-builder that for hollowing out logs

> he found the stone tool better adapted than any of the European implements. Unfortunately at that time my interests were chiefly concentrated on Ornithology so that I missed obtaining much valuable

information from this native shipbuilder, and it was alas! the first and last opportunity of seeing a stone adze used in Fiji for its legitimate work.[12]

His initiation into collecting was undoubtedly due to three of those living in Government House who were already keen collectors of ethnographica. The most serious was Arthur Gordon, who had been asked by A. W. Franks of the British Museum to collect for him; another was the Governor himself;[13] and the third was a young guest of the Governor's who must now be introduced, Baron Anatole von Hügel.

Only twenty years old when he arrived in Fiji, thus four years younger than Maudslay, von Hügel was the son of a Scottish mother and an Austrian father, a man of considerable distinction as a soldier, diplomat, and naturalist-explorer. A year after leaving boarding school, Anatole had been felled by an illness, probably rheumatic fever, and made a fair recovery, but his doctor advised him to complete it by making a round-trip to Australia on a sailing ship. Once there, however, he chose to remain in Australasia for four years, with the initial aim of collecting zoological specimens, particularly birds.[14]

Fetching up by chance in Fiji, he soon discovered that three other ornithologists had already worked there, and, as to the flora, it had been described rather fully by Seemann. Yet no one had even begun to take a serious interest in the Fijians themselves or their artefacts; they 'might have been so many cabbages for anything their white fellow creatures cared to know of them, their customs or their history'. Realizing that enormous changes had already occurred, and would continue under colonial rule, he decided to concentrate on ethnographic collections, for it might well be the last chance to study the people in anything resembling their original condition.

Von Hügel reached Fiji in May 1875 (a month before Gordon), and at once set off into the interior of Viti Levu accompanied only by an interpreter, a white lad, and bringing with him a large stock of trade goods with which to barter for spears, clubs, ceremonial bowls, bark-cloth, etc. After six weeks, with his money and trade goods exhausted, he was on his way back to Levuka, weakened by eating little but yams, troubled by rheumatism provoked by long marches in the rain, and with his clothes bereft of buttons because he had cut them off to trade for native ornaments, when unexpectedly he ran into Carew and Arthur Gordon. They helped him on his way back to Levuka, and there introduced him to the Governor, who, sensing the charm and enthusiasm of this remarkable young man, gave him the run of Government House.

When Maudslay arrived with Lady Gordon in mid-October, the two men soon became close friends, Maudslay regarding von Hügel as 'a most delightful companion', and von Hügel writing of Maudslay in his journal: 'he is such a jolly, hearty, frank young fellow, full of life and spirit and sense (thank goodness).' Maudslay was given a bedroom next to that of von Hügel, who often sat up very late writing his journal and letters, and therefore tended not to stir very early. Maudslay tells that he 'usually got him out of bed in the morning with the aid of a native fish spear which was easily passed through the reed partition between our rooms. Then we all went off to bathe from the jetty in front of the house'.

As von Hügel wrote in his journal, 'it was not long before the house took on a Museum look – and the price of artefacts in the islands rose tenfold'. He helped Maudslay decorate a room: 'he displays much taste and the *masi* [bark-cloth] and clubs, bowls, etc, look very well'. As will later be recounted more fully, the governor and Maudslay were both to give their collections to Cambridge University, where they formed the nucleus of a new museum, the direction of which would be entrusted to von Hügel.

It is clear that both men fell for the charm of their many Fijian friends, although Maudslay, because he had work to do, could not spare as much time for hanging out with them as von Hügel. The baron was often at a loose end in Ovalau or Mbau, sometimes because he was unwell, or recuperating from inland journeys, and during one period suffering a much worse episode of 'Fiji leg' than Maudslay's (a complaint possibly caused by coral abrasions).

Von Hügel felt especially at home in the house of Andi (Lady) Kuila, one of Thakombau's daughters, a lady of ample proportions who treated him like a son. Maudslay and he both enjoyed lazy evenings lying on comfortable mats, joking with her, teasing and flirting with girls, and drinking *yangona* (kava), a potion brewed from a root that first has to be chewed.[15] It was a drink von Hügel became rather addicted to, and, as he commented, 'it makes a great difference if it is chewed by an ivory set of teeth set in a radiant little face, [rather] than by the smoke-blackened grinders of a dirty mountaineer'. They made firm friendships with many Fijian men, too. Maudslay thought 'many Mbau men . . . so handsome and well made that I think they would look well anywhere (provided, of course, they are not dressed up in blue velvet coats and knickerbockers and tall white hats, the costume in which the late Prime Minister, Mr Woods, insisted on the *vunivalu* appearing in public)'.

In sum, there is no question that Maudslay very much enjoyed his time in Fiji. He had tasted adventure, even a little danger, and gained administrative experience. He had made friends and acquaintances of the most varied kind (while wondering, I am sure, at the contradictory blend of gentleness and violence that some of them had exhibited until a few years earlier). Among other aspects of Fijian life that intrigued him were the *mekes* or dances, and the extraordinary ocean-going canoes. Most delightful of all was the beauty of the land, its vegetation, and its birds.

In fact he had managed to tame several birds, and had them living around the house.

My greatest pet is a little lorikeet about the size of a bullfinch; his back and tail are the most beautiful golden green, his breast and the ring round his neck are a bright crimson, and the head and the feathers round his legs are purple. You cannot image anything more lovely. There is nothing of the vulgarity of a gaudy-coloured parrot about him, and he has a pretty little beak and a long brush tongue. He is perfectly tame and likes to sit upon my head and pass his feather tongue along a single hair. He lives just outside my bedroom and his favourite perch is on a branch of a brilliant yellow croton, which suits his style exactly.

At the end of the year it was arranged that Lady Gordon and the children should go to New Zealand, to escape the hot weather in Fiji. The Governor suggested that Maudslay go with them; or, as the latter wrote to his sister Isabel,

> personally he would like me to go, but officially he could very ill spare me. . . . So I put it to [him] this way: If I am to hold the post [of Colonial Secretary] for any length of time I will stay and make the most of my time, but if only for a few months I would just as soon go now when the bad weather is beginning, and have a few months in the cool climate of N.Z.
>
> And another consideration which I did not mention to him: having been Colonial Secretary, it was as well [or better] to go away holding that position than change back to a less important position. I know his own wish was to make me his Private Secretary and to add the office of Receiver General, which would give me a seat on the Council, an arrangement that I hardly think would work very well.

So, as he really felt in need of a change in climate, it was finally decided that he should accompany Lady Gordon, her children, and nanny to New Zealand. They all boarded 'a huge American steamer' of 3000 tons, equipped with a President's Chamber and a Social Hall, and arrived at Auckland on New Year's Eve 1876.

In the same letter to his sister, he confided to her some other tentative but revealing plans for the future.

> I am in hopes at no very distant date to get some work under the High Commission [for the Western Pacific] which would suit me even better than Colonial work and this was a further inducement for me to go now. Look on the map for the Tongan or Friendly Islands – you will find them just to the East of Fiji. Well, they are ruled over by King George who is eighty years old. The succession to the crown is very uncertain; there will in every probability be a row over it. . . . Things although quiet now are likely to be upset when the present king dies and my idea is to go there from New Zealand if I can get a passage

and loaf about the country for a month or so to pick up information. The Germans evidently have an eye to the place as they are trying to make treaties and conventions, etc., with the present king, and the missionaries seem to be in favour of them, and there is nothing to lose if we are to try and establish our influence there. If I were to go from Fiji, everybody would know about me and would 'smell a rat,' so I much prefer going from N.Z. Of course when the High Commission arrives, H.E. can make me a Deputy Commissioner as soon as it is convenient, and if I do good work there up to the time of the King's death – when I suppose the crisis will come – I shall have a claim for pretty nearly anything I like in the Western Pacific.

Two months earlier von Hügel had written in his journal, '[Then] we retire to Maudslay's room and talk over prospects of island Commissionerships! His dream is New Guinea or thereabouts. He intends sounding H.E., but I fear he'll have little chance, though he intends bearing all the expenses himself.'[16]

Chapter 5

Samoa

A s soon as he had settled Lady Gordon and her children at an
hotel in Auckland, Maudslay went off on excursions to both
North and South Islands.[1] First, he went by steamer to Tauranga,
about 60 miles south of Auckland, where he hired a horse and engaged a
Maori-speaking guide for a 40-mile ride. This took him through an extraordinary forest, one that he considered the most beautiful he'd seen
outside of the tropics. At a Maori village on the shore of Lake Ohinimotu
he tried bathing in the hot springs, and wallowed in the soft, delicious
mud. Then, engaging another guide, a Maori with whom he got on very
well, he went on to see the famous terraces at Rotomahana before returning to Auckland.

There he visited Sir George Grey, the former Governor, and the
originator of the phrase 'one man, one vote', so it is hardly possible that
they failed to discuss the rather similar problems that had afflicted Fiji
and New Zealand. Then Grey, hearing of his desire to meet the independent Maori king, gave him letters of introduction to His Majesty and
some of the principal chiefs.

Following the eruption in the 1840s of various land-wars between
Maoris and settlers, a group of Maoris began to suspect that British
superiority derived from their unity under a monarch. So they started a
movement to unite Maoris under their own king, and in 1856 'King
Country' came into being along the Wanganui River. It would retain its
independence until King Tawhiao abdicated in 1881.

On arrival at the border, Maudslay presented Grey's letter to a
friendly chief in government employ. By next morning this man had
come to the conclusion that, since the native disturbances in Fiji had been
settled so quickly, then the Queen must have sent Maudslay to the
Maoris to find out why the same settlement could not be reached in New
Zealand. Accordingly he had written to the King's chief minister to tell
him so. This was a blow, since Maudslay wanted to come discreetly, as a
private citizen.

As it was, when he reached the house of a chief a few miles in, he
could not avoid talking about Fiji and the little war, and the problems of

other islands of the Pacific, to a highly interested crowd squeezed into a small hut. Then, after a meal,

> hearing a great din from the hammering of iron bars on kerosene tins, I asked what it meant, and was told it was Sunday, and those were bells for church! I made it Thursday, but the Maoris had started a new religion, and I was told that the King had decided that four Sundays in the month were too many, so they had a Sunday every ten days.[2]

When Maudslay showed the Maoris photographs he'd taken in Fiji, they looked at them with keen interest, but were shocked by the undress of the girls, remarking that it was even worse than that of the ladies at Government House balls.

Eventually, Maudslay convinced them that he really hadn't come on political business, and they were very disappointed, even incredulous, for they could not understand his motive for coming at all. And he never got permission to see the King.

To round off his holiday travels, Maudslay then went down to the South Island, where he wandered for two or three weeks before returning to Auckland in time to join Lady Gordon on the mail steamer for the return journey to Fiji.

'Two days after our arrival in Suva', as Maudslay later wrote,

> letters came to say that a deputation of chiefs was on its way from Samoa to petition the Governor for British protection. . . . The Governor and I immediately returned to Levuka. . . . The chiefs did not appear to know what they wanted; and since the commissions as High Commissioner [for the Western Pacific] and Consul-General had not yet reached the Governor, he had no power to act, and could do no more than say that the petition would be forwarded to the Queen.

The creation of these offices had been authorized under the Pacific Islanders Protection Bill, but the Order in Council creating them did not follow as expected, and Gordon was furious at the delay.

> I had intended not to leave England without it, but was at last persuaded . . . to start in March [1875] on the distinct promise in writing that it should be sent after me immediately [by telegraph], and that I should probably find it awaiting me in Sydney on my arrival there. I did not find it there.[3]

(A principal cause of the delay, it appears, had been Foreign Office jealousy of Colonial Office infringement of their authority.)

So now Gordon asked Maudslay to go to England and try to hurry up the commissions, explain the financial position of Fiji, and see to certain other matters. As Maudslay described it, 'my instructions were very short, very liberal, and practically placed the Governor's resignation in my hands, if I found his wishes were not acceded to'. The urgency that Sir Arthur attached to this mission is indicated by the fact that he himself would pay for the travel expenses.

Maudslay departed on 11 May 1877 by way of Hawaii, San Francisco and New York, reaching England ten weeks later.[4] There, in Westminster, he found people distracted by South African affairs, the Russo-Turkish war, and approaching summer holidays, but in *Life in the Pacific Fifty Years Ago* he wrote that he had a very interesting time, met many distinguished people, and, among other engagements, had breakfast alone with Mr Gladstone.[5] He was sure that he worried the Colonial and Foreign Offices a good deal, but at last he did succeed in getting both commissions telegraphed to Australia for Sir Arthur.

The principal task that Sir Arthur had given Maudslay was that of working out a scheme for the efficient functioning of the High Commission. Gladstone, the Prime Minister, had long been opposed to expansion of British dominion, and during discussions about acceptance of Fiji's offer of cession he had said had no wish 'to be a party to any arrangement for adding Fiji and all that lies beyond it to the cares of this overdone and overburdened Government and Empire', though he would admit to being much 'exercised in his mind about the Fiji Islands'.

The Order in Council for creating the High Commission was, nevetheless, passed, and shortly afterwards Maudslay presented the Colonial Office with his plan to extend British control over affairs in 'all that lay beyond Fiji' – an area, in fact, of nine million square miles. Basing it on Gordon's views, as he understood them, Maudslay suggested the installation of two more deputy commissioners (in addition to those covering Tonga and Samoa);[6] one would be resident in the New Hebrides and be given a sailing vessel of 20–30 tons for his use; the other would cover the Solomons, New Guinea, and other groups, and, in view of the vast area of his bailiwick, he would live aboard a steamship of 150 tons. Robert Herbert, Permanent Under-Secretary for the Colonies, called it 'as usual, much too grand' – but before the end of the century Britain's protection had indeed been extended to the Solomons, Gilbert and Ellis Islands, and Tonga, and the New Hebrides had become an Anglo-French condominium (now Vanuatu, which achieved independence in 1980).

In his book Maudslay tells how at the last moment before his departure, 'there was a hitch over the Great Seal. Mr. Herbert tried to persuade me to start for Fiji, saying that the seal would be sent after me, but I refused to budge. "The seal will be a very heavy package for you to carry across Europe", said Mr. Herbert. But I would not let that alter my determination.' At last it was ready, and Maudslay set off with it, packed in an official mail bag stamped with Colonial Office and Foreign Office seals. He travelled by way of Brindisi, the Suez Canal, Galle (Ceylon), and Melbourne, arriving in Fiji on 21 January. There he was told that the

Colonial Office had praised his negotiations with them, and the Governor also seemed pleased.

A week after his return Maudslay was appointed Lands Commissioner, and went off to the mouth of the Navua River to try land claims. There hordes of mosquitoes obliged the court to move some miles up river to the house of a celebrated character, Harry Danford, better known as 'Harry the Jew' (who was not, in fact, Jewish). He had lived in Fiji for over fifty years, after running away from a whaler in Tonga, and then had crossed to Fiji in a canoe. As Maudslay remarked, not so much was thought of a voyage of two or three hundred miles out to sea in a native canoe in those days. Harry had lived on the best of terms with the most ferocious cannibals, but being a sailor and a handy man he was invaluable to a tribe always at war, as he understood the mystery of the locks of guns, and how to bargain with the white men when they began to penetrate. When Maudslay left, Harry made him a present of one of his sons, aged about sixteen, who stayed with him until he was about to leave the Pacific. Then he returned him to his father.[7]

With this mission completed, Maudslay and Harry's lad canoed most of the way up the river, assisted presumably by the canoe's owner, and walked through the mountains till they came to the headwaters of the Rewa River. (Mention of canoeing may suggest lightweight American-Indian canoes or their modern descendants, but of course Maudslay and his lad were using an outrigger dug-out, as had von Hügel on the Rewa River three years before.) Two days of canoeing brought them down to Rewa Town, and thence to Levuka. There Maudslay was met on the pier by the Governor with the startling news that HMS *Sapphire* was in harbour, and that Maudslay was to leave in her at once for Samoa. He had to plead for two days' respite in order to write up his land reports, hear the Samoan news, and receive his instructions.

Samoa lies about 600 miles north of Tonga, and consists of four principal islands, or groups, strung out in a nearly east–west line; another very small one, Manono, was also the seat of considerable power, just as Mbau had been in Fiji (also like Mbau, it became at one point a centre of heathen practices after the other islands had adopted Christianity). The political situation in these islands, as he would learn, in some ways resembled that of Fiji in comprising both a problem with imported labour and a long tradition of warfare. Though cannibalism had never been common practice, a missionary visiting Manono in 1832 was shown a record of battles kept by means of collected stones: they numbered 197. Along with the similarities there came one marked difference: the degree of international rivalry and power-plays over the island.[8]

In the preceding century the islands had seldom been under the rule of a single king; instead, power was shared between five ruling families, with rather frequent changes in the share of it that each enjoyed. There were also five political districts, the central and most fertile island, Upolu, being divided into three. For a time in the 1830s there had been a king of all the islands, Malietoa, the first of his family to hold the title, but near the end of his life he declared his wish to be also the last. At his death in 1841 recurrent struggles began once more, the principal contestants being Laupepa and Pe'a, who faced each other across Apia Bay. Early in 1869 the two sides advanced towards each other, both sides putting up breastworks, until a battle broke out that lasted three days and nights. Curiously, care was taken not to harm the whites; a fight would even halt to allow them to pass. Nothing was resolved by the battle, and the power struggle continued, with lulls, until 1873, when British and US gunboats arrived and enforced a settlement giving Laupepa control.

Apart from missionary activity, there were then two factors responsible for increased European and American rivalry in Samoa. One was the establishment in 1857 of an agency (later, its Pacific headquarters) of the great Hamburg trading firm, J. C. Godeffroy and Son, the pioneers in shipping copra to Germany, rather than coconut oil extracted from it locally. In Germany the oil was squeezed out by hydraulic presses and used for making stearine-coconut oil candles; the pulp went for cattle feed.[9]

This company had bought about 25,000 acres of land, and worked it with imported labourers, mostly from the Gilbert Islands. The local manager was a shrewd, perhaps even machiavellian, man named Theodor Weber who came to wield considerable political power. Although in the present work unfavourable mention will be made of certain secret agreements entered into by the company, it should be emphasized that in general its operations appear to have been conducted scrupulously, and Caesar Godeffroy (as his fellow Hamburger Berthold Seemann called him) deserves credit for devoting a good part of the profits to supporting the Godeffroy Museum (of ethnography) in Hamburg, and its publications.[10]

The second cause of rivalry was the completion of the Union Pacific Railroad line to San Francisco in 1869. This opened up a new horizon for shipping lines, because the route between Europe and Australia via North America would be both quicker and cheaper than those crossing the Isthmus of Panama or going round Cape Horn. First, however, an intermediate coaling station would be needed, and, when it was known that the shipbuilder W. H. Webb was hoping to establish one in Samoa, Theodor Weber, by then serving also as German Consul, hinted that his government was intending to claim the whole of Samoa in order to establish a naval base there. The rumour was denied by Berlin, which at that time scarcely had a navy, but it may have spurred the US Government in 1872 to send a warship to choose a site for a naval coaling station of its own. Pango Pango, on Tutuila Island, was found to be the best site, and the chief of the island signed an agreement granting exclusive use of it to the USA. This, however, was never ratified by Washington.

In the following year there arrived in Samoa a remarkable rogue, Colonel A. B. Steinberger. He had been recommended to President Grant by Webb, and now he came as the President's special confidential agent charged with reporting on the harbours of Samoa, the fertility of the soil, and the disposition of the inhabitants. After a few months, Steinberger returned to Washington to submit his report; and also deliver a letter, together with various presents, from Samoan chiefs, who now requested not only annexation but also the appointment of Steinberger himself as Governor. This task done, he made a quick visit to Germany, where he concluded a secret agreement at Godeffroy's head office in Hamburg by which the firm would promote Germany's recognition of the government he hoped to head, and he, in return for patronage of the company, would receive $2 per ton of copra and ten per cent on other transactions with the firm.

On his return to Washington, Steinberger was disappointed to find there was no hope of annexation, but he was given a letter from President Grant to deliver to the chiefs, thanking them for their presents, and a quantity of arms as a further gift. Permission to return to Samoa in an American man-of-war was conceded, although he was required to pay his passage.

On 1 April 1875 he arrived in the USS *Tuscarora*, and after delivering the letter Steinberger's activity as an agent should have been strictly limited to gathering information. His ambitions, however, knew no limits, for, having come in a warship, he easily persuaded the Samoans that he had been sent to them by the President in answer to their request. Their constitution was then revised so that a parliament would be elected; kings would be appointed for four-year terms (with the rival claimants to the throne occupying it alternately), and the king would appoint a premier. In May Laupepa assumed the kingship, and in July Steinberger became premier and virtual dictator. Soon after, his schooner arrived, a vessel he had purchased in San Francisco with covert financing from Godeffroy's, and then he armed it with some of the weapons brought on the *Tuscarora*. This was a flagrant offence for a boat flying the American flag.

In many ways Steinberger's government was the best Samoa had seen, but it rested on a fraudulent claim of American backing, and his arrangements with the Godeffroy Company were hopelessly irregular. On discovering these facts, the US and British Consuls and the missionaries actively opposed him, and the king wavered in his loyalty.

Steinberger's dominion lasted only five months, and in December a preliminary account of its end was received in Fiji and relayed by Maudslay to his sister:

It seems that Captain Stevens of the *Barracouta*, who has been backed up by the American Consul, has taken prisoner Colonel Steinberger (the American Filibuster . . .), and has now got him safely locked up on board the *Barracouta*, and I suppose Captain Stevens is playing at being king of Samoa, an amusement that gallant captain will enjoy exceedingly. I don't suppose Stevens has the slightest right to imprison Steinberger, and some very amusing complications may arise. One good thing should come of it; it will wake up the people at home, and hurry on the preparation of the Governor's commission as High Commissioner. . . . Report says that when Steinberger was arrested his *Commission from Washington* about which he boasted, and pretended it gave him great powers, proved to be two old passports pasted together [and that in fact was the case].

Maudslay, who had known Captain Stevens since his voyage on the *Barracouta* from Melbourne to Brisbane, had obviously formed some idea of his excitable character (and after the event von Hügel noted 'his blundering, bouncing, self-willed stupidity'). But the complications that did indeed arise in this case were not particularly amusing. Apparently, when the *Barracouta* came in to Apia on a routine visit, Stevens had been urged by the consuls and the missionaries to demand Steinberger's American credentials. In hearings conducted by the King, Stevens became so excited that he even referred to the US President in quite undiplomatic terms: 'This man Grant's letter is simply a friendly letter; it means nothing!' When no credentials were forthcoming, Steinberger was denounced to the King, who was then persuaded to request his arrest as an impostor. On Steinberger's being taken on board ship under armed guard, the chiefs' and people's councils blamed their fickle king and he in turn was deposed. The zealous Stevens then made the mistake of taking him with a guard of honour to meet the chiefs, apparently hoping to secure his reinstatement. Instead a miniature battle ensued, resulting in the death of three sailors and eight Samoans, with others wounded.[11]

Steinberger was then taken to Fiji in the *Barracouta* and there put ashore. Eventually he made his way to London, where he sued the British government for damages, and obtained a compromise settlement. Captain Stevens was found guilty by court martial of actions grossly exceeding his authority, and dismissed; and the British and American Consuls were recalled. No one came out of the incident with much credit, and Samoa fell once more into disarray.

At this point the native councils seem to have decided that, in view of the growing commercial interests of Germany, Britain, and the USA, no hope remained of a native government surviving without foreign support. They would therefore put out feelers seeking foreign protection. This had been the purpose of that deputation of Samoan chiefs which had arrived in Fiji to see the Governor soon after Maudslay's return from

New Zealand, and had thereby galvanized the Governor into dispatching him to London to expedite the commission, since without it he could do little for them. In contrast, the Samoan delegate sent to Washington did succeed in negotiating a treaty of peace with the USA, one that also bound the USA to use its good offices in case Samoa became engaged in dispute with a third nation.

In 1877 two attempts were made by the former King Laupepa's party to overthrow the government, the second resulting in a rout which would have ended in a massacre had they not been given shelter in the British consulate. So, as soon as he received his commission, Sir Arthur went to Samoa, where he found that the Consul, whom he had from the beginning described as 'puzzle-headed', had just died of mental illness. Gordon managed to have an agreement drafted that established Apia as an extraterritorial municipality – neutral ground so far as native wars were concerned. His other objectives were to obtain compensation for the sailors killed in the skirmish and to settle the problem of the defeated chieftains who still languished within the grounds of the consulate. Sir Arthur then seized a schooner belonging to the Samoan government as partial reparation, and sailed off to Fiji with it in tow. The remaining problems he would leave for Maudslay to settle.

'It was into this turmoil', Maudslay wrote, 'with no previous knowledge of a Consul's duties, and with my instructions dotted down on a half-sheet of notepaper, that I was suddenly launched'. How lonely he must have felt when, on 12 March 1878, he arrived at Apia, not knowing a soul on those islands!

The new Acting Consul and Deputy Commissioner began by delivering letters from Sir Arthur and the Colonial Office to the chiefs. Then he explained to them that, if the terms offered were accepted, the schooner would be returned to them. Negotiations went on for days, with the various clauses being approved, but signature was not forthcoming. Finally, he cut down the clauses to two – payment of a $1000 fine, and a written pledge for the safety of the chieftains still confined within the fence of the consulate. They were given twenty-four hours to settle the matter; failing this, punitive action would be taken by the Navy. The deadline was extended, and at the very last moment the chiefs came with money tied up in coloured handkerchiefs, consisting of an assortment of coins ranging from French francs to cast-iron Bolivian dollars.[12]

> The absurd part of it is that the Government, pleading great poverty (which is not true), spent the whole afternoon going from house to house in Apia begging assistance . . . although I heard on good authority that they had got the thousand dollars together among themselves before they started on their begging expedition; and what confirmed it is that when we came to count the money we found that they had brought some hundreds of dollars too much, which were of

course returned to them, and they had a feast and a spree on the strength of it next day.

At last the Consul's widow left, and Maudslay was able move into the consulate. It was filthy and all the furniture had been sold off, but after a good scrub down and the purchase of a table and a few chairs he made himself comfortable, with Harry the Jew's son doing the cooking. But as things were quiet in Apia, Maudslay took the opportunity to see more of the country and sound out people's political views.

> I am now beginning to see for myself what I have often been told . . . that the essence of native politics is to be found in the 'king question', that is, whether Malietoa [Laupepa] or [his rival] shall be nominally king of all Samoa. . . . Personal fitness [has] very little to do with it. Malietoa himself behaved like a cur during the last war, and deserted his party in the most cowardly way, yet his claim to be king is not much affected by his behaviour.

Maudslay visited Manono, then crossed over to Savai'i, the big western island, for the specific purpose of enquiring into labour conditions on a plantation. He had written to Gordon:

> I shall take the opportunity to investigate Cornwall's case – I mean the charge against him of ill-treating his labourers. I fear it is a very disgraceful affair altogether, and the Overseer, who appears to be a fiend, is not a British subject but an American, so unfortunately I cannot deal with him as Deputy Commissioner.[13]

It was indeed disgraceful. Cornwall, an Englishman who at one time had served as Acting Consul, was now employed by MacArthur and Co., a New Zealand company, and had established for them a plantation on Upolo, the central island. Recently he had started another on Savai'i, importing labourers from Tabiteuea in the Gilbert Islands. One shipment brought seventy men, women, and children plus crew, all crowded on to a 13-ton cutter. They were landed on the coast where construction of shelters for them had not even started. Six weeks later many of these wretched people were still sleeping in the open. Food was insufficient, and consisted mostly of maize, and the water was so bad that it was obviously responsible for several deaths from dysentery.

In fact mortality was shockingly high. Of the two boat-loads totalling 131 islanders, twenty-two had died in the course of five months. In his seventy-four-page report, Maudslay listed by name the four men, eleven women, two boys and five girls.

Arriving at the plantation, he found that Moors, the overseer, was away, so he could walk around freely; he also found he could converse with many of the men because they had formerly worked in Fiji and knew the language. What they told him left him in no doubt that Moors was a brute. One deposition Maudslay obtained for his report concerned a woman who left the plantation to seek help for her sick child from a Tahitian missionary living some distance away. The child did not survive the journey. The woman was brought back; but ran away a second time. This time she was carried back tied to a pole like a pig, and on arrival was flogged in the presence of other labourers. She ran away a third time, only to die herself.

Maudslay ended his report expressing 'regret that the Pacific Islands Protection Act which deals so fully with the recruiting and shipping of labourers, gives no power to Consuls or Commissioners to enforce regulations for their proper treatment when they are employed on the Estates of British subjects'.

After ten weeks in Samoa, during which time he had received no communication from Fiji, Maudslay was relieved by Robert Swanston, an old hand in the South Pacific, who spoke Samoan. He was told that the Governor was about to start for England on leave of absence, and was anxious to see him before he left. Gordon had recently visited Tonga, and wanted Maudslay to establish himself there not only as Deputy Commissioner and Vice-Consul, but also, during his absence on leave, as Acting Consul-General for the Western Pacific. Maudslay then sailed the 600 miles back to Fiji in a 20-ton cutter.

Chapter 6

Tonga

S ir Arthur's concerns about Tonga stemmed from Germany's growing influence there. He had approved of Maudslay's statement in
1876 that

during the first few years of the existence of the High Commission . . .
there are two matters to be attended to: the extension of British influence in these islands, and the prevention of their annexation by any
other power. . . . Annexation of Samoa or Tonga – especially Tonga –
by any other power would be . . . a severe blow to Fiji's interests.

Tasman had seen no weapons in the Tongan group of islands, nor had
Captain Cook, so he named them The Friendly Islands (although the
natives were then planning to kill him and seize his ship). At that time,
Tonga had been at peace, but soon the taste for war among adventurous
chiefs, acquired during protracted sojourns in Fiji, resulted in the outbreak of civil war. Other Fijian practices such as cannibalism and widow-
strangling also began to be adopted. From about 1800 Tonga was to know
forty years of horror; not only horror but unnecessary famine, as gardens
were laid waste, and hunger then provoked further cannibalism.[1]

The paramount Tongan lineage, of mythic origin, had wielded both
spiritual and administrative power from before the Norman Conquest of
England; but then in the fifteenth century the Tui Tonga transferred
administrative power to a collateral branch. It was a member of this
branch, Taufa'ahau, who emerged as the dominant leader in the 1830s,
first as the ruler of the central island, and then of the northern island
upon the death of its ruler, who had named him heir. Then as we have
seen, Taufa'ahau, on embracing Christianity, was baptized George
Tupou.

On the southern and principal island, Tongatapu, civil war still raged,
and its ruler twice had to send for George Tupou to subdue his antago-
nists. When the ruler died in 1845, he too named George his successor,
thus making him king of a united Tonga. His claim could have been disputed by his kinsman Ma'afu (whom we've already met in Fiji), but the
King had adroitly removed him from the scene by sending him to Fiji to
organize the Tongans there.

Thus, when the British High Commission for the Western Pacific was established, Tonga was unusual – indeed unique – in having a centralized government, and equally so in having enjoyed peace for three decades. Nor were there disputes over land, for the King, on a visit to Sydney in 1853, had become acquainted with the leasehold system employed there. Impressed by it, he introduced it into Tonga, with the result that ownership of the land remained vested in the crown. Land could be leased but never sold.

And yet, for the High Commissioner there were still two causes for concern. One was the growing influence of Germany; the other, not unconnected with the first, was the dictatorial regime of a Wesleyan missionary. This man, the Reverend Shirley Baker, was truly one of the most extraordinary whites to have arisen in the Pacific, and a genius in his way: his particular gifts lying in the realm of gaining power and personal fortune, and knowing how to work up the feelings of the faithful and encourage them to pile high the collection-plate. While he had indeed performed a valuable service to Tonga by transforming it from a semi-feudal society into a political entity with a constitution, thus rendering it a less legitimate prey for colonial powers, his political ambitions eventually brought about his banishment from Tonga – not once but twice.

The Wesleyan Methodists had sent their first missionaries to Tonga in the 1820s. Following the conversion of some of the chiefs on two islands, the ranks of the faithful swelled rapidly, though some resistance was encountered, due in large part to the narrow-mindedness of most missionaries, and their overbearing attitude towards the chieftains (one must suppose the Fijians to have been unusually lucky in the missionaries they were sent, the Reverends William Cross and William Cargill, for they seem to have been more adaptable to circumstances).

Commodore Erskine of the Royal Navy, who visited the central island of Tonga in 1853, commented that

> a dictatorial spirit towards the chiefs and people seemed to show itself, and one of the missionaries in my presence sharply reproved Vuke, a man of high rank in his own country, for presuming to speak to him in a standing posture – a breach of discipline for which, if reprehensible, I was probably answerable, having encouraged the chief on all occasions to put himself on an equal footing with myself and other officers.

Nor were the Roman Catholics quite above criticism. In fact Lord Pembroke and Dr Kingsley, in their jaunty account of visits to the islands of the Pacific, entitled *South Sea Bubbles*, wrote scathingly about missionaries of every stripe, excepting only the Presbyterians and Congregationals of the London Missionary Society.[2] Basil Thomson, the official sent to Tonga in 1890 to settle the last serious problem caused by

Shirley Baker, refers to an *Apologia* printed in France 'in atrocious Tongan' in which Martin Luther is described as 'a disgusting fellow', and Wesley as 'a lying teacher'. But apparently the Catholics did not disdain adopting elements of Protestant hellfire-and-brimstone teaching, for Maudslay described a print widely distributed among Catholic missions in the Pacific as 'a large brightly-coloured print of some dark-complex-ioned gentlemen and ladies being roasted by some darker-looking horned attendants, with a beautiful background of yellow and red flames'.

Baker arrived in Tonga in 1860. Within two years a constitution, largely of his own devising but based on that of Hawaii, was introduced; within ten years he was head of the mission (a dependency of the Australian Wesleyan Missionary Society); and in 1875 he imposed a more elaborate version of his constitution. With this, Tonga's thousand-year-old polity was essentially wiped out at one blow. Fornication now became a criminal offence – and in fact the measure that would be most rigorously enforced. A rigid dress code was established, under which a woman found without a pinafore, even in her own house, was fined $2 and a man caught without a shirt had to pay $10.

These laws, though long repealed, have had enduring effects: to this day one never sees a woman with bare arms, nor a man without a shirt, even when engaged in heavy labour. Nevertheless, it has to be admitted that the 1875 constitution, with its later amendments, remains the law of the land, and it has ensured that most of the land is still in Tongan hands. The consequent absence of European plantations has made it unneces-sary to import labourers from other places, and ethnic tension within the population such as now exists in Fiji is non-existent.

Sir Arthur had come away from Tonga feeling that Tongans were oppressed by Baker's influence, and that the King was somehow writhing under his tyranny, but could not, and would not, shake it off. Baker, having established himself in two crucial roles as the King's political mentor and his personal medical adviser, was able to exercise a lightly veiled dictatorship. Through his influence Germany had been granted the best harbour in the group as a coaling station, and he had arranged for Tongan government business in Sydney to be transferred from one firm to another managed by Herr Stahl, the German Consul. In gratitude the Germans invested Baker with the Imperial Order of the Red Eagle. He was also involved commercially with the J. C. Godeffroy Company. When Weber visited in a German warship, he persuaded the King to discard the man he had chosen as Secretary, and instead accept on trial a man selected by the Emperor of Germany; Baker explained that a man from Germany would need only a small salary.

Some of these activities may have been improper, and some unfitting for a man of God (though not at all unusual, since the realms of church and state have always overlapped in Tongan history); but none was illegal. Baker's fund-raising activities, however, were clearly classifiable as exploitation of the Tongans by a British subject, and as such fell within the competence of the High Commissioner. Maudslay's principal task was to investigate and if possible put an end to these abuses.

Luckily for Sir Arthur, during his visit to Tonga, Baker had been absent in New Zealand, and according to Maudslay, 'when Sir Arthur expressed his regret [about this] to the King, the King replied that it was a good thing, for had Mr. Baker been present, he would never have been allowed to have such pleasant and instructive interviews'. But by the time Maudslay arrived, Baker had returned, and he

> only paid me a most formal visit, which of course I returned, and he was profuse in his expressions of regard. . . . But he never introduced me to his wife and family, which he has had good opportunities of doing, and has never really asked me to his house, so I thought the best thing was to ask him, so I had him to dinner . . . and we got on very well, although he is undoubtedly a snob.[3]

Maudslay had an audience with the King, a dignified old gentleman dressed in black, who received him very graciously. In a letter home he described the lengthy Constitution Act,

> which the native authorities neither read nor understand; indeed half of it is written in English, and has never been translated into Tongan. The greatest crime, as far as I can make out by the laws, is murder, the next being the making of native cloth (*tapa*), an industry which we are doing our best to encourage in Fiji. . . . At the King's orders about a hundred natives came to my house a few days ago, to sing mékés to me, and they sang the old songs of the land, which had not been heard for years. Baker, at a large Church meeting the next day, told them how Fiji was lost, given over utterly to sin and ruin, ruined even more politically and socially than morally, that the chiefs were now no more than common people, and why was this? Because they had clung to the old songs of the land.

Maudslay continues:

At the same meeting he publicly reprimanded a native minister for coupling his (Baker's) name with that of a native minister in his prayers, telling him that the white Missionary should always be prayed for first and alone. This was all reported to me by the native Prime Minister [David Unga, the King's son] the next day. . . .

The European clothes movement is most amusing. It is tabu to appear at the big church in native dress, and in consequence the miscellaneous collection of seedy black clothes and trousers is something wonderful. The ladies are resplendent in silks and satins, and tight lacing has lately come into fashion, but as the hill on which the [Zion] church stands is steep (the only hillock on the island) and the ladies are not used to stays, a good deal of unlacing goes on when the service is over at the church doors.

(From that tiny hill, now named Old Zion, communication with the heavens is maintained – by means of massive microwave towers now standing upon it.)

Shyly at first, the native chiefs began visiting Maudslay, and he had many of them to dinner. It was suggested to him that he build a house in the old town, the exclusively Tongan quarter near the Old Zion hill, and away from the white traders, so he obtained a house lot near the present British High Commission. Then having decided that the wooden shanties imported from New Zealand, which Baker had been persuading the chiefs to live in, would be neither comfortable nor attractive, he bought an old Roman Catholic church and had it transported and rebuilt.

The old church had four splendid great greenheart posts, which we scraped and polished, supporting the usual cross-beams. All the crossings of the beams and of the narrow rafters of the birdcage-like roof were tied with sinnet (coconut fibre string) of three colours worked into elaborate patterns, which were most effective; for the King had sent all the old native craftsmen to do it skilfully.

The floor of the old church . . . had been laid in blue gum timber from Australia, and we had the greatest difficulty relaying it, for it had been down for fifty years and was as hard as iron. . . . The walls of the new house were of crossed reeds, Tongan fashion, and the ten glass doors I imported from New Zealand. The inner lining was of reeds, each panel worked in a different pattern with coloured sinnet. The bedrooms were separate native houses. Mine was a gem. When out riding one day near Mua, I had taken refuge in what was used as a cart-shed; but on looking up into the roof I beheld the best native roof I had ever seen. I then learned that a [woman of the sacred Tui Tonga family] had died in the house some years before, and the house had to be abandoned.

Maudslay bought it, had the thatch removed, and the roof carried in four pieces to the Consulate. The narrow rafters and crosspieces of this roof were not of the usual coconut wood, but of greenheart from the hull of a great Fijian war-canoe that had been presented to the Tui Tonga.[4]

Two photographs of the interior of this house exist, one of them a pair of stereophotos – but how sad it is that these are apparently the only survivors of the many pictures that Maudslay, a superb photographer, must have taken in the Pacific with that 'big camera' mentioned by Lady Gordon. In these photos two tennis rackets and a ball may be seem – artefacts testifying to extraordinarily rapid cultural transmission, when one remembers that lawn tennis had been invented only three years earlier. And on the table a stereoscope can just be made out.

'Housekeeping', Maudslay wrote, 'was not an easy matter. . . .

A few chickens, a little fish and some yams could be bought, but we were often hard put to it for food. When an occasional trading schooner called, we always rowed off to see what we could secure. If she came from New Zealand, we could sometimes get a bag of onions or a cheese, and if from San Francisco some tins of asparagus; but we often drew a blank. I must now record a curious coincidence. Among the stores I had from home were six small jars of Maille's French Mustard, and on the day when the last of our stores was consumed, and the last spoonful had been scraped from the mustard-pot, a schooner appeared in sight. Frank Symonds [an acqaintance from New Zealand who was staying with him] asked me if he could row off to her, and I said it was hardly worthwhile, since we had drawn so many blanks lately. 'However,' he replied, 'I think I will try.' As he shoved off, he called out, 'What shall I bring you back?' and I cried, 'Six jars of Maille's French Mustard.' I might as well have asked for the moon.

When he returned I said, 'What luck, Frank?' and he replied, 'Six jars of Maille's French Mustard.' I thought he was joking, but there were the jars sure enough. Frank told me that when he rowed along-side the schooner the skipper called out, 'What can I do for you?' and Frank answered 'Sell me six jars of Maille's French Mustard.' 'All right,' said the skipper, 'come aboard,' and diving into his cabin he produced the six jars, and told Frank that about two years earlier a Frenchman in Samoa had asked him to procure them from . . . Auckland . . . or Sydney, and that he managed to [do]; but when next he returned to Samoa the Frenchman was dead, and he had carried them about the Pacific for a couple of years, and was glad to get rid of them.

The new cases from Fortnum and Mason's arrived on Christmas Eve, just in time for me to be able to give a good dinner to the home-less Britishers . . . on Christmas Day.

In a report to Sir Arthur, Maudslay gives us another glimpse of his unofficial occupations. He had just made a week-long visit to Mua, the old capital of the Tui Tongas, 12 miles away, and there he had

spent a day or two clearing the undergrowth away from the tombs of the ancient Tui Tongas, built of huge stones. Many of these were brought in canoes from the Island of Uvea (Wallis Island), about 500 miles to the north. . . . The canoes must have been of great size, for the story is undoubtedly true, and the Uveans show the quarries they were taken from. One stone I measured was 24 feet by 10 feet, and it was not the heaviest. . . . I managed to interest Gara-ni-valu ('spoiling for a fight'), a descendant of the Tui Tongas (with a Fijian name), in the tombs of his ancestors, and we spent the day clearing the scrub from one of them. I have got the chief to promise that when the yam planting is over we will have a feast, and turn out the whole village and clear them properly. I found twelve tombs, some with one tier, others with two, three, four, and five tiers of stones.[5]

As for that 'intolerably irksome and repressive legislation' (Gordon's description of the social and sumptuary laws), his conversations with the King must have allayed the latter's fear of Baker's recriminations enough for the King's Council to relax them. Soon after his arrival Maudslay was able to report that the King was walking about the town in a *sulu* in the daytime, and that the unpopular taboo on bark-cloth also appeared to be nearly over, so too the prohibition of smoking except for pregnant women and those under sixteen years of age. Maudslay's 'ostentatiously *fakatonga* [traditional Tonga-style] behaviour' – as a recent critic, Noel Rutherford, has termed it – also suggested that the previous headlong and superficial Europeanization was arrested. The chiefs were pleased that for the first time the parliament was free from outside pressure, so that they could 'talk like Tongans and didn't have new things shoved down their throats'. Maudslay was kept informed by the chiefs about 'the latest Bakerian moves, and much to my amusement I find myself becoming the rallying-point of a Conservative reaction'.

Gordon's disquiet about Baker had first been aroused by accounts of his exorbitant extraction of contributions to the mission. Layard had previously reported on this, and in 1872 Lord Pembroke had written:

> Can it be believed that out of the kindly credulous Tonga Islanders, just struggling into civilisation, and whose every dollar, hardly earned, should and would be spent on the improvements of their country, were it not for those canting sharks; they [the missionaries] get the noble and astonishing sum of . . . £6,000, being £3,500 above the current expenses of the Mission.

The islands had become the golden milch cow of the Australasian Mission, for, in the nine years following Baker's appointment as head of it, the Tongan mission sent £39,375 to Sydney. After subtracting the cost of the missionaries' salaries and Tonga's share in running the mission ship, there was a surplus of nearly £2000 per annum. Maudslay therefore brought with him Taniela (or Daniel) 'Afu, a Tongan Wesleyan minister who had spent many years in Fiji, and soon after his arrival Maudslay obtained permission from the King to hold an inquiry into the way in which the Tongans were having their possessions sold up under distress warrants brought against them for debts to white traders; and, because subscriptions to the Missionary Church were the cause of many of those debts, he asked Baker to join in the inquiry, or to send a representative. But Baker declined to have anything to do with it.

The principal object of this inquiry was to gather enough solid evidence of Baker's extortions to convince the Wesleyan Conference in Sydney that some action should be taken against him. In Maudslay's words, his modus operandi was as follows:

> The villagers were worked up into a state of excitement by means of . . . night-services before the collection day, and when that day arrived Mr. Baker would drive to the principal church of the district, having made arrangements with one of the agents of Godeffroys' firm to be in attendance with a supply of money. This money the agent advanced to any native applying for a loan, the amount to be repaid in copra. Sometimes Mr. Baker would himself advance the money to the trader, and receive an order on the firm of Godeffroy for the amount.

It was an ingenious method of rendering unto God what was God's, while not forgetting to render something unto J. Caesar Godeffroy, the 'king of the South Seas'.

> The villagers would march round the church in procession, depositing silver in the plate each time they passed the altar, and see who could keep it up longest, village vieing with village, and individual with individual; and when their store was exhausted, in the heat of excitement they would run out and borrow money from the trader, who set up his table near the church door.

The excitement was often heightened by the noise of kerosene tins being beaten, and since the copra was entered in the accounts at much below its market price there was room for a large profit, which Maudslay suspected that Baker shared in, though this couldn't be proved.

Having a 20-ton cutter at his disposal for a short while, Maudslay availed himself of it to visit Niuafo'u, a small volcanic island about 300 miles north of Tongatapu (the main island) and about half-way between Samoa and Fiji. This he knew to be one of Baker's pet hunting grounds, and so remote that it was seldom visited by outsiders. Upon arrival he found the chiefs

> loud in their complaints of missionary rule. All the males over sixteen pay taxes, and there are only 300 taxpayers, but the Mission manages to squeeze $10,000 to $12,000 a year out of them in Mission subscriptions, which is paid in copra at trade price, so there is room for profit; money is given as well, and the people pay all building expenses for church, schools and teachers' houses. There were two white traders living on the island, agents for Godeffroy and Hedemann, and both confirmed what the chiefs told me, and said that great pressure

was put upon the natives to subscribe more than they could really afford.

For unforeseeable reasons the return journey was unpleasant. A local chief had requested passage to Tongatapu, readily granted him by Maudslay. When some miles from land it was discovered that twenty men and two women had swum out, scrambled aboard and hidden in the hold, perhaps shortly before Maudslay himself came aboard. 'The chief had no hesitation; he said "Throw them all overboard, they will swim ashore all right".' But he would not do so. Then during the night the native helmsman carelessly jibed the boat with all sail set, and was rewarded by a blow on the head from the boom. Maudslay thought it was lucky the mast didn't carry away, since he found that a penknife could be run into it anywhere near its foot. The five-day return journey left them entirely without food at its end.

In September 1878 Maudslay wrote a letter to the Wesleyan Conference in Sydney reporting some of his preliminary findings. It included further evidence in support of his case against Baker: the large number of debts for mission contributions that had been brought before native courts. Since some debts were still outstanding, distress warrants had been issued that could lead to seizure of all of a debtor's chattels, and Baker, now alarmed by the inquiry, paid off the debts himself, thus restoring, in the eyes of his flock, some lustre to his tarnished image. At the same time he retaliated against any who had given Maudslay information by suspending them from church appointments.

The following January Maudslay gave the King, through an interpreter, a detailed account of his investigations, and was complimented by him on it. He also sent reports on the matter to the Foreign Secretary, Lord Salisbury, and to Gordon, who forwarded a copy to the Wesleyan Conference in Sydney. There it was decided to send a commission of enquiry to Tonga, and in the meantime to recall Baker temporarily.

Next month (February 1879) Maudslay was asked to return to Fiji to lend a hand there, as the Acting Governor was very short-handed. During the voyage they endured a terrific gale lasting five days, probably the tail-end of the hurricane that severely damaged Tonga – as he would see when he returned in May. The new Roman Catholic church had disappeared, as had the large wooden warehouse which had been his first home on the island. The Consulate, however, had suffered little damage, as he had been careful to cover the thatched roof with large-meshed wire netting attached to guy-wires secured to large stones buried in the ground.

But within a month, and much to his disgust, Maudslay received a telegram from Lord Salisbury, sent to Auckland and brought by schooner, ordering him to go at once to Samoa, where disturbances were expected. On arrival he found German and American warships in harbour, the *Bismarck* and the *Lackawanna* respectively. 'I am not expecting an English vessel', he wrote, 'and don't want one, although everyone here seems to think I carry a man-of-war in my pocket.'

Apia had now been taken over by the foreign Consuls, and Maudslay, as Consul-General, had to take the chair at their meetings.

> [I] was faced by Weber, the German Consul, the American Consul . . .
> the Captain of the German man-of-war, [the Captain of the
> *Lackawanna*] and the British Consul, Mr. Swanston (whom I did not
> trust). . . . I had a rather difficult position, for I was under thirty, a
> good deal younger than the rest of them. However, Captain Chandler,
> the American, was an old dear; he saw that I was in rather a tight
> place, and did all he could to back me up.

Maudslay must have rather enjoyed the twelve-gun salutes given him by the German and American ships whenever he made official visits, but he was not sanguine about the future, having come to the conclusion that the indigenous political system was still showing no sign of developing the settled, reliable chain of authority necessary to a state that was to bear the trials and responsibilities of autonomy on conditions imposed by Europeans.

In August a British ship, HMS *Cormorant*, did arrive, and its captain brought news that Sir Arthur was on his way from San Francisco on a mail steamer which would call at Pango Pango. Another interesting fact he learnt was, that when Sir Arthur reached England, he found that it had not been within his power to appoint anyone Acting Consul-General without consulting the Foreign Office; but as the Foreign Secretary himself had ordered Maudslay to take charge in Samoa, where there was already a British Consul, he supposed that the Foreign Office acquiesced in his appointment.

When the time came, he sailed in the *Cormorant* for Pango Pango to pick up Sir Arthur, bringing with him a document that had been handed to him just before leaving Apia, signed by Malietoa Talavou and the fourteen *taimua* chiefs: it offered the cession of Samoa to Britain. In fact, as Sir Arthur stepped ashore Maudslay was triumphantly waving this document. Sir Arthur simply said, 'Put that in your pocket, my boy. The day before I sailed the Cabinet decided that Britain would relinquish its claim to suzerainty in the Samoan Group.' It made this decision because of an earlier pledge given by Samoa to Germany; so Maudslay had to hand the document back to the chiefs, and tell the other consuls what he had done.

It was hard on Maudslay that he was unable to enjoy credit for a outstanding personal achievement. Gordon himself was greatly in favour of annexation, not only as a measure assuring peace within Samoa but also for Fiji's sake, but he probably knew that both the Foreign and Colonial

Offices were likely to disavow any such agreement. The crux of the matter seems to have lain in the imperial policy of the day, Treasury parsimony, and a feeling of colonial surfeit.

At meetings that followed, it was agreed that Malietoa should be acknowledged as king of Samoa, and the next day all the foreign officials and the chiefs were assembled for his installation, to be followed by feasting. 'Just as we were arriving', Maudslay relates, 'old Sanga, one of the chiefs whom I had freed from his refuge in the Consulate the year before, caught sight of me, and insisted on embracing me and rubbing noses. Luckily, I was able to dodge behind a coconut tree, and I don't think the other foreigners present witnessed the performance.'

Sir Arthur then sailed for Fiji on the *Cormorant*, dropping Maudslay off in Tonga on the way. A month later, the Wesleyan Mission ship arrived from Sydney with two missionaries on board who had been appointed to inquire into the charges he had made against Baker. Maudslay objected that, with a year gone by, and the censure – indeed near-excommunication – visited on those who had given him information, there was little chance he would be able to get them to repeat what they had told him. It would be far better for them to make their own inquiries. The missionaries would not agree, so he gave in, and the investigation took place in his house over the next three weeks.

Six charges against Baker had been formulated by the Wesleyan Conference on the basis of complaints addressed by Gordon to London, conveyed to the Wesleyan headquarters there, and relayed to Sydney. Three were political, concerning his supposed lobbying in the cause of Germany, connections with Godeffroy's, and involvement with Tongan government business, and these charges Maudslay declined to press, since they were based on reports he had sent to London in unofficial correspondence, qualifying some of them therein as unsubstantiated.

The other three charges accused Baker of putting under censure the church officers who had assisted Maudslay in his enquiries; of making advances of money to Godeffroy's agents immediately before or during mission collections; and of being responsible for the issue of distress warrants arising out of Mission collections, as suggested by the fact that few had been made while Baker was out of the country, and that it was only after Maudslay's inquiries had started that Baker began to stay the proceedings by paying the debts himself.

In support of these charges he produced affidavits sworn by both Tongans and traders. A trader, Francis Payne, affirmed that he received $2000 from Baker, and handed receipts from the natives to Godeffroy's agent; a Tongan complained that in his village the people had subscribed more than they could afford because the collection was supposedly for building a church, but no church had been built; David Unga, the King's son, put his signature to notes of a meeting held in his own house with the chief of Niuafu and two others from that island, which corroborated Maudslay's report on collections there; and some of those suspended or disciplined for speaking to Maudslay did provide written statements to that effect.

In answering these charges, Baker began by declaring sarcastically that he had been unable to find the least evidence that investigation into church affairs formed any part of a consul's duties – a pretty argument for a man who had himself so completely ignored boundaries between church and state in his activities, and had even become a money-changer in the temple. Baker also, of course, produced depositions supporting his case, but in reading some of them one can't help wondering about pressure on the deponents, or perhaps the lack of need for any pressure, since their fervent loyalty to the church included absolute loyalty to its leader.

In his account of the hearings, Rutherford has called them 'an almost complete vindication of Baker'. In some instances his opinion rests on questionable judgments, such as calling a witness, Robert Hanslip, 'one of the least reliable of the whites', whereas Maudslay, who knew the man well because he was his translator, called him 'a thoroughly honest man'; yet it is quite likely that often he was feeding Maudslay the opinions of 'the beach' – that is, the European traders. In another instance (his discussion of whether Baker had a financial arrangement with the Godeffroy company) Rutherford takes Weber's word in denying any such thing (of course, he wouldn't lie about *that*, any more than Steinberger would), and produces what he calls corroborative evidence. 'In March 1875 Godeffroy's detained their vessel, the *Samoa*, for a considerable time in Nuku'alofa to allow two mission families to come aboard, and then transferred them to Sydney, all without charge. This [was done] to retain the mission's goodwill', hardly necessary if Baker were a paid operative. One might as convincingly argue that the $17,000 so generously disbursed by Godeffroy's for the purchase and fitting out of Steinberger's schooner in San Francisco disproved the existence of any potentially profitable contract between him and the firm.

Rutherford gives the impression that Maudslay's case fell apart pathetically during the hearings, basing this view on a résumé of the proceedings edited by Baker himself and printed for him;[6] nevertheless, he does concede that Maudslay proved his principal accusation against Baker: that he had lent money to traders on the understanding that it would be redistributed to Tongans for missionary collections. It also emerged that Baker, somehow or other, had managed to amass a large personal fortune, since he had provided half of the £15,000 paid-up capital of the Bank of Tonga, had made a loan of £1200 to the government and another of £600 to the Mission, and was about to build a two-storey weatherboard house, which, after the

King's palace, would be the most imposing in Tonga.[7]

When the inquiry was over, Maudslay felt exhausted, but confident that he had proved his case (as is generally agreed in respect of the Mission collections; the other accusations were much weaker). He asked the Commissioners for their decision, and was astonished at their telling him they were not empowered to make any, but must report the matter back to Sydney. Nevertheless, they told him eventually that they were quite satisfied with what he had done.

In its own good time the Conference decided that Baker should be recalled, and then sent to spend a year in New Zealand as an unpaid supernumerary. Soon after Baker had left, Sir Arthur arrived in Tonga, and with Maudslay's help negotiated with the King a new treaty to supersede the one Maudslay had drawn up a year earlier. This had been signed by the King, but in London technical faults had been found in it concerning suits against British subjects in the High Commissioner's Court – hardly surprising in a treaty drafted hundreds of miles from the nearest lawyer.

Maudslay then requested a leave of absence, and in January 1880 left for Sydney. From there, a month later, he sailed for Calcutta to rendez-vous with Charles and Isabel, his favourite brother and sister.

Upon reaching London, several months later, Maudslay learnt that Sir Arthur had been offered the governorship of New Zealand, and had accepted it, while nominally retaining his position as High Commissioner for the Western Pacific. Under these circumstances, and with the British government still reluctant to extend its sway in the Pacific, Maudslay must have concluded that little chance remained of obtaining the kind of appointment he and von Hügel had once dreamt of. Accordingly he tendered his resignation from government service.

For five years he had worked in the Pacific, and had certainly matured. In a sense, this had been his 'coming of age in Samoa'. The process had taken longer than expected, for on accepting Cairns's first offer of a position in Trinidad he told his mother that a couple of years in the job would teach him all he needed to know; but in what framework he expected this knowledge to be useful he failed to specify – and in fact it may be doubted that he had at the time any clear idea on this point. Now, nearly six years later, if he had any plans for the future other than colonial service, he kept them to himself.

His situation, however, was enviable. For all his modesty, he must have become aware that he was endowed more than the usual allotment of brains and common sense; the tropics had proved his constitution to be strong; he was well educated, and enterprising; the world was at peace; and in choosing his course he didn't have to pay much attention to financial recompense.

As Henry James makes one of his characters say, 'I call people rich when they're able to meet the requirements of their imagination.' Alfred Maudslay would show that he had imagination enough to open up an entirely new field, and good fortune had blessed him with the means to do it.

A POSTSCRIPT ON THE WESTERN PACIFIC

In case there are some whose curiousity has been aroused about the further course of events in those South Sea Islands, this coda is provided.

Any reader so cynical as to harbour a suspicion that worldly ambition lurked in the Reverend Mr Baker's breast may wonder whether he was capable of enduring a whole year's banishment in New Zealand. To such a person, then, it will come as no surprise that before long he found a pretext for returning to Tonga.

The opportunity arose when King George's son, David Unga, died in New Zealand. Baker, with his German connections, was able to arrange for his body to be taken back to Tonga in a German man-of-war, with himself in the role of coffin-watcher. On arrival, he took up residence in the Mission House, ostensibly to gather materials for a biography of the King.

The book was never written. Instead, by exerting his old influence on the monarch, Baker obtained the position of Foreign Minister and Comptroller of the Revenue. Six months later he resigned from the Mission and became Prime Minister. A new Constitution was introduced, containing various new measures: a minor one, which stemmed from his observation that Tongans were neglecting agriculture in favour of cricket, regulated the times and places for playing this game, which had lately become popular.[8]

In a later and more serious move, all leases held by the Australian Wesleyan Conference were cancelled, and in its place the Free Church of Tonga was established, which would manage its own affairs without interference from Sydney. Persecution of Wesleyans loyal to the old church then ensued; there was an attempt to murder Baker; and finally he was removed by the High Commissioner 'as being a person dangerous to the peace and good order of the Western Pacific'.

King George, who had so confounded Maudslay's earlier prediction of his imminent demise, died at last in 1893, at the age of about ninety-six. From 1900 until 1970 Tonga, although under British protection, was not a British colony, and it is now an independent member of the Commonwealth. It is worth remarking that no other polity in the Pacific has survived without being colonized by one of the great powers, and for this proud condition Sir Arthur Gordon deserves much credit.

A more depressing situation prevailed in Samoa, one that wouldn't be resolved for another nineteen years. The Samoans had an impossible task conforming to the separate treaties they had with Germany, Britain, and the United States. As Maudslay wrote in a memorandum addressed to the Foreign Office after his return home,

One cannot help noticing that no representative of a foreign Power ever misses the opportunity of telling the natives that there is nothing his Government desires to see more than the establishment of a strong and independent Government in Samoa, yet some of the stipulations of the treaties are such that even if the Samoans had the highest capacity for government, the formation of a strong and independent Government is rendered impossible.

Matters may be left to drift for a few years yet, and we shall hear of more native disturbances, for it is always worth while to encourage a native dispute when it creates a demand for muskets, and lowers the price of land: the taste for gin will increase, and when the natives have become hopelessly demoralized and have lost all claim to their lands, and a misled government have succeeded in involving the country in debt, there will be an outcry from the 'owners of the soil' against native depredations and a demand for Chinamen and Indian coolies, and the large estates of Germans and Englishmen will be urged as a strong reason for foreign interference and annexation.

Maudslay recommended annexation by Britain, as the power preferred by the Samoans (at one stage, Samoans took to wearing lava-lava waistbands printed with the Union Jack, to show their preference); but if that could not be arranged, then Germany should take over. But none of the three wanted sole responsibility, and none would agree to relinquish its part.

Chapter 7

Quiriguá and Tikal

O n 20 February 1880 Maudslay left Sydney aboard a steamer
bound for Calcutta. There he joined Charles and Isabel, who, by
the time he arrived, had been in Calcutta for a month already,
and were going on to Japan.

Charles and Isabel were not due to return from their round-the-world
tour until October, and it is almost certain that Alfred remained with
them for the entire second half of it. As evidence there is a photograph of
Charles and 'Bob' in Japan, an albumen print which looks more like the
work of their brother than of a street photographer.[1] Also surviving are
four magnificent photographs of his, taken in Banff, Alberta, which
cannot be attributed to any of his other journeyings.[2] Moreover, if he had
been hurrying home from Japan, leaving Charles and Isabel to pursue
their way in a more leisurely manner, he would have taken the quickest
route via San Francisco, rather than make a detour through Banff.

Uncertainty arises only from the fact that, after leaving Sydney,
Maudslay disappears from written records, drops out of sight entirely,
and isn't heard of again for eleven months. Maudslay was a fairly good
correspondent, but, of all his brothers and sisters, it was to Isabel he
wrote most often, so the very fact that no letter of his to her has survived
from this period tends to confirm, albeit weakly, that for most of this
period he had no need to write, for the simple reason that she and
Charles were with him.

This gap in the record occurs at a stage in his life that for those
interested in him is unfortunate, since it may well have been during
those months that he made the decision to try his hand at archaeological
exploration. If only he had kept a journal! But the very lack of firm facts
may excuse our imagining how he may have spent some of his time on
returning to England.

We may be sure that he went to see Osbert Salvin, primarily as a
friend, but also to discuss the birds he had seen in the South Seas, and
perhaps to give him specimens collected on his travels. Salvin in turn
would have told him more about his last and longest sojourn in
Guatemala, lasting the whole of 1874, from which he had returned

shortly after Maudslay's departure for Australia. Salvin probably had new photographs to show him, besides those he had taken long before of Quiriguá and Copán; and Caroline, his wife, would have brought out the vivid watercolours of various scenes that she had painted in Guatemala.[3] Among them were two views of great carved stelae lying in a jumble and utterly neglected at a site in the Pacific piedmont called Santa Lucía Cotzumalguapa, on the south side of the Atitlán volcano, near its foot.[4] These would certainly have interested him.

Nor could he have failed to visit J. W. Clark, with so much to tell him, not only about Fiji and the ethnographic collections he had made there, but also about the ruins in Ceylon he had seen, perhaps in that very year on his way from Australia to Calcutta, or possibly during an earlier stop-over at Galle en route between England and Australia. Whichever these were – and they are likely to have been Anuradhapura and Pollonaruwa – he later avowed that he had found them very interesting.[5]

For his part, Clark could have brought him up to date on archaeological work then in progress in the Greek, Roman, and Near Eastern worlds. Archaeological investigation was expanding as never before: buildings embellished with splendid sculptures were being brought to light at Pergamum by the Berlin Royal Museum; the French were excavating at Delos; the Forum in Rome was being cleared of its heavy overburden; and excavators from the British Museum were continuing to find marvels at Nineveh, following up on discoveries made by Layard more than thirty years earlier. But of archaeological news from Mexico or Guatemala there was none.

Further encouragement of his nascent interest in archaeology may have come from a much older cousin, Henry Maudslay, junior (1822–99). After some years of activity in the family firm, Henry had turned to other pursuits, one of them archaeology. While Alfred was in Trinidad, Henry had been busy excavating in Jerusalem on his own initiative and at his own expense. From a point then well outside the walls of the city, between Bishop Gobat's School and the English cemetery, he was sinking a shaft and driving a tunnel into the scarp, hoping to find the tombs of David and Solomon and all the kings of Judah.[6] Although he was disappointed in this modest ambition, his efforts were appreciated by the Palestine Exploration Fund. And if Henry, junior, helped convince his cousin to try his hand in a similar field, then his contribution to archaeology was vastly greater.

After remaining for so many months hidden from our sight, Maudslay emerges at long last into the brilliant sunlight of the Caribbean. He is on board the SS *Bernard Hall*, lying in St Thomas Harbour. It is 27 December 1880, and the letter that he now writes to Isabel has survived. In it he tells her that after a smooth passage the ship had called at Port-au-Prince and then Kingston, Jamaica, and was expected to reach Belize within a week.

But the letter also contains some far more interesting information. He tells his sister:

> Mr. Sarg, whom Charlie will remember as the German we met at San José and Amatitlan, is on board with his wife and children. He is very civil, and his assistance will be most useful to me in Guatemala. At present he acts as my Spanish Master, and I really have made some progress. He excites me by an account of a newly discovered and undescribed ruined city near Flores which is said to be as fine as Palenque [this, of course, was Tikal].
>
> Guatemala has become, you will be pleased to hear, quite civilized now – a strong government and no revolution in sight for years, regular posts and telegraph lines all over the country! – and no one thinks any longer of riding around with revolvers. This is really true and not said to make your mind easy. . . . I enclose some Gulf Weed fished up in the middle of the Atlantic, and you must give a bit to Cousin Anne with my love.[7]

In fact, a dried-up tangle of Sargasso weed still remains in the envelope.

Having reached Belize, British Honduras, Maudslay began a journal, its first entry dated 9 January. He was staying at Government House as the guest of Sir Frederick Barlee, the Governor.[8] The two had met and become friendly when Barlee was Colonial Secretary of Western Australia, and the informal briefing he gave Maudslay about affairs in his colony during the six days he spent with him must have been very helpful.[9]

Barlee, who had become accustomed to riding long distances in Australia, kept up this practice in his new post, and so had come to know the colony better, probably, than any of his predecessors. He had ridden several times up to the Mexican frontier, where there had been recurrent raids involving bloodshed by the independent Maya of Santa Cruz – they were the next generation of those who had risen in 1847 in the so-called War of the Castes against Spanish-Mexican dominion in Yucatán.[10] In Maudslay's words, 'The Indians have a grievance arising out of a disputed boundary, and they apparently have a good cause' – the territory they claimed being that lying within the loop of the Río Hondo at the extreme north of the colony. But Barlee's personal negotiation with them had reduced the tension, and raids had ceased.

During Maudslay's brief stay in Belize, the Santa Cruz chiefs arrived to purchase foreign goods (largely powder and shot), and he spoke with them through an interpreter. 'I explained to them that the purpose of my visit to Central America was to study the works of art of their forefathers, and they very courteously asked me to visit them in their own country, an invitation which I greatly regretted my arrangements did not permit me to accept.'[11] When back in Belize a year later he was still hoping to take advantage of that invitation.

In a last entry in his diary before going on his way, Maudslay summed up his impressions of Belize:

> Apart from remembrances of the kindest hospitality, I carry away from Belize the recollection of a town out of which there is nowhere to go except into the swamp, and absolutely nothing to do, and never shall I forget the sandflies. In most parts of the town, whenever during the day the breeze dies away, they rise in their thousands and render life almost unendurable, and one is only freed from them at night, to be delivered as prey to the mosquitoes. The sandflies quite eclipse the weather as a topic of conversation.

On 15 January he boarded the *Wanderer*, the mail steamer from New Orleans, for an overnight passage to Livingston. This village, at the mouth of the Río Dulce in Guatemala, was then the country's only port of entry on the Caribbean coast for ocean-going vessels, although passengers and goods had to be landed in small boats because of two obstructing sand-bars. There passengers, luggage and freight were transferred to a small stern-wheel steamer that plied up the river to Yzabal, a village on the south shore of Lake Izabal (as the name is now spelt).[12] Since Maudslay described the steamer as a terrible old rattle-trap, it might even have been the very vessel that forty years earlier had taken Stephens and Catherwood up the same route.

Those two immortal travellers had been on their way to Copán, and were quite ignorant then of the existence of Quiriguá. It was not until Catherwood was in Chiquimula, returning alone from Copán to Guatemala (while Stephens was elsewhere in Central America, witnessing its breakup), that he heard mention of it. A man there told him that Colonel Juan Galindo was working at those ruins – which in fact was untrue – and Catherwood considered going there at once, 'but being much worn with his labours at Copán, he was incredulous to the whole'. But he did go alone later, and his brief description, with two engravings of stelae almost hidden within mats of creepers and moss, was published in Stephens's *Incidents of Travel in Central America*.[13]

Over the next forty years a mere handful of interested travellers visited Quiriguá, one of them with a mission that nowadays seems a trifle reprehensible. He was Carl Scherzer, who in 1854 was engaged by the British Consul in Guatemala to report on the feasibility of removing some pieces of sculpture. They would be dragged to the riverbank, floated downstream on rafts, and trans-shipped for delivery to London. In this enterprise the consul was acting on the instructions of Lord Palmerston, who had heard that attempts had been made to purchase

Copán and Palenque on behalf of the United States, and was anxious lest Great Britain be left without monuments of similar calibre in its collections. But Scherzer reported that the monuments were too heavy to be moved.[14]

Maudslay had brought with him the two volumes of Stephens's work, and during his passage up the Río Dulce made no attempt, when writing his journal, to rival the marvellous description of it given by Stephens. But he was able to describe making the same journey by night:

> The moon was full and the scene most beautiful. The river was closed in by banks some hundreds of feet high, clothed with vegetation to the very summit, with here and there a bare rock jutting out. Now and then in the sudden turns of the river the moon was hidden from us and it appeared as though we were steering right against a dark mass of forest ahead, then another sudden turn and another moonlit reach would open to view. . . .
>
> On landing at Yzabal [next morning] we had to walk along a wooden pier that was so rotten that it [was] actually tumbling to pieces, and one had to look carefully at each step one took.

A tedious Customs examination of all his baggage, including three wooden boxes containing a riding saddle and pack-saddles, was eventually curtailed by the intervention of Francis Sarg.

He was then taken to see the Jefe Político,

> a courteous gentleman who spoke English well . . . [and] who on hearing that I wished to visit the ruins near Quirigua sent off orders immediately to have a path cut through the forest from the village to the ruins. He advised me to stay with a certain Don Onofre Alvarez who is managing a cattle ranch at Mico, not far from the village, and in the afternoon sent Don Onofre to visit me.
>
> I found Don Onofre to be . . . a gentleman of colour who was a major in the Guatemalan army, and district official. He had been thirty years in the Government service and was well known for his good nature. His visit to Yzabal was an important one – he was to be married next day, and I was to go back to Mico with him and his wife. I naturally made some apologies about the inopportuneness of my visit, [but] he did not seem to be at all put out at it, the reason being that the ceremony might just as well have been performed some years ago, and I could hardly be considered as interrupting a honeymoon.

Returning later to the *posada* (inn), he found that

> Don O was celebrating his wedding day with a dance given in the room next to mine, and as there is only a wooden partition about 8ft. high and then all open to the roof there seems little chance of sleep for

me. The minstrelsy consists of Don O. on the guitar, assisted by a fiddle & a very noisy clarionette. . . . The Polka seemed the favourite dance. The musicians were indefatigable, the fiddle knew most about it, but the clarionette determined to drown him and perpetrated the most frightful discords in the attempt.

Next morning, the muleteers were late in arriving (predictably, under the circumstances), but there was a further cause of delay.

Remembering the trouble I had had during my short trip in Guatemala eight years ago, I brought out my own pack-saddles from England, [with] all my packages fitted to them. I had tried them most successfully in other countries, and produced them to the *arriero* [mule-driver] with not a little pride, and I [had] told him I should use my own pack-saddles when I engaged him the day before. Now he looked at them and said they would go very well on top of the pack! Nothing I could do would persuade him to use them.

In explanation the *arriero* simply stated, 'those things would kill my mules', and Maudslay had to give in.

A ride of about 15 miles over the Mico range brought them to Don Onofre's ranch. Maudslay must have been surprised and greatly relieved to find the track in fair condition, since Stephens had experienced unimaginable hardship and danger on the same route. Next morning Maudslay was up early (thanks to the fleas), roused Don Onofre, and within two-and-a-half hours they had reached a clearing where three of the 'Idols' stood in line; then a little farther on they found two more and an altar. 'The stones were covered with orchids and other plants and had a thick coating of moss, so that I thought at first that the hyroglifics, which were in low relief, were much worn and not likely to repay the trouble of cleaning them.' It was not easy in fact to distinguish the stelae from dead tree-trunks, but to Maudslay's delight he found that the moss came off very easily. Don Onofre and the *arriero* worked hard at making ladders out of saplings, and brushes out of bundles of palm leaflets, and Maudslay sacrificed a hair-brush to clean out some of the more delicate carving.

That night Maudslay slept very comfortably with his mosquito net slung from one of the Idols, but next day the weather looked threatening, so he hastened to take some photographs with what he judged to be adequate exposure. Soon it was raining hard, and since Don Onofre had to return, and Maudslay didn't much relish a wet night in the forest, they packed up and went back to Don Onofre's hacienda.

That evening Maudslay took the opportunity to develop some of his plates, and to his horror found them badly underexposed.[15] So he and Luis, the *arriero*, went back to the ruins.

I took 12 photos, but the light was very changeable and uncertain [because] it was still cloudy. For about 4 hours I dodged about from one idol to another trying to get a bright sunlight on the image. . . . Altogether it was rather troublesome work. Luis seemed quite happy, when not employed cutting down palm trees, lying on his back and shouting anything but melodious songs, stopping abruptly every now and then to ask me why I did not sing too.

Writing a decade later about this, the first of four visits he would make to Quiriguá, Maudslay enlarged on one detail of the cleaning procedure already described.

The final scrubbing was done with an ivory-backed hair-brush out of my dressing bag; and I well remember the fire of chaff I was subjected to on my return home, when the wreck of that hair-brush was pounced upon by an old servant, who wanted to know 'what Mr. Alfred could have been doing with his hair whilst in foreign parts!'[16]
    We slept only one night in the forest, and I cannot give a better instance of the denseness of the vegetation than by saying that I cleared a space for my camp cot on the south side of [Stela] A; yet it was only by chance that late in the following afternoon I became aware of the existence of the splendid [Zoomorph] B within twelve yards of my sleeping place. It was the unexpected magnificence of the monuments which that day came into view that led me to devote so many years to securing copies of them, which, preserved in the museums of Europe and America, are likely to survive the originals.

This statement of Maudslay's has often been quoted as evidence of his having experienced an epiphany – a conversion from a mere seeker of winter warmth to a committed archaeological explorer. But there is good reason to regard that statement of his as an over-simplification, and to reconsider its significance.
    One can well believe that the experience of pulling mats of moss away from a shapeless bulk, to reveal well-preserved inscriptions, was an astonishing experience, indeed a revelation, an epiphany, since a more vivid demonstration of the need to make an accurate record of those sculptures can hardly be imagined. One can imagine something of his immediate thoughts, and even an unspoken exclamation: 'Surely, these inscriptions should be recorded as soon as possible!' – and then, 'but isn't this exactly the kind of challenge I've been hoping to find?'
    For it seems very likely that well before experiencing this revelation Maudslay had been searching for some task of just this kind. The idea could easily have come to him from looking at the engravings in Stephens's book, for, no matter how brilliant a draughtsman and painter Catherwood was, he very seldom had the opportunity to record more

than a general impression of the sculptures – a rare exception being his more detailed drawing of the inscription on Altar Q at Copán. But now Maudslay was ready to apply photography to the task, and to spend time in doing so.

An argument against this supposition might be that in preparing for this first tour through Quiriguá and Copán Maudslay brought with him no special equipment beyond a camera and chemicals for developing the plates (not to mention pack-saddles and who knows what else, for Maudslay did not travel light);[17] and that he spent less than three days at either site. But if he had indeed made such a commitment, no matter how tentative, then surely a quick reconnaissance of suitable sites would be a necessary first step, simply to determine what useful ends his investigations might achieve, and what practical problems he would have to cope with.

Three pieces of evidence point to Maudslay's prior interest in investigating Central American ruins. One was the excitement that he felt when told by Sarg while still on the high seas of the 'recently discovered and undescribed ruins near Flores', coupled with the fact that he felt no need to explain the importance of this information to his sister – presumably because she already knew of his intentions, or at least, hopes. Next, he gave the game away inadvertently in recounting how, soon after landing at Belize, he told the Santa Cruz chiefs that the purpose of his visit was to study the works of art of their forefathers. And lastly, there is an anecdote told by the archaeologist James Cooper Clark: Maudslay confessed to him, at a luncheon given by the British Minister to Mexico in 1905, that at the start it had been for him 'just a toss-up' whether he had gone to Ceylon or Central America to excavate. What it was that tipped the balance he did not explain, but the fact that he chose Central America as his goal in the winter of 1880, and not Ceylon, seems to suggest a more purposeful motivation than simple avoidance of bronchitis.[18]

So why should he have wanted to conceal his original intentions, even after his work had been acclaimed? It is hard to say. Perhaps such a very modest man may have thought it pretentious, or over-ambitious, to announce a plan of engaging in such a novel and formidable enterprise; or even, much later, to admit having had such a plan. Much better, he may have thought, to leave for Central America ostensibly for the benefit of his health – and then quietly go to work.

We return to Mico. There, on the following morning, Maudslay said goodbye to Don Onofre and his lady; they had both been so kind and attentive that he was quite sorry to leave them. Now alone with Luis, they set off for Zacapa, but Luis seems to have taken him by a round-about route for his own devious purposes, and relations between them steadily deteriorated throughout their journey. At Zacapa Maudslay tried to enlist another *arriero* and more mules, but his journal records a depressing series of broken engagements, delayed departures, whole days lost, even some trouble with his own pack-saddles, which were at last in use.

They reached Copán on 3 February, and the *cabildo* (town- or village-council office) was opened up for them. This was 'a wretched, one-roomed plastered hovel with a mud floor and furnished with a rickety bed and two benches. Inside, a cross and altarpiece painted on wood, I suppose for service. Against the outside wall is a cell about six foot by four with a strong grated door, which is the village prison.'

Maudslay then spent three days wandering around the ruins with Stephens's book in hand. He found a few items that Stephens and Catherwood appear to have missed, and took some photographs (which proved to be over-exposed). His scanty notes end with an imprecation: 'Oh, the ticks, garrapatas as they call them, the brush swarmed with them . . . every leaf harbours some.'

On the 7th they left Copán, reaching Esquipulas two days later. After a day there they went on to spend nights at Amatillo, Chapara, Jalapa, and Agua Caliente. The ride to Amatillo proved to be longer than Maudslay expected, nearly 30 miles, 'and the mules were so tired that as it was a beautiful cool moonlit evening I footed the last two leagues'. A few hours beyond Agua Caliente,

> a turn in the track brought the lofty peaks of Agua and Fuego into view. The perfect cone of Volcan de Agua stood out against the blue sky whilst Fuego was partly rolled in silvery sunlit clouds. It was a lovely sight, and the impressions I had taken of the beauty of those peaks eight years ago was in no way corrected.

After a night at Palencia, a ride of some 20 miles brought them on 15 February to Guatemala City.

How long he remained there is unknown, but eventually he went on to Antigua, and determined to climb the Volcán de Agua. This must have been a very hard day-trip, for a mule path had yet to be made. He walked up to the crater hoping to take a photo of the view, but then, after waiting for four hours in vain for low cloud to clear, he had to pack up his camera and scramble down again.

Although unwilling to leave, he soon started for the Pacific slope along a road that passed between the volcanoes and then descended into lush, tropical vegetation.

> Towards evening black clouds began to gather over the mountains with occasional flashes of lightning. Thousands of big birds were circling high overhead and at first I took them to be the carrion crows which are so plentiful and so useful all over the country, but as some

of them swooped down and came near enough I found them to be hawks who had assembled – so my man told me – to feast on the locusts which for the past hour had been so numerous.

The next day, he rode on to Santa Lucía Cotzumalguapa, passing several well kept coffee and sugar estates.

An 'Hotel' proclaimed itself in large letters . . . and a wretched, dirty little inn it proved to be. I walked out in the afternoon to see some of the ruins, but found very little indeed, for all sculptured stones worth seeing have been bought up, and after being cut to make them as light as possible, have been taken off to Germany for the Berlin Museum . . . . I was by no means prepared for such a wholesale clearance.

But enough remained for Maudslay to see how different were these sculptures in both style and content from anything he had previously encountered.

Next morning he rode on westwards, and after about three hours was overtaken by a man who told him that 'the only ruins in the area worth seeing were at Pantaleón, where there were six large, well carved blocks of stone a league on the other side of Santa Lucía – muy hermosos – he said'. Maudslay had half a mind to turn back, but doing so would cost him three days, and time was running short. So he continued on his way to Patulul and then up to Lake Atitlán. There he spent a day at an Indian town, San Lucás, wandering along the shore and trying to take photographs of the market in the town, but found it difficult, because, as soon as he had the camera set up, half the people he had focused on would rush up to see what he was doing.

I am a terrible puzzle to the people in the hotels and elsewhere, for a stranger travelling merely to see the country is a thing almost unknown to them. Of course, I am usually taken for a professional photographer, and have raised no little anger by refusing to take portraits, and no amount of explanation will satisfy them that it is not mere caprice. . . . But at the hotel at Quesaltenango I was given a new character, for the boy belonging to the hotel came somewhat cautiously to my room to ask if I had any 'remedio' to sell him to make his hair lie straight.[19]

Then he set out on a ride of about 140 miles, heading in a northeasterly direction to Cobán, in Alta Verapaz. Although no 'log', or diary, covering this part of his travels has come to hand, at least the route he took is shown on the map published with the report of his Royal Geographical Society lecture, given in December of 1892 (as is the route he and his brother followed in 1872). But of his adventures or observations along the way nothing is known. The route he now followed took him through Totonicapán, Chich, Joyabaj, Cubulco, Rabinal, Salamá, and at last Cobán.

His objective now was clearly Tikal, that 'recently discovered and undescribed ruined city near Flores'. The man who had told him about it, Frank (or Franz) Sarg, was a resident of Cobán, which besides being the largest town in the highlands of Alta Verapaz, also lies on the route to Flores. Presumably Sarg had also told him that he could supply a guide and any equipment needed for the journey.

Sarg was a native of Frankfurt, but he had an English mother and an English wife, so the language they spoke at home was English. When Charles and Alfred had met him eight years earlier at the port of San José, he had been working for a shipping agency there. After an unsuccessful attempt to operate a lead mine near San Cristóbal, Alta Verapaz, he started a store in Cobán, and a coffee-exporting business, too. In 1875 he became the US Consular agent in Cobán (Livingston, incidentally, lying within his area of responsibility); and in 1879 he was appointed German Vice-Consul – since there had been a considerable immigration of Germans into Alta Verapaz during the previous ten years. The Sargs were a talented family. Francis was an amateur painter and musician, with a serious interest in natural history and anthropology. During his residence in Cobán, any expeditionary traveller heading north into Petén tended to consult him and borrow or hire the necessary equipment. Then, having on many occasions engaged various members of a Ladino family named López (from Cahabón, east of Cobán) as hunters, collectors and guides, and having also learnt to appreciate their reliability and knowledge, he encouraged other travellers to employ them.[20]

One of Sarg's visitors had been an English globetrotter and author, J. W. Boddham-Whetham, who in 1875 had found his way to Flores, Petén, and had there been offered, and then bought, two fragments of zapote-wood carved in low relief. They had been hacked out of lintels at Tikal, ruins which at that time had only once been mentioned in print, and then in an obscure German journal. These fragments he presumably showed to Sarg.[21]

Two years later a Swiss physician and botanist, Gustav Bernoulli, arrived at Sarg's house, on his way home from a wide-ranging tour that had taken him to Palenque, and then actually to Tikal. There, he had been greatly impressed by the finely carved wooden lintels, and had noticed the damage recently done to them by crude attempts to hack parts of them out. This made him resolve to remove the finest intact lintel (composed of three beams) and a beam each from two others, to protect them against such damage, and to send them for safekeeping to a Swiss museum. He had started to lower the beams to the ground, but found they were too heavy to handle. Accordingly on reaching Cobán he commissioned Sarg to send a party of men to complete the work, and ship the beams to Switzerland. In spite of the enormous difficulty of this task it was accomplished successfully, and the lintel has ever since been in Basel. Sarg himself seems not to have taken part in the operation. But that is how Sarg knew enough about Tikal to excite Maudslay's keen interest.

Of the López family, so highly esteemed by Sarg, the most intelligent, reliable, and good-natured was Gorgonio, who would become a much-loved adjutant to Maudslay on most of his expeditions. But on this occasion he must have been engaged elsewhere, since it was his brother Carlos who was appointed to accompany Maudslay to Flores.

On 31 March they set out from Cobán, with Maudslay mounted on a good mule. A party of *mozos* (hired men) carrying food supplies had been sent on ahead. The route to Chisec climbed up and down steep hills over muddy and rocky tracks, with various obstacles along the way, among them a deep river to cross. During this three-day leg of the journey Maudslay was suffering from an upset stomach, and unable to eat.

On the next leg, from Chisec to Chinajá, no longer were there steep hills to negotiate, but instead many streams to cross. These were spanned by rough log-bridges, and in leading his mule over one of them (as Maudslay set down in his notebook)[22]

> I heard a crack just as I was on the [other] side and turned round to see my mule with his feet hanging just above the water and his body wedged between two logs of the bridge – the centre log had given way. I scrambled up to him and managed to loosen his girths – the poor head struggled a good deal at first and was then tolerably quiet whilst I and Carlos got poles and levered one of the logs aside and dropped the mule down into the stream, and then with some little difficulty we got [him] up the bank. I had an awful vision for the moment of journeying the rest of the way to Peten on foot.

Fortunately the mule was none the worse for its tumble.

Soon after passing Chinajá both the road and the bridges improved, and two days' travelling brought them to Laguna Petex-batún, then another day's ride to the wide and sluggish Río de la Pasión. But while riding through the forest that day, as Maudslay noted,

> I suppose we had disturbed a wasps' nest, for both Carlos and I were stung. I opened a bottle of liquid ammonia which I kept in my saddle bags in case of snakebite or scorpion, and I suppose, owing to the knocking about and the high temperature, on loosening the stopper nearly the whole of the contents flew up into my face. I dropped the bottle and stumbled along the road gasping for breath, blinded and choked by the ammonia, and it was some minutes before I could breathe freely or open my eyes, which continued to be painful for an hour or more.

The ferryman, maintained there by the government, took the men across in a canoe, then the mules were swum across. They went on to Paso Subín, where they passed 'a most unpleasant night as fleas, mosquitoes, sandflies, horseflies, garrapatas [ticks] and every other sort of noxious insect seemed to abound'.

A ride of five hours next day, half of it through an oven-hot savanna, brought the little expedition to Sacluk, a village sustained by mahogany-cutters, but a poor-looking place consisting of a few dozen wattle-and-plaster-walled houses with thatched roofs built in the vicinity of some shallow ponds. The water taken from these, which remained the only source of water for precisely another century, was filthy, since the unfenced ponds were open to cattle and pigs, and were also used for washing clothes. 'A woodcutter', Maudslay remarked, 'is indeed to be pitied who has to seek recreation in such a hot, dull, dreary place as Sacluk; the condition of the water alone would justify his preference for aguardiente.'

Sacluk had recently become the *cabecera* or administrative centre of Petén, and, as Maudslay observes,

> had been euphemistically renamed 'La Libertad,' possibly to hide the fact that a condition not very far from slavery was more noticeable there than in other parts of the Republic. . . . Mozos are openly bought and sold, or at least their debts (and they are all deeply in debt) are passed from one creditor to another, and the services of the debtor pass with the debt until he has worked it off, which means never.
>
> Soon after my arrival I received a visit from an elderly Englishman [a Mr Denning] who told me he resided there 'because the climate suited him'; he was an eccentric waif who had at one time served with the British army, in what capacity I could not discover, although he gave me many unavailing hints that it was as a commissioned officer, and he was fond of talking about his 'little place' in Somersetshire. The poor fellow earned an occasional dollar by taking very imperfect photographs, and his visit to me was in order to learn my intentions, as he had heard that I was a 'retratista' and was sadly afraid I would cut him out of his business. He told me that some years earlier when on the road to Peten he had lost his way in the forest and nearly died of starvation, and that some Peteneros who found him had carried him to their village and treated him with the greatest kindness during an illness which followed from the hardships he had gone through, although they knew he had nothing with which to repay them. . . . I met the poor old fellow another year when he was in broken health and almost penniless, and was able to help him on his way to Guatemala, where the foreign residents got him into the infirmary and he passed quietly away.

The Jefe Político told Maudslay that in response to Sarg's request the ruins at Tikal had been cleared on his orders a fortnight before, so next morning Maudslay and his party set off for San Benito, an eight-hour journey, leaving at 4.30 a.m. so as to get through the savanna portion in the cool hours.

San Benito stands on the south shore of Lago Petén-Itzá, almost opposite the island-town of Flores, which had until lately been the *cabecera* of Petén – and before long would be again. Maudslay took a quick nap at the San Benito *cabildo* (town hall, if that is not too grand a term), and then received a visit from the Alcalde of Flores, who arranged for a boat to take them over to San Andrés on the northwest shore of the lake. Maya-speaking men from this village, and from San José a mile down the shore, had been recruited because they were more accustomed to life in the forest, and a few of them had some knowledge of the Tikal area. Evidently, the Flores Alcalde also arranged for the Comandante, Don Estanislaus, to join the expedition.

They would embark for San Andrés as soon as the wind fell that evening, but because of the usual Holy Week excitements they didn't get off until 11 p.m. The lake was smooth and an Easter full moon lit their way. On arrival, the Comandante sent for the Alcalde of San Andrés, who proved to be agreeable, in spite of the hour, and assured Maudslay that everything would be ready for departure next evening. But he had to confess that the ruins had not, in fact, been cleared because he had not had the men to do it.

The next evening Maudslay, Carlos, and the Comandante set out in a bad canoe with eight *mozos*, then called in at San José to pick up another eight in a larger canoe. They were blessed with another windless, moonlit night, and without trouble reached El Remate, the starting point for their march to Tikal. After a few hours' sleep, they hunted for six more *mozos* who were to have joined them, but they were nowhere to be seen. Leaving a man to watch for them, Maudslay got his men on the road, but soon discovered that, unlike the Cobaneros, these were no good as carriers, for at first they refused to carry loads heavier than 65 lb. At this the Comandante must have exerted his authority, for off they went, and after four hours' walk made camp at an unfortunately waterless spot. Next morning the other six *mozos* turned up, so now Maudslay had a respectable force of twenty-two.

Within an hour's walk of their destination they found some water in a hollow tree, and then, a little farther on, four coconuts in the *champa*, or hut, of an abandoned *milpa* (maize field), enough to provide all of them, at last, with a good drink. As guide they had the only survivor of a party of men from the lake who a few years earlier had attempted to form a settlement near the ruins. All the others had died of fever. Now, for a time, he lost the trail, but eventually they began to find minor mounds, and then reached the towering temples that face each other across the great plaza. It was 17 April when Maudslay reached this goal.

Losing no time in climbing up these temples, Maudslay found that from those heights he could see two others that appeared to be even higher. But in the two he first climbed, Temples I and II, the carved zapote-wood lintels were either badly eaten away or else (as he must have been prepared to find) missing.[23]

After some searching, Maudslay found a suitable lodging in a well-preserved vaulted chamber in the Central Acropolis. But the first impressions jotted down in his notebook were these:

> On the whole I must own to being much disappointed. The forest was over everything. The work of clearing would be much more than I could do and there appeared to be very little hope of taking satisfactory photos. No doubt I was on the site of a very large city, larger than anything mentioned by Stephens, but although the houses were large and numerous there was little sign of carving or ornamental work, and my mozos told me I had seen the best there was to be seen. I returned to my house rather downhearted, all the mozos having fled back to the plain, being frightened to sleep in the ruins because of the 'Duendes de las casas' – goblins of the temples.
>
> I got some of them to bring water, which had to be fetched from some distance and was very bad and dirty, and got some of them to work to clear the two inches of dust and loose plaster from the floor of my house, and then made myself pretty comfortable. Carlos and the Comandante prepared to string their hammocks to the trees outside, being also I think a little frightened of ghosts in the house. However, after hearing a tiger prowling about a little too close to them to be comfortable, they too strung their hammocks in the house. There were certainly strange noises in the night but they were nothing worse than the howls of the howling monkeys.

One day Carlos went out shooting, 'and shot two Curasows different to what I had seen before[24] [perhaps they or the other birds had been Penelopes] and captured two young ones alive, old enough to feed themselves, and I intend to carry them home – such pretty little beasts'. Next day he could report: 'my little Curasows are already quite tame and do not attempt to run away when let out, but I am afraid of them getting into the fire. They are always hungry.'

Maudslay could not afford to stay at Tikal for longer than a week, since he was anxious to board the mail steamer *Wanderer* at Belize when she called in on 4 May. During the rest of his stay he had to spend some time supervising the *mozos* clearing the surroundings of Temples I, II, and III, as he found they were disinclined to work unless watched. He scrubbed one of the stelae in the plaza for its portrait, and measured the chambers of the tall temples. On his last day there, he photographed ruins that had been cleared, and then in the evening had to unload the glass plates from their slides.

> In shifting the dry plates just before going to bed I have great fear that some of the views I had taken were spoilt. I had told the boy to let the camp fire burn low, and when there was nothing of a flame, only smouldering embers, I set to work inside our house with the red lantern, but just as I had taken six plates out of the slides a sudden flare of light came through the open door [and] I yelled to the boy and tried to cover up the plates. The light only lasted a moment and then died out again, and the boy told me that it was caused by a dry leaf of the tree above falling on the embers. I hope the plates are not much damaged. . . . My little Curasows are most delightfully tame and run after me everywhere about the camp and are always ready to eat.

On the 23rd the men came for their loads at 6.30, and then all made off, carelessly leaving behind one of the loads. The Comandante went off in pursuit, but it was an hour before one of the men returned for the last pack. Then, astonishingly, they went the whole way to the lake – about 30 miles – in one long march. Maudslay expected to camp there by the lake, but the Comandante, who had had an attack of fever, was all for getting home, and Maudslay had no objection to offer, so, leaving some of the men at Remate, and dropping off others at their *milpas* (corn fields) along the shore, they reached San Andrés at 3 a.m.

Then in Flores, Maudslay met Don Chencho, who had been recommended to him by a friend of Sarg's in Sacluk. He was to leave next day for El Cayo, in British Honduras, with twelve cargo mules, and he agreed to take Maudslay and his baggage. They were to start next morning.

Start they did, although later than planned, but Don Chencho insisted that they would travel eight leagues (20 miles, or eight hours' walk at cargo-mule speed). But, Maudslay wrote,

> after we had ridden two leagues we came to a few shanties round a filthily dirty pond, and here the arriero stopped in spite of all my bad language and entreaties that we should push on. It was only two o'clock and I was most reluctant to waste time. But it was no good, I had to give in. The only drinking water was from that pond; the banks were muddy, and cattle and pigs were wallowing in the mud. The water was the colour of pea soup and full of tadpoles and innumerable insects. I boiled it and let the filth subside and then it was evil looking enough, and I possibly swallowed the germs of many fevers. One of the mozos had a bad calentura [fever] towards evening and lay groaning all night. I mended my birds' cage, then strolled about when the heat passed off. I reluctantly came to the conclusion that don Chencho had sold me, and had only bundled me out of Flores because I worried him about starting.

Next morning they got under way early.

No bribes would induce any of the mozos to take charge of my little birds, so I had to carry them myself. I tried all sorts of dodges, but the jolting of the mule was most uncomfortable for them and I had fears that I should fail in keeping them alive. I first of all tried to carry them in a basket, but that was too tiring for me as I had to hold the basket in my hand all the time. Then I tried if they would sit quietly on the peak of my saddle, but the motion was too much for them. At last I put one in each of the side pockets of my coat, and cut a small hole for their heads to come through, and in this way they travelled fairly comfortably, but every now and then one of them would fly out, and I was in great fear of losing them, but they never attempted to fly away, [but] only landed in the track and began to peck about. Once, one escaped without my noticing it, and I rode back some distance to find it, when luckily I came upon don Chencho who had picked the bird up in the pathway.

That evening, Maudslay sewed buttons on to his pockets to prevent his pets from escaping again.

At last, on 28 April they reached the border, crossed the river into British territory, and went on to El Cayo, the head of navigation of the Belize River. There he made the acquaintance of a Mr O'Brien, described as a Hispano-Anglo-Negro, 'who was most civil and obliging, and gave me a good supper, but told me the Wanderer had left Belize on the 18th or 19th.' Maudslay was appalled, until at the Alcalde's he was able to consult the sailing dates given in the *Gazette*, and found the *Wanderer* was, in fact, to sail on the 4th, as expected.

Mr O'Brien then put himself out to find a boat and boatmen to take Maudslay down the river. Neither the boat nor the boatmen that he was able to find proved to be ideal, but after four days of paddling they arrived at a narrow and, to the newcomer, unexpected branch close to its mouth, which runs down to Belize City. This last stretch Maudslay chose to walk, perhaps to ease the boatmen's labours on that shallow creek. He had arrived with twenty-four hours to spare.

The *Wanderer* took him to New Orleans, where he went to a lager beer saloon to hear the music. Next day he took a train to New York, arrived early in the morning, and had the good luck to obtain an excellent cabin, which had just been given up by an intending passenger, on the White Star liner *Celtic*.

Chapter 8

Yaxchilán

O f Maudslay's activities following his return from Guatemala nothing is known, but one may imagine the enthusiastic, even excited, tales that he had to tell his family – and his friends, such as J. W. Clark and Osbert Salvin. He must also have told them that he meant to resume his explorations there before long.

On setting out for Guatemala in the previous winter, the travels he'd had in mind were probably quite modest. He would follow in the footsteps of Stephens and Catherwood – and Salvin – to Quiriguá and Copán, and afterwards revive his memories of Antigua and Lake Atitlán, after an absence of ten years. But quite unexpectedly he had found himself drawn into the terra incognita of the central Maya lowlands, and had discovered there a richer field for archaeological work than he could have imagined.

Now, a year later, he seems to have held in check any temptation to mount at once an ambitious expedition. From past experience of travel in undeveloped countries, he probably thought it prudent to limit his activities at that stage to further reconnaissance, to learning more about local conditions and the customs of the country, and to picking up more Spanish. For obviously there were many matters to look into: shipping arrangements, overland transport, government permissions, Customs concessions, letters of credit, food supplies, availability of labour, and, among many others, advice as to the best months in the year for working in various areas of the country. All of these and more he would have to enquire about as opportunities arose.

Regarding possible activities for this second venture, he seems to have decided beforehand to set Copán aside for another year. Instead, he chose Quiriguá and Tikal as his goals, and, since this expedition was intended to be scarcely more elaborate than the last, there would be no need to spend much time buying stores and shipping them before leaving.

When ready – having remained in England for less than six months in fact – he sailed from Southampton on 17 November 1881, aboard the Royal Mail steamer *Medway*, to retrace the route he had taken years before with Charles, crossing the Isthmus of Panama, and landing at San José.[1]

The ship dropped anchor there at 11 p.m. on 19 December, but it was not until 3 a.m. that Maudslay was landed. Having seen his cargo safely brought ashore, he rolled himself up in a blanket in the cargo shed for a few hours of sleep.

Since his arrival ten years earlier there had been one tremendous change: San José was now linked to Escuintla by a narrow-gauge railway, but he still had to ride the rest of the way to Guatemala on mule-back, arriving there a few days before Christmas. In one of his notebooks comments are found on the state of the roads, perhaps inspired by this journey:

> These roads are only in parts fit for native two-wheeled bullock carts to crawl over, and although a diligence does run from the capital to Escuintla and another plies between the capital and Quesaltenango, what induces anyone to travel in them it is difficult to imagine. Surely not the inability to sit a mule, for no mule in the country could buck and jolt and jump as do these vehicles over the stones and ruts in the worse parts of the tracks.

On reaching Guatemala City he called on a scientist at the Instituto Nacional, whom he had met a year earlier at Sarg's house in Cobán. This was Edwin Rockstroh, a man with German training who had already explored the Balkans and Turkey before being commissioned by a Dresden newspaper to report on the great Centennial Exposition held at Philadelphia in 1876.[2] There he met Dr C. H. Berendt, a physician who spent years of his life wandering about Central America and Mexico, collecting or copying manuscripts, compiling vocabularies, and studying ruins, and he it was who recommended Rockstroh to visit Guatemala.[3] Having been supplied by him with information and letters of recommendation, Rockstroh decided to go, planning to recoup his expenses by collecting zoological specimens for sale.

Accordingly, he made his way to Guatemala City, and then to Cobán, where he called on another man he had met at the Philadelphia Exposition, Frank Sarg. Sarg and his wife hospitably took him in as a guest, but Rockstroh, after spending three months there, concluded that there was little money to be made by such collecting. It was then that Sarg managed to obtain a post for him at the Instituto Nacional.

On meeting Rockstroh again soon after his arrival in the capital, Maudslay found he had interesting news to tell him. He had now made a second expedition down the Usumacinta – the river which now serves, over nearly half its course, as part of the boundary between Guatemala and Mexico. As the river had never been surveyed, cartographers had not the slightest idea of the course it took in making its way through a vast and almost trackless jungle before reaching Tenosique and the coastal plains of Tabasco. Clearly, its course as shown on maps of that period was the result of pure guesswork. But now the immense area of forested land lying to the west of this uncharted river was in dispute; Mexican army units had been brought into the area, and an offer of arbitration by the United States had been rejected by Mexico as an unjustified intrusion into its affairs.

Until 1820, the whole of Chiapas had been part of Guatemala, but following an invasion of it during the brief regime of the Mexican Emperor Iturbide, and then another by General López de Santa Ana, most of the state had become indisputably part of Mexico. In spite of this, no serious interest in defining the border was shown until 1874, when Mexico began asserting its claim to terrain that Guatemalans still regarded as theirs: Soconusco, the fertile southeasternmost portion of Chiapas along the Pacific coast.

Eight years later, when military action between the two countries seemed imminent, the Guatemalan President, Justo Rufino Barrios, indicated that he was ready to cede Soconusco to the United States – or if the offer should be refused, then to a European country – so as to have a buffer state between his own country and Mexico. The State Department, however, showed no interest in the offer, although it did became concerned that a European power might step in to purchase it.[4]

Eventually, in 1880, Barrios realized he could do nothing but yield, and agreed to discuss boundary proposals with the Mexican government. Two years later a preliminary accord was signed, and the frontier lines therein proposed remain in force today, apart from a couple of changes. Of course it then became necessary to survey and mark boundary lines, which in the treaty had been defined only in words. This task was to involve so much work (and not a little dispute) that the final Convention would not be signed until 5 May 1899.[5]

To carry out this survey, the Mexican government appointed a surveyor named Manuel Pastrana, while the Guatemalans were obliged to import one from the United States named Miles Rock, a surveyor and expert in celestial navigation at the Naval Observatory in Washington, D.C. Edwin Rockstroh was then appointed as his assistant.

Rockstroh was a keen explorer who on his own initiative had already investigated the headwaters of the Río Usumacinta. On this bold journey into the little-known Lacandón country he had set out from Huehuetenango in the Cuchumatanes mountains, passed down the Río Ixcán and into the Río Lacantún, followed this into the Usumacinta, and then down that great river for some distance before turning back. His return route then took him up the Río de la Pasión, one of the Usumacinta's other two principal affluents.

Since the Usumacinta was now going to serve as part of the proposed border, accurate knowledge of its course had become a priority, and Rockstroh, as the only employee of the Guatemalan Commission of Limits with any knowledge of it, was clearly the best man to carry out further reconnaissance of it. His instructions were probably to follow it as far as rapids well known to be impassable by conventional craft – these lying just upstream from Tenosique – and then to continue on foot as far as that little Mexican town on the riverbank.

What, then, was the news Rockstroh gave Maudslay? It was that some considerable way down that river he had come upon a neatly constructed stone pyramid or pier, built on a rocky ledge within its course, near the left bank. Intrigued by this, he had investigated the riverbank behind the pile, and discovered a ruined city hidden there in dense forest, with standing buildings and fine pieces of relief sculpture. He was anxious, therefore, for Maudslay to explore these ruins, and hoped to accompany him if he could get leave of absence from his employers.

In Guatemala Maudslay also found waiting for him a letter from Sarg written from Cobán, and in his reply he requested Sarg to make various arrangements for his Petén trip. That trip, however, was planned for two months ahead, for it was still too early in the year to consider going to Petén: the track leading there from Cobán would still be flooded and impassable.

Maudslay's immediate plan was to send a gang of men to Quiriguá in advance to clear out some of the thick underbrush from the ruins, and instructions about this were either sent to Gorgonio López or relayed to him by Sarg. In the meantime Maudslay would climb a volcano or two, and revisit Lake Atitlán, as planned. Then he would proceed to Quiriguá to do his work there; and only when this had been accomplished would he go on to Petén via Cobán.

Before leaving, Maudslay, accompanied by the British Minister, paid a call on President Barrios and presented him with an album of photographs taken during his previous visit. (Maudslay noted that the President's room reminded him of the King of Tonga's, since it was 'full of odds and ends piled up anyhow. Saddles, barometers, clocks, samples of cartridges etc.'.) On hearing his plans, the President promised to send a letter of recommendation to the Jefe Político in Sacluk – then the administrative centre of Petén.

No sooner had Maudslay arrived in Antigua Guatemala than he set off to climb Volcán de Agua, the extinct volcano that looms above the old capital. Then a few days later he chanced to meet Otto Stoll, a Swiss doctor who was practising medicine there, while at the same time collecting the valuable notes on Indian languages that he would later publish. They agreed to climb the Volcán de Fuego together.[6]

This would be a volcano far more arduous to climb than Agua. They set off with porters, and at 11,000 feet, having enjoyed memorable views, they camped for the night. Maudslay put on three jerseys, two flannel shirts, a knitted waistcoat under his jacket, and trousers, and in spite of a double rug over him, felt intensely cold. Poor Stoll, he thought, got no sleep. At sun-up they resumed the climb. Stoll, recovering from an illness, was in poor condition and found the climb extremely hard. On reaching the cone, about 400 feet high, they scrambled, sometimes on all fours, up the cinder slope to a ridge of rocks which they thought must be the edge of the crater. 'Maudslay's ambition was greater than mine', Stoll wrote, 'But now, oh misery!' – there was a further steep slope of scree to ascend!

'Once at the top, Stoll was more venturesome than I,' Maudslay noted, 'and induced me to follow him round the smoking edge of the crater. . . . After a short rest on the summit we returned . . . shooting down the cinder slope as if it were snow, somewhat to the damage of our boots'.

During his visit to Lake Atitlán, Maudslay ran into trouble in the large Indian village of Santiago Atitlán.

I had taken one instantaneous picture of the women in the market-place before they observed me, but after that they ran after me and shook their fists, and used what I am sure must have been the strongest language whenever I appeared. Then I was waited on in the Cabildo by a deputation of about two hundred men, who apparently wanted to know my business, but as only one of them could speak Spanish and he was very drunk, it did not mend matters. This sort of thing went on for two days, and then I received notice to clear out of town, but luckily I was delivered from my difficulties by the arrival of the Ladino magistrate, who was making the round of the district, and who satisfied the Indians that I was quite harmless.

On 30 January, soon after his return to Guatemala City, Maudslay set out for Quiriguá, with Rockstroh seeing him off, but telling him regretfully that he would not after all be able to accompany him to Petén. On reaching the village of Quiriguá five days later, Maudslay was welcomed by Don Onofre Alvarez and his wife, his friends from the previous year. For Don Onofre he had brought a violin as a present.

At the ruins he was pleased to find that Gorgonio López had cleared them already, although much cleaning of the sculpture would be needed before he could take photographs. And now he had his first view of Zoomorph P, declaring it

the largest and best of all the monuments in Quiriguá. It is . . . a sort of tortoise shape with a huge grotesque human head and turtle's fins, but although one can just make out this general plan, the stone is so covered with hieroglyphics, intertwining grotesque figures and faces that it was some time before I could make out any general plan at all.

Maudslay made a rough plan of the site, and had a path cut through to the river, with a view to possible use of it for access and carriage of supplies, but found there was no beach or landing-place for boats within half a league (1.2 miles). He also decided that the weather in February was too uncertain; March to May would be more propitious for work at Quiriguá. Then a small discovery was made by Gorgonio while bushing the site, a little 'Chacmool' statue, which they took to the village for safe-keeping.

Recumbent figures of this type, named Chacmools by the eccentric Auguste Le Plongeon when he found the largest and best-preserved example at Chichén Itzá, are associated with a Central Mexican cult that arose near the end of the Classic Period. Of course, when the Quiriguá Chacmool was found, the chronological element of the surprise was not apparent, for there was no clear idea yet of when cities like Quiriguá had flourished. That would come only later when it was understood (partly in consequence of Maudslay's own work) that the great Classic Maya cities, including Quiriguá, were being abandoned at about the time that Toltec influence from central Mexico was reaching the area. Or so it appeared until recently. Now the presence of that Chacmool at Quiriguá seems less anomalous, with the recognition of considerable cultural interchange between Central Mexico and the Maya area during the Classic Period.

Having achieved his limited goals at Quiriguá for the year, Maudslay rode over the hills to Yzabal, meaning to take the ancient shallow-draught steamboat to Panzos, and from there ride on to Cobán. But the boat had just left, obliging him to go by canoe. With six men in this canoe, plus saddles and other baggage, there were only a few inches of free-board, and more than once as they crossed to the western end of the lake they were in danger of being swamped. There still remained about 25 miles of paddling up the Río Polochic before reaching Panzos. But there they found Sarg waiting for them, and he had brought Maudslay the same excellent mule that he'd ridden to Petén the previous year. Three days of riding brought them to Cobán, where Maudslay spent ten days hospitably entertained by the Sargs.

Maudslay's party set out for Petén on 2 March: it was made up of Gorgonio, Carlos and Dionicio López, and thirteen *mozos*. They reached Sacluk on the 11th, and from there Carlos and Dionicio were sent off with two other mozos to Lake Petén-Itzá, with orders to recruit yet more men from around it, and take them in to Tikal, where further clearing of the ruins was required.[7]

In the meantime Maudslay intended to visit the ruins Rockstroh had described to him. The letter the President had promised to send to Sacluk had evidently arrived, and was effective, since Maudslay was able to obtain a note to the ferryman at Paso Real (a government employee who had been with Rockstroh to Menché the previous year), ordering him to accompany Maudslay as guide. This order the ferryman, a Mexican named Carmenate, complied with very reluctantly. Maudslay also secured the company of a Mr Schulte, manager of the lumber company working in that area, who was going as far as the mouth of the Lacantún River to set up a new lumber camp a short way upriver (with a name that now resonates oddly, Acapulco).

Then, having dropped off Mr Schulte, they paddled on down the Río Usumacinta through increasingly turbulent water to the *encajonada*, a stretch where the river has cut through a rocky ridge, and in that narrow defile swirls into dangerous whirlpools. They passed through it safely, and continued downriver as far as a landing on the left bank, almost opposite the mouth of a stream named Yalchilán, and went ashore hoping to see some Lacandón Maya.

The path they took was marked at intervals by jaguar skulls set on sticks, and after half an hour's walk they came to a group of three houses in a clearing. A woman came out to meet them, and fortunately, as some of his boys knew Yucatec (which resembles Lacandón Maya), conversation was possible. As Maudslay wrote in his journal,

> She had not the slightest trace of fear; she smiled quite happily and received us most courteously, asked us to go into the small open house (shed) and said that all the men were away hunting cacao and would not return for five days. She was dressed in the same sort of garment as the man I saw in the morning [described as one long sack-like garment of brown, splashed with round blots of some red dye], but was ornamented with many strings of many-coloured beads round her neck and amongst the beads were many silver coins – half-dollars etc. which she told me she got in Tabasco. She had black straight hair hanging loose and her complexion was quite light coloured, a great deal lighter than my mosos.
>
> The biggest house had walls of sticks, and out of this came another woman. I wanted to go into the house, but my mosos advised me not to as the dogs were shut up there and were very savage, and they certainly gave tongue freely. The houses are much the same as ordinary ranches, except for the low walls. The woman had features exactly like the faces at Palenque and Menché, receding forehead, hooked nose and big lips. She was quite pleasant and talkative, much more so than most of the Indian women I have seen. The clearing was planted with maize, plantain, chile, tobacco, tomatoes, gourds, calabash and cotton, and they seemed very well off. We got four bunches of plantains, some small sort of yams and tomatoes in exchange for a little salt, without any haggling – and the woman promised to make *totoposte* for us (to be sent for) and said she wanted a coin like [the

one] she had on her neck (a dollar). [Totoposte are large, thin, dried tortillas of maize meal.]

Next morning an hour's paddling brought them to the stone pier, or rather, mound, which now, with the river so low, stood high and dry on its rock ledge. They scrambled up the sandy bank and began their search. As Maudslay recorded, 'the forest was rather thick but one could get through the undergrowth at a fair pace. It was some time before we could find a house good enough for me to live in, but at last we came upon one at the top of many terraces and steps, which was in fairly good preservation and rather wider than any I had seen at Tikal.' The floor was covered in loose stones and broken plaster.

In one of the recesses stands a large Idol with its head broken off, and lying beside it, and scattered about in all parts of the house and especially near the Idol were a large number of earthen vessels in which some resinous substance had been burned. These I believe had been brought by the Caribes, and they certainly could not have been in the position in which they were if they had been left since the houses were deserted.

('Caribes' was another term for Lacandóns, a group of Indians famous for having resisted conversion to Christianity and incorporation into the state.)

Maudslay's journal continues: 'Whilst I was looking at the house a cry came from the men that there were some peccaries [wild pig] and I bolted after them with my gun. Carmenate was ahead of me with his gun. When I asked the boy how many there were he said they were like ants. Carmenate got the first shot, and knocked one over.' Maudslay wounded one which got to its feet and came towards him. He had no time to reload, and having heard that they charge fiercely when wounded, he climbed a tree. Soon after, he was able to kill it.

Two *coches de monte* were a great help to our larder as we were fourteen in all. We went back, [and] cleared out part of the house. . . . It has carved lintels over each of the three doors very well done, generally two figures in elaborate costume presenting something one to another. . . . Gorgonio and I only sleep there, the mozos and bogas [boatmen] prefer the river bank.

19th March. . . . In the afternoon found the fallen carved lintel on which Rockstroh had broken his axes – set men to work to shave it down.

20th March. Worked at general plan – on the whole fairly pleased. Mozos worked well. . . . Sent off three men in canoe in morning to bring food from the caribal [Lacandón settlement]. Work on carved stone goes on fairly but some of tools broken.

21st March. Chino returned in the evening bringing very little food, no totoposte or plantains – much to my astonishment he said he had a note for me. I opened the paper and was not best pleased to see the card of Désiré Charnay, 'Mission Franco-Américaine.' Chino said that he had lots of people with him and that he sent word that I was not to put myself out about food as he was bringing plenty for all, and he asked for the loan of my canoe to bring him down from the Paso de Yalchilan. Three of his 'bogas' came down in my canoe and I further learnt from them that there were three 'estrangeros' and that they had all come from Tenosique. I expect a small scientific expedition which will swamp my work. The bogas say that there is no Mexican officer with them, so they can hardly throw difficulties in the way of moving the stone.

The name of Désiré Charnay was familiar to Maudslay. As early as 1858 Charnay had been dispatched by the French Ministry of Education to photograph pre-Columbian ruins in Mexico, and the superb prints that resulted were published three years later in portfolios of huge format and limited edition (Maudslay had probably seen the British Museum copy).

Charnay was less a scholar than an explorer-cum-travel-writer, and as such he was exceedingly anxious to discover some ruined city of importance, the existence of which could be revealed to the world in his forthcoming book. He earned a place in the history of Mesoamerican archaeology, however, by making extensive excavations at Tula – but until then, the unknown ruined cities he was so anxious to find had eluded him. It must therefore have been with the greatest excitement and anticipation that Charnay left Tenosique; he was even wondering if this could be the Phantom City of which John Lloyd Stephens had heard tell.[8]

Because of those rapids impossible to navigate upstream from Tenosique, Charnay, his secretary, and baggage train were obliged to travel overland, taking a trail which would lead them in about four days to Paso Yalchilán (or Jachilan, as Charnay had heard it called, but now known as Paso Yaxchilán). On arrival there, they would be faced with the problem of reaching the ruins, which lay on the opposite bank, nearly 4 miles downstream, so, before leaving Tenosique, Charnay had sent four men on ahead to the Paso with instructions to fell a tree there and make from it a dugout canoe. But upon arrival Charnay found it would be at least a week before the canoe could be ready, so they were obliged to wait in the hope that someone, Ladino or Lacandón, might come by and ferry them to the ruins.[9]

Then a canoe did come into view, and Charnay's excitement, now at fever pitch since he was on the point of adding lustre to his name as discoverer of the Phantom City, turned to gall as he caught sight of European belongings in it. Asking whose they were, he was told they belonged to Don Alfredo, who was working at the ruins.

He could only ask to be taken to the ruins; and there, as he describes in his book, *The Ancient Cities of the New World,* he was welcomed by Don Alfredo 'whose fair looks and elastic step shewed him to be an Englishman.' The truly magnanimous reception that Charnay received is best told by him, though we may take his account with a pinch of salt:

> We shook hands; he knew my name, he told me his: Alfred Maudslay, Esq., from London; and as my looks betrayed the inward annoyance I felt: 'It's all right,' he said, 'there is no reason why you should look so distressed. My having had the start of you was a mere chance, as it would have been the other way. You need have no fear on my account, for I am only an amateur, travelling for pleasure. With you the case of course is different. But I do not intend to publish anything. Come, I have had a place got ready; and as for the ruins I make them over to you. You can name the town, claim to have discovered it, in fact do what you please. I shall not interfere with you in any way, and you may even dispense with mentioning my name if you so please.' I was deeply touched by his kind manner, and I am only too charmed to share with him the glory of having explored this city. We lived and worked like two brothers, and we parted the best friends in the world.

Taking him at his word, Charnay named the site 'La Ville Lorillard' ('Lorillard City' in the English edition of his book), to honour the manu-facturer of tobacco and snuff who was his co-sponsor with the French government. But poor Charnay! For all his egoism, surely he must have suffered embarrassment and chagrin at the tone of that passage when in time he saw the magisterial volumes produced by the 'mere amateur'.

As to the name given the site, Maudslay simply called it 'Usumacinta' in his first published description, a paper read before the Royal Geographical Society in December 1882. Surprisingly he appears to have been unaware that Rockstroh had already in 1881 used another name, 'Menche', in a brief note reporting his discovery which appeared in a German geographical journal. Later he was to call it 'Menche Tinamit', and, on learning this, Maudslay immediately adopted the name Menché (with accent), including the 'Tinamit' only on a very few occasions.[10]

'Menche Tinamit' has been criticized as a hybrid construction (*tinamit* being a Nahua word for town), even though the ancients were not above using such hybrid terms themselves. No one could be more scathing in his objections to that name than Teobert Maler, an archaeological explorer of belligerent tendency, who became jealous of Maudslay and was not above disparaging him when the opportunity arose. When Maler came to write up a report on the valuable work that he himself would do at 'Menché' a few years later, he used the name 'Yaxchilán', borrowed from the stream, and this is the name that has stuck.[11]

Thanks to the survival of Maudslay's journal, another version of his remarkable encounter with Charnay at Menché/Lorillard/Yaxchilán can be given.

22nd March. Worked away all the morning. After breakfast whilst I was away hunting for ruins in the bush Gorgonio came to say that the strangers had arrived – and I went off to see them. I had sent both my canoes up with a note to Charnay – but only Charnay himself, his secretary (about 25 years old) and four men turned up. Charnay told me that he had after 25 years' travelling had an attack of fever this morning for the first time in his life. I took them off at once to show them the 'casa subterránea' (as the men call it) which I have had cleared out for them, and a path cut to the river – it is much more convenient than my house which is so high up the hill. Then as Charnay said he had eaten nothing for I forget how many hours, I took him up to my house and gave him the best breakfast that I could. He gave me rice and frijoles for my men.

23rd March. Showed Charnay round the ruins and he immediately set his secretary at work to make paper moulds of some of the carved lintels. It is a very easy process and I wish I had known of it before. Charnay tells me he has been two years working in Central America [southern Mexico was often loosely included in this term] at antiquities on behalf of the French Government. Lorillard's share in the matter seems a curious one. Charnay says that Lorillard telegraphed him asking him to take charge of an expedition of this kind, but Charnay had already arranged to do so for the French . . . so Lorillard merely agreed to pay part of the expenses with no gain as far as I can see either to himself or his country except the ribbon of the Legion of Honour. Charnay's work comes to an end here and he returns to Mexico and then to Paris and does not travel again, says he begins to feel it too much [he was fifty-three]. He does not strike me as a Scientific traveller of much class – he is a pleasant talkative gentleman, thirsting for glory and wishes to be professor of the history of American Civilisation in Paris – burst on me in the first few minutes of our acquaintance with the fact that he had established a great theory about the ruined cities and that the work was done now once and for all – which means that he had set to work to upset the utterly unnecessary theory that the cities are of great antiquity – and had clinched his argument by finding in Yucatan the figure of a Spaniard on horseback amongst the sculptures – he says that as soon as he found that, all further interest in the work was ended!!

Charnay was very civil to me and I breakfasted with him and am to do so during the rest of his stay – he is well off for provisions and has plenty of wine. Hearing that I had already cleared the ruins he left his men (14) at the Paso de Yachilan. This trip from Tenosique costs him about $1500.

Charnay only takes a mould of a few sculptures here and there and a few photos and he is going to be good enough to give me what paper for moulds etc. he has left. Unluckily for me it is not much but will enable me to take the monuments at Tikal. He is evidently always thinking of the grand opening of his exhibition at the Trocadero when all his moulds will be complete, and can't help describing it to me frequently in anticipation of the glory of an official opening with the Ministers, President, etc. He is just my idea of a French traveller but not of a careful scientific observer.

Where, then, in Yucatán had Charnay seen the remarkable figure of a Spaniard on horseback that clinched his arguments? We find it was in the ruins of Kabah, for upon arrival there, about a month earlier:

Hardly had we trod the ground when I made a discovery of very exceptional importance. I write these notes in a state of veritable intoxication: my joy knows no bounds, for this discovery is the most significant ever made in American archaeology. The question of the American civilization is settled, and I have the satisfaction of knowing that my theory of the modern origin of these civilizations is established beyond dispute.

In the middle apartment of the building called by Stephens Casa No. 2, on the front wall, is seen a design which, by itself alone, tells the whole story. It represents *a horse with a rider*.

Horse and rider are designed after the Indian manner by an inexperienced hand, guided by an excited imagination. Yet it is impossible not to recognize both figures. The horse has his trappings; we see the stirrups; the man wears his cuirass. . . .

Verily, excited imagination had played its part in settling this question, but after a time Charnay seems to have become doubtful about his interpretation of the damaged wall-painting (no trace of which now remains), for he quietly dropped his theory.[12]

On the 26th they all left Yaxchilán together. Navigating a canoe, especially a rather heavily laden canoe, upstream on the swiftly flowing Usumacinta is extremely hard work, the more so when there is no one on board who knows the river intimately. A boatman who does will make use of back eddies now on one side, now on the other, willing to be swept back from a hard-earned position whenever he crosses, to benefit eventually by having done so. Maudslay's men had to haul the boats with ropes for much of the way, contending with banks that are mostly either rock-strewn or of steeply sloping sand.

Before bidding each other adieu, Maudslay bought some tools from Charnay, and was given some more provisions for the *mozos*, also two bottles of wine and spirits for himself. Charnay travelled with ample supplies of Bordeaux, Aragon and Madeira wine; some years ago I crossed Charnay's route at a water-hole north of Yaxchilán, and there I found two wine-bottles of black glass, hand-blown into moulds, one of them miraculously unbroken. They could only have been Charnay's.[13]

On their way back, a quick visit was made to ruins on the riverbank near the mouth of the Río Salinas, ruins now known as Altar de Sacrificios. On 18 April the long haul upstream, which had lasted more than three weeks, ended as they reached Paso Real. Maudslay went on horseback straight to Sacluk, but as for the lintel, estimated by Maudslay still to weigh about a quarter of a ton even though reduced to half its original thickness, there was no other way to carry it than lashed to a pole borne on men's shoulders. Not surprisingly the men took several days to reach Sacluk. There Maudslay was able to reduce its thickness a little further with a saw he bought from a lumberman. From Sacluk he sent it on the next stage of its journey, across the savanna almost as far as Flores, on a solid-wheeled ox-cart, the solitary wheeled vehicle then existing in the province of Petén. But from there it had to be slung once more on a strong pole and carried by sixteen Indians as far as El Cayo, British Honduras, whence it could be taken downriver to Belize for shipment.

Some years later Maudslay would send Gorgonio López and his brothers back to Yaxchilán with instructions to make paper moulds of any lintels still in position, and to carry away others that had fallen from the door-ways of collapsed buildings and were well-preserved. This mission the López brothers accomplished very successfully – more so than Maudslay could have hoped, as they discovered a group of buildings they had missed before which formed a small acropolis, and there they found a few interesting lintels still in place, and the well-preserved upper half of another lying among rubble. The seven fallen lintels or fragments chosen by them were taken this time by a route involving a rather shorter porterage: up the Río Salinas to the head of navigation at Nueve Cerros, then overland (but up the steep mountainside) to Cobán, where they could be properly packed in crates and sent to Panzos by wagon, and thence by boat to Livingston, the Caribbean port.[14]

The lintels reached England safely, although something of a mystery surrounded the one now known as Lintel 56. The front edge was carved with an Initial Series date, but its underside was plain, so the inscribed edge had been sawn off to make carriage of it easier. In Maudslay's words, it was 'one of those removed from the ruins by Gorgonio Lopez and his brothers which were repacked in Coban for transmission to England. However, by some mistake this particular stone was put in the wrong case and sent to the Museum at Berlin, where I have allowed it to remain.'

Recently, however, a letter has come to light, written by Sarg to Dr Adolf Bastian, and dated 12 March 1886, telling Bastian (in Spanish) that he has shipped this hieroglyphic tablet to him at the Museum für Völkerkunde, Berlin. 'Although it is not as beautiful a piece as that which Maudslay removed, I believe it will be of interest, and welcome as representing a contrast with those from Santa Lucia [Cotzumalguapa] in the Berlin collection.' The explanation of what previously seemed a mystery lies in the date of its removal, for this lintel cannot have been one of those taken up the Río Salinas and up to Cobán in 1891; instead, Sarg must have dispatched Gorgonio López to Yaxchilán on his own initiative to obtain a Yaxchilán sculpture for Berlin.[15]

What, then, was the Mexican attitude to the removal of these lintels? Evidently this had been a matter of some concern to Maudslay, judging by the note in his diary about the absence of any Mexican officer accompanying Charnay's expedition, quoted above. Rockstroh would naturally have told him of impending efforts to settle the boundary, but in fact the first lintel was removed before even the initial agreement concerning the boundaries had been signed (on 27 September 1882). With regard to those that would be removed later by the López brothers, the situation is less clear. Although there's no evidence that Maudslay ever met Rockstroh again, he must have heard from other sources news of progress by the Joint Commission of Limits. But maps showing the new boundaries were slow in appearing. One, for example, prepared by Antonio García Cubas, Mexico's most active geographer and principal adviser to the the Mexican Secretary of Foreign Relations, continued to show the old and vague boundaries in an edition published as late as 1886.[16]

In any case, no objection was made at the time. For one thing, no one in the capital knew of the existence of Yaxchilán, much less of its sculptures; indeed the central authorities were to remain poorly informed about them for years to come. Even the fiercely nationalist Inspector-General of Monuments, Leopoldo Batres, would remain unsure about the location of this great ruined city for another two decades. This became evident in 1905, when Justo Sierra, the Secretary of State for Foreign Affairs, received a letter from Policarpo Valenzuela, holder of the lumber concession surrounding Yaxchilán. He wrote to inform him that marauders were damaging these ruins, and, in view of this, he asked permission to build a house there at his own expense for guards.

Sierra referred the matter to Batres, who replied:

In the first place, I am uncertain whether the ruins of Yaxchilan lie within Mexico's border with Guatemala, so that while we are unsure about this, we might give concessions within foreign territory which could bring about international difficulties, as already happened once before, unless I am mistaken, when a similar matter involving the same company nearly resulted in armed conflict between Mexico and its neighbour, the Republic of Guatemala.[17]

In fact, Batres's objections were overruled, and consent for the building was given by E. A. Chávez of the Secretaría del Estado, but there is no evidence that Valenzuela ever built a house, or installed guards in it.

In our narrative of Maudslay's return from Yaxchilán we left him attending to the carriage of the lintel, and as will be remembered, still intending to visit Tikal for a second time. In late April, then, as he had done the previous year, Maudslay recruited about twenty men from hamlets along the shores of Lake Petén-Itzá, and walked into Tikal. There is little to tell of his stay there: the men continued clearing the ruins so that the main temples could be photographed – very large clearings being necessary for the camera to capture the whole of such tall buildings. Maudslay spent much of his time mapping and measuring buildings, and perhaps he tried his hand at making moulds with the paper Charnay had given him. He remained there only a week, and then set off briskly to catch a steamer at Belize, overhauling the party carrying the lintel, which had to be sent by a later sailing.

Chapter 9

Quiriguá

Maudslay must have been extremely busy during the second half of 1882 because, even while making preparations for another expedition, he was also considering the use of a radically new technique for recording Maya sculpture. This would involve taking moulds of the sculpture, from which casts could later be made – a scheme that had everything in its favour as an ideal, but from the practical point of view, at least three serious disadvantages. First, a highly skilled technician would have to come as a member of the expedition; second, much more elaborate planning would be needed for the purchasing and shipping of a greatly increased volume of supplies, and last, the expenses incurred would be enormously increased.

This new plan grew out of the experience Maudslay had gained of recording sculpture at Quiriguá, Copán, Tikal, and Yaxchilán. In doing so, he had found it difficult to acquire an adequate record of certain monuments, and very likely he foresaw other difficulties arising. He had come to understand that scholars would not be fully satisfied by the provision of photographs alone, no matter how good they were, or how well reproduced; they would want line drawings too. In reaching this conclusion (and putting it into practice) Maudslay made one of his greatest and most distinctive contributions to the study of Maya sculpture and inscriptions. More than a century later, the principle he established remains valid, and the usefulness of good drawings is more than ever appreciated, now that they can be copied so easily for circulation among colleagues.

But then: if drawings were going to be so valuable, how were they to be prepared? This was a challenge, since a technical illustrator could not be expected to produce good work in a steamy, mosquito-ridden tropical forest – least of all when perched on improvised scaffolding, as he would have to be in order to draw the upper portions of a towering Quiriguá stela; or crouched beneath a door lintel to draw its underside, with head craned awkwardly upwards. Furthermore, lightly engraved details in a weathered sculpture do not show up clearly in the diffused light that percolates through the forest canopy – if they show at all – whereas these may spring to the eye when illuminated by a beam of raking light.[1]

The answer, Maudslay thought, lay in plaster casts. Charnay's moulds had given him the idea. Their usefulness probably first struck him in connection with Yaxchilán lintels that were still in situ, like those in Structure 33, the temple he had adopted as his living quarters.

For several reasons, photographing these would be difficult. First, a wide-angle lens would be necessary on account of the short working distance, but such lenses were still imperfect. Then, lighting the under-side of a lintel for photography presented a problem, although not one that was any longer totally insoluble, since magnesium flash powder and ribbon were both available. Another difficulty was that the carved surfaces to be photographed would often be blemished by patches of almost ineradicable black or white stains left on the surface by lichen.

All these problems would be solved if casts could be made. But the practical difficulties of making them were daunting, and the trouble and expense involved in just packing and transporting fragile piece-moulds would have discouraged almost anyone else.

Charnay's motive for making casts had been to provide both exhibits for the Trocadéro Museum, and illustrations for his book in the form of engravings based on them. Maudslay realized that casts could serve his purposes too. The artist could make drawings from them under com-fortable conditions, with lighting arranged to bring out the relief to best advantage; indeed, if well made, a cast should be far more legible than a lichen-stained original.

With his new interest in casts, Maudslay must have visited the South Kensington Museum (now the Victoria and Albert) to see the superb casts exhibited in the Architectural Courts, which had been opened to the public in 1873. The 1870s had seen the culmination of widespread enthu-siasm for plaster casts, spurred by the signing of the impressively named International Convention for promoting universally Reproductions of Works of Art for the Benefit of all Countries. In addition to the large national collections that were being formed in various countries for educational and reference purposes, commercial casters were also selling plasters to the public for embellishment of the home. In London, D. Brucciani's gallery in Covent Garden offered the largest selection, comprising about 1200 items. Their Venus de Milo, for example, cost seven shillings for a full-size cast, while three shillings would buy a machine-reduced version of the same.[2]

Through enquiries Maudslay would have learnt that while paper 'squeezes' or papier mâché casts such as those Charnay made yield good copies of low-relief carving on flat surfaces of moderate size, the same technique is less satisfactory for large monuments carved in deep relief, especially where there is any degree of undercutting in the relief. In such cases the mould may prove impossible to remove from the original, like a dove-tailed joint. A further point: paper moulds cannot reproduce fine detail quite as well as those of plaster.

Instead, as the experts probably told him, the way to obtain first-class copies of those Copán stelae carved almost in the round, or of the carved boulders (later called zoomorphs) at Quiriguá was to make rigid moulds of plaster of Paris. But there was a difficulty with plaster moulds: only one small area at a time could be moulded because of the difficulty just mentioned. Re-entrant angles in the original would make a plaster mould impossible to remove without breakage. Thus, coverage of such an area had to be divided between several separate moulds. These were termed 'piece-moulds', and in extreme cases, such as the zoomorphs, the complete mould might consist of several hundred pieces.

Maudslay would have grasped at once that the technique of doing this was far beyond his capabilities, or those of any amateur. Plaster of Paris is a tricky substance which can be mastered only through years of experience, and skill is particularly necessary in planning and executing the divisions between the many piece-moulds needed for a large monument. This involves the provision, in the mating faces of each piece, of pairs of conical bosses and sockets that fit together when the piece-moulds are reassembled for casting the final product, thus ensuring accurate registration between them.

Maudslay laid his plans accordingly, having decided to return to Quiriguá and take moulds of the principal stelae and zoomorphs. Paper moulds would suffice for casts of hieroglyphic texts intended only for his artists to work from, but he wanted the national collections to have the best casts possible of the finest monuments. That meant piece-moulds. Accordingly he engaged the services of a professional plaster-worker who had been employed for many years at Brucciani's: this was Lorenzo Giuntini (whose name Maudslay often misspelt as 'Guintini').[3] For his use at Quiriguá, nearly 4 tons of plaster of Paris was purchased, special-ly packed in metal-lined barrels. This and all the other supplies they would need for a lengthy stay were dispatched to Livingston.

On the very eve of his departure, Maudslay gave for the first time a public lecture on his work in the Maya area, with the title 'Explorations in Guatemala and examination of the old Indian cities, Tikal and Usumacinta'. This was presented by the Royal Geographical Society, and, since the Society's building lacked a suitable lecture hall, the talk was given in the splendid new administration building of London University, just across Burlington Gardens. By happy coincidence, this very building would house, some ninety years later, the Museum of Mankind, its impressive stairway flanked by two of Maudslay's finest plaster casts.[4]

Maudslay and Giuntini sailed for Belize in early January 1883, and were met there by Charles Blockley, a young but inexperienced surveyor living in the colony, who was coming with them to map the ruins. But before taking the steamer to Livingston, Maudslay paid a call on his friend Barlee, the Governor, to enquire if the Mayas of Santa Cruz were still peaceable. As Maudslay noted:

> He [the Governor] replied that he thought everything was favourable for such an expedition and that a very pleasant and learned ethnologist [whom Maudslay calls Dr X] had just been to see him on the same subject, and no doubt it would be agreeable for us to travel together. Dr X had gone out of town for a few days, so I was not able to see him before my steamer sailed for Livingston; but I learnt that he did not intend starting for Santa Cruz country before April.

Tentative arrangements were therefore made through the Governor for him to make the trip in company with the learned doctor upon his return from Guatemala.

Maudslay, Giuntini, and Blockley then took the steamer to Livingston. Because of sand-bars, they and all their supplies were transferred to Carib dug-out dories, and from them to the steam launch that would take them to Yzabal, which they reached on 18 February. Two days later Carlos and Gorgonio López arrived, bringing with them twenty Kekchi *mozos* from Cobán. Their first job was to carry some of the provisions and a little of the plaster, now repacked in waterproof sacks, to Quiriguá. The rest was carried over the next ten days in many trips, sometimes on the few mules available but more usually on men's backs, over a range of hills and along a track which proved almost impassable in bad weather.

From Yzabal, Maudslay and Giuntini rode off on horseback to Mico, but Giuntini had a wretched saddle, and this was the first ride he had ever taken, apart from a shillingsworth one day in Epping Forest. To ease his discomfort, Maudslay exchanged horses with him part way. At Mico they spent the night in the house of Don Onofre and his wife, Maudslay's hosts of two years before, for whom he had brought a violin as a present.

Next day they went to the ruins, where one good-sized shelter had already been built. Giuntini was very pleased with the sculpture he was to mould, and Maudslay equally pleased with Giuntini, finding him 'a very good fellow and good companion – does not grumble'.

The ruins stand on the flood-plain of the Motagua River which now comes no closer than about 1000 yards from them, though it appears that when the ceremonial centre was built the river ran close by. For a site of no great size, the main plaza, a rectangle of about 200 by 350 yards, seems disproportionately large. In it are found ten stelae and several boulders carved in the form of mythological animals, the so-called zoomorphs.

The stelae are all large, the tallest being a shaft 33 feet high and weighing about 65 tons – the largest sculptured monolith erected by the Maya anywhere. The largest of the carved boulders is 10 feet across and weighs perhaps 20 tons. As, of course, there is no stone to be found in the alluvial plain, all these heavy shafts and boulders had of necessity to be dragged by the Maya (presumably on rollers) a distance of 3 miles from quarries in the foot-hills, and all the stone used in construction of stairways, platforms, and temples must have been carried a similar distance.

At the south end of the Great Plaza stands an irregularly shaped acropolis built round a large courtyard. But the acropolis does not seem to present its face to the plaza; instead, one is led from the southwest corner of the plaza into a smaller one defined on its north side by a large mound, and on the other three sides by the acropolis itself and wings built out from it. Within this precinct are found a ball-court and several carved altars and boulders, including Maudslay's Great Turtle (later called Zoomorph P, and now renamed Monument 16). This space, it is safe to say, was the heart of the ceremonial area, and the long ranges of steps on three sides would have functioned as viewing stands.

In February – or so Maudslay had been given to understand – the seasonal rains should have ended, and their failure to do so until well into March caused severe difficulties. As he later reported to the Royal Geographical Society,

> Excavations filled with water as soon as made, and no moulding could be done unless a water-tight roof was first built over the monument which was to be worked at. At one time, the floods covered all but a few feet round the knoll on which we had built our palm-leaf shanty, everything in the camp turned green with mould and mildew, and snakes and scorpions were very troublesome, and mosquitoes were innumerable. Worst of all, the sick list increased, until at last twelve Indians were ill with fever on the same day, and the sound ones all ran home.

Blockley fell ill and was sent in to the village; indeed by 3 March Maudslay was on the point of withdrawing everyone to the village until the weather should clear up. Giuntini was firmly against leaving, saying it was 'capital weather to work in', and he was longing to start work on the Great Turtle. For the next day, Maudslay's diary records: 'Of an evening I read "Gil Blas" aloud to the Ladinos, which delights them.'[5] (Lately, this congenial feature of camp life seems to have fallen into desuetude.)

As Maudslay wrote,

> the work of examining and copying the carvings at Quiriguá was one of no small difficulty. It was necessary, after clearing away the thick undergrowth, to fell the forest trees, and after an interval of about ten days, to run fire through the clearing. The earth round the monuments had to be cleared away usually to a depth of two or three feet, as, probably owing to floods from the river, the level of the ground

had altered considerably since they were originally placed in position; a scaffold had then to be built round each monument and the carving subjected to a careful and thorough cleaning. This cleaning proved to be the most tedious part of the work, as the stone was always covered with thick and adhesive growths of moss and lichen. Two of the animal-shaped monoliths were almost completely buried under huge forest trees, which had grown exactly on top of them, and it was only by a chance notice of some carved stone appearing between the roots that I became aware of their existence.

Occasionally, Maudslay could be hard-hearted in the interests of discipline, as when one of the *mozos* who had run away returned because he was sick. He was told to clear out again as he was not wanted. Good workers, though, were very badly needed, and Maudslay telegraphed Sarg asking him to procure twenty more. When Sarg replied that none would be willing to leave until after Easter, and advised him to send Carlos López to collect them, Maudslay resolved to do that himself. Giuntini and Blockley (now recovered) could carry on with their work, and there was not much for him to do himself until later, when the moulds of some monuments had been completed, since only then would they be in the cleanest possible condition for photography. In the meantime a 'photographic house' would be built; it would not have to be very light-tight for use at night, but probably would have to be screened to prevent insects entering and getting on to the plates as they dried after development.

Maudslay's journey to Cobán, although ultimately successful, was not enjoyable. To begin with, on reaching Yzabal he learnt that the steamboat *Esperanza*, which he was relying on to take him and Gorgonio across the lake and up the Polochic River to Panzos, would be out of action for three weeks. The *Esperanza* was not the rickety vessel that had carried Maudslay to Yzabal two years earlier but a new stern-wheeler brought down from Columbus, Ohio. It was designed to carry 50 tons of cargo and yet have a draught of only 26 inches, so that it could ascend the river to Panzos. It provided a valuable service for the coffee-growers of Cobán, but was lost in a storm two months after the end of Maudslay's season at Quiriguá.

Maudslay spent the night with the Potts family at Yzabal. William Potts, a native of Tennessee and the chief merchant at Livingston and Yzabal, was known as 'Old Forty Drops' from his habit of dividing his prodigious consumption of rye whiskey into portions of just forty drops.[6] (Captain Owen, a native of Maryland, and the owner and skipper of the *Esperanza*, was married to Mrs Potts's niece.) It is said that some years later an unfortunate relaxation by Mr Potts of his self-imposed rule during a Fourth of July celebration resulted in his demise.

The next day Maudslay found a canoeman willing to make the

journey, so they set off – he and Gorgonio, three canoemen, a small boy, and a Ladino who begged a passage. In his journal Maudslay describes the trip laconically:

> 15 March. Started at 4 a.m., crossed the end of the lake and got into the river about 10 a.m. Mosquitoes came off the shore in thousands whenever we passed close to the banks. River very full. No playas [sandbanks] dry so that we had to land on the banks and cut away a little of the bush before we could make a fire to make tea, etc. Very crowded in canoe but had to sleep in it as best we could as it was impossible to sleep on the damp mosqitoey banks. Passed bad night, men paddled as long as they could then rested by hitching on a tree as far out from the bank as possible, slept and rested thus until the mosquitoes became unbearable then paddled on again. . . . 16 March. Expected to get to Panzos today but the river was too high and the current so strong it was impossible, men working very well. No sandbanks above water – got to mouth of Cajabón [river] about 11 p.m. Gorgonio surprised an alligator laying eggs and secured a large number. Same sort of night again in canoe.

They arrived at Panzos next morning. There they found it difficult to engage a *mozo* to carry Maudslay's small bundle; the danger of jaguars was mentioned, but the offer of a little more pay and the promise not to ride away from him persuaded one man to do it. That night they managed to repair some of the sleep lost in the two previous nights on the hard benches of the *cabildo* at La Tinta. The following day's ride took them to Tamahú, where next morning it was found that the horse and mule had run away. After several hours of fruitless search they hired the one available horse, which Maudslay rode, while Gorgonio walked and a porter carried his saddle for some distance until another animal was found. Late that evening they reached Cobán.[7]

The following day, Maudslay went to stay with the Sargs while Gorgonio went on to San Pedro Carchá, an Indian town, to recruit labourers, then on to Cahabón to see his wife.

It would be tedious to recount in detail the frustrations they experienced in attempting to round up twenty men. Eight were found and given advance payment, and the Alcalde of San Pedro promised to find twelve more. When ready, six of these were brought the nearly 5 miles to Cobán by Gorgonio, who reported that the other six had been accommodated by the Alcalde in prison, so that they should not bolt. Maudslay, having now decided to make the return journey to Panzos by a different route passing through San Pedro, said goodbye to the Sargs and set off with the six *mozos*, and there in prison found the next six, but in the meantime the eight who had been paid were nowhere to be found. Then a Ladino claimed that he had engaged two of the men before Maudslay.

'The whole business was pure slave-driving – at last I got tired of it and started back for Cobán leaving Gorgonio to worry the alcalde. . . and made up my mind to return to Panzos by the old road.' Finally on 4 April they set off with eighteen Indians. One succeeded in running away en route, but they reached Quiriguá safely with the remainder on the 10th. The recruiting trip had thus cost Maudslay exactly three weeks, but at least he was now able to pay off those of the original crew who had remained faithful, and resume work.

On 26 April Giuntini finished his plaster mould of the Great Turtle, a mould of over six hundred pieces which had consumed nearly 2 tons of plaster. He had also moulded the most interesting portions of two other monuments. Maudslay and helpers had taken paper moulds of every inscription then known at the site, and the whole of one monument; casts from these paper moulds would serve well in supplementing photographs for the artists making drawings. Blockley had finished his plan of the site, and Maudslay had taken a complete set of photographs of each of the monuments. Now, after three months at the ruins, it was time to leave.

> The work of packing and transporting the moulds to the port was one of even greater difficulty than bringing the material, for there were over a thousand pieces of plaster moulding of all shapes and sizes with delicate points and edges which had to be protected from the slightest jar, and large paper moulds, some of which measured nearly five feet square. The last loads were not over the mountains when the rains commenced again with tremendous thunder-storms, and the mountain tracks were again an alternation of mud-holes and watercourses. A few of the paper moulds were damaged by damp on the passage home, but, on the whole, the result of the expedition has been very satisfactory.

Meeting the Governor of British Honduras again, as Maudslay relates, during his passage through Belize homeward bound, he was walking with him towards the dock to board the boat with little time to spare, when it occurred to him to ask him how Dr X had fared in his expedition to Santa Cruz. 'Thank God [he replied], I have got rid of that fellow! I found out that he had been concerned in the most abominable practices.' As Maudslay describes it:

> At that moment my baggage came up and I had no time to ask any further questions even had it been discreet to do so, and although I was rather mystified the matter passed out of my mind.
>
> On my return home, one of my first visits was paid to my old friend Mr. Bates, then Secretary to the Royal Geographical Society, and in the midst of his kindly greeting he stopped short and said, 'By

the way, did you come across Dr. X?' I said no, that he had already left Belize. 'Thank God for that!' he said, and then rapidly changed the subject. . . . I told Bates how mystified I had been at the Governor's last words to me, and how nearly Dr. X and I were to becoming travelling companions. He shook me by the hand again and said, 'Well you have had a lucky escape; perhaps I had better tell you the whole story,' which he did as follows: 'Not long ago Dr. X came to me with good introductions, and said he intended to visit Belize; he asked my advice and assistance, and as he seemed a very well-informed and pleasant man I gave him a note to the Governor. A few months later I had a visit from the Colonial Office clerk, who asked me if I knew anything of the whereabouts of Dr. X; and when he heard what I had to tell him, he informed me that a Foreign Embassy in London had been in touch with our Foreign Office regarding Dr. X's career. . . .'

Rather than following the rest of Maudslay's account of Bates's story, we can turn instead to the very memorandum received by the Foreign Office in 1881. It came from the German embassy:

In the first half of this year there resided in Berlin a certain Dr. Otto Wien, a Doctor of Law and subject of the State of Mecklenburg-Schwerin, who contrived to procure for himself letters of introduction from German men of science for a pretended projected journey of investigation to Central America. In the meantime official reports which have been received give grounds for supposing that this Otto Wien who in previous years had spent a considerable time in La Plata, is a skilful and daring swindler. He managed to insinuate himself into the confidence of the German residents under the guise of a scientific traveller, and then took advantage of the hospitality extended to him to commit burglaries of very considerable importance. He is further accused, likewise with mercenary intent, of having committed a murder by poison there, a suspicion which is supported by the fact that the said Otto Wien, as is proved by testimony from several quarters, was in the habit of carrying about with him a supply of the deadliest poisons.

Positive evidence, which would be sufficient to justify prosecution of Dr. Wien for the acts imputed to him has not, it is true, been obtained. In no. 43 of the journal *Export*, which is published at Berlin, of the 25th ultimo, Dr. O. Wien published a letter dated Belize, 16 Sept. 1881, stating that he had arrived there in the month of August of this year, and in consideration of a letter of introduction from the Royal Geographical Society, had been received in the most friendly manner by the Governor and the Colonial Secretary.

Beyond this there is only an abstract in the Colonial Office Register of a memorandum received from British Honduras in 1882: 'Wien, Otto:

Has arrived at Greytown [Honduras] where he is practising as a physician. Describes him and encloses his photograph.' Unfortunately this now bears the notation 'Destroyed under statute'.

So Dr Otto Wien has disappeared from view – although Maudslay expressed his hope that 'if he had been trying more interesting experiments he may have tried them successfully on himself'.

Maudslay would return to Quiriguá eleven years later for a short spell, as will be described in due course, but in 1886, after finding that excavations at Copán were rewarding, he sent Gorgonio off to Quiriguá to carry out two missions for him. One was to do some excavating in the large mound at the north end of the Great Plaza. It had been his discovery at Copán of well-preserved architectural remains lying within unpromising mounds that now suggested the possibility of similar finds at Quiriguá.

Gorgonio, however, found nothing of the kind in that mound (nor would archaeologists from the University of Pennsylvania in the 1970s: evidently the Maya had denuded it of all its worked stone for reuse elsewhere). He then turned to the mound standing at the north side of the south court, and by digging into the top of this uncovered a complex arrangement of a central chamber connected to lateral chambers; he found, too, that part of the vaulted stone roof remained. An American engineer named Walter Heston (involved perhaps in construction of the railway then being built within about a mile of the ruins) found Gorgonio at work, and, having made a sketch plan of these chambers, sent it and brief report to Maudslay. His letter ends with: 'Your friend Gorgonio did his work very well, and deserves credit for it.'[8]

The other task that Gorgonio was charged with was to make a paper mould of the back of Stela J. As will be clear from Plate 45 in volume 2 of *Archaeology*, this monument had fallen on its back and broken, so that only partial and oblique views of the sides and front are reproduced; clearly, no photograph could be taken of the back. And yet the inscription on the back, sixteen rows of well-preserved glyphs, is reproduced in Plate 46. How this could this be? The explanation is that Gorgonio burrowed under the shaft and made a paper mould of it from underneath – an extraordinary achievement in view of the difficulty of persuading the paper to dry on a stone shaft that was presumably damp through and through, having been for untold years in contact with moist earth.

Now Maudslay was faced with the problem of how to make use of the results of this very satisfactory, if also very expensive, expedition; and, of course, the results of the earlier expeditions to Tikal and Yaxchilán. One can scarcely doubt that he'd already decided to prepare a report lavishly illustrated, not only with photographs but also with drawings – these to be prepared by professional illustrators working from the casts Giuntini would make from the moulds.

The initial difficulty would be to find a place in London where, first of all, casts could be made from assemblages of piece-moulds, and then the resulting sections joined together to form complete facsimiles of monuments. The finished plaster casts would, of course, have to be stored with enough space left between them for illustrators to be able to work conveniently while drawing them.

An even more serious difficulty was the matter of publication. How could he find a publisher willing to arrange for all this material, gathered at such cost in time and money, to be printed in a way that would do it justice? The photographs deserved the best available reproduction technique, and the drawings a large format and lithographic printing. The publisher would have to accept that the publication might eventually run into several volumes, as one expedition succeeded another. In short, the outlay for such a work would be very large, and the chances of ever recovering it from sales, decidedly slim.

At some point – but exactly when is unknown – the question of publication was resolved in a surprising but most satisfactory way by Maudslay's old friend Osbert Salvin and his collaborator Frederick DuCane Godman: they offered to publish the archaeological material as a special section within the prodigious series of volumes they were producing on the natural history of Central America. More will be said about this ideal arrangement later. But immediately it provided encouragement for Maudslay to begin work on his material, and to engage Giuntini for the rest of the year to make casts. He may also have begun at that time to try out artists with some of the casts as test pieces.

In the autumn he found time to visit Seville to look for documents in the Archives of the Indies that might throw light on knowledge of Maya ruins in early Colonial times. With the help of the Director, Dr Marimón, he was able to find various reports of official *entradas* and missionary ventures into the Lacandón area, and early maps. And, as on other visits to Spain, he had a large quantity of the paper used in Valencia for wrapping oranges shipped to him in England, having found this paper ideal for making paper moulds.

In the 1880s no one had a clear idea of the period during which Maya cities such as Yaxchilán and Quiriguá had flourished. Some thought they had still been occupied at the time of the Conquest, the more credulous among them even being disposed to believe the story that Stephens heard from the laughing padre of Santa Cruz Quiché, that on a clear day the white towers of a distant city in the jungle could be seen, where an Indian community still carried on their ancient traditions. Others of course put the heyday of those cities much further back in time, even thousands of years.

On this question, Maudslay was now willing to take a tentative position. On 3 December 1883, soon after returning from Seville, he gave a lecture before the Cambridge Antiquarian Society, of which the President during that year was his old friend from undergraduate years, J. W. Clark. He brought photographs and small casts from his expeditions to display in the lecture theatre, and in his talk reasoned that, as Cortés must have passed close to Palenque in 1524 without being aware of it, and because early descriptions of the Lacandóns showed them to be at much the same cultural level as those he had visited near Yaxchilán, then it seemed to him that both great centres had ceased to exist as living towns well before the Conquest. In his remarks after the lecture, the President expressed his hope that the University would help Maudslay in his explorations with a grant from the Worts Fund.

This it eventually did, with a grant of £300, the only financial aid that Maudslay would ever receive for his work. In today's currency that may seem a paltry sum, but then it was enough to pay Giuntini's salary for two whole years.

Meanwhile, the foothold of archaeology in the Cambridge University curriculum had become firmer. By 1880 the Classics tripos had been divided into two parts, one of them including the study of art and archaeology. The need then arose for a museum with space for plaster casts and a lecture room. The Fitzwilliam Museum itself could not provide these, but its management actively supported both the construction of a separate museum and the appointment of a curator for it. One argument put forward in favour of this plan was the report of a promised donation of ethnological collections from the South Seas.

These, of course, were the collections of Maudslay and Sir Arthur Gordon, and the two donors proposed Anatole von Hügel as Director. Since von Hügel had a private income, the salary he would need to be offered was low, and when that was trimmed even further it was argued 'that it was not improbable that the pleasure of residing in Cambridge and having work to do there might induce the gentleman to accept the smaller sum'. There was another difficulty, less easily solved: von Hügel was a Roman Catholic, but somehow this obstacle, too, was overcome and von Hügel was appointed Director, and would remain in that post until 1928. His own collection, of course, was added to the Museum.

In 1884 the Gordon and Maudslay collections from Fiji and Maudslay's plaster casts were installed in the Museum of Classical Archaeology, and a formal opening ceremony was held, but in 1903, owing to lack of space, the casts were removed to a warehouse near Newnham College. Efforts continued, however, to amass the money needed to build the Museum of Archaeology and Ethnology. In the words of an obituary writer, 'von Hügel was such a charming beggar for the Museum that his friends could not resist his appeals', and in 1913 the new museum opened, with the Central American casts displayed in the 'Maudslay Hall'.[9]

Having now decided, as it seems, to dedicate his life to archaeological exploration, Maudslay must then have spent some time acquainting himself with recent literature pertaining to the archaeology of Mesoamerica (although this term, denoting the area of pre-Columbian high culture, had yet to be introduced).

A great deal had been published since about 1820. Some of the illustrated reports of Mayan ruins by pioneering travellers were important in diffusing knowledge of remarkable sites previously unknown to scholars, an outstanding example being *The Description of the Ruins of an Ancient City, discovered near Palenque*, by Antonio del Río, published in 1822.[10] As illustrations, this contained drawings he had made in 1786, engraved for reproduction by an extraordinary character who styled himself 'Count' Jean Frédéric Maximilien Waldeck, a man who would himself travel widely and publish highly finished but unreliable illustrations of antiquities, accompanied by equally unreliable texts.[11]

In fact, much of what was published before about 1850 was unreliable; but on the positive side, several Mexican scholars throughout the nineteenth century became avid collectors and transcribers of historical texts, the most notable, perhaps, being Joaquín García Icazbalceta, who not only published a vast number of them in a long series of volumes, but also became the leading bibliographer. (The late Dr Ignacio Bernal García-Pimentel, Mexico's greatest archaeologist and a grandson of his, among all his other work found time, appropriately, to produce a great bibliography of Mesoamerican archaeology.)[12]

There was, however, one early magnum opus that never could be overlooked, or forgotten once seen, and that was the set of the nine huge and gorgeous elephant-folios produced by the ill-fated Lord Kingsborough. These, published in 1830, contained remarkably accurate reproductions in colour of pre-Columbian codices, illustrations of ruins (somewhat less accurate), and transcriptions of a few sixteenth-century documents, but they were accompanied by a text in which Kingsborough sought to prove at tedious length that the ancient Mexicans were none other than the lost tribes of Israel. One can be sure that once Maudslay had become interested in the Maya, he would have examined this work, either in the British Museum Library, or in that of his friend Frederick Godman.[13]

Then, in the ten years that would pass between Maudslay's first arrival at San José and his return to engage in archaeology, various documents of the greatest importance had come to light. The most notable was Bishop Diego de Landa's *Relación de las Cosas de Yucatán*, a rich source of ethnographic information compiled by that sixteenth-century

Spanish bishop;[14] and then another was found of equal importance, the *Popol Vuh*. This is the creation myth of the Quiché Maya, transcribed into European writing, perhaps in the seventeenth or eighteenth century, from a text in some script once employed in the Guatemalan highlands.[15]

During the same period, much of this documentary material, both new and old, was being gathered together, picked apart, sorted by subject-matter, synthesized into a comprehensible narrative description, and published in heavy quarto volumes in a most extraordinary publishing venture.

Hubert Howe Bancroft was a San Francisco printer and publisher who conceived the idea of producing a comprehensive history of the states bordering the Pacific coast of North America. For this purpose he had already amassed by 1868 a library of ten thousand relevant books, which over the next twelve years would grow to sixty thousand. Initially he had planned to write the work himself, but with such an influx of source material the project expanded, and soon assistants had to be engaged. Some were employed in preparing index slips, while others made abstracts. The latter were filed by subject-matter in paper bags fastened by clothes-pins on a clothes-line, ready for use by the writers.

Regrettably, in these volumes the writers were not credited by name for their contributions, Bancroft appearing as the sole author of all thirty-nine volumes. As Howard Cline has written, 'to Bancroft's historiography were applied most of the classical elements of mass production: specialization, uniformity of procedures, scheduled and integrated work flow, even quality control'. And, of course, the products of that factory all bore the same brand-name![16]

In the first five volumes, entitled *Native Races of the Pacific States*, the lion's share of attention is naturally given to the well documented Aztecs, but volume II has six chapters (more than two hundred pages) on Maya ethnography, including matter taken from Bishop Landa's work (which had been published only just in time to be processed by the production line); volume III is devoted to myths and languages; volume IV has three hundred pages on Maya antiquities, largely drawn from Ephraim G. Squier, John Lloyd Stephens, and the unreliable 'Count' Waldeck, while volume V is a general overview of the origins and historical relationships of various language groups. These tomes, published just six years before Maudslay reached the ruins of Quiriguá for the first time, must have proved invaluable to him during his years of active investigation of Maya sites. As reference works, or compendia, they provided starting points from which his work, and that of others, could take off.[17]

Archaeology cannot be said to have existed as a discipline before about 1860, despite the fact that since the sixteenth century European antiquarians had been busy collecting pottery, carved stones, worked flints, metal objects, bones, and so on, amassing in the process heaps of incoherent data – data which no one knew how to use fruitfully. Surprisingly, perhaps, it was Latin texts that finally provided clues to chronology. As Lucretius, for example, wrote in the first century BC, 'The earliest weapons were hands, nails and teeth, as well as stones, pieces of wood, flames and fire as they [became] known. Later the properties of iron and bronze were discovered, but bronze came first, the use of iron not being known until later'.[18]

This hint may have been taken up by the French savant Montfaucon, who in 1734 proposed three successive ages in antiquity – stone, bronze and iron. A century later, this seminal idea was developed by two Danes, Christian Thomsen and Jens Worsaae, and from then on, relative chronologies of increasingly fine grain would be established – although more than another century would have to pass before those 'ages', and their artefacts, could be placed with confidence in an absolute chronology, tied to our calendar.

Nineteenth-century antiquarians who studied American prehistoric artefacts soon realized that the European scheme of 'ages' had no validity in the New World. In the Maya area, for example, already famous for its elaborate architecture, superb sculpture and a unique writing system, no tools had been found dating from the Classic Period save those of basalt, flint, and obsidian. Copper began to appear only shortly before the Spanish invasion, and soon it became clear that iron had been unknown anywhere in the Americas before the Conquest.

Regarding the native peoples, it was generally accepted that they were descendants of hunters who had wandered across the Bering Straits, although there were many who held that the advanced cultures of Mesoamerica (a term denoting central and southern Mexico, and the northern part of the Central American states) owed everything to Egyptians or Phoenicians, and even today a few enthusiasts cling to such beliefs.

No one in the twentieth century, however, has questioned the accepted opinion that the famous ruined cities of Yucatán were built by the ancestors of the Mayas who still, in large numbers, inhabit that area (although sadly, not all the living Maya can believe that those builders were their own ancestors, for they find it difficult to imagine that they, unaided, could possibly have raised those enormously heavy blocks of stone right up to the tops of pyramids). But in the 1840s and 1850s, controversy did arise concerning the builders of the large mounds found in the Ohio and Mississippi River valleys. Although these were far removed geographically from the Maya area, the eventual resolution of that controversy has some bearing on Mesoamerican archaeology.

Common opinion then held that ancestors of the Indians living in the vicinity would have been incapable of constructing those mounds, or of fashioning the well-finished artefacts found buried in them. So it seemed obvious that another tribe or race of people had been responsible, these having later migrated to another territory, perhaps even to Mexico. For lack of a better name, then, these people were called 'The Moundbuilders'.

However, a study commissioned in the 1850s and 1860s by the Smithsonian Institution convinced many that the mound-builders had not gone far, as there were similarities between artefacts that had been dug up and those of current Indian groups in the eastern USA.[19] More convincing proof was provided thirty years later by Cyrus Thomas, in a report based on his own excavations. He was able to demonstrate a clear and continuous evolution in the form and decoration of excavated arte-facts, in a series leading from the earliest examples to later ones resembling those of contemporary Indians. Thomas's work, published in 1894, is now regarded as the first work of authentic archaeology in North America. (Thomas also made an early contribution to the decipherment of Maya writing.)[20]

The fame bestowed by Stephens and Catherwood on the great ruined cities of the Maya fortunately didn't result in an outbreak of enthusiastic digging; on the contrary, interest in them dwindled. One cause of this was the isolation of Yucatán, another, political unrest, for after a series of uprisings in the 1850s, Spanish and British troops occupied Veracruz in 1861; then French troops invaded, reaching Mexico City in 1863; a year later, Maximilian arrived to be crowned Emperor, only to be defeated and shot in 1867. In 1877, following ten more years of revolutions, Porfirio Díaz was declared president, and after an interregnum became president again in 1884. From that year until 1910 calm was restored in Mexico, and both ethnologists and archaeologists moved in to avail themselves of a long-awaited opportunity.

The situation in Yucatán, however, differed from that prevailing elsewhere. Owing to a total lack of road, rail or telegraph communication, the peninsula was isolated from the rest of the country and its political upheavals. But in 1847, a large proportion of the Mayas in Yucatán rose in rebellion against the small Spanish-speaking population, and almost succeeded in taking control. Something of a guerrilla war ensued, with the south-eastern region remaining potentially dangerous for outsiders even into the early 1900s.

As a result, very few antiquarians, photographers, or other travellers interested in Maya ruins entered that region in the middle decades of the century, but two who did deserve mention. One was Augustus Le Plongeon, a Channel Islander and American immigrant, who, with his valiant wife Alice, dug at Chichén Itzá in the 1870s – we shall encounter him later in this book.[21] The other well-known visitor to Mesoamerica in the middle of the nineteenth century was Désiré Charnay. In 1857, during the Second Empire, he was commissioned by the French Ministry of Education to photograph the great ruins of Mexico, and the photographs that he took with a huge camera, often under very difficult conditions, were truly remarkable.

In 1880, he returned to Mexico and stayed for four years, patronized jointly this time by the same French ministry and Pierre Lorillard, a tobacco manufacturer. A target of particular interest for Charnay was Tula, a complex of ruins about 100 miles north of Mexico City. This was the legendary centre of the Toltecs, a powerful and still somewhat mysterious people (mostly Nahua-speakers, like the Aztecs), who exerted great influence over a vast area between about AD 800 and 1200. There, Charnay cleared out all the overburden of soil and crumbled adobe from a many-roomed 'palace,' as well as from two smaller structures, finding carved stone, pottery, and other artefacts. These he intended to send to the Musée de l'Homme in Paris, but the permit he requested sparked a famous debate in the Mexican Congress, and it was voted down. Charnay's technique in carrying out these excavations appears to have fallen short of the best contemporary practice in the Old World or in the United States, yet perhaps they marked an advance on previous excavations south of the border. It is also disappointing that he failed to publish any details of his work.[22]

Until the mid nineteenth century, attempts at reconstructing the past of pre-literate peoples, such as those of the Americas, Africa, or Oceania, were either fruitless or purely imaginative. One problem seemed insuperable: the globe was peopled with uncounted tribes of various physical types, languages, and customs, and yet the time available for all this differentiation to have occurred among the descendants of Adam and Eve was decidedly short – less than six thousand years, according to Archbishop Ussher's Bible-based dating of the Creation. The only recourse was to assume the rapid creation of a number of distinguishable tribes, which then migrated hither and thither, leaving behind signs of their passage. In North America, the Toltecs had an enviable reputation in this regard, for they were credited by some antiquarians with mound-building in Ohio, as well as dominating Yucatán. (Another possible origin of American Indians, still being supported by a few scholars even at the close of the nineteenth century, was the genesis in the New World of a distinct branch of the human race.)

Then suddenly, the intellectual landscape suffered a volcanic upheaval. Charles Lyell's work in geology, and Charles Darwin's in biology (triggered by Lyell's findings), expanded the scope of prehistory into a far, far deeper past, so that now there was time enough for the simplest forms of life to develop, in the course of many millions of years, into primates, and from primates into *homo sapiens*. A similar liberation was to affect prehistoric anthropology, in that slow processes of social and technical development from stone age to modern thought and technology were now conceivable. Thus, within a decade or two it became possible for archaeology to transform itself from not much more than the cataloguing of curiosities into a nascent scientific discipline.

In the wake of these developments, some ethnologists (or social anthropologists, as they came to be known) attempted to apply the concepts of biological evolution to the rise of civilizations, with some of the most influential of them maintaining that all of these transformations were bound to follow a set and unvarying course. This attempt to link the two processes was mistaken, since the essential factor in the evolution of species is competition, whereas it is the accumulation of knowledge that propels social evolution.

In North America the leading exponent of this 'unilinear' theory was Lewis H. Morgan, a man generally regarded as the founder of American anthropology. Convinced of the basic unity embracing all American Indian peoples (all of them 'Red Indians' in his terminology), he defined the stages through which any society was bound to pass on its upward progress to civilization. Tribes lacking the craft of pottery were mired in Savagery; those making pottery, but unable to build with adobe or stone were in the Lower Status of Barbarism; while tribes that constructed houses but were ignorant of iron were in the Middle Status of Barbarism. The Mayas and the Aztecs, then, belonged in this third category.

When Morgan came to review the second volume of Bancroft's *Native Races*, he launched a scathing attack on it. Bancroft had done no more than amalgamate the descriptions, or recollections, left by Cortés and other *conquistadores* of the splendours of Moctezuma's palace. But Morgan, entitling his review 'Montezuma's Breakfast', poured scorn on the author for his credulity in believing those descriptions. The Aztecs were in Middle Barbarism, and Moctezuma, far from savouring delicacies served on golden plates, would instead have squatted on the floor in a communal tenement, and eaten his portion of a shared dinner off rough pottery.[23]

Academic attention to American archaeology had been scant until, in 1866, the Peabody Museum of American Archaeology and Ethnology of Harvard University came into being as the first university museum of its kind in the Americas. Field research, both in archaeology and ethnology, began there at once, but for more than twenty years it would send no expedition south of the border; and when at last one was sent to Yucatán, Mexico, in the winter of 1888, its formation was largely due to the enthusiasm of a remarkable man, Charles Pickering Bowditch, and his willingness to back it financially.

Bowditch, a grandson of Nathaniel Bowditch, the famous mathematician and navigator, was a banker and a man of enquiring mind; he was also a friend of Stephen Salisbury, director of the American Antiquarian Society, based in nearby Worcester. Since Salisbury had encouraged the work of two Maya enthusiasts in Yucatán, first Le Plongeon, and then a young man named Edward H. Thompson, he is likely to have played a part in stirring Bowditch's interest in the Maya. As Bowditch himself had visited Yucatán earlier in that year, coming away impressed by the importance of starting research there, it was undoubtedly his advocacy that led the director of the Peabody Museum, Frederick Ward Putnam, to initiate exploration in the Peninsula.

Such, in brief, was the chain of events that led to the dispatch for the first time of an archaeological expedition by any national or academic institution to a Maya site. We shall encounter Bowditch, Putnam, and Thompson once again in a later chapter, as they turn to Alfred Maudslay for advice and co-operation – he, by then, being a seasoned researcher in that area.

Chapter 10

Copán

The work at Quiriguá had concluded triumphantly; there remained, however, the delicate task of transporting tons of fragile cargo loaded on mules down a path that under the best of circumstances was rough, and could quickly be rendered almost impassable by heavy rain. This too was accomplished with only slight rain-damage to the moulds. Then these precious items had been repacked in crates, the crates had been loaded from rickety dock on to lake-steamer, at Livingston off-loaded into lighters able to cross the sand-bar, and finally hoisted up into an ocean-going steamer. At this point, a sigh of relief may have seemed appropriate, because the next stage, an ocean voyage – even one traversing one-third of the earth's circumference – might not appear risky, but in fact the ship did run aground somewhere, but was towed or floated off by some means. (Nine years later, though, as we shall see, Maudslay's casts did suffer serious damage in the course of an ocean voyage.)

In general, then, this expedition had met its goals, or more likely had exceeded them, so it may be worth attempting to identify some of the factors responsible for the success of this and other expeditions mounted by Maudslay. Two are obvious: meticulous planning and the expenditure of a great deal of money. The importance of the former can hardly be exaggerated, for it could only have been by dint of concentrated and imaginative thought that Maudslay was able to list what was needed: the dry and canned foodstuffs, the tools, photographic and moulding materials, tents and camp furniture, medical supplies, packing materials, and a host of other items, all of which had to be shipped out from England; and much of this planning he had done without prior experience.

Because practically nothing useful was going to be available locally, he must also have consulted closely with shipping-and-forwarding and Customs agencies. Shipments did on a few occasions go astray (disastrously so, on one expedition), but in general the system of agencies must have worked fairly well, since on a few later occasions he was able to send to New York or London for items badly needed, and have them arrive in good time: once, it was for a 12 by 10 inch camera that by mistake had not been shipped, and another time to obtain a new half-chronometer watch.

Success had also depended, of course, upon technical factors, such as the use of highly developed techniques for making moulds, and mastery of photography. When all these are taken into account, Maudslay's first serious venture into the field emerges as a milestone in the history of archaeological field research in the Americas. Nothing approaching it in any of these respects had been attempted before. To begin with, virtually all earlier work had been carried out at relatively accessible sites: Squier and Davis, for example, conducted their investigations of the 'Moundbuilder' ruins of Ohio in an area that had long been settled and under cultivation, so they were spared any serious problems of labour, health, logistics, or environment.[1]

In fact, during the thirty-five years following the completion of their work in Ohio, very little other fieldwork would be done elsewhere in the United States (or anywhere in the Americas, for that matter) until 1882, when the Division of Mound Exploration was created within the Bureau of American Ethnology of the Smithsonian Institution, a year after Maudslay entered the field.[2]

Fortunately for Maudslay, those intervening years had seen technical progress of the greatest importance for his work. One was the invention of factory-made, ready-to-use, photographic dry plates, which all at once rendered obsolete the wet plate, the portable (and in the tropics, insupportable) dark-tent, and the challenging procedures that a photographer had to wrestle with inside it. These dry plates had become available only about three years earlier.

Also relevant for Maudslay's publication plans were new techniques for printing photographs directly on the pages of books. Previously the only way to use photographic illustrations had been to paste silver prints onto the page – a very expensive procedure, although sometimes justifiable for small editions of art books or scientific publications, the images being far superior to engravings or lithographs made from the same photographs. But by the time Maudslay was ready to start publishing his work, there were two techniques available: the halftone process (still widely employed), and the much finer, although more expensive, photogravure process.

In the course of the Quiriguá expedition, tons of plaster had been transformed in the middle of a rain-forest into a thousand intricate and fragile moulds; the moulds, shipped back across the Atlantic, had then been assembled and used to cast a few more tons of wet plaster into faultless reproductions of enormous monuments. As to the photographs of the monuments themselves, they constitute, as a set, the finest ever achieved, in spite of their having been taken under extremely difficult conditions. Many of them remain unexcelled in quality, even one hundred and twenty years later.

Maudslay and Giuntini, aided by the López family, had faced hardships and difficulties of many kinds, and had won through. Their season at Quiriguá had been a test of physical robustness, but even more had it been a test of character and *savoir-faire*, and of Maudslay's skill in dealing with people of entirely different culture, in spite of his still rudimentary knowledge of Spanish.

In the large and varied literature of travel in Latin America the misadventures that befell travellers during their explorations tend not to be made light of – since they often they make good reading. But to judge by their own accounts, some explorers were plagued with such a succession of mischances, and unpleasant or even dangerous confrontations, that one does wonder whether some of them were not partly responsible for their own predicaments. Others have had less trouble or none at all, and Maudslay has to be numbered among these fortunate few, for never, as far as one knows, did he find himself in a really awkward confrontation with anyone during his travels, either in the Pacific or in Latin America.

How, then, in the course of so much pioneering, this could have been the case? The answer may be simple to state, but not to emulate, for it would seem to have been mainly a matter of character and human understanding. All the evidence we have shows Maudslay as a man who was never anything but calm and genial, and sensitive to the self-esteem of others; but no fool. And perhaps the ease with which he usually gained the confidence of strangers can be attributed partly to his open countenance and good manners.

With this expedition Maudslay had proved himself, and the praise soon given to his work at Cambridge and the Royal Geographical Society must have reassured him about its value. Bolstered, then, with new confidence he prepared to tackle his next objective, Copán. This famous ruined city offered some advantages in comparison with Quiriguá. The climate would be much pleasanter, with a lower rainfall, absence of floods, and fewer mosquitoes; it should also be less difficult to recruit labourers, as there were villages much closer to Copán than Quiriguá had been to distant Alta Verapaz, his previous source of workers.

The difficulties of supply, on the other hand, would be greater, since Copán was a three-day ride from Yzabal, or a week's journey for packmules, and the task facing him more formidable, simply because there was much more work to be done there than at Quiriguá. Not only were there more stelae and other sculptures to mould and photograph, there were also many mounds inviting excavation. The mapping, too, would be a bigger task, and this Maudslay would have to do himself, as no suitable surveyor had been found.

Well aware of the inaccuracy of the best available maps of the region, and of his own lack of proficiency in celestial navigation, Maudslay was anxious to receive some instruction in both celestial navigation and surveying before he set off for Copán. Equipped with suitable instruments, he should then be able to include in the eventual report of his explorations a map showing the major ruins and some of the principal towns in their correct location.[3]

So he wrote to the Royal Geographical Society asking for the loan of several pieces of apparatus: a 5-inch theodolite, a sextant, an artificial horizon, a half-chronometer watch, a hypsometric apparatus (for measuring altitudes), and draughting instruments – requesting also instruction in the use of them. Both requests were granted. Maudslay was then given a thorough grounding by John Coles of the Society, following which Coles returned to him his original letter endorsed with a note certifying that he was now competent to use the instruments.[4]

Many years later, in comments following a paper given at the Royal Geographical Society, Maudslay made this confession:

> When I first came across a ruin in Central America, I did not know what to do with it; it looked so very big and formidable, and I did not know how to set about recording my observations. Luckily for me, when I came home I fell into the hands of Mr. Coles, and anything I have since been able to do has been much owing to the instruction he gave me.[5]

Thus encouraged by the co-operation of the Royal Geographical Society, Maudslay wrote again in November, a week before leaving for Copán, making another request, this time for a grant towards the expenses of his expedition – £300 was the sum he suggested. The total cost, he wrote, was expected to exceed £1600, the whole of which he himself would otherwise have to bear. Mentioning the casts given to Cambridge University, and the £300 received from them, he let it be known that he had applied to the University once again for a similar sum of money which as before would be devoted to the making of casts.

He was to be disappointed, for both requests were denied. The University's decision may have been influenced by its unwillingness to receive any more casts, owing to the fact that, as we shall see, there was nowhere to put them.

By then, vast quantities of stores and equipment had been assembled, packed, and shipped. The plan this time was for Maudslay to leave first, make preliminary arrangements in Copán, then after ten days go down to Yzabal to meet Giuntini who would be arriving with the cargo.

While still in England Maudslay had discussed with the Foreign Office his plans for working at Copán. Control of archaeological work being in most countries practically non-existent at that time, all that was necessary was a word between the British Minister to the Central American States and the President of Honduras, and the matter would be arranged. Maudslay describes the unexpected result:

> On arrival in Copán, I entered the village under triumphal arches, and was received by a guard of honour of barefoot soldiers, and by an ex-Minister of State and a professor from the Government College, who presented me with an official-looking document addressed to 'El Sabio' [the Sage, or Learned One] which informed me that they had been appointed by the President of the Republic of Honduras as his commissioners to assist me in my labours. These gentlemen had already been awaiting my arrival for more than a week, and it was an evident relief to the villagers when, at the end of another week, I was able to impress upon them the value of the work they had accomplished, and recommend them to rest from their labours and return to their homes.

Ten days after his triumphal entry into Copán on 10 January 1885, Maudslay went down to meet Giuntini at Yzabal, only to receive the bad news that the ship in which he was travelling had broken its propeller shaft and had gone into Cork for repairs. His arrival would be delayed a month. This was a serious blow, since the time available for moulding before the onset of the rainy season would be reduced by a quarter. Taking stock, Maudslay realized there was little for him to do in the ruins until the surveying instruments and other equipment arrived; so, leaving the clearing of the bush and the cleaning of monuments to Gorgonio and his brother José Domingo, he went off on a reconnaissance trip with Carlos López.

They crossed the lake, and, following a trail leading in a north-westerly direction through uninhabited hilly country, came after six days to Chahal, at the foot of the mountains and close to the southern border of Petén. Chahal itself had no special attraction for Maudslay – it was just a village of Kekchis who had settled there in the wilds not long before in the hope of avoiding taxes. What led him into that remote area was the hope of hearing about ruins, and the desire to see for himself a region that Hernán Cortés must have passed through in 1524, although his exact route was unknown.

The march of Cortés from Tenochtitlán (now Mexico City) to Honduras, described in his Fifth Letter to the Emperor Charles V, was regarded by Maudslay with good reason as a valuable source of information about the political geography and level of culture in the Maya Lowlands at the time of the Conquest. Its potential value, however, would not be realized until the route he took was more accurately determined, the Indian towns identified (all of them presumably long abandoned, with the exception of Tayasal), and these studied, preferably by means of excavation.

Disappointed on this trek by their failure to find ruins, Maudslay and Carlos headed back from Chahal into the mountains to visit Cahabón, the López family's home town. From there they rode to Panzos to have a look at ruins lying a few miles away south of the Polochic River. He was hoping they might correspond to a town raided by Cortés when he was searching desperately for provisions during his great trek to Honduras in 1525. In his letter to the King, Cortés reported that when he had 'asked some of the Indian prisoners whether they knew of any other village where dry maize could be obtained they answered me that they knew of one called Chacujál, a very populous and ancient one, where all manner of provisions might be found in abundance'. Having raided this town successfully, Cortés had rafts built to transport the corn they had captured down the Polochic and on to the Caribbean coast.

Two years earlier, while at Quiriguá, Maudslay had sent a man up the Polochic to look for Chacujál, who came back with news of ruins known locally as Pueblo Viejo, which lay in the right area. So now he and Carlos spent a day looking at these heavily overgrown ruins, and Maudslay came away convinced that, although there was no certainty they were Chacujál itself, they indeed differed from Copán or Quiriguá in type of construction, resembling instead other sites which nowadays we would probably recognize as Postclassic.

The fact that Cortés described Chacujál as being of greater importance than any town he had seen since Acalán (a town not yet located precisely, but evidently somewhere east of Tenosique), was regarded by Maudslay as evidence that Cortés had heard nothing of any of the great Classic period cities, thereby confirming his view that none of the great centres of Maya art and architecture was functioning when Cortés passed through the country.

From Panzos they travelled by canoe down the Polochic to Yzabal, in time to meet Giuntini, and then arranged for the carriage of the stores by mule train to Copán, a task that would take many weeks to complete. Maudslay gives the following rough list: axes, machetes, pickaxes, spades, crowbars, wheelbarrows, surveying equipment, photographic apparatus, photographic chemicals and dry plates, a barrel of lime, 4 tons of plaster of Paris, and about 500 lb of moulding paper. He neglected to mention several hundred pounds of tow (coarse hemp fibre) and quantities of brown paper and American cloth for packing the delicate plaster moulds, and lumber for making crates for them; besides that, of course, there were food supplies, personal baggage, and camp kit.

The plaster of Paris was shipped from England to Livingston in tin-lined barrels; at that port it was landed and re-shipped in a small steamer which carried it up the river and across the Golfo Dulce to Yzabal; there the barrels were opened and the plaster put into waterproof sacks, which we had brought out from England for the purpose, and thence it was carried on mule-back over the mountains to Copán. I remember making a calculation at the time which showed me that the plaster for which I had originally paid fifty shillings a ton in Carlisle had cost £50 by the time it had reached Copán [that is, twenty times as much].

Now work could begin in earnest at the ruins. A thatched shelter had been built near the acropolis to accommodate the López brothers and Giuntini, while Maudslay took up his quarters in the village in that small mud-walled *cabildo*. The particular attraction of this place of residence was the prison cell attached to it, measuring about 7 feet by 4 feet, which was speedily turned into a darkroom for developing photographs.

The village of Copán consisted then of about a dozen houses grouped round a plaza, in the midst of which stood a sculptured altar, for the village had been built over an outlying portion of the ancient city. As we have seen, the river runs past the core area of the ruins, and then, about 1.5 miles downstream, runs past the village, before turning north to join the Motagua River. During the centuries of abandonment the river cut over towards the acropolis and began eating it away, until by the nineteenth century it was running below a vertical cliff nearly 100 feet high in which were visible patches of masonry belonging to early structures buried beneath later additions, and two or three passageways looking (in section) like windows. (In the 1930s steps were taken to force the river back into its earlier course to prevent further erosion.)

The ruins of Copán were among the first Maya ruins to become known to the Spaniards. As early as 1576 a description of them by a government official, Diego García de Palacio, was sent to King Philip II. This excellent account provoked no investigation, but was simply filed away until disinterred and published in 1860. By then the ruins had become famous because of the description by John Lloyd Stephens, with its remarkable illustrations by Frederick Catherwood, in their work, *Incidents of Travel in Central America, Chiapas, and Yucatan*. It may be wondered how Stephens, living in New York, ever came to hear about Copán? The answer seems to lie in a brief account of the ruins inserted in a New York newspaper by Colonel Juan Galindo – or perhaps in the longer versions of those descriptions published in London and Paris.

In spite of his name, Galindo was an Englishman. Born into a theatrical family, and originally named John, he set out (strangely prefiguring Maudslay) to take up farming in Jamaica, but landed up instead in Guatemala where he became an officer and administrator. Because of his interest in antiquities he was commissioned to make an official report on the ruins of Copán in 1834, and a version of that report was sent to the Société de Géographie in Paris, along with plans and drawings of a few monuments. But only the text was published by the Société.

The principal, and most impressive, feature of this ruined city is the acropolis, a huge construction covering nearly 10 acres. This is the result of several stages of construction, one upon another – an agglomeration, in fact, of many structures raised to support temples that are now ruined, or partly so. With the passage of time, terraces and ancillary structures were built around them, resulting in the formation of two courts of irregular shape which stand at a level far above the surrounding terrain.

At the very edge of the 'cliff' along the edge of the Eastern Court caused by this erosion, Maudslay examined a building he called no. 20, and recognized it as the 'tower' mentioned by Palacio three hundred years earlier. This he considered the most curious building his excavations had brought to light, for he found a stairway leading into the building from the court, but then came upon a chamber that had been sealed off. He could only suppose this had been done to safeguard the building's stability, but now, a century later, recent work suggests a more interesting explanation. Apparently the structure had been built with the intention of closing the chamber from the *outside*, and the fact that its façade had been embellished by figures of bats with death signs on their pectorals suggests that victims were incarcerated there from time to time, just as the Hero Twins of the *Popol Vuh*, the ancient Maya Creation myth, were shut up in the House of Bats – one of their trials by the Lords of the Underworld.

The north side of the acropolis is dominated by two large temples, Structures 11 and 26. The former overlooks the entire length of a vast ceremonial space about 270 yards long. It was here that most of the famous stelae of Copán were erected. Looking down from it at the southern end of the plaza, one has a good view of the large ball-court below; indeed the broad steps leading up to it must have provided, as at Quiriguá, a grandstand view of games being played there. But at the eastern extremity of this range of steps there is another great stairway, this one ascending Structure 26, a pyramid united on one side with the acropolis, and facing west.

Maudslay did not fail to notice that a run of these steps, apparently still in situ, were carved on their risers with hieroglyphs. Puzzled, however, at their abrupt termination about a quarter of the way up, he had a trench dug horizontally into the mound above the top step, but this revealed nothing but unshaped stones and soil until, 17 feet in, a vertical wall was encountered. The explanation eluded him, and it would be found only in the course of the Peabody Museum's large-scale excavations some years later. It then became apparent that the section of steps examined by Maudslay had originally been set higher up, but at some time in the not too distant past, when the lower reaches of the stairway were already covered over with rubble from decay of the temple and upper portions of the pyramidal substructure, this middle section of the stairway, shaken loose perhaps by an earthquake, slid down *en bloc* and came to rest over the loose soil and rubble. Removal of those displaced steps and rubble beneath them revealed the lowermost fifteen steps still in position

The stelae, though not as tall as some at Quiriguá, are in general more ornate, more varied, and more graceful. The style of the later monuments, in particular the employment of deep relief, is peculiar to Copán, and its development owes much to the nature of the stone available there – a volcanic tuff which is easy to carve and yet weather-resistant. The personages represented on the stelae stand out from the shaft almost in the round; while the figures themselves are rather stiff and formal as their dignity requires, the general effect is enlivened by swirling feathers, entwined serpents, and a multitude of other elements represented quite freely, sometimes with a few of them undercut and free-standing. One thing was certain: Giuntini would find sculpture of this kind even more challenging to cast than the Great Turtle of Quiriguá.

As soon as Maudslay had returned to Copán with Giuntini, and the first consignments of stores had arrived, he began to survey the site; Giuntini started making plaster moulds; and the López brothers making paper moulds of the inscriptions. Maudslay was busy also with excavations: some were only small trenches through rubble at the base of the acropolis or other mounds, aimed at locating the foot of each slope or retaining wall for the survey; in other cases he was having rubble and soil cleared out of buildings that were still partially preserved; and in yet other cases he was probing into or under structures. These, it is worth pointing out, were the first careful excavations ever done at any Maya site.

At first sight the pyramids, great rounded masses of stone blocks, shaped and unshaped, mixed with soil, did not seem to be crowned with any trace of buildings, but Maudslay found it difficult to believe they had been built for any other purpose than to serve as foundations for buildings such as those he'd seen at Tikal. As the vegetation was cleared away and the outlines became clearer, he began to notice that many of the higher mounds had a depression running across its summit, which might be accounted for by the collapse of a central doorway.

> Judge, then, of my delight when, on digging into the top of the mound on the north side of the eastern court, I came on the unmistakable signs of the sides of a doorway and the remains of an elaborate cornice running along the top of the interior wall of a chamber. Digging on with the greatest care we finally unearthed the fine ornamental doorway between the two chambers of the temple, of which a drawing (with the fallen stones restored to their places) is here given.

Cyrus Thomas, in 1899, was to write of such passages:

As we follow Mr Maudslay while he slowly and laboriously plows his way into the bowels of the forest-covered mounds, viewing in his excellent photographs the sights he beheld as the covering of earth and debris was removed, it is difficult to realize the fact that all this is the work of native Americans artists, and not the crumbling temples and palaces of the Orient.[6]

Indeed, nothing comparable had been revealed in previous excavations, and this work at Copán inaugurated a new era in Maya archaeology.

By clearing rubble off various mounds Maudslay showed that most of the structures at Copán had been raised to support buildings, some of them doubtless temples, thereby demonstrating that they were not the defensive walls that earlier visitors had taken them to be. Going a step further, he engaged in a more fundamental kind of excavation by trenching downwards into one side of the pyramidal mound standing in the centre of the Great Plaza. This fair-sized mound had almost entirely lost its casing of masonry, although a stairway on the east side was still discernible. No trace remained of any building on top.

The upper part was composed of rough unworked blocks of stone and mud, with occasional layers of cement and sand, and the lower two-thirds of stone and mud only. The excavation was then continued below the level of the plain through about twelve feet of hard-rammed earth, free from stones, below which the natural soil appeared to have been undisturbed. In the centre of the mound, about six feet from the top, an earthen pot was found containing a bead-shaped piece of greenstone, pierced, diameter two-and-three-quarter inches, the jade whorl of a spindle, the remains of a necklace of nine beads, four pearls, some rough figures and other ornaments cut out of pearl oyster-shell, and other irregular pieces of roughly carved pearl-shell. At the bottom of the pot was some red powder (which proved to be finely ground cinnabar), and several ounces of quicksilver. . . . About eight to nine feet below the level of the plain a skeleton of a jaguar was found lying under a layer of charcoal. I was able to preserve some of the teeth and part of the jaw as well as a few small pieces of the other bones by dropping them into glue. The teeth and part of the skeleton had been painted red.

About 100 yards south of this mound he excavated a smaller one, and there found parts of another jaguar's skeleton mixed with a few small fragments of human bones and other objects.

In descriptions such as this a great advance is seen from the kind of excavations made in Mesoamerican ruins by earlier enthusiasts who did little more than break open blocked-up doorways with crowbars, looking for treasure. Here by contrast was Maudslay, investigating the construction of a mound, digging a long way down to sterile earth, carefully noting and photographing the contents of a cache vessel, attempting to preserve extremely crumbly bones by dropping them into glue (and who else at that time would have brought glue?), having the red powder analysed in London, having also the bones from the other mound studied by experts, so that 'a few small bones could be identified as human bones'. The one conclusion he didn't reach was that 'the occasional layers of cement and sand' might have been the floors of structures which were later demolished and built over, but that was not surprising at that date. Nor does it seem that he recorded on paper the section revealed by his trench. (As a photograph of the plaza taken by the Peabody Museum project reveals, the cut was not back-filled either, but doing so would have been exceptional at the time. Even forty years later, the trenches dug at Uaxactun by Carnegie Institution archaeologists were left open.)

All this work, however, had not proceeded without difficulties. Hardly had it begun when war broke out, with Guatemala and Honduras on one side, and El Salvador and Nicaragua on the other. Nearly all Maudslay's labourers were carried off to serve – very unwillingly – as soldiers, leaving him with only a few who were lame or beyond military age. Every now and then a report would come that troops were marching towards the village, and Maudslay's neighbours there would prepare to betake themselves to the bush with their few valuables, leaving the village in the care of some ancient ladies. Wild rumours were flying about, and it was impossible to get trustworthy information.

Apart from safety, another pressing problem arose as a result of the war. As Maudslay describes it:

I had made arrangements when in Guatemala City, for a supply of silver coin to be sent to me from time to time with which to pay the labourers; but at the end of a few weeks the supply suddenly ceased, and my correspondents sent a telegram to Zacapa, which was forwarded to me, to say that owing to the disturbed state of the country it was unsafe to send a messenger with the money, that the tide of war was surging my way, and it was advisable that I should make a speedy retreat to the coast.

I walked about for an hour with that telegram in my pocket, trying to think out the chances of our being left unmolested; I knew by this time that we had won the goodwill of the villagers, and I was loth to leave the work which was daily growing more interesting, so finally I tore up the telegram and said not a word about its contents to anyone. But my silver was nearly at an end, and some of the workmen who had come from a distance, and were naturally perturbed at the rumours of war, wanted to get back to look after their own homes, and they had to be paid off. It was then that the Niña Chica came to the front.

The Niña Chica was an old lady, and the outstanding personality in the village. She was to develop an unshakeable loyalty to Maudslay, and now showed it by coming to his aid in a most unexpected fashion.

> While she was boiling my kettle for me that evening I told her some of the difficulties I was in, to which she listened attentively and then left without expressing any opinion. An hour or so later she returned and placed a small bag of silver on the table. It seemed she had gone round the village and borrowed every cent she could scrape together, and to this she added her own little store of dollars, and then handed it over to me. It was done with such perfectly good grace that it was impossible to refuse her help, but I had to explain that she had not altogether caught my meaning. I had enough silver to pay all the workmen up to date, but if I stayed on there was not enough to pay such labourers as I might be able to engage in the weeks to come. 'Don't trouble yourself, Don Alfredo', she replied, 'those that are left in the village will go on working for you just the same; we know well enough that you will pay us when these troubles are over'.
>
> I went to sleep that night in a happier frame of mind, but was careful, before turning in, to bar the door and place a revolver handy. [There had been reports of marauding bands near the frontiers.] I asked the Niña Chica what chance there was of the villagers standing by me in case of a night raid; perhaps I did not express myself as though I had sufficient confidence in their courage, for the old lady's eyes flashed and she cried 'What! do you think all my boys wear petticoats? You fire a shot for warning and just see if we don't all turn out and give the rascals a good drubbing.'

Finally, a considerable battle was fought at about one-and-a-half days' journey to the southwest, in which President Barrios, who had helped Maudslay in his previous expeditions, was killed, and the war came to an end. Some of the labourers then returned.

With the end of hostilities the village of Copán was visited by a General in the Honduran army.

> I am told that in the army of that Republic Generals are plentiful, and that the Government find it well to keep them harmlessly employed, lest the devil should find some mischief for their idle hands to do, in the shape of drawing up 'pronunciamentos'; and this particular General was in the employment of the department of excise – that is to say, with the aid of a somewhat ragged following of soldiers he was hunting through the country for illicit stills. Of course we paid one another formal visits and I had some very pretty speeches made to me

about Progress, and Liberty, and Science, which, had they been printed with liberal use of Capital letters, would have read like a leading article in a Spanish-American newspaper. The General thanked me formally for the distinguished service I was rendering to his country, and accepted with effusion my offer to show him what discoveries had been made.

On the next morning he appeared with notebook and pencil in hand, and we set off for the ruins, where I did my best in the capacity of showman. We examined all the excavations, and then returned to have another look at the monuments in the Great Plaza; but throughout our walk, although the General's fingers played caressingly round his pencil, he never took a note. At last we stood looking at the back of Stela A, which is covered with a particularly well-preserved inscription inclosed in a flat undecorated margin, on which some former visitor had rendered himself conspicuous by deeply carving his distinguished name, J. HIGGINS, in letters about three inches long. I was holding forth, in my best Spanish, about the probability of an interpretation being found to the hieroglyphics, and pointing out some glyphs which I had also met with on monuments in Chiapas and Petén, when the General opened his notebook, as I thought to make a drawing of the glyphs in question. When his pencil had been at work for a few moments I glanced at the sheet to see how proficient he might be as a draughtsman, and found that he had got down J. HIG, and was carefully printing the second G, when he turned to me and said 'Señor Don Alfredo, after all, these hieroglyphics are very much like the characters we use now!'

Before coming to Copán Maudslay had heard unflattering stories about its inhabitants, and indeed at first they did not make him feel welcome. But, as the story of the silver loan shows, he gained their trust and kept on excellent terms with them.

Ignorant, lazy, dirty, and drunken as these people undoubtedly are, I found them to be cheerful, kindly, and honest. My hut was full of things which were of value to them, and although at first I was always careful to padlock the door when I went off to the ruins and to give the key to the Niña Chica, later on it was often left open nearly all day long, yet nothing was ever touched.

As soon as the war was over, Maudslay began sending mules and porters to Yzabal with cargoes of paper and plaster moulds.

The paper moulds, after being well dried in the sun, were given a good dressing with boiled linseed oil, and then made up into packages covered first with 'scrims,' a sort of loosely woven canvas, and then with an outer coat of shiny waterproof cloth. Each package was then fixed in a crate made of long light stems of a species of hibiscus, which we had previously cut and dried. They were unwieldy burdens, but as none of them weighed more than sixty pounds, we had no great difficulty in engaging mozos who carried them on their backs in safety to the port. The conveyance of the plaster moulds was a more difficult matter, as there were in all about fourteen hundred pieces of various shapes and sizes, which needed the greatest care in handling and packing. Each piece was first of all wrapped in tow, which I had brought from England for the purpose, and then tied up with string in a sheet of strong brown paper. Thirty-two of these packets could on the average be packed into the two boxes which each mule carried. We usually managed to send off about ten cargoes at a time, with instructions that the boxes (which were those in which our stores had been brought from home) should be unpacked and sent back empty.

At the end of May, with showers beginning to herald the rainy season, Maudslay judged it prudent to leave. In five months of work, photographs and moulds had been taken of over a dozen complete stelae as well as altars and other kinds of sculpture. A number of fruitful excavations had been made, and an accurate plan of the site. To have accomplished so much was an extraordinary achievement, especially in the face of the unforeseeable difficulties, and others such as a plague of ticks, and a threatening epidemic of smallpox nearby.

Now it was time to consider the problem of ensuring the safety of the many small pieces of sculpture that had come to light in the clearing of rubble and in the course of excavations. The document authorizing him to work at the ruins does not seem to have referred to this matter, since Maudslay raises it in a telegram he dispatched to the President, Luis Bográn. In a Spanish that was, perhaps, no better than could be expected, he announced the approaching termination of his work, and his intention of handing over, before he left, those pieces of sculpture into the care of the Alcalde. At the same time he hoped the President might permit him to remove certain pieces to place in the museum alongside his plaster casts. In conclusion he thanked the President for his favourable interest.

In reply came a telegram from the President, dated June 3rd. It reads (in translation) 'I rejoice at the successful completion of your work. You can take away what you like. I shall have pleasure in helping you in your explorations for the benefit of science. Bográn.'[7]

The four pieces Maudslay chose to remove were: a bust, carved in the round, of a youthful figure making a gesture reminiscent of a bodhisattva (Maudslay called this the 'singing girl'; others have identified it as a youthful corn god); two bas-relief panels that were part of a largely ruined interior frieze of Temple II; and a beautiful panel set at floor level in the back wall of a wide gallery in the same temple. At its centre the panel served as riser for a rather high step up to the threshold of a doorway leading into a sanctuary, and from that, out to the Western Court of the acropolis. This panel, nearly 6 yards wide and 18 inches deep, is carved with a short hieroglyphic text in the centre, flanked by ten men of high rank on either side, each seated on a hieroglyph and further distinguished by headdresses and pectoral ornaments of various designs. As the rubble-filled chamber was being cleared out, part or all of some of these figures were found among the debris, having split off from the panel. Such fragments were carefully preserved for eventual re-attachment to the panel. From Maudslay's point of view it was fortunate that the panel was made in two sections; even so, each of them was 9 feet long, and how such long stone slabs were ever transported to Yzabal remains a mystery.

When at last their work at Copán was over, and everything had been packed up and transported to Yzabal,

a week was spent at the port making strong wooden cases out of a supply of timber which I had fortunately had the foresight to order to be sent from New Orleans, and in re-packing the moulds for shipment to England. I have gone into these rather uninteresting details about packing to show how absolutely necessary it is, when starting on an expedition of this kind, to think out every detail beforehand.

It was lucky, indeed, that the moulds were well packed and the cases strong and well made, for the vessel in which they were shipped ran on a reef off the coast of Florida, and the cargo had to be trans-shipped under difficulties; and when the freight came to be paid I was initiated into the mysteries of a 'general average' which added largely to the cost.

Throughout this expedition it seemed as though the sea had a spite against us. The vessel in which Mr. Giuntini sailed from England broke her shaft [as already told]; then the vessel which held the precious results of our work ran on shore; and lastly the small steamer [the SS *Dallas*] in which Mr. Giuntini and I took passage on our way home from Livingston to New Orleans broke her shaft when sixty miles off the north coast of Yucatan, and we lay for some days helplessly drifting into the Gulf of Mexico, until we were able to anchor on the great Bank of Yucatan, about fifty miles from land and in forty-five fathoms of water.

The weather fortunately held fine, but it proved too hot for the preservation of the cargo of fruit, which was thrown overboard as it ripened, until a broad yellow band of floating bananas stretched out astern as far as the eye could reach. At the end of a week our signals of distress were most fortunately sighted by a small fruit steamer which had strayed somewhat out of its course; and the passengers were carried in her to New Orleans, whence tugs were sent out to rescue the disabled vessel and tow her into port.

Chapter 11

Highlands and Pine Ridge

I
n planning his next venture into Maya territory Maudslay again allowed rather more than a full year to pass between return from one expedition and departure for the next. Since sea voyages to Guatemala and back took six or seven weeks, there would never have been enough time between yearly expeditions for working up the results of one expedition and making preparations for the next, to say nothing of time for recuperation of his health, both physical and financial.

In 1887, though, Maudslay chose to leave earlier than usual, sailing in October rather than December. This time his plan was to reconnoitre a wide swath of terrain extending from the Guatemalan highlands towards British Honduras. By spending the first half of this season in the highlands, where the climate in winter is far more agreeable than in the lowlands, an earlier start would be feasible.

In the course of this journey through the highlands Maudslay hoped he would be able to compare Conquest-period accounts of Maya towns with their archaeological presence, as he had done three years earlier when he made that already described side excursion to Pueblo Viejo.[1]

This time he had his sights set on the ruins of Utatlán and Iximché, the ancient strongholds of the Quiché and Cakchiquel Maya realms respectively. Since Pedro de Alvarado's conquest of these towns had cost him some trouble, it was a rather full account of them that he despatched to Cortés; but for a more detailed description of Utatlán itself one can turn to Francisco Fuentes y Guzman, whose work, partly based on older manuscripts, was written a century and a half later.[2]

The town, he says, stood on a small plateau surrounded by a deep *barranca*, or ravine; this formed a natural fosse, leaving only two very narrow roads as entrances to the city, both of which were so well defended by the 'Castle of the Resguardo' as to render it impregnable. The castle was five storeys high and measured 188 by 230 paces. Among other marvels were a superb seminary where between five and six thousand children were educated, and the Grand Alcázar, or Palace of the Kings, which surpassed every other edifice, and in the opinion of Torquemeda could compete in opulence with that of Moctezuma in Mexico, or that of the Incas in Peru.

To show how far these and other statements could be relied upon, Maudslay surveyed both sites. Utatlán lies 2 miles from Santa Cruz del Quiché, and, as he reported, 'on the left of the track from the town, just before reaching the great barranca, there is a natural mound, the sides of which have been terraced, and on the top is a more or less level space measuring 200 by 150 feet. Within this space are several mounds surrounding a level plaza.' Two of the mounds were square (temples, perhaps) while two others may have supported long houses. All the stone had long before been stripped from these mounds by the people of Santa Cruz, who had used them as a quarry, but Maudslay felt confident in identifying this group of mounds as the Resguardo. 'The position they occupy', he wrote, 'is naturally a strong one . . . but there is nothing especially characteristic of a fortress about the buildings themselves.' As for the Palace, he failed to see where there could have been room for it.

Writing of these towns, and others sited on hilltops that he was later to see in Baja Verapaz, and of towns built on islands in Lakes Lacandón and Petén-Itzá, he concluded that 'all were placed in naturally strong positions, and were easily defensible, and their existence tends to the conclusion that the condition of society was one of continual intertribal warfare'.

> None of the sites of these strongholds have yielded any examples of the carved hieroglyphic inscriptions, highly ornamented stone buildings, or elaborately-sculptured monolithic monuments which are to be found at Copan, Quirigua or Palenque; and it cannot be too strongly insisted on that between the civilization revealed to us by those great ruins and the culture of the Indian tribes conquered by the Spaniards there is a great gap which at present we have no means of bridging.

On his way from Santa Cruz to Cobán Maudslay halted at Rabinal, in Baja Verapaz, a town near the site of an earlier one founded by Bishop Las Casas, for the purpose of gathering the scattered Quiché Maya into a community and thereby speeding their conversion to the faith. It had been in Rabinal, only thirty years before Maudslay's visit, that the Abbé Brasseur de Bourbourg, famous for his discovery of Landa's manuscript, the Codex Troano, and other important documents, had recorded the Rabinal Achi, the most important Maya drama to have been preserved, although by then somewhat corrupted. Before the Conquest the dance had probably been performed in Cahyup, the now ruined but clearly defensible Quiché centre close to Rabinal. But instead of visiting Cahyup, Maudslay chose to ride for two-and-a-half hours to another considerable town from the late pre-Conquest period, Chuitinamit.[3] There he spent five hours to good effect: his sketch map shows seven of the eight groups that Ledyard Smith mapped eighty years later, he recognized the ball-court as such, and his hastily surveyed plan of Group E (Smith's Group D) is excellent.[4]

Having seen Chuitinamit, Maudslay resolved to study the ruins in that area more closely, should the opportunity arise. And arise it did, when he made another survey of the highlands seven years later. But, as will be told in a later chapter, he was obliged to abandon the planned investigation.[5]

By January he was once again comfortably ensconced at the Sargs' house in Cobán. This time he had no settled plan of work, but hoped to do some amateur map-making (as he called it) around the headwaters of the Río de la Pasión, and then to look at ruins in Petén reported to exist near the frontier of British Honduras.

Carlos López was sent ahead to the village of Cahabón to engage porters for the journey, but, since the 'dry season' (a relative term, in that rainy region) was not yet at hand, he decided to spend a fortnight mapping by compass and pace the track between Cobán and Cahabón, a distance of about 60 miles, a labour that seems difficult to justify, for how could the precise course of the road have mattered very much to him or anyone else in the foreseeable future? But he must have had his reasons. He intended also to determine the position of Cahabón by astronomical observation, because he suspected it was shown too far north on existing maps.

After several days' work along the road he saw Carlos returning with a deputation of Cahabón Indians; they were going to the Jefe Político in Cobán to protest against his having ordered them to accompany Maudslay on this journey north. It was well known, they said, that 'los Ingleses comen gente' – the English eat people. Maudslay could only hope that on reaching Cahabón he might persuade them that he at least abstained from that practice.

The rain continued, but Maudslay and his small group usually managed to stay dry at night in *ermitas* – 'hermitages' literally, but actually open-sided, thatched-roof shelters which served also as shrines. At one end there would be a rough wooden altar, and behind it a collection of wooden crosses.

> It is in these Ermitas that the Indians hold their fiestas, meet to transact local business, get drunk, and bury their dead. I had several times noticed the unevenness of the hard mud floor when I was setting up my camp bed, but it was not until I was trying to get the bed level above a more than usually distinct mound, that I asked a question and found out that I was about to sleep above the latest addition to the majority.

Having surveyed as far as Lanquín, Maudslay decided to move on directly to Cahabón, and establish a temporary base there for measuring the rest of it. As they got nearer, Gorgonio told Maudslay he didn't think he would be very comfortable at his brother Cornelio's house, and suggested the Convento, where the Padre was known to be hospitable. Maudslay describes how, as he dismounted at the foot of the steps up to the Convento, he was greeted with

'Come in, come in! I very glad to see you. I do speak de Engleesh very well.' Looking up I saw a small, sandy-haired, grey-eyed man dressed in blue-and-white-striped cotton trousers, a spotted cotton shirt, and a pair of rough brown native shoes; he ran down the steps, grasped my hand, patted me on the back, roared with laughter, and kept up a stream of greetings in the most delicious broken English. . . . I had chanced on, of all people in the world – a Dutchman!

Cornelio and the Padre, as the only 'gente de razón' in the place, generally spent their evenings together. I asked the Padre if they had any books to read, and he said that he had none, but added with some pride that Cornelio possessed a 'History of the World,' in two volumes, and that they had often read that. My offer to see if I could spare him any books did not seem to arouse much interest; apparently he had never read a novel, and hardly seemed to know what it meant.

Maudslay gave him a copy of 'Pepita Jiménez'.[6] He thanked him listlessly and put it aside.

That evening I said goodnight to my host early, as I had some writing to do, and later spent an hour or two shooting stars with a sextant and working out our position. It was past one o'clock when I was ready to turn in, and to my surprise I saw a light under the Padre's door and heard the sound of a voice. I called out, and hearing no reply, pushed at the big wooden door, which swung open. The feeble rays of light from one small oil-lamp were lost in the gloom of the far corners of the great bare room; but I could just make out Cornelio seated on the bench against the wall with his elbows pushed over the heavy well-worn table, his head resting on his hands, in rapt attention, whilst the Padre – a candle in one hand and a book in the other – was pacing up and down in front of the table, reading aloud from the pages of 'Pepita Jiménez'. 'Hush!' he cried, holding up the book at me and not stopping in his walk, 'he is just going to do it'; and I sat quietly on the bench whilst he read page after page of that delightful story. Then I crept quietly off to bed – my departure unobserved by them, so absorbed were they both in the story – and fell asleep to the distant murmur of the Padre's voice.

By 18 February the traverse from Lanquín to Cahabón was finished: *cargadores* had been engaged; their loads were ready; and it was time to bid farewell to the Padre and Cornelio with many handshakes and expressions of goodwill. Maudslay was now accompanied by Gorgonio,

Carlos and José Domingo López, and about twenty *cargadores*. They took also a horse and three mules, even though many years had passed since anyone had attempted to take animals over the track; but they would be very useful once they emerged from the forest into savanna country.

Up to this point, Maudslay had been making regular use of his sextant and chronometer, but now, on entering uncharted territory, he was to take sights even more frequently. His notebook is full of calculations of latitude from observations of the Meridian Altitude of the Sun's Lower Limb, or of Sirius or Capella, these usually proving quite accurate.

Estimation of longitude was a far more difficult and uncertain matter, since it depended entirely on comparison of local time with Greenwich Mean Time, the former as determined by astronomical observation with a sextant, the latter as indicated by a watch that had been set, perhaps many weeks in the past, by a ship's chronometer or a telegraphic time-signal. But while box chronometers were very accurate and proved reliable for shipboard use, they were found to be much too delicate for rough overland journeys. Pocket chronometers were available, but they too had disadvantages, such as a tendency to stop when jolted. Instead, travellers found 'half-chronometer watches' the only satisfactory time-keepers, in spite of being less accurate.

Half-chronometers were English-lever watches, with temperature-compensated balance wheels and carefully tempered balance springs. At about £40 they were not cheap (their price being about a year's wages for ordinary labourers) and they still needed to be cosseted by being wound with great regularity, and carried as far as possible in an unchanging position, and above all by having their going rate checked at least every six days. This procedure involved taking a shot on the sun or a star, and noting the disparity on repeating it a couple of days later at the identical time and place. As may be imagined, these obligatory two-day halts could be extremely inconvenient.

Two years earlier, on his expedition to Copán, Maudslay had been carrying two half-chronometer watches, which by the time he reached Belize on his way home were showing a difference between them of 9 minutes and 40 seconds. Then on boarding the SS *Dallas* there, he compared one of them with the ship's chronometer and found it to be 46 minutes and 31 seconds fast. This gave him the total drift, and since he had rated his watches throughout the journey, he was able to recalculate all his measurements so as to reduce, if not eliminate, the errors. Performing those complicated calculations with six-figure logarithms may have helped him pass the time when the *Dallas* broke its propeller shaft on the second day out and drifted off the coast of Yucatán – if they didn't drive him to distraction.

On leaving Cahabón the course Maudslay and his men now followed took them through a region that is still quite far from any road passable by wheeled vehicles. One passage through limestone hills took them over a rough surface likened by Maudslay 'to a gigantic fossil bath-sponge with innumerable pits, sharp edges, and projecting points. We frequently had to use the backs of our axes to break away the points and edges of the rock before it was possible for our animals to pass . . . ; even the sure-footed Indians had much difficulty picking their way.' On reaching a tributary of the Sarstoon River, too deep to ford, the Indians 'with great judgment and skill felled two trees from opposite sides of the stream, whose branches interlaced, and along this rough bridge the cargadores carried their loads in safety'. Maudslay himself then swam the animals across.[7]

One of the men had been brought by Maudslay from Cobán on the strength of his claim to have found, some years before and near the track to San Luis they would be following, a cave in which there stood three great idols carved out of stone. In spite of burning incense to propitiate the spirits, as the man had suggested, they failed to find it.

Another of the men was then bitten by a poisonous snake, and was beginning to recover when they encountered two hunters, returning to Cahabón. Maudslay suggested that the sick man return home with them, and in a speech translated into Kekchi by Gorgonio he expressed the hope they might already have found that Englishmen were not man-eaters, and, as for himself, he was anxious to take good care of them, and he proposed generous compensation for the man. The only comment elicited by this was, 'If Pedro was fool enough to put his foot on a snake, of course we know it was not the Patrón's fault.' But Maudslay thought the men's attitude had already improved.

At last they arrived at San Luis, which had been one of the larger villages in Petén, but now, Maudslay saw,

> nearly all the houses . . . were empty and fast falling into decay. About two years before my visit the inhabitants, worried and wearied by the constant interference of the Government in their concerns, and especially resenting an extra tax [levied for building a railway from the capital to the Atlantic coast], determined to abandon their homes and seek shelter in British territory. In all about one hundred families fled across the border and founded the village of San Antonio between the frontier and Punta Gorda.
>
> The Colonial Government did not interfere with them and they lived on in taxless peace; but even so their happiness was not complete, for had they not left the sacred images of the saints behind them, and had not their chosen Alcalde, fearing the long arm of the President, refused to accompany them? The loss was intolerable and a council was called to discuss the matter, when it was settled to make

an attempt to recover the saints and their Alcalde whatever the risks might be. A number of the younger men then recrossed the frontier, seized the church bells and the images of the saints, and called their Alcalde to follow them; but he, wise man, knew the value of forms, and refused to leave unless they would first bind him with cords. This was soon done, and then conscience being satisfied he cheerfully marched off to join his family on the other side of the frontier.

The fate of the bells of San Luis nearly became an international dispute, 'but, fortunately for the peace of the world, after a few despatches had passed between the governments interested, the matter was allowed to drop'.

On reaching the grassy savannas, streams, and scented pine woods of Poptún in early March, Maudslay resisted the temptation of lingering there, and pressed on to one of his goals, the village of Dolores. Some years earlier, the Jefe Político of Petén had spoken to him of ruins in this area, their existence being known to him perhaps from records in his office, for in 1853 a predecessor, the Corregidor Modesto Méndez, had visited two sites with carved monuments near Dolores. But now it seemed that with the passage of twenty-five years both of these had again been forgotten; eventually, though, a guide to one of them, Ixkún, was found. The other, Ixtutz, had relapsed into an oblivion that would endure for 120 years.

Gorgonio and Carlos López were sent off at once with this guide to inspect the site, reporting on their return that it lay about two hours' walk north, and had been rendered almost impenetrable by a thick tangle of woody vines. It was fortunate, then, that Maudslay had so many men with him (twenty, in fact), for they were able to make short work of clearing both trail and ruins.

For the first few days he himself stayed mostly in Dolores working out the astronomical observations he had taken along the route from Cobán, and presumably rating his chronometers by equal-altitude observations; but making occasional visits to the site. Then, once the ruins were cleared, he settled into a *champa*, or hut, that had been built for him, and started mapping them – producing in fact a remarkably accurate plan. Meanwhile Gorgonio began making a paper mould of a magnificent stela that was still standing. This monument, 12 feet tall, shows two standing rulers facing each other, and two bound captives crouching in a lower panel.

To Maudslay, whose acquaintance with Maya sculpture was still limited to that of Copán, Quiriguá, and Yaxchilán, the representation of captives was a novelty. Thinking that a clue might lie in the marked difference in physiognomy between captives and conquerors, he suggested that the stela might celebrate the conquest of the aboriginal inhabitants of the land, or the defeat of some of those barbarous invaders from the north whom some writers believe to have finally caused the overthrow of the Maya civilization. It is also worth noting that the Mayas carry only ornamental staves in their hands and make no show of weapons of war.

Maudslay and his men then moved on in a northeasterly direction towards Benque Viejo, the crossing point into British Honduras. Along the way one halt was made in order to investigate ruins at Yaxché, where, as also at Ixkún, cuts were dug through a few mounds to obtain information on architecture and burials.

At Yaxché, one of the Indians shot a howler monkey, which fell from the tree dead, and was found to have a baby clinging to its breast.

> The poor little beast was uninjured, and was brought to me howling piteously; for the second time I had to be nurse to an infant monkey, and I don't think any human child could have demanded more attention [the first time had been at Quiriguá]. . . . The new baby was a little older . . . and could take its food from a spoon, but unluckily there was not much food to be had which suited him. However, I heard that there was a company of mahogany-cutters in the neighbourhood, and sent one of my mozos to their temporary head-quarters or 'Montería,' which was distant two days' journey, to try to buy a tin of condensed milk from their stores. Running after ruins and sculptured stones was a sufficiently incomprehensible proceeding to the Indian mind, but journeying four days to buy a tin of food for a juvenile monkey must have seemed an act of sheer madness; when the order was given a look of incredulous surprise was visible on the usually stolid faces of my mozos, and I believe that in their eyes it was the wildest eccentricity in which I was ever known to indulge.

The monkey soon became devoted to its foster parent, and objected strongly to travelling on top of a pack carried by one of the men.

> I usually had to give in to him. . . ; and then he would sit contentedly on my shoulder with his tail round my neck crooning to himself; or if he were sleepy he would find his way inside my flannel shirt. [One night they had a serious disagreement, which Maudslay tried to settle by taking him into his bed.] By this time he was in a towering rage, and instead of going to sleep where I placed him under the blanket, he dashed out and danced a sort of war-dance on my chest, gesticulating fiercely. Then, after the manner of nurses, I had to give him a good spanking which only made him angrier than ever; but he knew that he was beaten, he gave up his war-dance and went to the bottom of the cot, covering his head with a rug. Then, like a naughty child, every

few minutes he would raise his head to [peeka] boo at me, and then hide it again under the rug, until at last, tired out, he fell asleep.

It was a moonlit night, and for some time longer I lay awake listening to the sounds of the alligators clashing their teeth – which sounds like a traveller's tale, but is not fiction. The river literally swarmed with these hideous creatures, and they have a queer habit of opening their mouths wide and bringing their teeth together with a snapping sound which can be heard from a long distance.

While passing through Benque Viejo Maudslay learnt of ruins across the river, which he mistakenly supposed to lie on the Guatemalan side of the border. This was the city now known as Xunantunich, where he noted 'several carved stelae, but unfortunately all the monuments are broken and much weather-worn. I was only able to give a few hours to examination of these ruins, and could not attempt to make any plan of the many-chambered buildings, which I feel sure would well repay further exploration.'

Having reached El Cayo and replenished his supplies, Maudslay sent off Carlos and José Domingo López and several men on a journey of five or six days to Tikal, with instructions to take paper moulds of the three stelae he had photographed five years earlier; he himself had not taken moulds of them because at that time he had not yet mastered the technique.[8]

A few days later, on 23 April, Maudslay started out on his last journey planned for the year, a reconnaissance of the Great Southern Pine Ridge (an uninhabited and little-known area south of El Cayo). He would also investigate the course of the Macal river, or 'Eastern Branch' of the Belize River, which comes from the south to join the 'Western Branch' or Río Mopán, flowing in from Petén. His motive on this trip was not simply archaeological (though it was that, too), but also political and economic. For as Wayne Clegern has shown, Maudslay wished to contribute usefully to the debates then current about commercial development in the Colony, and to do this he needed to enlarge his personal knowledge of the territory.[9]

It was not that he had any thought of personal involvement in local business. Instead, he seems to have regarded himself (with good reason) as unusually well qualified to offer advice on policies aimed at restoring the Colony's economic well-being. He could contribute his experience of the politics, economics, and internal communications of the Colony's neighbours, first-hand knowledge of the physical geography of a large part of the region and of living conditions within it, and then, of course, past experience of diplomacy and colonial administration.

The issues then in contention within government and business circles in the Colony arose from a worsening economic depression, largely due to the growing difficulty and expense of obtaining mahogany for export. The only feasible way to bring logs to the coast for trimming and loading for export was by floating them downriver, but as commercially workable stands of trees close to the river-banks became exhausted, and loggers had to go deeper into the forests, the expense of having them dragged by teams of oxen to the river banks increased proportionately. Then, to make matters worse, revenue from logwood, once valued as a source of brown dye, was falling as cheaper synthetic dyestuffs became available.

By this time, loggers from the Colony were already poised to penetrate beyond the border into Petén, where they could cut mahogany under licence from the Guatemalan government, but they faced a difficulty: the upper reaches of the Belize River were unsuited for transporting logs. It was then the idea of building a railway began to find support, since this was an era of railway promotions in Central America and Mexico, especially for the ambitious inter-oceanic links such as the Tehuantepec and Honduran railways.

Railway fever in Belize broke out with a mass demonstration held in 1884, but agreement as to best destination for a railway line was lacking. Some favoured a route terminating in Petén, whereas others boldly advocated a route running southwestward to Cobán, and thence to the capital, to link up with the line to San José. Yet another inter-oceanic route would thus come into being, albeit an extremely long one.

The first plan would have presented no serious engineering difficulties, but the second could have found support only at a time when reliable relief maps of the area were not yet available. The contorted and steep-sided valleys leading up to Cobán, and the three mountain ranges running from east to west, barring the way to Guatemala City, made this scheme quite hopeless; yet its advocates persevered in the hope that the British government would help underwrite its costs as a way of satisfying Guatemala's claim, based on the boundary treaty of 1859, that Britain was obliged to establish a cart road from Guatemala City to the Caribbean.

This, then, was one issue upon which Maudslay was thinking of offering his opinion to the Foreign Office. Another was the matter of encouraging immigration: a contribution to this could certainly be made by opening up fertile and well-watered land so long as road or rail connections were provided for transport of produce. One area that Maudslay evidently regarded as worth investigating for both settlement and railway construction was the Great Southern Pine Ridge, and it was for this reason that he was now setting out to reconnoitre it with the help of Gorgonio, eight men, and a French naturalist then living in El Cayo.

Their first night was spent at a small village in the high forest, San Antonio. Next day they passed into more open country, then into a great stretch of undulating terrain clothed with coarse grass and scattered pine trees. By the third day they found themselves gradually ascending to the top of a range known as the Blue Mountains, where the altitude as measured by Maudslay was 2600 feet. Continuing southwards and downhill, they came at last within sight of the Macal River, somewhere near the point where the Rascaculo branch flows into it, and they camped near it. Then, while the men were fetching water, the naturalist made the mistake of setting fire to the *camalote* reeds. Soon the thicket was a mass of flames, but luckily the wind carried the fire down to the riverbank and off to the west.

They turned in for the night, but awoke before dawn to find the wind had changed and the fire was coming at them. They all set to work firing the grass round camp and beating it out again with green boughs, until all of them were black with ash. Then the wind shifted again and the fire retreated.

> During the next few days [Maudslay wrote] we passed the time in a way that a school-boy fresh from Robinson Crusoe would have considered almost perfect, for we attempted to make a raft and float our baggage down the stream, whilst the mozos unencumbered with loads should cut their way through the thickets that lined the banks. However, it was not a success, as the following extracts from my scrappy journal will show: '29th April. The Pine Ridge is still burning to the NE of us. Have seen many tracks of tapir and deer, but cannot catch sight of the animals themselves. Started with the raft in the afternoon. Hard work hauling it over a shallow rapid before putting the luggage on board. Rapids rather close together. At the last rapid the raft caught on a snag and the food-box went overboard; recovered with difficulty, biscuits all sodden. – 30th April. Lashed more cross pieces to the raft, and then gave each mozo a small load to carry so as to lighten the cargo, but after a hard day's work only succeeded in rafting about a mile and a half, and had to unload the raft once in that short distance. Very hard work in the shallow rapids: determined to abandon the raft.'

They found an alligator's nest on a small island in the river and the men had a glorious supper off the thirty eggs they took out of it. The nest consisted of a great pile of dry sticks, leaves, grass, and sand, which the animal had scraped together to cover up the eggs. Walking back, partly over ground that the fire had cleared, they reached El Cayo on the 4th, and there found Carlos López and his party awaiting them with a doleful story to tell of their expedition:

> They had reached Tikal safely, but had met with no water to drink during the latter part of their journey, and when they arrived at the small lagoon near the ruins which had afforded us a supply in 1881

and 1882 it was only to find that it was completely dry. There was nothing to do but make the best of their way back again, and their sufferings were severe, as for three days they had nothing to drink beyond what they could collect from the water-lianas growing in the forest.

Having received their wages, the men set off on the long journey back to Cahabón, and Maudslay took a shallow-draught boat known as a *pitpan*, propelled by six paddlers, and reached Belize four days later. There is no record of whether he had time to kill before the next sailing, but if so he is likely to have made use of it by consulting merchants, colonial officials, and others about the colony's problems, and very likely putting some of his thoughts on paper.

Five months later he delivered a seven-thousand-word memorandum addressed to the Foreign Secretary, Lord Salisbury. Maudslay begins it with a reminder that Britain had yet to honour the commitment it assumed under the terms of the 1859 treaty with Guatemala, which stipulated that, in return for Guatemala's relinquishing its claim to the colony's territory, Britain was to construct a cart road from Guatemala City to some point on or near the Caribbean coast, such as Yzabal.

A Royal Engineers team was to survey the terrain for the road, and £50,000 would be provided for its construction. This money Guatemala expected to receive as a lump sum, whereas the Foreign Office insisted on it being paid in five instalments, all but the first of these payments being contingent on evidence of satisfactory progress with the road. The stalemate that ensued has endured ever since, and it has been responsible, until recently, for continuing tension and recrimination between the two countries.

Maudslay then surveys Guatemala's commercial routes, both maritime and internal. Until a few years earlier, Guatemala had had no port of entry on either coast, so that merchandise had to be shipped through the agency of merchants in Belize, for reshipment in small craft able to cross the bar at Livingston and land it at Yzabal, whence it was conveyed inland on pack-mules. This trade had benefited the Belize economy.

But just as the treaty was being negotiated, an effort was being made to open Guatemala's Pacific coast to international trade, a development which, if successful, would deprive Belize of its function as an entrepôt. Furthermore, three other more recent developments were threatening to eliminate Belize from Guatemala's trade altogether: the railway already connecting Guatemala City with San José, on the Pacific coast; a port of entry lately established at Livingston; and a railway planned to link the capital with a new deep-water port to be built south of Livingston. Construction of this had begun, but had not progressed far before the government ran out of funds. The first 30 miles might be built in connection with a plan to grow bananas in the lower Motagua valley, but

Maudslay considered completion of the whole line in the foreseeable future as unlikely.

It was his view that the British government had always intended the money to be spent on a project of mutual benefit to Guatemala and British Honduras (a debatable assumption, for it could be interpreted as simply a *quid pro quo* for obtaining title to the colony). In any case, he saw no advantage in the money being spent in that area; better it be devoted to building a railway from Belize to Petén.

As to the route, his trip into the Blue Mountains had convinced him of the unsuitablity of that area for railway construction. A route through El Cayo presented fewer problems, and it would serve several purposes. The mahogany cutters could bring their logs from a wider area, especially if tram-lines were run out into the forest. He foresaw the line enjoying good business in bringing into Petén all the trade goods that were currently being carried in by porters from Cobán, or brought by mules from Tenosique, in Mexico, which were therefore very expensive. The line would pass within reach of the Pine Ridge, which he thought held promise as cattle country (but this opinion was almost certainly mistaken, for in that area the limestone capping has gone, and the soils, which overlie sedimentary beds of shale, quartzite, and intrusive granite, are low in natural plant food; also, the tall, coarse grass and reeds are more regularly swept by fires than he could have realized).

He predicted a future for banana cultivation, too. There were already many small plantations, but co-ordination of their cutting for shipment was impossible without a telegraph service for giving notice of the arrival of a steamer, and a railway was needed for prompt delivery of fruit to the pier, such as existed in Costa Rica. It was because fruit from the colony didn't reach the wholesalers in New Orleans in such uniformly fresh condition as that from Costa Rica, that it commanded only half the price.

Maudslay's prophesy of a future for bananas was to be fulfilled a quarter of a century later, when a 25-mile-long narrow-gauge railway was built from the pier at Stann Creek, south of Belize, to Middlesex for carriage of fruit. This industry made a promising start, but ended in failure when Panama disease struck the plantations. The railway struggled on for a while transporting lumber.

Wayne Clegern, who discovered and published this document, describes the fate of Maudslay's memorandum after he delivered it:

> [Its] odyssey in the Foreign Office is indicative both of its authoritative quality and of the low priority which concerns of British Honduras commanded in London. Its arrival at the Foreign Office late in 1887 went almost unnoticed in the midst of that department's rather heated three-way dialogue with the Colonial Office and the Treasury. For reasons unexplained it was pigeonholed for more than

two years; for practical purposes it was lost. Maudslay had very generously sent along two explanatory maps, one of them in manuscript. On several occasions he requested the return of the maps, but the Foreign Office Librarian denied all knowledge of them.

On 18 February 1890, the memorandum and maps were rediscovered. Sir Edward Hertslet, Foreign Office Librarian, legal consultant, and famed editor of many volumes of British treaties and state papers, arrived at his office that morning to find Maudslay's memorandum and maps lying on his desk. Hertslet apparently had not seen these papers before, and knew of them only through Maudslay's requests for the return of his maps. Upon inquiry Hertslet found that the janitor had retrieved them from a trash box ready for the incinerator. Attracted by the technical appearance of the maps, the man had brought the entire roll of papers to Hertslet's desk to be checked before destruction. Hertslet then perceived that the report and maps were quite important. He forwarded them to the office of the Under-Secretary for Foreign Affairs, where a subordinate summed up in a line the misadventure of maps and memorandum: 'It is a pity we have not had this Report sooner.'

The memorandum was printed for circulation within the government, more copies of the published map were ordered, and the manuscript map was sent to the Intelligence Department to be reproduced. Letters were dispatched to Maudslay, who was now in Egypt, thanking him for his efforts, and apologizing for the long delay in returning his map.

Once recovered, the Maudslay memorandum was very influential within government councils. Great Britain had refused to discuss the road and boundary questions with Guatemala since 1884 because the British government simply had been unable to arrive at a consensus on these questions, and the Guatemalan government was in no position to force a decision.[10]

Clegern reports that a joint Foreign Office–Colonial Office conference was then held, and the newly appointed British minister to Guatemala was briefed in the light of Maudslay's information. In the few discussions held with Guatemala in the 1890s, 'one of the notable characteristics of those negotiations was that the British negotiator grasped, more firmly than did the Guatemalan, the facts of the dispute and the relationship of the dispute to the entire Central American situation'.

Chapter 12

Chichén Itzá

Having investigated four great Maya cities, as well as some smaller ones, Maudslay had reached the conclusion that each of them – including Palenque, as far as he could tell from published pictures – shared a common tradition of art, iconography, hieroglyphic writing, and architecture, although there were regional differences among them, as might be expected. Regarding the question of their antiquity, he now felt sure that all of the great cities known to him at first hand had been abandoned well before the arrival of Spaniards in the early sixteenth century. This view was consistent with evidence found in early colonial documents (partial and indirect though such evidence might be), and it tallied with the degree of delapidation that he found among the ruins.

But what of Chichén Itzá? It was possible that at the time of the Conquest this great centre had not long passed its heyday, and might even have retained a vestigial population, as suggested by the fact that, when the Spaniards arrived, rites were still being performed at the Cenote of Sacrifice, or Sacred Well. There were known to be hieroglyphic inscriptions at these ruins, as well as great quantities of figurative sculpture and many well-preserved buildings. If Chichén did represent a late period of Maya history, then it would be worth comparing its remains with those of sites further south. Such a comparison could be of crucial importance in attempts to reconstruct the prehistory of the Maya, and place them more firmly in the sequence of prehistoric Mexican civilizations.

On grounds such as these, Maudslay chose Chichén Itzá as the focus of his field season for 1889. In going to this site he would be breaking new ground, since he was a complete stranger to Yucatán, having had no closer acquaintance with it than distant views of its coastline from a steamer. Worse, he had few contacts there and no information about the availability of labourers at Chichén; nor had he arranged for any of his reliable Guatemalan helpers, the López family, to meet him there – a decision he later came to regret.

Once again Maudslay obtained from the Royal Geographical Society the loan of a half-chronometer watch and other instruments, and then, in his own terse account,

Chichén Itzá

Towards the end of the year 1888 I journeyed by way of New York and Havana to Progreso, the chief port of Yucatan. Here I passed a month in much discomfort, waiting for the arrival of my heavy baggage from England, and for letters which had been promised me from Government authorities in Mexico. . . . The vessel with the baggage met with such heavy weather in the Gulf that she passed Progreso [where there is no harbour or shelter] without attempting to land cargo, and went for a trip round the other Gulf ports, returning finally a fortnight later. During this time I was able to make a flying visit to Mr. E. H. Thompson, the American Consul, who was engaged upon a most thorough examination of the ruins of Labna, and also to spend one day at the great ruins of Uxmal. Then followed the usual delay in passing the baggage through the Custom-house, although orders had come from Mexico that all my stores should be entered free of duty. . . . At the end of the month I was heartily tired of Merida, and was delighted to turn my back on it. I was able to travel along the new railroad as far as Cacalchen and carry with me as much of my baggage as had come to hand. Unluckily this did not include the moulding-paper, which despite telegrams and letters was delayed for a month or more in Havana, and at last arrived half destroyed by salt water.

Maudslay may have expected Mérida to be the charming, sleepy town that Stephens described. He found instead a modernized town in the throes of a sisal hemp boom. The stony soil of Yucatán will grow just one crop very well: *henequén*, a kind of aloe, from the leaves of which the sisal fibre is obtained. With McCormick's invention of the mechanical reaper-and-binder, and the cultivation of wheat over vast areas of the Middle West, demand soon soared for sisal binder-twine ('beendery-tweeny', as Yucatecs used to call it). The McCormick-Deering Company, in fact, exerted immense influence on the destiny of the province. For several decades Yucatán was to enjoy new prosperity, and a network of narrow-gauge railways was just then being built to transport the sisal to Progreso (formerly it had been taken for shipment to another port, Sisal, from which the hemp takes its common name in English).

But the destruction of the Manila hemp crop by a typhoon in the Philippines not long before had caused the price of sisal to rise from 2 to 13 cents a pound. For Maudslay, this boom was not a fortunate state of affairs:

I had need of many hands to help in clearing the ruins, and now that every proprietor was eager to increase the size of his henequen plantation, field-labourers were in great demand; I could only hope that as Chichen lay far from the centre of commercial activity, the villages in its neighbourhood might for some time yet escape the effects of the 'boom'.

In Guatemala and Honduras Maudslay had depended on local officials for help in engaging labourers, but in Yucatán, in spite of bearing recommendations from the Mexican government to the local authorities, he found these authorities seldom to be in a position to oblige, as the Indian labourers were firmly under the control of a few large land-owners.

From the rail-head at Cacalchén Maudslay continued his journey over a long and rocky road to Valladolid by *volan-coche*, a two-wheeled spring-less cart usually drawn by three mules abreast, and provided with a mat-tress for the traveller to lie on. There he presented his papers to the local authorities and made the best arrangements he could for a supply of labourers. Then from Valladolid he had to backtrack to a village where there would be horses and porters available to carry the baggage over the last stage of the journey, 12 miles through the forest to Pisté, the nearest village to Chichén.[1]

Pisté had been completely abandoned because of raids during the Indian rising known as the War of the Castes, which began in 1847 and in the Tulum area did not peter out completely until the First World War. Only two years before Maudslay's arrival, his friend Frederick Godman had been told in Mérida that it would be unsafe for him to visit Chichén Itzá.[2] But now Pisté was beginning to be repopulated, and a few houses had been repaired. There Maudslay managed to recruit a few workers, so on about 11 February he moved to Chichén and took up his quarters in the Casa Colorada. From that time onwards until 2 July he was continu-ously at work at the ruins, save for about two weeks spent in visits to Valladolid and Izamal trying to recruit more labourers.[3]

Although accurate data on Chichén were lacking, the ruins were far better known than the others Maudslay had worked at. In 1532, during the hard-won conquest of Yucatán, Francisco Montejo the younger estab-lished a base among these ruins. The Maya chieftains of the area, the Cupules, initially showed – or feigned – tolerance of the invaders coming to a place which had, for them, great political, religious, and military significance. Montejo confidently named his new town Ciudad Real, but, before it had become well established the Cupules rose against the Spaniards and laid siege to them. In defending themselves the latter turned several of the ruined buildings into forts, and installed a gun in the western corridor of the Castillo (the tallest temple), having made a breach in the wall through which to point it. For several months they held out until imminent starvation forced the survivors to slip away during the night.

After that, not much is heard of Chichén Itzá until 1843, when Stephens published his book, famously embellished with Catherwood's illustrations. And then, some four years later, the War of the Castes broke out, keeping most visitors away for nearly forty years, although two bold

Frenchmen did come to Chichén: one was Désiré Charnay in 1860 (escorted by a troop of soldiers), and the other, Augustus Le Plongeon.[4] The latter, who arrived in 1873, remained there long enough to take a large number of excellent photographs, many of them stereoscopic, and to indulge in excavation.

Le Plongeon was the very archetype of the imaginative and deluded antiquary. Turning the tables on those who saw the rise of American cultures as resulting from transatlantic contacts, he demonstrated to his own satisfaction that the true cradle of civilization was Mesoamerica. Transatlantic contacts, he insisted, went the other way, and the Greek alphabet, alpha, beta, gamma, delta was but a hymn in Mayan. At Chichén Itzá, following clues in hieroglyphic inscriptions, which he claimed to read with perfect ease (except for those of Palenque), Le Plongeon dug at a spot indicated by these texts and found a splendid large Chacmool statue (this term was his coinage), supposedly at a depth of 25 feet, though its discovery at such a depth seems highly unlikely, for the soil cover there is shallow.

With his bald head, penetrating gaze, long straggly beard, and confident knowledge of recondite histories, Augustus Le Plongeon must have made a deep impression in Yucatán. Some, however, were less deeply impressed, including the Mexican government, which confiscated his Chacmool, to his acute indignation.

Apart from Le Plongeon's photographs, and those of Charnay, little had been added in forty years to the store of reliable information about the site, with most of that still being owed to Stephens and Catherwood. Maudslay's arrival was therefore opportune.

Quite soon after he had begun work at Chichén Itzá Maudslay realized that the man he had engaged in Mérida as overseer was useless. This man invented a story about his dying mother as pretext for a leave of absence, and tried to trick Maudslay out of a month's pay in advance, clearly not intending to return.

> I then gave up all hopes of finding another overseer and chose the most intelligent amongst my workmen to take charge of the tools and act as 'caporal.' During the first few weeks all my men were from Pisté, and as they returned to their homes before dark, I was left to sleep in the ruins alone. For a few nights I paid one of the Indians an extra 'real' to stop for the night; but as he could speak no Spanish, conversation was impossible, and the way he sat silently on the floor and followed my every movement with his eyes was worse than a nightmare, so I soon gave up the experiment, infinitely preferring the solitude of the ruins to his company.

He set to work clearing the earth and rubble which had accumulated round the base of the buildings.

As usual, I had been laughed at by my acquaintances for bringing with me wheelbarrows and spades, being assured by them that the Indians would never be persuaded to use them. They told me that an Indian's method of digging was to scrape a little earth together with his hands and, in a leisurely way, to ladle it into a small basket of plaited leaves or into his straw hat, if a basket were not at hand, and then to saunter off and empty the contents at a few yards distance. I must own that there was some difficulty in persuading the newcomers that four men were not needed to take charge of one wheelbarrow, one to fill it half-full of stones, and three to look on and see that the load was not unduly heavy, and then with united effort to lift it by the wheel and two handles and carry it off bodily. I did once see an Indian load a wheelbarrow with a few stones, and (with the help of two friends to raise it up) carry off the loaded barrow on the top of his head. However . . . as soon as they found the wheels went round, and that their labour was lightened by the use of them, they always took kindly to wheelbarrows.

In March Mr Thompson paid me a short visit accompanied by Mr. H. Sweet, who had been assisting him in his work at Labná. Mr. Sweet was about to return home to Boston, but he was much attracted by the work to be done at Chichén, and I exerted my powers of persuasion to the utmost to induce him to stay with me. At last he promised that should the letters he expected to receive on his return to Mérida enable him to prolong his stay in Yucatán, he would come back to pay me another visit. Not many days later to my great delight he rode into camp, and I secured a charming companion for the remainder of my stay at the ruins.

Henry Sweet, a native of Lancaster, New Hampshire, was twenty-nine when he came to Yucatán with Thompson. After studying at the Massachusetts Institute of Technology he spent some time working in Florida as a surveyor, some of it in company with his boyhood friend John Weeks. At the time of Sweet's departure for Yucatán a successful banker named Henry Hornblower had taken Weeks into partnership to form a brokerage house, Hornblower and Weeks (which became very well known), and it may be that Sweet was hoping that among the letters he went back to collect in Mérida he might find one inviting him to join them in some capacity. Such an offer was several years in coming, but Sweet did later join the firm, and went on to become a partner.

Sweet had been engaged for the Labná expedition by Charles P. Bowditch, the Boston banker, whose enthusiasm for Maya archaeology, and ability to persuade his rich friends to join him in financing expeditions, were responsible for the dispatch of several Peabody Museum expeditions over the next twenty-five years. This one to Labná would be the first, and in its planning and direction Bowditch naturally collaborated with and deferred to Frederick W. Putnam, Curator of the Museum and Professor of American Archaeology at Harvard University. But as yet there was no course of study in archaeology, hence no students, and a team of outsiders had to be recruited. Edward H. Thompson was engaged as field director, Sweet as photographer, and another man as surveyor.

As Putnam wrote in a memo to Bowditch,

> Mr Thompson must understand how little information we have that is of importance in determining who were the people who made the great structures, beyond that obtained from the misty history of the time of Cortes, and the Maya and Nahuatl myths. . . . That the Mayas have lived in Yucatan for a considerable time cannot be questioned. Were they the first race that came there, or did they take possession of the deserted country and occupy the structures they found?[5]

Their hopes of settling these questions lay in excavation, and Thompson was sent instructions by mail as to how he should proceed; among other things he was encouraged to collect skulls.

Thompson did make some useful contributions. His identification of small mounds scattered throughout the site as being house mounds convincingly demonstrated that such ruins were not exclusively ceremonial centres, but residential as well; and, by emptying out a number of *chultuns* (bottle-shaped subterranean storage chambers), he drew attention to the fact that some were used, puzzlingly, for purposes other than their primary one of serving as rain-water cisterns. With this expedition, the Peabody Museum, under the aegis of Bowditch and Putnam, took its first tentative steps into the world of Mesoamerican archaeology, thereby initiating a series of more productive expeditions.

When young, Thompson, a native of Worcester, Massachusetts, had written an article entitled 'Atlantis not a Myth',[6] thereby attracting the attention of Stephen Salisbury, president of the American Antiquarian Society (based in the same town), since Salisbury tended to encourage those propounding exotic and mystical interpretations of antiquity – among them, for a time, Le Plongeon.

Thompson was taken on by Putnam largely because he already had some experience in exploring ruins in Yucatán, for Salisbury had managed to have him appointed as US Consul in Mérida, a post from which he was able to take an annual three-month leave of absence. He seems to have been a man of strong physique, practical and self-assured, a good photographer, and a good story-teller, though not endowed with good judgment, nor gifted enough to overcome the disadvantage of a mediocre education. He also had a pronounced streak of the romantic adventurer in his make-up.

During their visit to Maudslay at Chichén Itzá, Sweet was greatly impressed by Maudslay and his manner of working – as he seems not to have been by Thompson.[7] The latter, for his part, regarded Sweet's decision to stay on in Yucatán and help Maudslay as a defection, even though he had completed the full period of work at Labná that he had contracted to do. Thompson thought Maudslay was working for the British Museum or some other institution, and was afraid the Englishman would learn from Sweet the details of his work and plans.

> It is not very pleasant [as Thompson complained to Putnam] to think that the expedition has furnished a man to work for a rival Society of a rival nation, but Mr Maudslay is rich and generous, has no thought of the money he spends while at work, consequently he probably makes it to the advantage of Mr S. in some way to work for him. . . . Of one thing I am certain, that Maudslay's work will not in any way approach in value our work done and to be done in the future. A dozen different people have been to Chichen Itza and Uxmal and taken moulds and made plans of a portion of the group only, and Maudslay has done the same only on a more accurate basis and on a larger scale.[8]

By the time Sweet arrived, a considerable amount of clearing had been done, and Maudslay had shifted his quarters to the large building known as the 'Monjas', choosing the long central chamber on the south side of the second level as his study and sleeping quarters. This has three doorways, and since it stands on a basement structure 30 feet high it catches the breeze and gives a fine view over the scrub-forest. Wattle 'doors' were installed to reduce the heat and glare in the middle of the day, and to keep out animals at night.

> To the southward, [in Maudslay's words] where no clearing had yet been made, the sea of verdure spread unbroken from our feet. During the lovely tropical nights, when a gentle breeze swayed the tree-tops, and the moonlight rippled over the foliage, it seemed to be a real sea in motion below us, and one almost expected to feel the pulsation of ocean waves against the walls. In the daytime the woods were alive with birds; the beautiful motmots were so tame that they flew fearlessly in and out of our rooms, and the mocking-birds and scarlet cardinals poured forth a flood of melody such as I have never heard equalled.

Later on, the heat became intense by day and showers were frequent; then the cloud effects were most beautiful, and they never tired of watching the storm-clouds, three or four at a time in different directions, travelling across the country.

To Sweet's arrival at the most critical moment the success of my expedition was very largely due. He was keenly interested in his work, and . . . we spent a very happy three months together. Sweet undertook all the photography, and was also of the greatest assistance in the survey; and with his ever-ready help and cheery companion-ship I could make light of the numberless petty annoyances and delays which were so hard to bear when I was alone; moreover he supplied that invaluable stimulus to work which came from dis-cussing with an intelligent companion the various problems which presented themselves for solution as the clearings widened out and the remains of the ancient city were disclosed to our view.

The presence of Henry Sweet was never more of a blessing than when fever struck them.[9]

'During the month of May', Maudslay tells, 'we were both ill with fever, but as our attacks fortunately occurred on alternate days we could each take it in turn to be nurse and patient'. The fever left them both very weak, and as they were at that time entirely deserted by their workmen they had the greatest difficulty in supplying themselves with firewood and water. Bringing a bucket of water up from the steep-sided Xtoloc cenote, then across 400 yards of level ground and up the steep and par-tially dislocated stairway of the Monjas was an ordeal requiring frequent rests along the way. Fortunately by dosing themselves with quinine both men recovered and were able to resume work, although they still felt very feeble for many days.

Once the central area of the ruins had been cleared, Maudslay began making a quite detailed examination of the buildings, and having them cleared of earth, tree-roots, and rubble – as far as the uncertain supply of labor permitted. One motive for doing this was to reveal corners, door-ways, and other features of buildings so as to plot them securely on his map, but over and above this he was studying the architecture and build-ing sequences.

Maudslay can be credited with several specific contributions to knowledge of Chichén Itzá architecture. One concerns the serpent-columns found at the entrance to the upper ball-court temple and in other buildings: large stone serpent-heads are set at the foot of the columns, but in all cases the capitals and portions of the façade supported by them had fallen.[10] Maudslay found broken stones carved to represent rattlesnake tails, and these he was able to show had each formed one limb of an L-shaped capital, set with the rattle turned upward – a feature missed by the archaeologist W. H. Holmes, usually a careful observer. Maudslay also showed that tenoned frets found in debris fallen from various buildings had originally been set vertically along the edges of the roof, like the antefixes on Doric temples. Such observations added to the accuracy of the reconstruction drawings which he afterwards had an artist prepare of a few buildings, including the upper temple of the ball-court.

When Maudslay's plan of Chichén Itzá is laid over the Carnegie Institution of Washington's professionally surveyed plan (which, of course, was produced under very much easier conditions), the close correspondence between them speaks well for Maudslay's work. He appears to have used a plane-table and alidade for the survey – equipment that makes an exceedingly awkward load to carry from one surveying 'station' to another, especially when the whole site is littered with heaps of rubble, felled trees and bushes. And because triangulation may sometimes have been blocked by large buildings, and extension of a metal tape across a lot of rubbbish would also be difficult to achieve, he must occasionally have had to rely on the less accurate stadia rod for measurement of the distance between two 'stations'.

Maudslay's plotting of the 'Caracol' provides a good example of his careful work. A slipshod archaeological surveyor, working under pressure of time and in debilitating heat, might simply have taken 'shots' on two adjacent corners of the main substructure, thus defining the length and orientation of one side, then measured a neighbouring side with a tape-measure, and drawn the substructure as rectangular in plan. Upon this substructure stands a smaller and much lower platform which serves as the base for the Caracol itself, a round structure. This platform, measured in similar time-saving fashion, might also have been represented as rectangular, with sides parallel to those of the substructure. This is how the two structures were described and illustrated by Holmes after his 1894 visit. Maudslay, however, correctly shows the irregular shape of this platform with its sides unequal, and none of them parallel to those of the similarly unsymmetrical substructure.

When in June a few labourers once more presented themselves, Maudslay and Sweet began making paper moulds with the damaged paper that had come so late. The most important and successful mould was of the decoration in the Lower Temple of the Jaguars chamber, the interior walls of which are embellished all over with low-relief carvings showing a procession of warriors dressed in an interesting variety of raiment and equipped with instruments of ceremony and war. The façade had collapsed, filling the interior with rubble up to the spring of the vault, so that when Charnay visited Chichén in 1860 only the rear half of the vault could be photographed. Maudslay had the chamber carefully cleared, finding in the process a jaguar altar in the doorway.

The scene of our labours was about three-quarters of a mile from our house and nearly half a mile from the cenote [again, the Xtoloc cenote, not the Sacred Well], from which all the water had to be carried on men's backs. The heat was terrific, for the ruined chamber formed a sort of shallow cave facing E.S.E., into which the June sun poured its rays until past noon, raising it to the heat of an oven. We could not begin work until three o'clock in the afternoon, and even then the wall was so hot that the damp paper refused to adhere to it, and the precious water had to be freely used to cool it down; time after time a half-finished mould would fall away from the heated surface and the labour would have to be gone through again. All the moulding had to be done with our own hands, as no native could be found competent to help us; and as I was still busy on the survey, the heavier share fell on Mr. Sweet.

By the end of June the food stores were nearly exhausted, and there was scarcely anything to be bought locally.[11] For the last day or two they lived on nothing more than a little rice and some beef-tea, and thus on 2 July were obliged to pack up and start out on the return journey to Mérida.

So ended the longest and most gruelling of Maudslay's expeditions. Earlier, he and Sweet had intended, on leaving Chichén Itzá, to put in two or three weeks' work at Uxmal, but in their state of exhaustion this was out of the question, and had to be postponed for the following year. Five months' hard work in the heat of Yucatán under very difficult conditions, plus a bout of malaria, was more than most Europeans could endure. As it was, Maudslay thought he had left for a change of climate just in time to save him from a serious illness, and it took more than six months for him to recover his usual health.

The moulds reached London safely, and an excellent cast was obtained of the back wall of the Lower Temple of the Jaguars. Maudslay directed the painting of it to correspond with traces of colour still visible on the original.

For some reason the expedition to Uxmal planned for the following year never happened (although it was revived as a secondary goal for the year after that), nor did Henry Sweet ever again take part in archaeological fieldwork. Yet the experience that he had at Chichén must have affected him profoundly, for when he died, two years after Maudslay, it was found that he had bequeathed one-tenth of his estate to the Peabody Museum.

Chapter 13

Palenque

It does seem unlikely that Maudslay would seriously have considered putting into effect his notion of working at Uxmal in the winter of 1889–90. For one thing, if comfort were a consideration, the climate of Yucatán practically required him to leave England by early December, and to do this he would have had to start mailing tentative plans to agents in Yucatán by September. Yet at that time he may still have felt unsure of recouping enough of his strength for such an expedition by the end of the year. And besides, never before had he made major expeditions in two successive years, for reasons already suggested.

Whatever his reasons may have been, Maudslay did indeed give up the idea of going – and just as well, because Uxmal, for all its glorious architecture, would have yielded sparse hieroglyphic and iconographic material of the kind he had become so adept at recording. Besides, Uxmal was notoriously malarious.

Instead, he decided to avoid the ever-present threat of British bronchitis by escaping to Egypt, taking some of his family with him. We catch glimpses of him in the Egyptologist Charles Wilbour's book *Travels in Egypt*, composed of letters he wrote home.

11 February 1890: 'We had brought to the boat [Wilbour's *dahabeeyeh* or Nile boat, *The Seven Hathors*] the seat of a statue with unknown letters on the back like this: [drawing of signs omitted]. In the evening Ned and I went to the *Timsaah* (an English *dahabeeyeh*) and Mr. A. P. Maudslay, who has worked seven seasons on the Mayan antiquities in Central America, showed and explained to us many fine photographs taken by him at Copan. He with four others of his family are on one of [Thomas] Cook's new *dahabeeyehs*, the one he showed me, the *Osiris*, at a cost of twelve pounds and a half a day, Mr. Robertson says.' [p. 553]

25 February 1890: 'Mohammed had shown us, and Mr. Maudslay has now purchased, the gold-shod breast scarab of the Heretic King, the finest scarab I ever saw.' [p. 558]

26 February 1890: 'Sayce and Robertson had been to Karnak with the girls and the Maudslays, and we all tea-ed on the *Timsaah*.' [p. 558]

3 March 1890: 'The Laimbeers called on us and we saw the *Osiris* folk, our Mr. Maudslay suffering from his Nicaraguan malaria.' [p. 560][1]

The scarab bought by Maudslay is described as having a base of gold, and being inscribed with the name of Akhenaton, allegedly from the Royal Tomb at Amarna in Middle Egypt. Unfortunately the scarab's whereabouts are now unknown.[2]

A year later Maudslay was back in Mexico, with Palenque his goal. It may seem strange that he hadn't settled years earlier on this queen of Maya cities as an objective, so famous had it become since the visit of Stephens and Catherwood nearly fifty years before. At that great ruined city so many buildings of distinctive and elegant architecture were still standing, their walls inset with panels of fine-grained limestone carved in well-preserved relief, or embellished with moulded stucco figures. The setting of this city, as shown in Catherwood's views, is also without peer, for it is built on a ledge near the foot of a chain of hills (the nearest being of almost conical shape), yet it stands high enough above the flood-plain below to furnish a splendid view over its broad expanse towards the Gulf of Mexico.

Maudslay gives us no hint, but it seems likely that he reserved Palenque for his very last expedition in the Maya area, hoping that through his work at Chichén Itzá he would have earned the trust of government officials in Mexico City. But having also learnt to his cost how difficult labourers had been to obtain at Chichén, he must have been concerned about an even worse situation confronting him in a region more sparsely populated, and provided with even poorer communications. So if an adequate supply of manpower was to be obtained, government orders addressed to state and local officials would be essential.[3]

Accordingly, he went first to Mexico City, and with the help of the British Minister, Sir Spencer St John, procured from the Minister of Foreign Affairs, Ignacio Mariscal, a letter of recommendation to the Governor of Chiapas; also a general letter addressed to all local officials. Then, shortly before Christmas 1890, he took passage at Veracruz on a Ward Line vessel for Progreso, and there transferred, with great misgivings, to a coaster bound for Frontera, at the mouth of the Grijalva River – this taking him, in fact, halfway back to Veracruz.

It was the season of *nortes*, fierce north winds, and this boat was a stern-wheel river boat with 7 feet of hull underwater, and 20 feet of cabins and flying bridge above. 'The captain owned to me that he had very nearly been blown over on his last voyage down the coast, and that should he be caught in really bad weather there would be no alternative but to turn the ship's head to the shore and pile her up on the beach.' A few days later, when they crossed the bar and anchored at Laguna, the sky was so threatening that he thought it wiser to unload all his equipment there instead of at Frontera. (The Usumacinta River flows into the Gulf through two navigable rivers, one debouching at Frontera, the other into the Laguna de Términos, with the port of Ciudad del Carmen at one side of the lagoon's principal outlet to the Gulf.)

At Laguna, as Ciudad del Carmen was called in Maudslay's day, he found about twenty-three sailing vessels of various nationalities loading timber,

> and one might say that twenty-three mates were feeling very hot and using strong language as the mahogany logs were hauled on board, and that twenty-three sea-captains were on shore on a spree. . . . Three-card Monte began, as far as I could make out, at about nine o'clock in the morning, but I am not sure that in some cases it was not a continuation of the game of the night before. . . . [However,] I never heard the slightest dispute which was not settled at once and quite amicably.
>
> During the last part of the two weary weeks I had to pass in town, much of my time was passed in the Custom House. Orders had come to pass all my stores free of duty; but this did not prevent the Custom House officers opening every case and weighing the contents, and making out endless unnecessary lists. . . . At last my preparations were finished; Mr. Price, who had volunteered to come out from England and assist as a surveyor, had joined me, and I had secured a small steamer . . . to take us up the river.

In the hotel he had met another lodger, a Frenchman named Louis (or in Mexico, Ludovico) Chambon. This young man was in Mexico with the idea of writing a book about his travels, and now, having read Charnay's *Ancient Cities of the New World*, was hoping to visit 'La Ville Lorillard' himself.[4] But many days had passed without the arrival of any steamer to take him up-river to Tenosique, so Maudslay offered to take him on his as far as Montecristo (now known as Emiliano Zapata).

> As usual there was some delay in starting, and after we had crossed the big lagoon [on 2 January], and passed through the narrow passage into the smaller one our troubles began. We had missed the top of the tide and found it running out strongly against us and we stuck on one sandbank after another; at last we reached the mouth of the river, where huge alligators lay sunning themselves on the sand-spits, and here, where the stream was at its narrowest, we stuck fast; there was no chance of getting off until the tide rose on the morrow. Then began a night of torment. The mosquitoes were monsters and they came off to us in myriads; we had no nets to protect us against their attacks, and the only thing to do was to roll one's self up in a rug in a beddingless bunk and swelter until morning. Soon after sunrise we were afloat again and entered the broad stream of the river. . . . On the

third day we reached the little village of Monte Cristo, which was to be our starting-place for the ruins of Palenque.

At Monte Cristo we fell into good hands. Don Carlos Majares, who kept the largest of the two or three village stores, gave us a big shed in which to house our baggage and hang up our hammocks, and he and Don Adolfo Erezuma did their best to help us on our way, but the difficulties could not be overcome in a hurry. The ruins of Palenque lay buried in the forest forty miles away, and as pack-mules and carriers were equally scarce nearly a fortnight passed before we had succeeded in despatching the most necessary part of our stores to Santo Domingo, a village six miles distant from the ruins.

Maudslay found some diversion from forced idleness in wandering along the banks of lagoons or the river, and watching the innumerable aquatic birds, especially the beautiful little parras running over water-weeds;

but the most beautiful of all were the great flocks of rose-coloured 'chocoloteras,' spoon-billed wading-birds as big as cranes and more brilliant than flamingos. They were not very quick to take fright, and now and then I could so manage that a flight would pass in long line close overhead, and I could watch them until they faded from sight in a sunset sky. . . .

At last the day came that we were able to make a start for Palenque: Don Adolfo lent us horses for ourselves, and four or five wretched pack-mules carried part of the baggage. Luckily for us some half-dozen Indians from the Sierra had just paid their yearly visit to Monte Cristo to sell their cargoes of wild cacao and buy machetes and a supply of salt, and as their return loads were not heavy, after much persuasion they agreed to carry some of our things, and it was to their care that we had to confide our surveying instruments and such articles as could not safely be put on a mule's back. As the Indians had all been hopelessly drunk the night before, we did not get off very early, although our efforts to start commenced before dawn, and what with bad mules, sulky muleteers, and half-drunken Indians we had a hard day of it.

Around noon the next day they arrived at Santo Domingo, and with some difficulty managed to hire an empty hut as a lodging – it could hardly be called a house. In times past, when Chiapas was part of Guatemala, Palenque had been a town of some importance on the main road to Guatemala, but with the abandonment of this road Palenque had dwindled to a sleepy little village of twenty houses.

It lies so far out of the world that it was strange to find the two inhabitants of most importance to be one the son of a Frenchman, the other the son of a Swiss doctor, and the latest addition to the society to be a

Corsican, who, though poverty forced him to live the life of the poorer class of native, had not yet lost all his energy and was wildly excited about some minerals which had been found in the sierra, on which he was building golden hopes of a return in riches to his own country. Alas! the specimens with which he loaded my boxes on my return home proved to be nothing but valueless pyrites, and I fear the sandalled feet of the cheery fellow still tread the grass-grown street of Santo Domingo.

As the track to the ruins was, we were told, entirely overgrown, our first business was to get it cleared, so I made a play with [my] letter from the Minister of Foreign Affairs in Mexico . . . [and] by this means I managed to secure a few labourers until arrangements could be made with the higher authorities for a regular supply of workmen.

His letter to the Governor in San Cristóbal had already been sent from Laguna, but an answer could not yet be expected; meanwhile he sent a messenger to the Jefe Político in El Salto, only two days' journey away. When they came, the answers were satisfactory, but unfortunately free voluntary labour was almost an unknown thing in those countries, and without the help of the local authorities nothing could be done. He had asked for thirty labourers, and these were promised, but the number, though at first exceeding fifteen, gradually dwindled to three or four. This was very disheartening, and he telegraphed both Mexico and San Cristóbal, knowing quite well, though, that it would be of little use. On 16 February he received a visit from the Jefe, and he at last was able to produce twenty men from the Chol Maya village of Tumbalá.

Before the end of a week the track to the ruins had been cleared, and Hugh Price had engineered log-bridges over the muddy-banked streamlets which crossed the path, so that pack-mules could pass in safety, and we prepared to leave the village and take up our quarters in the Palace. . . . On arriving at the ruins we tied up our mules at the foot of the Palace mound and set to work to carry up our baggage and arrange our beds and camp-furniture in the house on the west side of the Eastern Court, which was chosen as the driest place to be found.

The mozos had already done something towards clearing the house of rubbish and cutting away with their knives the rank vegetation immediately around it. When I used the word 'driest' it was only as a term of comparison, for the house was anything but dry. The great forest around us hung heavy with wet, the roof above us was dripping water like a slow and heavy rainfall, and the walls were glistening and running with moisture, so that it took time to select places for our beds, where the drip was lightest, and then to protect them with water-proof coverings.

An hour before sunset the *mozos* went back to the village with the mules, and Maudslay, Price, and Chambon, who had come with them to Palenque, were left alone to shift for themselves in their damp abode.

Day by day, as the vegetation was cleared away and the sunlight let in on it, our house became drier and some of the discomfort disappeared; then there came the repetition of the old old trouble, which has haunted me since my expeditions began – a message was sent from the village that no mozos could come to work for some days on account of a fiesta. There was no help for it, so I determined to use the time in a journey to Monte Cristo, to arrange for the transport of the rest of my baggage which was still stored there.

He engaged a muleteer and some pack-mules in Santo Domingo, and expected to complete the journey in one day, but soon lost patience with the continual stoppages and delays caused by the surliest and most ill-mannered *arriero* it had ever been his fate to encounter, so he and Louis Chambon went on by themselves, and found their way before nightfall to Monte Cristo, where Don Carlos gave them a kindly welcome.

In front of Don Carlos's house an awning had been stretched across the grass-grown street, and a wooden floor laid down to form a ball-room for the villagers, for the morrow was Shrove Tuesday, and we learnt that in Monte Cristo the Carnival is a matter of no small impor-tance. All was quiet when we arrived, but we were told that dancing had been kept up the night before from dusk to dawn, and we had hardly finished our supper when the company began to flock in to resume the revels. The wooden steps of the house formed seats on one side of the floor, chairs and benches were set round on the others, and every seat was soon occupied, whilst a happy crowd – smoking, chatting and laughing – filled up the street. Then the band of six musicians, three of them performers on the most strident of brass instruments, struck up a Zapateado, and dancing began. Zapateado followed Zapateado with scarcely an attempt at any other dance . . . ; however, if the dancing was dull the scene in itself was bright enough, for all were dressed in their best, and the women had decked them-selves freely with streamers of brightly coloured ribbons.

By eleven o'clock Maudslay and Chambon were so tired that not even the brazen strains of the band could keep them from a sound night's sleep. But there was one more night of revelry to go.

It is the one great excitement of the year, and I was told that the women would pledge their labour as servants for months ahead in order to raise a few dollars with which to buy ribbons and artificial flowers so as to enjoy three days of butterfly life, to be inevitably followed by month after month of monotonous labour of grinding corn and toasting tortillas, until three happy days come round again.

That night Maudslay found the noise made sleep impossible, and was just falling into a doze at about four when the *arriero* came hammering on the door, asking for the loads for his mules. He was as impudent and surly as ever, and the worse for drink, but Maudslay gave him the cargo and told him to go on ahead.

Chambon and I turned out of our hammocks at about six o'clock and were only half-dressed when the music ceased, and there came a thundering knock at the door. As soon as I opened it three or four dancers pushed their way in, and their spokesman told me, in a most polite and measured tone, that they had been appointed as a deputation to wait on me and inform me that a resolution had been unanimously carried to the effect that the Carnival could not finish until Don Alfredo had danced a Zapateado.

Meanwhile laughing faces were thrust through the crack of the door, which almost before we knew it was pushed open and the dancers and their friends flocked in and ranged themselves round the walls of our great barn-like chamber. The band took up its position at the far end and with much gravity and a low bow the spokesman led out the 'Capitana' [a handsome woman who had been elected to lead the revels] in front of me where I was standing with a sponge in one hand and a towel in the other; another damsel was led up to Chambon, who had his night garments hanging over his arm; the band struck up and we had to dance our first Zapateado amidst a chorus of hand-clapping and 'bravos'. It was all as orderly and good-tempered a frolic as possible, and when the dance was over we were overwhelmed with kindly and pretty speeches; then the whole company formed up in couples, with the band leading, and marched round the village, each man leaving his partner at her own door.[5]

An hour or so later I strolled up the village street, and much to my astonishment found the loaded pack-mules wandering about in different directions, and the arriero, who should have been well on his way to Palenque, quietly sitting on a doorstep smoking a cigarette. In spite of his grumbles and growls I soon had his mules together again and hustled him off; but just as he was passing the Comandante's house, at the edge of the village, he fired a parting speech over his shoulder at me, the exact words of which I did not catch, but it was certainly not complimentary. However, I took no notice of it . . . but I reckoned without the Comandante, who had overheard the speech from his house, and before I could understand what was up, had darted out, caught the arriero by his collar, pulled him off his mule, and called two of his men to carry him off to prison. As soon as the torrent of words with which he overwhelmed his prisoner was at an end, he turned to me and offered a thousand apologies for the insult I had received from a savage, a bushman, who did not know how to treat a gentleman, or how to conduct himself with decency when he left his native wilds and entered a civilised town, but the lesson must be learnt and an example should be made of him. Of course I expressed my profound thanks and then dashed off to catch one of the pack-mules who was trying to scrape off his pack against the overhanging bough of a tree, whilst the Comandante, having vindicated the civilisation of Monte Cristo, returned to his hammock to finish his broken sleep.

All hope of making a start for Palenque was at an end, so I collected the straying mules together and drove them back along the silent street. Luckily Don Adolfo . . . was up and about, and he kindly helped me to unload the mules, and then asked me to stay and share his breakfast. . . . Later on I ventured to call on [the Comandante], and after many polite speeches, in which we deplored the wanton ways of ignorant and savage men who were not 'gente de razón', at last in deference to my urgent request (which I was assured showed the goodness of my heart even when dealing with an unworthy subject), and in order that I should personally suffer no inconvenience, the Comandante said that he would on this one occasion overlook the arriero's offence and order his immediate release. As soon as the fellow was free I made him load up his mules and bundled him out of the village, as I knew there was a wayside rancho a few miles distant which he could reach before nightfall.

I accepted Don Adolfo's hospitality for the night, and was ready to set off early the next morning on a good horse he had lent me; but Don Carlos and Don Adolfo had put their heads together and agreed that it was out of the question that I should ride the forty miles to Santo Domingo alone.

They insisted that a guide accompany him, and found one for him. Having negotiated the first few miles, made slow by tree-roots, Maudslay pushed his horse to a gentle canter, but the guide lagged behind. After waiting some time, he went back and found the guide sitting on the ground, his mule grazing nearby. He explained that he needed his breakfast, and appeared to have made it solely off a large bottle of *aguardiente*, which was by then quite empty.

With some difficulty I got him on his mule again, whilst he kept muttering 'Galope, galope! con los Ingleses es siempre así, galope, galope!' and for the remaining twenty miles, with the aid of a long stick, I kept his mule in front of me at a 'galope', or rather at a sort of shuffling canter which was all she was up to. The guide swayed fearfully in his saddle, and at times I thought he must come off, but somehow or other he always managed to save himself just in the nick of time; by degrees he got better, and, much to my astonishment, when he dismounted at Santo Domingo he was as sober as a judge. There we parted on the best of terms, and as I learnt that the arriero had also arrived safely with the pack-mules, I mounted my horse again and rode on to join Mr. Price at the ruins.

On 20 February Gorgonio, with his brother, José Domingo and fifteen-year-old son Caralampio, arrived at Palenque, having ridden overland from Guatemala, and they set to work at once making paper moulds of the inscriptions in the four temples. By the end of three weeks a large number of moulds had been dried and stored on scaffolds and shelves in the temples; and others in process of making were still adhering to the sculptured slabs, when, late one evening, a heavy rain-storm unexpectedly burst upon them.

It was impossible in the dark to reach the temples where the moulds were stored, as the whole of the intervening space was covered with felled trees, and even in the daytime it was a severe gymnastic exercise to get from one building to another. When daylight came and we were able to reach the temples, we found that the waterproof sheets with which the moulds were covered had not sufficed to keep out the driving rain, and that half of the moulds had been reduced to a pulpy mass, and those in process of making had been almost washed away. The rain continued to fall all day, the rooms where we were living were partly flooded, the walls were running with water, and the drip came through the roof in all directions. It was not until the next day that the remnant of the moulds could be carried out to dry in the returning sunshine, and then we made certain that the greater part of the work would have to be done over again.

Labour troubles continued: at one time there were over fifty men at work, and during the next week, none.

For many days our only connection with the village was kept up by the two small boys who brought over the supply of tortillas for which a contract had been made. These plucky little fellows walked the twelve miles through the forest alone, although they were so small that on arriving at the ruins they had to help one another up and down the rather steep steps which led in and out of the Courts. Perhaps the chocolate and sweet biscuits with which they were rewarded had something to do with the persistence with which they stuck to their task.

The forest which surrounds the ruins is as heavy as any I have seen in Central America, and we were not able to clear away the undergrowth and fell the timber over more than three quarters of the area [embracing the principal structures]. A fortnight of sunshine is needed to dry up the leaves after the trees are felled, and it is of course of the greatest importance to burn off the whole clearing at the same time, as the dried leaves easily catch fire and the great heat ensures the destruction of all twigs and smaller branches; but unluckily we were denied a continuous fortnight of dry weather, and each succeeding rain-storm beat the dried leaves off the branches and reduced the amount of easily inflammable material. It was not until the 15th of April that we were able to run fire through the clearing, and as the result was not very satisfactory, a good deal of our time was taken up in heaping together the unburnt branches and starting secondary fires.

Price was then able to run out a base line for his plane-table survey, and Maudslay could resume photography. He had been able to take photographs of details before this, but general views had had to wait until the burn was completed. He had intended to take these with his 10 by 12 inch camera, but as this had not been forwarded from New York owing to an error by the shipping agent, he had to rely on his 6.5 by 8.5 inch camera (the 10 by 12 inch camera did arrive later).

During their long wait before burning, Maudslay and Price had been hard at work cleaning the stucco modelling on the piers. This was a work that could not be entrusted to others, as it needed not only great care but also some knowledge of the designs being uncovered.

In some instances these decorations have been preserved in a very curious way: the water continually dripping on them from above has passed through the dense mass of decaying vegetation which covers the roofs of the buildings, and has become charged with carbonic acid in the process; it has then filtered through the slabs of which the roof and cornice are built, dissolving some of the limestone on its way, and redepositing it in a stalactitic formation on the face of the piers.

Mr. Price and I worked for some weeks at clearing the carvings of this incrustation, which varied from a hardly perceptible film to five or even six inches in thickness. The thinner parts were the more difficult to deal with, as they were exceedingly hard; where the thickness exceeded two inches a few taps with a hammer would sometimes bring away pieces two or three inches square, and we were fortunate sometimes in finding the colours on the surface of the stucco ornament underneath still fresh and bright.

They found it necessary to wear glasses to protect the eyes from the hard, flint-like particles that flew off at the blow of the chisel.

Progress with the thin incrustations was sometimes so slow that only a few square inches could be cleaned in a day. In other cases the attempt at cleaning had to be given up altogether as the filtration had formed a hard crust whilst the stucco beneath had become disintegrated and soapy, and had no surface left. [But when, in other cases,] the incrustation could be removed in large pieces and the surface of the stucco was sound, we sometimes found the colours with which it had been painted still retaining something of their former brilliancy.

According to Maudslay's field notes, the period during which he and Price were occupied, perhaps intermittently, in cleaning the piers actually amounted to nearly six weeks. Now they had to be photographed, but as Maudslay noted, 'In order to secure good photographs I found it necessary to bring the stucco ornamentation to an even tone by washing it over with a distemper of wood-ash and flake white, which did no harm to the moulding and was all washed off again by the first shower of rain.' There was another small problem: the terraces in front of the piers were too narrow to allow the camera to be set up far enough away from the piers. The only solution was to have platforms built out on scaffolding, work that consumed a great deal of labour.

Among other tasks undertaken by Maudslay was rendering first-aid to the Palace tower.

The top storey is half destroyed, and the whole structure was in danger of being overthrown in a heavy gale from the weight of the huge trees which were growing out of it. At considerable risk of accident my men succeeded in felling all but one of these trees, and I hope that the safety of the tower is now secured for some years to come. It was perilous work, as the foothold was uncertain, and there was great danger of the trees tearing away the loose masonry in their fall. One tree alone was left standing, as its fall must inevitably have damaged the roof of a neighbouring building, so a ring of bark was stripped from its trunk, in the hope that it will cause it to die slowly and fall piecemeal.

Another operation was clearing out the Eastern court of the Palace. This was found to be so choked up with debris from the half-ruined buildings surrounding it, that it was necessary to dig it out in some places to a depth of 4 feet, a very laborious task.

Price began his survey on 18 April, and despite losing a week to sickness managed to finish it on 10 May. Two days later, Maudslay, Price, and the López contingent left Palenque for Monte Cristo. From there, Gorgonio and his brothers, apparently accompanied by Price, left for Tenosique on their way to Menché (Yaxchilán), having been commissioned by Maudslay, as has been mentioned in an earlier chapter, to collect some carved lintels that were lying exposed to the elements, and to take some paper moulds.

On 20 May Maudslay boarded the SS *México* at Laguna, arriving two days later at Progreso, and went on to Mérida. There he noted: 'Met don

Pedro Peon Contreras, the owner of Uxmal, who offers me every facility for working at the Ruins should I return.' Significantly, the next entry is: '27th. Havana. Telegraphed Sweet.'

Then he continued his journey home, well pleased with his four-and-a-half months' work. During their stay at Palenque their health had been good (except for Price's brief indisposition), and for all the difficulties they had encountered, and the hot and mosquito-plagued nights, there were pleasures to remember too. As Maudslay recalled,

> one could usually find some spot where there was a cool breeze and we could escape [the mosquitoes'] attacks, and the beauty of the moonlit nights when we sat smoking and chatting on the western terrace looking onto the illuminated face of the [Temple of the Inscriptions] and the dark forest behind it will never fade from my memory.

The labour involved in this venture had been tremendous, especially that devoted to the piers, but the superb illustrations that resulted were ample recompense.[6]

Chapter 14

Marriage

Maudslay's birthday was in March, but as he and his assistants at Palenque were then about halfway through their five months of hard work, it's quite possible that this day passed by unnoticed.[1] But now he was forty-one – and therefore well into middle age by the standards of the time – so he could scarcely have failed to consider the question of how to allot his time over the next few years between fieldwork and a more settled existence. For all we know, his health was still robust enough to see him through another expedition or two – though heaven forbid it should be another quite as gruelling as the one to Chichén Itzá!

In any case, he would need to spend more time in London, preparing his material for publication. There was much to be done: there were still plaster casts to be taken from moulds, and arrangements made for their storage; the artists drawing them would need supervision; he would have to select negatives for publication and see that prints of prime quality were made from them, scrutinize the gravure plates made from the prints, and settle the layout of pages; in addition, there was the work he would be doing himself – writing the text and drawing some of the plans. How much time, then, would all this take? Even two full years might not be enough.

It is quite possible that in view of these commitments, Maudslay may have felt ready to slacken his established rhythm of mounting expeditions in alternate years. And now a new factor demanded his attention: the state of his finances, for a marked decline in the prosperity of Maudslay, Sons and Field – and therefore of his income – called for retrenchment.

There was also the matter of his private life. One can imagine him weighing the possibility that, if there were to be no more expeditions, then perhaps he should consider getting married and settling down. In his case, giving up fieldwork would by no means lead to idleness at home, even after the results of all the expeditions had been published, for there was other work to do, such as translating and publishing some of the most important documents written in New Spain during the Conquest period.

Since in this narrative there has been no word of passionate affairs, or of any sentimental attachments, the reader may be wondering whether Alfred Maudslay were not a man so completely absorbed in his work, or in himself, as to fend off altogether any emotional entanglements; or whether, perhaps, he was one of those sad victims of Victorian respectability whose lives were made miserable by pent-up emotional pressures they were unable to express.

Neither of these profiles fits Maudslay. All that is known about him suggests a man blessed with easy manners, an uncomplicated psyche, and a gift for establishing warm friendships with both sexes. But owing to the disappearance of most of his correspondence, the apparent non-existence of intimate diaries, and the meagre information about him surviving within his family and their records, we know almost nothing about his personal affairs as a young man.

For a biographer this was a disappointing discovery. But I began to wonder whether there was much reason for regret; for what, after all, is the principal reason for writing the biography of an archaeologist, or a mathematician, or any person who has contributed to progress in technical fields? Surely the central aim is to identify as far as possible their subject's innate gifts, to track the moral and educational influences that may have encouraged their flowering, and to identify, if possible, crucial encounters or events that may have influenced them in some way.

For whereas emotional states caused by grief, sickness, poverty – or the bliss of a love-affair – may be expected to affect the work of artists, we may wonder whether such states have much influence on the work of those engaged in technical or intellectual fields. Possibly there have been highly strung or unbalanced geniuses in whose work the effect of emotional conflict can be detected, but they must be rare exceptions. On the other hand, it is easy to cite an example of the opposite extreme: Albert Einstein produced his paper 'On the special and general theory of relativity' (and ten other scientific papers within the same year) soon after his wife had left him, taking with her his much-loved sons. Their departure may well have been partly responsible for the duodenal ulcer that prostrated him a little later, but surely not for any diminution of intellectual power!

Nevertheless, it would have been satisfactory to know more of the emotional life of this pioneer archaeologist, even though such information would be unlikely to throw much light on his motivation in undertaking his great work, or on his success in accomplishing it so triumphantly.

There has been, it is true, one archaeologist whose personality did affect his work. This was Teobert Maler, that other tireless explorer of Maya ruins and near contemporary of Maudslay's, whose combative and jealous temperament did lead to a rupture of relations with his sponsor (the Peabody Museum) as a result of which he withheld work intended for publication. (It also seems frequently to have led to poor relations with the men employed by him in the jungle.)

As for Maudslay, there is nothing to suggest that he had anything but a normal interest in women. Twice, or perhaps three times, in his life he may have fallen in love, or so some slender evidence suggests. If the total were found to be much higher it would be surprising, for there is no sign of profligacy or hot blood in him (nor cold, for that matter), and the calm self-confidence with which he steered his way through an eventful life doesn't suggest a man who would easily become involved in passionate affairs or hopeless infatuations. And yet, for all that, he may not have been entirely spared the pain that affairs of the heart can cause, for if one reported episode in his life is true (the meagre details of which will be told later) it must have caused him lasting sadness.

An early disappointment came not long after his return from the Pacific, when he fell in love with Catherine, or Kitty, Brabazon, a niece of John (or General Sir John, as he became) Palmer Brabazon, of County Meath, Ireland. This information came from Dolly Maudslay, but how long the affair lasted she could not say. In any case, it came to nothing, and Kitty married another man, Clare Kendall by name, at some time prior to 1885 (on the evidence of Maudslay's field notebooks, which record in that year a letter received from Mrs Kendall).

But another close friendship with a woman proved to be enduring. It began when Alfred, with his brother Charles, encountered the Morris family en route to Yosemite in 1872. For the next twenty years he and Annie Morris kept in touch through correspondence and occasional visits.[2]

It is likely that Alfred managed to see her on one or two of the few occasions when he passed through New York on the way to or from Central America.[3] But as Annie later referred to the 'many rough and wintry passages'[4] she had made across the Atlantic before her marriage, she almost certainly saw more of Alfred in the warmer parts of Europe than in America – with maintenance of due decorum, we may be sure. Still, for most of those twenty years, according to family tradition, there was little evidence of anything more than ordinary friendship between them, at least on his part.

Then the next thing we know is that Alfred Maudslay and Ann Cary Morris were married at St Paul's Church (American Protestant Episcopal) in Rome, on 31 May 1892, the witnesses being her sister Mary and her other sister's husband Lewis Turner. Alfred was then forty-two years old, and Annie, as she liked to be called, forty-four. Nothing whatever is known about the course of events that led to their union.

Annie was intelligent, well-educated, and a good writer. She is avowed to have been 'sporting' – that is, willing to try anything, and to put up with discomfort when necessary, as she certainly had to do in her travels with Alfred after their marriage.[5] Another quality that would have endeared her to Alfred was the fondness for animals that we see her displaying during those travels. But Dolly Maudslay, Alfred's niece, who by her own admission was not one of Annie's more ardent admirers, described her as very impatient, and was sure she had chased Alfred to the altar.

In the only surviving photograph of her when young, in San Francisco, she appears fair-haired and attractive, with rather too prominent a nose for conventional beauty, and an intense look. In middle age her aspect became more formidable, with her nose appearing sharper, and the deepening lines in her face seeming to express more obvious determination. By then she had taken to carrying two pairs of pince-nez, the one on her nose pinching it and thereby exaggerating the two lines of concentration between her eyebrows and emphasizing that penetrating look; the other pair, for reading, she kept hanging round her neck.[6] But in 1892 Annie was still a handsome and distinguished-looking woman, and undoubtedly she had a good mind.

For some years prior to his marriage Maudslay's address in London had been number 11 Park Lane, but if this was a bachelor flat, then he must have obtained more spacious accommodation by the time of his marriage. About two years later, the Maudslays were evidently living in a house on the banks of the Thames, perhaps in Chelsea or Hammersmith, before settling on a house to buy in Knightsbridge: number 32 Montpelier Square (between Hyde Park and Harrods), a spacious and handsome house facing south on to the gardens in the square.

Annie came of distinguished forebears – Randolphs, Jeffersons, Carys, and Morrises. Through the Carys she was also a descendant of Powhatan and Pocahontas, and it was an odd coincidence that in old age she did rather resemble a Plains Indian woman. As to the Morrises, they were one of the first English families to obtain, after the Dutch left, the grant of a manor in New York, the parcel of land having previously been held by a Dutchman named Bronck. Among the Morrises, now lords of this manor, were two prominent eighteenth-century judges, a father and son both named Lewis. The younger Lewis, long after his first wife died, took as his second wife Sarah Gouverneur. She was a young woman from a well established New York family of Huguenot and Dutch origin; thus when a son was born to them in 1752, the name bestowed on him was Gouverneur (pronounced in the family 'Gouverneer'), following the common American practice of giving a mother's maiden name to her son (in this case a name that when borne by a statesman is unfortunately apt to be mistaken for a title).

This boy was to make a name for himself in American history as one of the Founding Fathers. He was also to be Annie's grandfather, and in this capacity he exerted a palpable influence on her. The story of his life, in fact, and that of Annie's grandmother Ann Cary Morris, whose full name she was given, is so extraordinary that it merits telling at some length.

Young Gouverneur soon showed himself to be lively and clever. For his first schooling he was placed in the family of Dominie Tetard in the Huguenot settlement of New Rochelle, where he learnt to speak fluent French, a rare accomplishment at that time among Americans. Then, at the age of twelve, he went on to Kings College, New York, the predecessor of Columbia University (notable then as a hot-bed of Toryism). After graduating from the college at the age of sixteen, he entered at once upon legal training, and completed it before his twentieth birthday.

He achieved this in 1771, and no sooner had he started to practise law than the revolutionary movement broke out in earnest. Initially, as a conservative from a background that was aristocratic by Colonial standards, Morris was reluctant to oppose the British, but gradually he became convinced that the patriot cause was just, and should prevail.

Having entered the fray, Morris acquired with astonishing speed a mature grasp of politics, and when still only twenty-three was elected a member of the first Provincial Congress of New York. Thereafter he worked hard and astutely for the cause, while always advocating moderation, for, though sincerely republican, he could not have been called a democratic republican, and he never ceased to regard the threat of mob rule with abhorrence.

Morris was soon a key figure in the state government, and later in the Continental Congress. As a member of the latter he was charged with reorganizing the army, and while executing this commission had many dealings with George Washington, whom he came to admire greatly. The two men developed a lifelong friendship, one that was firm enough for Washington not to feel inhibited from reproving his friend, when he found it necessary, for his frivolity and devil-may-care attitude.

Gouverneur Morris (known by his friends as 'Gouvero') was over 6 feet tall and well proportioned. But in 1780 he suffered an accident while trying to control runaway carriage horses in a street; his left leg got caught in a wheel and was so badly damaged that it had to be amputated below the knee.

According to his first biographer, 'the day after the accident a friend called to see him, who thought it his duty to offer as much consolation as he could, on an event so melancholy. He dwelt upon the good effects, which such a trial would have on his character and moral temperament, and the diminished inducements it would leave for seeking the pleasures and dissipations of life into which young men are only too easily seduced. "My good Sir", replied Mr Morris, "you argue the matter so handsomely, and point out so clearly the advantage of being without legs, that I am almost persuaded to part with the other".[7]

But his friend was mistaken. In the matter of amatory exploits, for which Morris was already notorious, his loss may only have spurred him to greater efforts to show that he was still capable of making conquests. And the rough oaken stick with a plain wooden knob at the bottom that he chose to wear (spurning a 'hambone leg') made him a yet more striking and sympathetic figure, not a whit less attractive to women.[8]

In 1787, with peace restored, Morris was appointed as one of the members representing Pennsylvania at the Federal Constitutional Convention, which had been called into being for the purpose of choosing the best form of government for the newly independent country, still at that time a loose association of states, and to draw up a constitution. The discussions, in which Morris played a prominent part, including an eloquent plea for the abolition of slavery, were brought to a close in less than four months with broad agreement on a draft document.

Morris and four other members were then nominated to produce a final draft. It was to Morris that the actual writing was delegated, and out of the awkward first draft beginning 'We the people of New Hampshire, Massachusetts, [etc.] do ordain, declare and establish the following Constitution for the Government of ourselves and our Posterity', Morris composed the more sonorous and memorable preamble: 'We the people of the United States, in Order to form a more perfect Union, establish Justice . . . and secure the Blessings of Liberty to ourselves and our Posterity, do ordain and establish this Constitution for the United States of America.'[9]

Morris's father had died in the year preceding the Constitutional Congress, bequeathing his estate, Upper Morrisania, to his eldest son Lewis, this being the northwestern half of 'the Broncks Lands' which lay along the Harlem River, across from Manhattan. The southeastern portion, 'Old Morrisania', with a house that looked over towards Randall's Island, was to be held by his widow as life tenant, and when she died, Gouverneur managed to purchase the property from his elder brothers. This he able to do only by taking out mortgages to the tune of £7500.

By then Morris had been engaged in business ventures for some years, and it was presumably the successful tendency of these that gave him the confidence to assume such a large debt. A good part of this business was done in association with Robert Morris, who was not a relative, his father having come from Liverpool; the two men had worked together before, when Robert Morris was Superintendant of Finance in the Continental Congress, and Gouverneur his deputy.

Robert Morris had a contract for a monopoly on the sale of tobacco to the French Farmers-General, but certain difficulties had arisen over this. There were also hopes, as yet unrealized, that Thomas Jefferson, then

American Minister in Paris, could arrange for the sale of tobacco to be applied in part towards the reduction of the American debt to France. The Morrises hoped to purchase the debt in France at a discount and sell it in the United States at par.

As a first step they spent several months of 1788 in Virginia, largely on tobacco business. While there, Gouverneur took the opportunity to repeat an earlier visit to Tuckahoe, Thomas Mann Randolph's plantation on the James River. In this house Jefferson had spent seven years of his childhood while his father was acting as Randolph's guardian during his minority. By the time Gouverneur Morris made his visit, Randolph's wife was mortally sick, her ill-health probably exacerbated by having borne her husband thirteen children. Among them were Thomas, junior, who was soon to marry Jefferson's daughter Martha, and Nancy, then fourteen, whom Morris would meet again twenty years later in a fateful encounter.

To carry out the other part of their plan – resolving difficulties with the tobacco contract at the French end, and promoting other business ventures – Gouverneur Morris sailed for France at the end of that same year. Once there, he found that as a French-speaker, with polished manners, a ready wit, and striking appearance, he was well received in Parisian society.

He had been there only a couple of months when he met Adèle, Comtesse de Flahaut, an intelligent and fascinating woman of twenty-eight whom he at once gauged to be 'not a sworn enemy of intrigue'. Her husband was an impecunious nobleman of sixty-three, whom she had already deceived by becoming Talleyrand's mistress, and then bearing his child. Morris effectively stole her away from that brilliant and calculating man – the 'mitred monster', as Morris liked to call Talleyrand in his capacity as Bishop of Autun.

Morris kept a private diary, in which he made long daily entries while in Paris – until at the height of the Terror he ceased doing so for fear of compromising his friends. These diaries provide one of the best eye-witness accounts of the French Revolution. They cover all aspects of his life, commercial, diplomatic, social, and amatory, and because they were never intended for publication the entries are unusually candid. They are also perceptive and vividly (if carelessly) written. These diaries have been published in three different editions of increasing completeness, and very tempting they are to quote from at length, but here there can be room for few quotations.

At first, perhaps, Morris may not have been much interested in what was going on in France in the spring of 1789, apparently sharing this lack of interest with Louis XVI, a dull-witted man chiefly interested in hunting. Morris's attention, though, was soon engaged by the rapidly developing situation, and before long he became convinced of the need for reform. As a New York Federalist he perceived both the lack of responsibility of the upper classes, and their total inability to implement any reforms they had agreed to. Morris could see, too, that unlike the Americans, with their provincial assemblies, the French people had no experience of self-government, and could hardly be expected to make a success of it.

Then the Bastille was stormed, and a regime that he dreaded began. He deplored especially the actions of misguided idealists such as Lafayette, who in turn denounced Morris as a counter-revolutionary. Morris was then recommending a limited monarchy for France, and was passing advice to the king through one of his ministers on such matters as the attitude he should take towards the constitution, and how he might win the support of the people.

In the spring of 1792 Morris was appointed Minister in Paris in place of Jefferson, who had returned home some two years earlier, leaving his post in the care of a chargé d'affaires. Morris's appointment was controversial, with eleven senators opposing it; and Washington himself had sufficient reservations to send him a stern warning: 'While your abilities, knowledge of the affairs of the country and disposition to serve it were adduced on one hand, you were charged on the other hand with levity and imprudence of conversation and conduct. It was agreed that your habits of expression indicated *hauteur*, disgusting to those who happen to differ from you in sentiment . . . that in France you were considered as a favorer of aristocracy and unfriendly to its Revolution, that . . . that . . . I will not go further into details. . . .' He reproves him for meddling in French politics, but declares his good opinion, friendship and regard. Morris replied to this with contrition: '*I now promise you* that Circumspection of Conduct which has hitherto I acknowledge form'd no Part of my Character.'

For a time he kept his promise, but as the King's position grew desperate Morris and a member of the royal household contrived a plan for the King and Queen to escape from Paris. Already, a year earlier, the King had tried unsuccessfully to slip out of the country, and now when the appointed day came he failed to go through with the plan. Some days later he asked Morris to look after his papers and his funds. These amounted to almost a million livres, part of which was to be used to pay a corps of men to protect him from conspirators and to support an expected rising in his favour. But the royal forces were routed, the monarchy came to an end, and six months later the king was executed.

Once his service as Minister had ended, Morris shipped home all the best pieces of furniture and decorative wares that he had bought for his house, and his English coach, too. The most splendid pieces of furniture he had purchased near the end of his time in Paris: these came from Versailles, from Marie-Antoinette's Grand Cabinet-Intérieur, and were bought at one of the year-long series of auctions of the contents of royal palaces. Morris himself did not return to America until late in 1798. By then the old Morrisania had been demolished and a new one built, expressly to hold his tapestries and furnishings from Paris.

Having served for a time as a senator for New York, and now past fifty years of age, Morris might well have been expected to give up public life entirely, and retreat to the pleasures of Morrisania, where, as a visitor recorded, 'He lives literally like a nobleman. . . . He has all this world can give but a good wife and amiable children. . . . He also laments that he did not, twenty years ago, unite his talents with some corresponding female mind to make each other happy.'

Then one day in October 1808 he went down to Greenwich Village in his coach, and drew up outside Mrs Pollack's boarding house. Nancy Randolph, by then thirty-four but still slender and pretty, if wan-looking, went to the window and recognized him, or at least knew him at once, for who else with such a fine physical presence, a wooden leg, and a splendid coach would be calling at those lodgings? She came down to meet him, but all we know of their conversation is that he told her he was looking for 'some reduced gentlewoman [who] would undertake to keep his house, as the lower class of house-keepers often provoked the servants to a riot in his dwelling'.

To few others could the term 'a reduced gentlewoman' have been applied more fittingly than to Nancy Randolph, as Morris must have been aware. Already he had sent her a note in which he told her: 'I once heard but have no distinct recollection of events which brought distress to your family. Dwell not in them now. If we ever happen to be alone you shall tell your tale of sorrow. . . .'

That tale had begun in 1791 when she quarrelled with her father and new step-mother, apparently because she refused to accept the man they had chosen for her to marry. So she left home and went to live with her older sister Judith, who two years earlier had married her second cousin Richard Randolph. They were living on a plantation near Farmville in Cumberland County, which bore a name that would soon seem strangely appropriate: 'Bizarre Plantation'.

Richard had two younger brothers, Theodorick and John, the former an undergraduate at Columbia who was twenty when Nancy came to Bizarre. The latter was to become known as Congressman John Randolph 'of Roanoke', and famous as an orator. Theodorick and Nancy fell in love, she being a strong-willed and attractive girl not yet seventeen, and he a dissipated and consumptive undergraduate.

One night when Judith, Richard and Nancy were staying at another

Randolph cousin's house, Nancy, who had evidently become inconspicuously pregnant, miscarried, and soon word spread of a foetus having been discovered by a slave among debris near the house. Rumour claimed that it was Richard who had seduced Nancy and then murdered the newborn. To clear his name Richard demanded a public hearing before a magistrate, engaging as counsel first his cousin John Marshall (later to be Chief Justice) and then the famous Patrick Henry. At the hearing, the magistrate found no cause for pursuing the case.

Nancy's prospects of matrimony were, of course, blighted by this affair, but she stayed on at Bizarre, for where else could she go? Then Richard died mysteriously, of poison it was suggested, and Judith took to treating Nancy almost as a servant. She remained there for nine years, engaged in menial work, until one day in the winter of 1805 John Randolph appeared, and drove her out of the house with the accusation that she took as many liberties as if she were in a tavern, later adding a charge of intimacy with one of the slaves. Nancy fled and made her way to Richmond, where John must have expected her to become a prostitute, there being then few other ways of surviving.

Somehow she gravitated to Newport, Rhode Island, and there for a time she remained, ill and destitute. Then at last she obtained a position as a teacher at a new boys' school in Stratford, Connecticut, established partly through the efforts of a man named William Johnson who had been a Connecticut delegate at the Federal Constitutional Convention, and was therefore likely to have known Gouverneur Morris, then a member of the five-man drafting committee. Later Johnson was appointed first President of Columbia College, of which Morris, an alumnus, had been made a trustee in 1805, so their old acquaintance is likely to have been renewed.

Perhaps then, Johnson happened to ask Morris if he knew the Randolphs of Tuckahoe, and if so, did he know that a daughter of theirs was teaching at this new school? When Morris answered that indeed he remembered her, Johnson may have suggested to Nancy that she write him a note. This proposed link is speculative, but no better explanation has emerged for their improbable rendezvous in Greenwich Village.

In his reply to her, Morris begins:

> Talk not of gratitude, but communicate so much of your situation as may enable me to be useful. I once heard but have no distinct recollection of events which brought distress into your family. Dwell not in them now. If we ever happen to be alone you shall tell your tale of sorrow when the tear from your cheek may fall in my bosom.[10]

The remainder of the letter is of a generally encouraging and philosophical description.

Morris then suggested that, since he had been obliged to discharge his housekeeper, she might consider taking up that position. Annie consented, and came to Morrisania early in 1809 to take up her duties. Mutual confidence gradually developed into intimacy, so that by November their changed relationship was noticed by certain of his friends.

As Christmas approached, they must have entered on a gay conspiracy, planned to the last detail for surprise. They would have a great Christmas dinner, to which some nephews and nieces were invited, and James Fennimore Cooper's father. During the festive meal in the library Nancy, wearing her old brown dress with the patched elbows, appeared from upstairs, and Morris broke their news to the company, causing consternation among relatives who were looking forward to substantial bequests upon their uncle's demise. No details of this dramatic event are recorded; merely Morris's diary entry, 'I marry this day Ann Cary Randolph. No small surprise for the guests.'

Spiteful reactions to the marriage were not long in coming. A niece in Philadelphia, who had taken the precaution of naming her first-born Gouverneur Morris Meredith, was first to write. Her letter has not survived, but Morris's answer has, and it begins:

> I received your letter, my dear Child, and perceive in it two Charges; viz. that I have committed a Folly in Marriage and have acted undutifully in not consulting you. I can only say to the first that I have not yet found Cause to repent, and to the second that I hope you will pardon me for violating an Obligation of which I was not apprized . . . . If I had married a rich Woman of seventy the World might think it wiser than to take one half that Age without a Farthing, and, if the World were to live with my Wife, I should certainly have consulted its Taste; but as that happens not to be the Case, I thought I might, without offending others, endeavor to suit myself, and look rather into the Head and Heart than into the Pocket.

The outbreak of war with Britain in 1812 was deeply deplored by Morris, but there was consolation in the news of Nancy's pregnancy; this stirred his pride and devotion. In February 1813 a healthy boy was born, and naturally he was given his father's name, Gouverneur.

Rejoicing over the event was not widespread in the family. A young Wilkins great-nephew (whose parents, like the Merediths, had expectantly given their eldest son the name Gouverneur Morris Wilkins) sourly joked that the child should be called Cutusoff, after the Russian General Kutusov, much in the news a year earlier for having turned back Napoleon's army before Moscow.

But this and other comments were mere pinpricks compared to the infamous letter, charged with concentrated venom, that John Randolph sent Morris some eighteen months later. It was Tudor Randolph, Judith's consumptive son, who was at least partly responsible for provoking this outburst. While on his way home from Harvard, and staying at Morrisania with his uncle and aunt, he had been taken with a severe haemorrhage. Nancy then nursed him with kindness, and at some cost to herself because at that time Gouverneur was also confined to bed, and of course she had also her son to look after. Eventually Judith, by then reconciled with Nancy, came up to help; and John Randolph visited for a night, showing apparent friendliness.

But just then Tudor revived John's ancient hatred for Nancy by telling his uncle he believed that it was she who had poisoned his father; that she still had loose morals; and that she cared nothing for her own son, save as a means of exercising power over her husband.

These charges, and others that had lain dormant in his mind, John Randolph spat out against Nancy in his letter, which he made sure was delivered to Morris, although it was addressed to Nancy. 'Madam', he begins, 'When at my departure from Morrisania, in your sister's presence, I bade you remember the past, I was not apprized of the whole extent of your guilty machinations.' He then dredges up, and distorts to suit his own purposes, the unhappy events of twenty years before. Throughout its length the rhetorical gifts that made him famous do not flag:

> Chance has again thrown you under my eye. What do I see? A vampire that, after sucking the best blood of my race, has flitted off to the North, and struck her harpy fangs into an infirm old man. To what condition of being have you reduced him? Have you made him a prisoner in his own house that there may be no witness of your lewd amours, or have you driven away his friends and old domestics that there may be no witness of his death?. . . 'Uncle,' said Tudor, 'if ever Mr Morris's eyes are opened, it will be through this child whom, with all her grimaces in her husband's presence, 'tis easy to see she cares nothing for except as an instrument of power. How shocking she looks!'
>
> I have done. Before this reaches your eyes, it will have been perused by him to whom, next to my brother, you are most deeply indebted, and whom, next to him, you have most deeply wronged. If he be not both blind and deaf, he must sooner or later unmask you unless *he too die of cramps in his stomach* . . . [a reference to Richard Randolph's having possibly been poisoned].

The blast of this explosive letter backfired, leaving Morris unruffled and its author indelibly besmirched. Prominent among all the qualities Morris possessed were worldly wisdom and sound judgment of character and motives. As he wrote to an acquaintance,

Mr Randolph's communication gave me no concern, for Mrs Morris had apprised me of the only fact in his possession, before she came to my house, so that her candor had blunted the point of his arrow. [But his heart was deeply touched for] 'the houseless child of want that I took to my bosom', [and he realized there were those who would] hate her because she is happy [while] we have among us curious women and flagitious men.

The plotters behind the letter, those curious women and flagitious men, waited for sounds of discord to break forth from Morrisania, but as Howard Swiggett comments, they would have been amazed to see the undisturbed Morris sitting next day in his library, engaged in writing very long letters to two political cronies.

Life at Morrisania soon went back to normal. 'I lead a quiet, and more than most of my fellow-mortals, a happy life', her husband wrote to a friend eighteen months later.

The woman to whom I am married has much genius, has been well educated and possesses, with an affectionate temper, industry and a love of order. Our little boy grows finely and is generally admired. You may, then, opening your mind's eye, behold your friend, as he approaches with tottering steps the bottom of life's hill, supported by a kind companion, a tender female friend, and cheered by a little prattler, who bids fair, if God shall spare his life, to fill in due time the space his father leaves.

Gouverneur Morris had indeed only a few months more to live, for in November 1816 he died in his sixty-fifth year. In his will, the first provision is one of the most gallant a man ever made for his widow: it confirms the ante-nuptial settlement of twenty-four hundred dollars a year (a large income for the time), gives her Morrisania and its contents for life, and 'in case my wife should marry, I give her six hundred dollars more per annum, to defray the increased expenditure, which may attend that connexion'. Young Gouverneur Wilkins was to have $25,000 at the age of thirty, 'provided his conduct shall be, in the opinion of my executor and executrix, such as becomes a good citizen'. There was nothing for the other nephews.[11]

The new master of Morrisania was a big man like his father, but he did not quite fill his place – as he could scarcely be expected to, with a father who had been, in Alexander Hamilton's words, 'by birth a native of this country, but by genius an exotic'. He made no mark in public affairs, and if he had any of his father's mastery of the English language, he made no use of it.

For some reason no longer discernible, his grandfather Lewis Morris, though educated at Yale, became deeply suspicious of the Yankees of New England, especially those of Connecticut, regarding them as too 'cute (that is, acute, or sharp) at bargains with their Dutch neighbours.[12] So, to protect the interests of his grandson or grandsons as yet unborn, he stipulated in his will dated 1762: 'It is my will and desire that every son of Gouverneur Morris may have the best education that is to be had in England or America. But my express will and directions are, that he never be sent for that purpose to the Colony of Connecticut, lest he should imbibe in his youth that low craft and cunning, so incident to the people of that country . . . though many of them, under the sanctified garb of Religion, have endeavored to impose themselves upon the world as honest men.' Young Gouverneur was therefore educated in New York.

Though one unreliable source describes Annie's father as 'a plain, unlettered farmer who daily sends his milk to the city', he was un-doubtedly just as much a business man, being an early and successful railroad promoter, and he developed part of the Morrisania acres into a model village.[13] But through reckless inattention to his grandfather's admonitions, he seriously impaired the great fortune he had inherited by using the services of some New England brokers on Wall Street to invest in the New Haven Railroad, only to find they were pioneers in the art of 'watering' railroad shares. The extent of his losses is unknown.

If he was heedless of grandfather Lewis's warnings, he did show him-self loyal to his mother's Randolph relatives and their habit of marrying cousins whenever possible, for his first wife was Patsey Jefferson Cary whose father, besides being a Cary, was a grandson of Thomas Jefferson's sister, while her mother was none other than Nancy's sister Virginia Randolph, the thirteenth and youngest of that brood. And when Patsey died, he found a new help-meet in Anna Morris, whose parents were both grandchildren of Gouverneur's half-brother Lewis.

The second Gouverneur Morris and his first wife had nine children, of whom four, including the romantically named Powhatan Randolph Morris, died young. The first-born was Gouverneur the third; then came Anne Cary or Annie, followed by two more sisters and a brother. Gouverneur the third left little to mark his passage through the world, beyond the *History of a Volunteer Regiment: Sixth Regiment of New York Volunteers, known as Wilson's Zouaves*, published in 1891. But in his son, the fourth and last Gouverneur, the literary heritage bursts forth with an end-of-the-line vigour, albeit not on the highest literary plane.[14]

His sister Annie, however, being possessed of both literary ability and a strong character, was indeed a worthy scion of her grandparents. Her debut as a writer was made in 1887 when the new *Scribner's Magazine* printed her article, 'Glimpses at the Diaries of Gouverneur Morris', in its very first issue. This was just a foretaste of the work she had already been working at diligently for some years: the transcription and editing of her grandfather's papers, then still preserved in the house at Morrisania. On its completion a year later, her work was published in two volumes by Scribners as *The Diary and Letters of Gouverneur Morris*.

Her edition contained a great deal of material not found in an 1832 publication which had drawn on the same material. It was soon translated into French, as might be expected, for only three other eye-witness accounts of the revolution exist, and none of these is a true diary, made up of freshly remembered conversations and scenes. Most of the events recorded by Morris were entered in his diary within twenty-four hours; and because he had no intention of publishing them, he did so with unrestrained frankness.

But he was a full-blooded man, much given to 'gallantry', and since Annie was preparing this edition for readers of the late Victorian period, she made considerable use of her scissors. They were plied partly in the interests of brevity and the production of a readable text, but by no means coincidentally they also cut out all mention of amatory affairs. So the reader learns nothing of her grandfather's long-running *affaire* with the Comtesse Adèle de Flahaut.

Her edition must also be faulted for failure to indicate cuts from sentences with the usual mark of elision, thus reducing its value for scholars. But she did show considerable skill in interweaving material from Morris's letters into the fabric of the diary, and in constructing a narrative exclusively from the letters for the later part of the 'Terror', when out of prudence Morris had ceased to keep the diary.

Chapter 15

To the Highlands and Copán with Annie

In 1889 Frederic Putnam and Charles Bowditch, inspired by Maudslay's productive work at Copán, submitted to the government of Honduras the Peabody Museum's proposal for a long-term archaeological investigation of that great city, and by March of the following year a ten-year contract for the same had been offered, accepted, and signed. One of its clauses required the Museum to carry out a season of excavations each year, failure to comply with which would result in cancellation of the contract.[1]

The scale of this expedition was to be far more ambitious than the museum's modest operations had been at Labná. To finance it Bowditch prevailed upon twenty of his wealthy Boston acquaintances to join with him as patrons; Putnam would direct the operation from Boston, and a staff of three at the site would consist of John G. Owens, Harvard's first graduate student in anthropology, as 'Executive Officer' (i.e. field director); Marshall Saville, another student, as 'Scientific Officer'; and a third man, still to be chosen, as 'Engineer' (or surveyor).

Maudslay, when consulted by Bowditch at an early stage of planning, responded by sending two lists of suggestions, one concerning the work that might profitably be done, and the other a list of the equipment they should take to Copán.[2] The former begins with: 'Excavations I made in Mound nos. 11, 16, 20–22 should be completed & better ground plans drawn out, & something further should be made out of the original form & design of Mound no. 26. . . . No. 27 should give really good results. . . .'

Even more valuable, perhaps, was the detailed list of equipment to bring, among them many items that no one without considerable experience could have imagined bringing. Maudslay also recommended the employment of both Hugh Price as surveyor and Gorgonio López, aided perhaps by other members of his family, as makers of paper moulds and potentially useful intermediaries in case of conflict with the workers.

Price, who had come from Cobán, punctually made his rendezvous with Owens and Saville at Yzabal, but, alas, antipathy developed at once between them, and Price left the expedition after about a month. Otherwise the work went well. A puzzling feature of the Hieroglyphic Stairway, for instance, was solved: Maudslay had dug a trench horizontally in from the top of an almost intact flight of these steps, and found, 17 feet in, only a vertical wall. Further excavation now showed that a considerable portion of the stairway had slipped down with little dislocation of its component stones (the cause perhaps being an earthquake), and come to rest on top of the lower steps, which had remained in situ. So Maudslay's opinion in this case proved to be mistaken.[3]

The following season was blighted by a disaster: John Owens died at Copán from a virulent tropical fever. His death now threw in doubt the museum's ability to mount its next expedition, scheduled for the winter of 1893–4, for lack of anyone competent to lead it. Then a warning was received: a letter written in Spanish on the Peabody's Honduras Expedition stationery and mailed from Honduras, but unsigned and undated (almost certainly sent by Carlos Mérida, the museum's agent) stating: 'I am informed that the Government does not intend to sustain the contract that you have, but according to what I have been told, is just waiting for an opportunity to break it.' (By then, Bográn's presidency had ended.)

It can scarcely be doubted that this letter prompted Bowditch to write to Maudslay with a suggestion, or at least a hint, of how he could help, for by late October 1893 Bowditch was telling Putnam 'Mr Maudslay thinks he would like to take some moulds at Copán, which we would be very glad to have him do. Would it not be a good idea for you to appoint him agent of the museum so that any work of that sort which he does would serve as part of our work under the decree?'

Putnam concurred, and by a document signed on 5 December 1893 Maudslay was appointed agent of the Peabody Museum, 'empowered with authority to make such arrangements as he may deem necessary with the explorations at Copán and with the Honduras Government, acting under the agreement made between the Honduras Government and the Peabody Museum'. Putnam also asked him to 'report on the condition of things and what is in your opinion necessary we should do in order to keep our rights intact and to keep the place protected from vandalism'.

Maudslay readily agreed to the plan, not only because he wanted to make those moulds but also, perhaps, because he had in mind a further reconnaissance of ruins in the Guatemalan highlands. And besides, with Annie accompanying him, this might also be considered as a kind of delayed honeymoon trip. Annie would have heard many tales about Copán, and the Niña Chica, and so much else, that she would be glad to go with him. Three or four weeks there could easily be fitted into the itinerary. And on the outward journey they could also take in the World's Columbian Exhibition at Chicago before it closed.

In the previous year, 1892, a great exhibition had been mounted in Seville to celebrate the fourth centenary of the voyage of discovery that brought Christopher Columbus to the New World. As a contribution to this Maudslay had offered to provide prints of some of his photographs for exhibition, and when this offer was accepted he commissioned his 'photo-lab' (as we would call it now) to make enlargements for that purpose. But making enlargements was not, then, the simple matter that it is nowadays, the reason being that the photographic paper available at that time scarcely responded to the yellowish light of carbon filament electric lamps. Thus, the only recourse was, first, to make a contact print from the negative, then to photograph that print with a camera using a negative of at least the size required for the enlargement, and finally, to make a contact print from that enlarged negative.

Since Maudslay wanted prints measuring 30 by 24 inches, a lab possessing a giant copy-camera had to be commissioned to make the necessary enlarged glass negatives. He had chosen more than forty of his best photographs of Maya monuments and buildings, and specified that pigment prints be made of them. Prints of this kind, very seldom made today, are widely considered to be the most beautiful of all monochrome photographic prints, and with reasonable care they don't deteriorate, because the use of mineral pigments (or carbon) instead of silver in the image makes them immune from the most common form of print degradation.

After plans for the great exhibition at Seville had been announced, planning began for a somewhat similar exhibition to be mounted in Chicago. This, 'The World's Columbian Exhibition', would follow a year later so that many of the original exhibits could be shown again, and reproductions of the *Pinta*, the *Niña,* and the *Santa María*, which had set out from Huelva, could be greeted upon arrival in Chicago during the exhibition. As Maudslay had apparently decided that his prints should go to the British Museum after the Seville exhibition closed, Professor Putnam, who had been charged with arranging the ethnographic and archaeological sections of the Chicago exhibition, asked Maudslay to have another set of forty pigment prints made for display in his hall. These were duly made and dispatched.[4]

On 10 October 1893 the Maudslays embarked from Liverpool on the Royal Mail Steamer *Teutonic*, bound for New York City. On arrival they are likely to have stayed in the city for a few days, as Annie would certainly have wanted to introduce her husband to friends and relatives, among them her old stepmother Anna, at Morrisania. Then they took a train to Chicago, to see the exhibition. While there they must surely have visited the Guatemalan pavilion,[5] if only to see the impressive display of artefacts and products from Petén, which included plaster casts from moulds of stelae made at the ruins of Seibal by Gorgonio López, who could not have failed to tell Maudslay about them.

After a delay of three or four days in Chicago, waiting to obtain sleeping berths on the train going west, they reached the western 'Morrisania', the ranch Annie's brother Gouverneur had created near Saint Joseph, Colorado.[6] Either then, or perhaps later, Gouverneur persuaded Alfred to help him run the ranch in an advisory capacity, for it was not doing well, partly owing to a general depression then affecting agriculture.[7] Then, a few days later, they went on to San Francisco, where they were booked to sail for San José, Guatemala, on 18 November. But no sooner had they moved into a hotel than both were struck down by influenza, and had to cancel their passage. When they were well enough to travel, a doctor advised them to complete their recuperation in the more benign climate of Monterey.

News of their presence having somehow reached Professor Holden, the astronomer in charge of the Lick Observatory on the top of Mount Hamilton, he telephoned to invite them to come up and visit. So they engaged a two-horse wagon, made the six-hour journey in pouring rain, and spent three days at the observatory hoping the weather would break. It never did; so they missed the chance of looking at the heavens through the world's biggest telescope.[8] When back in San Francisco once again, Alfred sought out Dr Gustav Eisen, a Swedish scientist who had become interested in the Maya calendar, and through him met his friend and collaborator. This man, Joseph Goodman, was to make significant contributions to the understanding of that calendar, some of which will be described in the next chapter.

At last, they boarded a Pacific Mail Steamship Company vessel, and set out to sea, encountering dull weather for the first few days. Then the sun broke through, and Annie, who was not a lover of ocean voyages in general, became enchanted when they had gone far enough south for flying fish to appear, and shoals of dolphins, four or five hundred together, played round our bows or dashed across our course, leaping and throwing up water in fountains of spray. Large turtles floated past lying asleep on the surface of the water, their shining backs catching the sunlight and reflecting it like mirrors. The sea-birds regarded them as convenient resting-places, and almost every turtle carried on his back a dozing bird which flapped lazily away, apparently shocked at the behaviour of the turtle when our ship caused him to take a sudden dive below.[9]

After calls at San Blas and Manzanillo, they arrived at Acapulco,

and sailed into the beautiful bay, through a tortuous channel between the high cliffs, guided by a feeble light perched on the rocks above us. The sea was a marvel of beauty, glowing with phosphorus, and alive with illuminated fish and dolphins darting about and leaving long streams of light behind them. Through this molten silver we glided to our anchorage near the town. As we neared the shore long narrow dug-out canoes lighted by great flaring pitch-pine torches carried by mahogany-coloured boys swarmed out of the darkness, and before the anchor was cast the ship was surrounded by a fringe of bumboats, filled with fruit, vegetables, and pottery, and presided over by swarthy Mexican men and women.

Resuming its voyage, the ship brought its passengers within sight of two great volcanoes near the Guatemalan border, and following a stop at the open roadstead of Champerico they soon came to the end of their voyage at the similar facilities of San José. Annie's observation of the landing operations at Champerico may not have allayed any fears about the ordeal that now faced her.

> When the time came to go ashore we were each in turn swung over the ship's side in a chair and deposited with a bump on top of the other passengers and piles of baggage in a large lighter which swayed alongside. This operation was reversed when we neared the shore, and a cage was lowered from the iron pier which loomed prodigiously and alarmingly high above us, and we were swung up in safety. Thank goodness there was no sea running, only the long undulations of the swell which beats ceaselessly on this coast.[10]

One marked improvement there was indeed: a narrow-gauge railway line from San José now took its passengers right up to the capital, and there the Maudslays were to spend three weeks, waiting until all their numerous boxes of equipment and provisions had been passed by Customs. These then had to be sorted and repacked in smaller boxes, some of which they would take with them on their first journey, while others would be forwarded to various destinations to await their arrival. Pack animals were scarce, and they had to take what they could find, but they did buy seven cargo-mules, none of them in very good condition.

No trained riding mule could be found for Annie, so she picked the smallest pack-mule, 'principally because she had a pretty head and held her ears well forward'. She proved to be miraculously sure-footed, and Annie soon learnt to leave the reins loose.

> Trusting in her superior knowledge and good sense, I was carried in safety for more than 500 miles, in daylight and in dark, over mountains and across rivers . . . without a stumble or a feeling of fear; and when I had to part with her at Yzabal, it was with real regret, and the feeling that I was saying good-bye to an old friend.

Their train was made up of six cargo mules, three saddle mules, and a saddle horse, and in addition four or five Indian *cargadores*, bearing loads which could not be conveniently carried on pack-saddles. In Annie's opinion Gorgonio held a unique position amongst his countrymen on account of his sympathy for dumb animals, and she noted that he never thought of refreshing himself until the mules had been attended to, and no beautiful scenery or convenient camping-ground had any charms for him if there was a scarcity of food 'para las pobres mulas'.

On reaching Antigua, Annie was disappointed by the hotel, supposedly the best in town, and by the food, almost all of which was ruined by too free a use of greasy lard. But when once outdoors, the charm of the surroundings banished all her thoughts of discomfort. The Maudslays then set out to climb the Volcán de Agua. The path was well graded, but dangerously undermined by gophers. Annie's mule, with singular intelligence and caution, never put her foot in a hole, but Alfred's horse floundered into them all.

> On one occasion, choosing for the performance the steepest and narrowest place in the path, right on the edge of a precipice, he managed, first to lose his forelegs in a burrow, and nearly crushed his rider's leg against a projecting rock, then in struggling out to lose his hind legs in another burrow, and to finish up by falling over backwards. . . . Luckily [Alfred] was soon on his feet again, and so was the horse, and we were all heartily thankful to have escaped what might have been a serious accident.

When more than half-way to the summit, they began noticing, on the shady side of the path, 'small cave-like recesses cut in the hill-side, which have a curious origin':

> The sloping surface of the soil is saturated with moisture slowly draining down the mountain-side, continually renewed by the clouds and mist which are ever gathering round the summit; every night this moisture is congealed into myriads of minute elongated crystals, which are so closely mixed with the disintegrated surface of the soil, that they almost escape notice. This mixture of earth and ice the Indians scoop out of these shady nooks and make into packages weighing about 170 lbs. each, neatly wrapped up in coarse mountain grass, and one of these heavy packages an Indian will carry on his back for sale in Antigua or Escuintla; but now the manufacture of artificial ice is putting an end to his trade.

The Maudslays camped for the night some way below the crater, and started off for the final ascent before dawn next morning, arriving in time to see, in Annie's words,

> a magnificent panorama of mountain peaks floating out of the mist, east and west and north, whilst to the south a grey hazy plain stretched away until it was lost in the mists of the ocean. Following the line of the coast the great bulwark of volcanic cones stood shoulder to shoulder, and in the far east we could just catch the faint

red from the active crater of Izalco in Salvador reflected on the morning sky. One by one the lofty peaks caught a pink glow from the coming sun, and as the mists rolled away we could see the pretty lake of Amatitlan nestled among the hills. . . . Very near to us on the west towered the beautiful volcano of Fuego, still clothed in the softest blue mist. As the sun rose clear and bright we beheld a sight so interesting and beautiful that it alone would have repaid us for the miseries of the night, for at that moment a ghost-like shadowy dark blue mountain rose high above all the others, and as we gazed wonderingly what this special visitor might mean, we saw it was the shadow of Agua itself projected on the atmosphere.

The Maudslays then rode off from Antigua, bent on making a lengthy reconnaissance of that portion of Los Altos (the highlands) lying to the west and north of that town. To begin with, their route was one already familiar to the more adventurous travellers. It took them, first, to a spot near Godines, high above Lake Atitlán and on the edge of a precipice, where there was a small spring, and a view so enchanting that they stayed for a week, riding and rambling, and always trying to get back early so as to finish dinner comfortably and take their seats in good time for the never-failing cloud display.

From 5 o'clock until dark there followed a scene which no pen and no brush could adequately portray. The clouds seemed to be bewitched: they came down on us in alternate black and sunlit masses, terrible in their majesty; then rolled aside to show us all the beauty of a sunset sky, tints of violet that shaded into pink, and pink that melted into the clearest blue, whilst far away beyond the mountains seaward rolled vast billowy masses, first red and yellow, and then pink, fading into the softest green.

Moving on, they sent their pack animals on to Panajachel, a few miles along the shore to the northwest, and made a detour to the entirely Indian village of San Antonio, built on a small promontory jutting into the lake. They spent a night there before going on to Panajachel, and there witnessed curious ceremonies of the Indian pilgrims returning from pilgrimages to the Black Christ in the great church at Esquipulas (about 25 miles southwest of Copán, and therefore a journey of many days on foot).

Annie described the scene:

As evening approached, little companies of pilgrims, bending under their burdens, filed into town, and as night fell the Plaza was lit up by numerous small fires, around which the pilgrims gathered for their supper. [When] this important meal ended, they began their religious functions by laying down *petates* (mats) in front of the *cacastes* [heavy back-packs], which had already been arranged in a line across the Plaza. Then each man produced from his cargo a small wooden box, usually glazed on one side, containing the image of a saint, and these were arranged in a row against the *cacastes*, between lighted candles, the place of honour in the middle being assigned to a box containing a figure of the Black Christ. When these arrangements were completed, the Indians, who were dressed in long black woollen garments, with long white veils fastened to their black straw hats, prostrated themselves in turn before each shrine, and crawled along from one end to the other on hands and knees, laying the forehead in the dust, offering up their prayers to each saint and kissing the box which contained its image. These acts of devotion were several times repeated, and then, grouping themselves on their knees before the shrine of the Black Christ, and led by one of their number, who seemed to have some sort of authority over them, they all chanted the quaint hymn we had so often heard in the early watches of the morning. After singing for nearly half an hour they withdrew to their fires, rolled themselves in their blankets, and were soon fast asleep.

From Panajachel the Maudslays had a stiff ride up to the small Indian town of Sololá. There, as elsewhere, Annie was enchanted by the Indian markets, in which she and Alfred bought several *huipiles* and other textiles, some of them straight off the wearers' backs.

The plan was now to head north, cross the River Motagua (which eventually flows into the Caribbean), and make for Uspantán, a Quiché Maya town about 70 miles northeast of Sololá as the crow flies, although considerably longer by any feasible route. From there they would swing east, cross the Chixoy River (which flows into the Gulf of Mexico), cross the Chixoy again (for it makes a great loop) and arrive at Santa Cruz Verapaz, about 15 miles south of Cobán, a notable town, and hub of the Kekchi Maya world. It would be a daunting ride, but fortunately Gorgonio had some knowledge of the area.

Having camped for the night along the way, they rode on, and at midday entered the large Indian town of Santo Tomás Chichicastenango, today the mecca of bus-loads of tourists, but then scarcely ever visited by outsiders. Although there was no inn, they managed to find something to eat, and then, in Annie's words,

> after breakfast we strolled into the picturesque plaza, bright with the gala costumes of the Indians. The women wore heavy chains of beads and coins round their necks, and were clothed in the most elaborately embroidered huipils we had yet seen. Almost every man carried a blue- or red-striped rug on his shoulder, and some queerly dressed old men wandered amongst the crowd, with distaff in hand, spinning woollen thread. . . .

At the top of the stone steps in front of the open church-door a large pile of wood-ashes smouldered and flickered faintly in the sun-light; the man who tended this fire every now and then threw on the embers small pieces of copal [incense] which scented the air with its heavy perfumed smoke, whilst around the fire groups of women knelt to pray before entering the building. We found the interior to be charmingly decorated with flowers. The floor had first been strewn with fragrant pine-needles, and on this carpet the flowers were arranged in the shape of a huge cross, extending almost the whole length of the church. In some parts the lines were traced in green and coloured leaves, and filled up with scattered rose-petals; in others, with clusters of all the flowers that could be found in bloom, edged with little groups of lighted candles. Picturesquely dressed Indians, singly or in couples, were dragging themselves on their knees the whole length of the cross, stopping at intervals to repeat prayers.

They went on their way, and after riding for about two hours came to a steep descent into the *barranca,* or ravine, through which the River Motagua flows, although it was there only a swift-flowing rivulet giving no indication of the great river it would become, about 250 miles down-stream. Having forded it, and climbed out of the ravine, they came to a group of mounds, some of which were 20 or 30 feet high. On the summits of the higher ones rough stone crosses had been set up, or shrines for burning copal incense. In the nearby village of Chiché the *cabildo* proved to be roofless and under repair, but they found shelter for the night in one room of a new, half-finished house.

We were now going altogether out of the beaten track and should have to take our chance for the night in cabildo, convento, or school-house, and when these failed we could take refuge in our tent (which proved to be the most comfortable lodging of them all), but it was to be used only as a last resort, so as to avoid the trouble of setting it up at night, when wearied by a long day's ride, and the extra packing which would delay the start in the morning.

They rode on through bare and uninteresting country till they came to Chinic (Chinique on modern maps), a village similar to Chiché except for its gardens of oranges and bananas, made possible by abundant water. Next morning they had a steep climb up to an altitude of 7000 feet to cross a mountain range:

The day was so enchantingly lovely that we lingered to enjoy the views [the volcanoes Agua, Fuego and Atitlán still being visible to the south], to pick wild flowers, to rest in the grateful shade of the woods, and gen-erally drink in the charm of our surroundings, and forgot to fulfil that never-ending task of hurrying up the loitering cargadores, who knew the length of the journey before them much better than we did, but who were more than willing to take advantage of a halt, as they had only partly recovered from the effects of the aguardiente imbibed during a fiesta the day before. When at last we began to urge them on they baulked us at every turn in the track, and were always halting on one excuse or another, so that during two hours we hardly made any progress at all; then about four in the afternoon, when we had hardly commenced the descent of the north side of the range, our Indians went on strike altogether and refused to go any further that day. Neither persuasion nor threats moved them from their purpose, and down they sat by the roadside and settled themselves in for the night.

We were still three or four leagues from our destination, and as the mules with our camp kit had pushed on ahead we could not possibly pass the night on the mountain. So making the best of a bad business, and trying to avoid the futility of losing one's temper with an obstinate Indian, we abandoned our dressing-bags and the other useful things which they were carrying, and pushed on as fast as our animals would travel in hope of reaching San Andrés Sacabajá before dark. Lofty mountains fenced us round, and the little river which ran down a narrow valley towards San Andrés was fully 3,000 feet below us. The descent was without a break and the track which zigzagged down the spur of a hill was rough beyond description. Before we were halfway down the sun set, the short tropical twilight faded, and night overtook us whilst we were groping our way through a thick wood. Gorgonio on his clever old mule led the way, I came next, and my husband, whose iron-shod horse was never too sure-footed even in the day, brought up the rear.

It soon became so dark that I could not see my own mule's head, but I felt sure that she was walking along the edges of precipices and I could feel that she was picking her way amidst boulders and stepping in and out of holes; sometimes she would stop, draw her feet together and slide down the smooth face of a rock. This sounds like a perilous feat, but it was all done with such extreme care and such perfect knowledge of what she was about, that although anxious I felt little real fear. The horse floundered about terribly; several times his rider dismounted and tried to grope his way on foot, but found the track so difficult and dangerous in the pitchy darkness that each time he was unwillingly obliged to mount again and trust to the guidance of his horse, whose stumbles continually alarmed me.

About halfway down the mountain, the lights of San Andrés appeared, as we thought, just below us; but never were lights more deceptive and illusive, for even after reaching the level of the valley we rode for at least two hours, crossing and recrossing the broad but shallow river several times. The night continued very dark, no stars came out, and only the light of the glow-worms cheered us along our path, while the flashing sparks of the fireflies deluded us into thinking that we were near to houses, and the air resounded with the harsh humming song of innumerable cicadas, broken now and again by the cry of some night-feeding bird.

It was nine o'clock when we arrived at the cabildo of San Andrés de Sacabajá, tired and hungry and with but small prospect of any supper, as our food-boxes were left behind with the mozos. The villagers were nearly all asleep, and we were told there was no water to be obtained without scrambling down in the dark to the river 200 feet below us. However, Gorgonio was sent out on a foraging expedition, and after a prolonged search returned in triumph with bread, eggs, and half a kettle full of water, so we made our coffee and ate our supper on the verandah surrounded by a pack of half-starved dogs.

Supper over, we looked about for a room to sleep in. The cabildo was under repair and the only inhabitable room in it was occupied by the half-caste 'secretario', who most politely offered to share his bedroom with us. On our refusal to put him to such inconvenience he suggested a visit to the convento on the other side of the plaza; so we all marched across to examine it by the light of a single candle. After passing in a ghostly procession through the huge empty rat-infested close-smelling rooms, we declined that lodging also, and finally put up our beds in an unfinished room in the cabildo, which was half-full of scaffolding, where the floor was inches deep in sand, the door refused to shut, and bats flitted in and out at their own sweet will; but even these discomforts and the howls of a drunken Indian locked in the prison next door could not keep sleep off after our long day's ride.

Next morning, they walked about to see what San Andrés had to offer, and were not impressed. There was not a green thing to be seen, saving one huge Ceiba tree standing alone in the middle of a great windswept plaza. They were told that 'the foolishness of a former Jefe Político had created this dreary waste by ordering all the trees in the village to be cut down, because in his enlightened opinion trees near houses were unhealthy'.

Then, while they were drinking their morning coffee on the verandah, the porters who had been left behind behind on the road came in, and before long they all set off for Uspantán. After riding about 5 miles over a fairly level plain they caught sight of some mounds on the far side of a gully.

Tying up our mules, we climbed down to the banks of a small rushing rivulet, crossed the stream, and scrambling up the opposite side, found ourselves on a detached bare plain surrounded on all sides by barrancas. At one end of this plain the mounds were symmetrically arranged. There was a clearly defined plaza about fifty yards across with low mounds on three sides of it, and on the fourth side a mound about forty feet high. . . . Two of the largest of the foundation mounds had been dug into by a German priest, father Heyde, who was formerly the cura of Joyabaj, one of the neighbouring towns. These excavations showed us that the mounds themselves were formed of cores of earth covered with a coating of rough stones, imbedded in mud, about 5 feet in thickness, and this again was faced with masonry of roughly squared stones and a thick coating of plaster. Patches of the outer casing of squared stones with the plaster facing still adhering to it could be seen where the surface had been left undisturbed. . . . Lying on the ground were two blocks of stone shaped into serpents' heads with human faces between their open jaws, undoubtedly of the same style and marked with the same conventional curves as those found at Copan and other more ancient ruins in Central America. Both of these carved stones had tenons about two feet long, by which they could be fixed into the masonry.

Observing that the deep *barrancas* surrounding the whole site formed a natural moat and made the position easily defensible, they rode on to overtake their pack-mules, which, as the country was open, they could still distinguish some miles ahead by the little cloud of dust that marked their progress.

About four o'clock we came to the edge of the gorge of the Río Negro and began a steep descent of twelve or thirteen hundred feet to the bridge over the river. The views which opened before us as we descended were very fine and of a peculiar character. Abrupt granite rocks jut out from the steep slopes, which are themselves curiously rounded in outline, and are covered with a coating of thick rough grass, giving them the appearance of being clothed in green velvet shot with gold. . . . The stream at the bottom of this gorge is swift and deep, and the water is of a beautiful greenish colour. It is not more than thirty yards wide, and we crossed it on a bridge of large roughly-squared logs, laid side by side without any attempt to fasten them or bind them together, and supported by four lofty and stoutly built piers.

They camped for the night by the river, and on setting out next morning on the long climb up they found that

the tracks, if such they could be called, were numerous and confused, and had been made by mules, cattle, and Indians wandering about in all directions seeking a firm foothold amongst the loose stones and slippery rocks. Our animals were suffering from want of food, and we left them to scramble up by themselves. . . . We clambered up about 3000 feet, and then mounting our animals rode over the ridge . . . [and then] continued our gradual ascent, and the oaks and pines increased in number until they formed patches of woodland. Great bunches of mistletoe of various sorts – green and orange and brown – were conspicuous amongst the oak-leaves, and the branches of the trees were laden with clusters of orchids and tillandsias. My companions gathered for me beautiful sprays of orchid blossoms and gorgeous crowns of crimson leaves which surround the flowering spikes of the tillandsias, and these, added to bunches of frangipani we had plucked on the arid hill-sides and the fresh green lycopodium . . . formed a decoration to my saddle that would have been the envy of Covent Garden.

And so they came to the straggling village of San Miguel Uspantán. The Alcalde alotted them a room in the convento, which had been swept and carpeted with fresh pine-needles in expectation of the arrival of the Jefe Político of the Department of Quiché – although this was only a monk's cell, windowless, and infested with rats and mice. 'The little village was in no way pretty, but the climate was exceedingly pleasant, the blossoms on the orange-trees in the plaza filled the air with perfume, the green hills round us were refreshing to look at, and our tired animals fared sumptuously.'

Maudslay and Gorgonio then began making enquiries about ruins in the area. In Annie's words, they set off one morning along a spur of the hill running out to the west, and

walked about a mile and a half without seeing any trace of mounds and were nearly giving up the search in that direction . . . when they noticed that the shrubs in front of them covered an artificial mound, and that there was a dip in the ground between them and it. This dip proved to be a ditch, which may originally may have been twenty feet deep, cut across a narrow neck of the ridge, and a long steep-sided mound barred the passage on the other side. Beyond this mound the top of the hill broadened out again into an extent of ground nearly the same as that of the site of Utatlán, and almost the whole of it was covered with foundation mounds. . . . In some cases the foundations retained part of their casing of well-dressed stone and cement facing. . . . In position and arrangement the ruins differed little from those at Iximché and Utatlán.

Maudslay wanted to make some excavations in one of the sites they visited before reaching Cobán, and perhaps it was this one, but he was thwarted by the land-owner's refusal to grant permission.

Maudslay's intention, on leaving Uspantán, had been to follow a track reported as heading southeast to the Río Chixoy, where they could cross it and reach Rabinal, some fifteen miles farther on in the same direction. This town was on his itinerary as a consequence of the brief examination he had made seven years earlier of the ruins of Chuitinamit, lying between Rabinal and Cubulco, as he had been planning to examine them more thoroughly. But now he was assured that no such track to the river existed – it was just a myth. This meant that they were trapped in the great loop of the river, the only escape from it being over a bridge sited far downstream to the north, and in exactly the wrong direction for Rabinal.

Then they learnt that another possibility did exist, although it involved a descent of nearly 4000 feet to the place where they and their baggage could be ferried across, but this was too steep for loaded pack-animals to negotiate. As Maudslay was so unwilling to turn back and make the detour, he decided to try this route. On reaching the beginning of the descent, they halted (in Annie's words)

> to unload the mules, and give over their burdens to the care of the Indian carriers. We did not unsaddle the animals, but were careful to remove stirrups and stirrup-leathers, and to see that all straps and girths were secure. My husband and I led the way, keeping well ahead of the mules, lest one of them should roll over us. It was an exceedingly rough and difficult walk, and we were more than three hours accomplishing it. Two of the mules fell, and the horse rolled over; but none of them were hurt, and we all arrived safely at the river.
>
> In answer to our shouts a man emerged from a house on the opposite bank and came over to us on a very small raft which he brought across the stream by hauling on a rope made fast to both banks. On this craft we were ferried over, two at a time. I dare say the passage was safe enough, but that was not exactly my impression whilst crossing, for the current was very swift and the raft almost entirely under water, and we had to curl ourselves up on a ricketty seat in order to keep dry. At our landing place, called Agua Blanca, there were only two houses, and these were inhabited by Cobaneros, friends of Gorgonio, who gave us food and shelter for the night, treated our tired animals most hospitably, and refused all payment.

From there, the way to Cobán presented no difficulty, and as the result of sending a telegram from San Cristóbal on their way they were met at Cobán by Moritz Thomae, a friend of Frank Sarg's, whose offer of hospitality they eagerly accepted (Sarg himself must have been absent). Cobán, a delightful and interesting town, had not been on the itinerary, but Maudslay probably felt that, since they were there, he couldn't deny Annie any of the pleasure and interest that the town had to offer. So they tarried there for a week.

In fact some elasticity had been added to Maudslay's schedule by a piece of unwelcome news that reached him there. This concerned the

cases of surveying instruments and boxes of provisions which should
have been forwarded to Salamá for his use at Rabinal; only now did he
learn that owing to some blunder they had never left Guatemala City. So
he was unable to do more than publish the hastily-made, yet very competent, plans he had made on his former visit. One is of the remains of a
building he found in one of the plazas, of which he provided a rough
ground-plan:

> It is an oblong enclosure with walls 10 feet thick, with recesses at the
> four corners. The walls are in some parts perfect to a height of 7 feet.
> I could not find that there had been any doorway to this enclosure. . . .
> It agrees in plan and dimensions with the building figured in
> Bancroft's 'Native races of the Pacific States,' as a type of the Tlachtli
> courts of Mexico, where a game (which is described by Herrera and
> others) was played with an indiarubber ball.

This may be the earliest recognition of ball-courts of this type, those
at Chichén Itzá and Copán being considerably different, and far larger.

The remainder of the long journey to Copán was accomplished with
no more than the usual difficulties over lodging, the hiring of *cargadores*,
and the fording of rivers almost too deep to ford. When they reached
Salamá, about 40 miles along the way from Cobán, Maudslay was obliged to send Caralampio to Rabinal to fetch boxes that should have been
forwarded there by the Alcalde of Chiché; but there was no sign of them,
so the unfortunate young man had to go all the way to Chiché to retrieve
them. But from there he could at least take a more direct route, passing
through Joyabaj.

In the Zacapa area *cargadores* were not a feature of the economy, so the
pack-train had to be increased to a total of twenty-five mules. They plod-
ded on, and on the third day after leaving Zacapa the Maudslays, at the
head of their impressive cavalcade, rejoiced at entering pine woods and
climbing up to higher ground; and soon, as Annie put it,

> they were scrambling down the last mile of the rugged path, and rode
> on into the modern village of Copan – a small collection of red-tiled
> dirty hovels grouped round a plaza which was glorified by the pres-
> ence of a fine stone altar, covered with the fantastic carving in which
> the Maya excelled, and we drew rein before the hut occupied by the
> Niña Chica, an old friend of my husband's and the presiding genius
> of the village.
> The arrival of our party had awakened the village from its siesta,
> and we were soon the centre of an admiring group of rag-clad men
> and women and bright-eyed and wholly unclad children. As soon as
> the Niña Chica emerged from her hut and recognised Don Alfredo
> she expressed her delight in the most flattering terms, throwing her

arms round him, as he sat in the saddle, in a fond embrace. In her youth the Niña Chica must have been a beauty, and even now in her old age her wrinkled face has a fine look, and she carries herself with an imperious air, in queer contrast to the dirt of her dress and the squalor of her surroundings. She seemed determined to take complete possession of my husband, and began to pour into his ears, with the greatest volubility and wit, the gossip of the village and the history of all that had happened during the eight years that had passed since his last visit. It required some tact and skill to disengage ourselves from this dirty but attractive old lady, and it was only achieved after many promises to visit her again soon and talk it over.

They rode on, and after crossing a small stream

at last had arrived and were in the actual presence of the strange stone monuments whose reproductions in plaster I knew so well. The bridle-path led over the steep side of a foundation mound into the Western Court, where I found myself face to face with an old friend, who has stood on guard for centuries at the foot of the great stairway. . . .

In the middle of the plaza stood the house we were to occupy, an airy structure something like a large bird-cage, which had been built [by the Peabody Museum crew], who for the last two seasons had been at work in the ruins. The walls were made of rough sticks placed side by side, about an inch apart, and bound together with lianes; the roof was thatched with sugar-cane leaves, one large opening in the wall serving as a doorway, and windows were certainly not needed, as every breath of air sighed through the gaping walls. One end of the house had been screened off and the walls thatched to the ground so as to form a dark room for photography.

Annie, however, soon decided that their bedroom lacked privacy and was too draughty, so the tent was put up as a bedroom instead.

'One great and important piece of work done by the Americans', Annie wrote, 'has been the building of a substantial stone wall which encircles and protects the principal ruined structures, so that there is no longer any danger of the sculptured monuments being damaged by fire, as has so often happened before from careless burning of fallen timber when the natives have been clearing the ground for plantation'. In addition, of course, much valuable excavation and surveying had been done by them.

In view of the hot weather that Maudslay would have remembered as beginning near the end of March, one imagines that he had intended to start work at Copán well before the end of February, but owing to the unexpected delays, and that week of rambling and enjoying sunsets over Lake Atitlán, he and Annie didn't reach Copán until the beginning of

March. Once there Alfred then seems to have devoted much of his time to photography and to checking Annie Hunter's and Edwin Lambert's drawings against the originals. Their great contribution to Maudslay's work is discussed in Chapter 17. Meanwhile Gorgonio and his sons, Carlos and Caralampio, were busy cleaning sculptures and making paper moulds of them. Annie, for her part, took charge of the house-keeping – since no one in the village had the slightest knowledge of cook-ing – and among other occupations found herself administering first aid to the sick or injured in the village.[11]

Her husband too, during his time at Copán in 1885, had felt obliged to try his hand at the profession that once he had intended to pursue.

Unfortunately, I soon gained a distinguished reputation as a surgeon. I say unfortunately, as it raised the hopes of all the sufferers, includ-ing every incurable cripple, for leagues around, and gave me the unpleasant task of telling them I was powerless to help them. The case that brought me fame was that of a poor fellow, a blacksmith by trade, living some twelve or fourteen leagues away, who came into camp one morning with his eyes in the most dreadful state of inflam-mation. He told me that about ten days before, when working at his forge, a hot spark from the metal had flown into his eyes, and that during the following week everyone in the village had tried in turn to get the speck out of his eye and that each one had failed. Then he heard of my arrival at the ruins, and had walked over to ask me to help him. It was no use my telling him that I was not a doctor, and that I might very easily destroy the sight of his eye altogether if I were to try any experiments: he only replied that he did not care whether I was or was not a doctor, and that I could not make him much blinder than he was, for he could not see at all with one eye, and very little with the other.

I was at my wits' end to know what to do for him, it seemed cruel to send him away; and my hands were so hot and shaky after work-ing with a crowbar and machete all the morning, that I could not even examine his eye satisfactorily. So I put a cold bandage over his eyes, gave him some food, and a seat in the darkest corner of the rancho, and told him to rest after his long walk, whilst I thought the matter over. When the sun had fallen low, Gorgonio led the man to my house in the village, and there we put him on his back, and I examined the eye with a magnifying glass. I could see a minute, almost transparent particle just on the outer rim of the iris, but the camel's hair brush which I passed over it failed to move it. Then I screwed up my courage and got Gorgonio to hold the eye down whilst, looking through the magnifying glass, I tried to remove the particle with the fine point of a knife. The first attempt failed but did no damage, and on the second trial I got the point of the knife under the particle and it came away. By the next morning the inflammation had very considerably subsided, the sight of the uninjured eye appeared almost normal, and that of the injured eye had to some extent recovered.

By the middle of the month, as Annie noted, 'the heat at noonday became excessive and the weather looked threatening. It was early for rain, but ominous thunder-clouds had hovered about for several days, and finally . . . the storm burst.' It proved to be just the prelude to a tremendous 'norther' which caused havoc throughout the Gulf of Mexico.

After a journey made unpleasant by heavy rain and exceptional cold they arrived at Quiriguá, shortly after crossing the newly cleared track of the railway line which soon would link the Guatemala City with Puerto Barrios on the Caribbean coast. On arrival at the ruins they were welcomed by Hugh Price, who had come at Maudslay's request, and had built a *rancho* for them near river bank.[12] But they found the nights unpleasant because of

herds of cattle roaming through the woods, and rival bulls would make the night hideous with their bellowings, and we were forced to get up repeatedly to ward off attacks on the rather frail fence . . . and drive off those animals who came stumbling among the tent ropes and threatened to bring the canvas down on our heads. Salt-stained clothing left on a line would be found chewed to unrecognizable mess in morning.

Annie had been told that

the climate at Quiriguá in April is usually clear and dry. But we had chanced upon one of those exceptional seasons . . . and the inevitable heat was made the more disagreeable by sudden deluges of rain, which falling on the sun-baked sands, turned the air into a great vapour bath. . . . On one bright and lovely day . . . the forest was beautiful and interesting beyond description, and seemed to be laid under a spell of enchantment. Nothing could exceed the wondrous beauty of the sinuous motion of coroza palms as the breeze gently stirred their splendid leaves and waved them lazily together in a lingering embrace. The forest resounded with the calls of birds, the gurgling note of the oropendula, the cries of parrots, and the screams of brilliant macaws, to which the hoarse roar of the *monos* [howler monkeys], hidden in the highest tree-tops, formed a monotonous accompaniment. The perfumed breeze shook down flowers from the invisible tree-tops and showered them in our path.

Maudslay had various reasons for returning to Quiriguá for a fourth visit. As at Copán, he wanted to check the drawings against the originals, and here, too, there were some paper moulds still to be made. Hugh Price was also going to make a more accurate plan of the ruins than the one that Blockley, a relative novice, had produced eleven years earlier.

Annie describes how, a few days before leaving

an exceptionally heavy shower had driven a party of women who were passing by to take shelter in our house; one of them carried in her dress a baby squirrel, a charming little brown creature with a long, grey, feather-like tail. I longed to possess it, and with some hesitation made an offer for it of five reales, about 1s. 6d. of our money, which was eagerly accepted, and the tiny thing became our property. I gave him a grass saddle-bag for a bed and hung him inside my mosquito curtain, where he slept through the night without disturbing me. During the day, when not cuddled up asleep in my hand, he was rushing about the house, prying into all corners, and amusing my lonely days by his pretty ways and the grace of his movements. [They named it Chico.]

Unfortunately, the Maudslays had to leave Quiriguá after spending no more than two weeks there so as to catch the next steamer from Livingston, the last of the season to carry passengers to New Orleans without a long detention in quarantine. On leaving Quiriguá, Annie admitted to a guilty feeling of relief as they left the steamy heat of the forest and rode up into pinewoods; then at nightfall they began the descent to the Golfo Dulce with 'the moonlight playing its usual tricks, lighting up the scattered palm-trees and throwing a glamour of beauty even over the white-washed houses of the village when we rode into Izabal'. On reaching Livingston, the Maudslays decided not to take the overcrowded mailboat, but instead a trading steamer. Its captain was bent on getting his cargo of eighteen thousand bunches of bananas to New Orleans as quickly as possible, and did so in ninety-three hours. There Annie developed malaria, but of a mild variety.

Price and Gorgonio were less fortunate. They had accompanied the Maudslays to Yzabal, and then returned to Quiriguá to continue their work there. The mounds had already been cleared, and sight-lines for triangulation cut, but, just as Price was beginning the survey, both he and Gorgonio were struck down by such virulent fevers that they had difficulty getting back to Yzabal. There they were kindly looked after by Mr and Mrs Potts. With both of them incapacitated, the task of repacking the moulds that had been taken at both Copán and Quiriguá had to be entrusted to a local carpenter at Yzabal. But most unfortunately his work was so incompetent that more than half of them were ruined by moisture during the voyage to England, the damage being exacerbated by an unexplained delay of six months in delivery. Maudslay had therefore to spend an unhappy day at the British Museum opening packing cases and rescuing the less-injured moulds from the evil-smelling mass of mildewed paper. Then Alfred also came down with a malaria of normal virulence, which he had presumably caught at Quiriguá.

And how had Chico, the squirrel, fared? 'His first day's journey into the great world had been rather trying to us both', Annie wrote.

> From the moment I mounted my mule until the arrival at Yzabal he never ceased running up and down from my saddle to the top of the mule's head, tugging at the string which held him and trying to jump into all the overhanging branches. He was so excited and wilful that I was sorely tempted to set him free . . . but when we reached Yzabal, all trouble with him was at an end, the poor little creature had so exhausted himself that he at once crept into his saddle-bag and slept without stirring for many hours. This was indeed the only day on which he gave us any trouble during the whole of our journey to London.

He made himself at home in the cabin of the steamer, and 'although during the long railway journey to New York, he took many a scamper round our state room, he used the utmost discretion in always retreating into his bag on the approach of the guard, as though he knew the stringent rules against carrying animals in a Pullman car'. Surviving various misadventures, Chico remained the Maudslays' much loved pet for two more years.

Chapter 16

Zavaleta

I n about 1898 Maudslay took over an hacienda and small gold mine near Oaxaca. After his death, one obituary writer attributed his own-ership of it to inheritance, but this improbable explanation can be discarded in favour of the one given by Arthur Laughton, the assayer, engineer, and later manager of the mine. As he wrote in a letter home dated 31 January, 1900, '[Maudslay] was principal shareholder in a com-pany wh[ich] went smash because they were a lot of fools, and he bought the whole show and is going to run it himself. His fortune is not too large however & if he can't make it, or at any rate pay expenses in 4 months, doubts if he can keep it on any longer.' Laughton was invited by the Maudslays to live in their house; and as it happened, he would develop another connection with the world of Americanists through his marriage to Nadine, the daughter of Zelia Nuttall and Alfonse Pinart.

In fact the mine was kept going, and the house which the Maudslays built close to it and named Zavaleta[1] served as their winter home until 1906. It stood in a delightful situation, overlooking a stream of crystal-clear water flowing from a spring at the foot of a high escarpment, with the mine entrance and ore-crushing plant on the other side of the stream. A young hardwood forest now covers the low hill above the mine, and there are no other dwellings in the vicinity. Oaxaca lies about 10 miles to the east along an unmade road that passes through the village of Cuilapan, and far above, near the edge of the escarpment, stands a Zapotec Indian village named San Pablo Cuatro Venados.

Since nothing now remains of the house, the walls must have been built of adobe. It was flat-roofed, and quite large, with room for servants, two of whom were old retainers who came with the Maudslays each year from England, and there was room for guests as well. The house stood on a hillock, probably built up of mine tailings, the sides of which still pre-serve the terracing made by Maudslay for his garden. There, Laughton says, he dug and planted, pruned and weeded for hours on end, every day.[2]

Maudslay's decision to have a settled home of his own in Mexico as a refuge from British winters is quite understandable in view of the work in which he was now engaged: translation of Bernal Díaz del Castillo's *Historia Verdadera de la Conquista de Nueva España*. But why in Oaxaca? Without question it is a delightful region, and not so very distant from Mexico City, but it's likely that a dominant factor was his ambition to investigate the important ruins of Monte Albán. And while Zavaleta wasn't in the immediate vicinity of the ruins, it cannot have been more than ninety minutes' ride away – or less if there existed a short cut through the hills.

No longer able to finance expeditions himself, Maudslay was quick off the mark in applying to the Carnegie Institution of Washington for funds. Andrew Carnegie had made his first deed of gift of $10 million to the newly formed Institution in January 1902, and, at the urging of D. C. Gilman, of Maryland, the Board of Trustees had agreed to support archaeology.[3] Maudslay sent in a request at once, but on 24 January of that year the executive Committee 'rejected the application of A. P. Maudslay for excavations on the site of the ancient city of Monte Albán, Mexico'.

Nevertheless, Maudslay seems to have been confident of obtaining support from the Carnegie Institution, because on 18 November 1902 the British Minister in Mexico informed Ignacio Mariscal, the Secretario de Relaciones Exteriores,[4] that Maudslay had asked him to transmit for consideration by the Mexican Government a proposal to clear and explore the ruins of Monte Albán. The whole cost would be borne by the Carnegie Institution. He went on to state that 'Mr. Maudslay, who was present at the Congress recently celebrated in Washington, was the only person elected by the mentioned Commissioners to explore the ruins of Monte Albán,[5] if the permission of the Mexican Government were forthcoming'. (This was the quadrennial International Congress of Americanists, which that year was held in New York City, not Washington.)[6] The Minister draws attention to Maudslay's promise not to remove any object of interest to antiquarians. Maudslay has lived several years in Mexico, interested in a mine near Monte Albán, and he cannot speak too highly of him. He is now in Mexico on his way to the mine, and would like to arrange a meeting with the President.

The proposal includes building a house among the ruins in which to store smaller finds.

> All sculpture would be left in place as far as possible, with measures taken to conserve them. He wishes to excavate, take moulds, photograph, and do whatever else is needed for a conscientious study in order to complete a report. He requests help in improving the road up to the ruins, and a supply of water.
>
> At the conclusion of his work, once the Government has chosen for the National Museum those pieces from among the collection of pieces that cannot be left in place, he requests the Government will

consider favourably the request of the Carnegie Commissioners to send the remaining objects to museums or institutions outside the republic, these to be chosen by the Carnegie Institution as doing most to encourage the study of American archaeology. One must bear in mind nevertheless that the Carnegie Institution possesses no museum of its own, nor has any special interest in other museums.

Teobert Maler, the Austrian explorer and photographer, who in certain respects was the equal of Maudslay (although quite unlike him in regard to judgment and temperament), is known to have met Maudslay in Mexico City in that same year, 1903. Of what passed between them there is no record, but for Maler the meeting may have been awkward, for he was extremely jealous of Maudslay. In a letter he wrote in that year to Charles P. Bowditch, Maler tells of efforts by Marshall Saville to get rid of Batres and replace him with someone less hostile to archaeological work by foreigners; he suspected that Zelia Nuttall and Maudslay were also involved in this plot.[7] 'It is true,' Maler wrote, 'that at the moment the personages at the head of the archaeology department are entirely opposed to give any foreigner concessions for exploring the ruins of the Land; but this has its reason in the impossible pretensions of some of them. For instance, the efforts of Mr. Maudslay to get a concession for "exploring" the ruins on the Monte Albán have been a complete failure!'[8]

But he was mistaken, for ten days after receiving the request the Secretaría de Instrucción Pública y Bellas Artes granted Maudslay the permission he sought. 'Se concede al Señor Alfred Maudslay la autorización que pide en nombre del Instituto Carnegie. . . .'[9] A new application by Maudslay to the Carnegie Institution for funding was considered on 27 October 1903, and this time it was 'ordered placed in a secondary list, to be recommended if funds were available'. But on 20 January 1904 it was 'resolved, that in view of the present condition of the funds, no further allotments be made for the year 1903–4 in astronomy, psychology, linguistics, archaeology and engineering'.

This 'present condition' of funds clearly resulted from the extremely generous support being given to Raphael Pumpelly, whose $18,000 grant had just a month earlier been increased by $8000.[10] There is no question that his archaeological work in the trans-Caspian region was of the highest importance, but at least to an interested party the allotment does seem lop-sided.

In September 1904 the Secretary of the Carnegie's Executive Board enquired of W. H. Holmes, now adviser in Pre-Historic Archaeology, if he knew whether Maudslay wished to renew his application to the Carnegie Institution for Monte Albán. Evidently he was, for as Carnegie Institution records show, at a meeting on 13 March 1905, 'The following were brought up and held for further consideration: A. P. Maudslay, $5583 to explore an ancient ruined city in Mexico.'

The same records show, however, that seven months later, on 16 October 1905, 'a letter from Dr. A. P. Maudslay was read, in which he stated that it would be impracticable for him to undertake archaeological researches in Central America' (sic). A likely explanation of Maudslay's abandonment of his evidently cherished plan was some failure of his health, for in January 1905 he had been admitted into a Denver, Colorado, hospital for treatment, and in June had undergone an operation.[11]

Some investigations of Monte Albán had already been made by Leopoldo Batres.[12] A self-educated man, he had been appointed to the position of Inspector General de Monumentos Antiguos as its first holder in 1886, and was to hold it until 1910. As such he became the first Mexican who could be termed an archaeologist, and the first to persuade the Mexican government to sponsor an archaeological project – an extremely large one, in fact: excavation and restoration at the vast ruined city of Teotihuacan. For this, as well as for his energy, he deserves recognition – but also criticism for the blunders he committed. As for the short season of work he did at Monte Albán, the late and great Mexican archaeologist Ignacio Bernal, who had an intimate knowledge of that site, told the author in a personal letter: 'As you know, Batres did some awful digging at Monte Albán.'

Highly opinionated, Batres was often badly mistaken in his judgments. According to some, he was not nationalistic, but he did cause trouble for several bona fide and respectable foreign archaeologists, and by 1903 he was already unpopular among them, to say the least. Marshall Saville, who by then held a position at the American Museum of Natural History in New York City, blamed him for ruining his planned expedition to Yaxchilán. As he wrote many years later, describing the débacle,

according to the terms of the [museum's] concession, the interests of the Mexican government were to be represented by the Inspector of Ancient Monuments, Leopoldo Batres. . . . On arrival in Chiapas [or more likely at the mouth of the Usumacinta in Tabasco], Batres refused to go to Yaxchilán, claiming that the site was within the Republic of Guatemala. Consequently the writer [Saville] was obliged to change his plans entirely, and Palenque seemed to be the best place to carry on operations. . . . After getting the outfit to the ruins [not a simple matter, since their supplies included several tons of special Spanish paper for making moulds of sculpture], Batres refused to take up his abode there, and remained in the village, making only one or two trips to the ruins during the six weeks the expedition remained in Chiapas.[13]

The adverse opinion of Maudslay that Batres shared with Maler was to be expressed even more forcibly to his own superiors four years later. The occasion was provided by an application made by the British Minister to the Secretario de Instrucción Pública on behalf of an unidentified British subject (who may well have been Maudslay himself) for permission to export examples of Zapotec ceramics to the British Museum. The request was forwarded to Batres for his opinion. Batres, who was then working at Teotihuacan, with his son Salvador as director of works, replied in January 1908 with strenuous arguments against granting permission, and next day dispatched another missive.

> To reinforce the opinion I had the honour to convey to you [yesterday] I will cite a deed, the principal author of which was the said museum [the British Museum] and the executive hand of this crime, the English subject Alfred P. Maudslay, who has a vandalic character highly significant for our historical and archaeological interests, one that would by itself be sufficient for Mexico to close its doors to him, and regard him with disdain, since neither the guilty Institution nor the hand employed in the crime can be brought to justice.
>
> In the years 1881 and 1882, Alfred P. Maudslay occupied, as Hernán Cortés would have done on his journey to Hibueras, the ruins of Yalchilan, situated on the right [sic] bank of the Usumacinta River, near the frontier of Mexico and Guatemala without worrying that this most important group of monuments belonged to the Mexican Republic, and destroyed without concern the most important temples which constitute that most interesting city in order to wrench from its walls the stone slabs which in high-relief sculpture and hieroglyphic inscriptions could teach posterity the history and myths of the most advanced Maya people, tablets of much greater importance because of their execution and high relief than those of Yucatán and the tablets of Palenque, since in the monuments stolen by the British Museum and Maudslay one sees the character of the highest artistic culture that was attained by the Maya people, and which flourished from there to Honduras. Maudslay committed this theft by thinning the tablets with a saw and transporting them to London via Belize. Later, the same Maudslay insinuated himself hypocritically into the ruins of Palenque, violated the sepulchres that were still sealed, and carried off more than two hundred boxes of antiquities for the British Museum. These facts, which I forgot to mention in my report of yesterday, I was reminded of by 'El Imparcial' [a newspaper] of today, on reading the name of Maudslay among those honoured by Mexico with the title of Honorary Professor of the National Museum. Mexico, January 3, 1908.[14]

It may be worth pointing out that Batres's grasp of recent history was as weak as his geography. He has Maudslay behaving like Cortés at

'Yalchilan' (whichever side of the river that was on) in 1881 and 1882; but in fact, as late as November 1881, the US Secretary of State was urging Mexico to withdraw the troops that had been sent, provocatively, to eastern Chiapas, and it is doubtful whether, even after the preliminary basis for a Mexican–Guatemalan agreement had been signed in September 1882, and a second one two years later, anyone in the area knew how the frontier would run. Even then, disputes and uncertainties persisted until a final agreement was signed in Mexico on 1 April 1895.

It does seem that Batres had only lately heard tales of Maudslay's supposedly nefarious operations (perhaps from Maler), because only two and a half years earlier Don Leopoldo had professed total ignorance about Yaxchilán. On 29 June 1905 Justo Sierra had written to him from the Secretaría de Estado, requesting his opinion on an application by a lumberman in Chiapas. This man had reported that marauders (*merodeadores*) were damaging the ruins of Yaxchilán, which lay within his concession, and to prevent further damage he requested permission to build a house among the ruins for guards, which his company would pay for.

Batres replied: 'In the first place, I doubt if the ruins of Yanchilan [*sic*] lie within the parallel [*sic*, once more] of the border between Mexico and Guatemala, so that while we remain unsure of this, we cannot run the risk of giving concessions in foreign territory which may run us into international disputes, as happened once before, if I remember right, with the same lumber company, and then caused Mexico to be on the brink of war with its neighbour, the Republic of Guatemala.'

And yet, in view of all the excitement about this ancient city, it is strange that Batres failed to include it on the very large archaeological map of the Republic that he compiled and published two years later, in celebration of the centenary of Mexican Independence.[15]

In the matter of the guard house, however, Batres was overruled by Chávez, and permission was given for its construction, but no confirmation has come to light of the lumberman's apparently public-spirited offer having actually resulted in the installation of guards.

While abuses by foreign explorers of antiquarian bent were indeed common enough in Mexico during this period to justify tighter supervision of their work, it is unfortunate that the task fell to a former cavalry officer lacking any useful preparation, other than acquiring the habit of command. Abundant energy Don Leopoldo certainly did have, but in this new field under his command there were few useful precedents for him to follow, and no guidelines to consult. But at the time of his appointment there may have been only a handful of men suitable for the task, and, in judging Batres's performance during the twenty-five years of his tenure, some positive actions do stand to his credit.

Among them was the installation of guardians at many archaeological sites in Yucatán and elsewhere; his campaign against the manufacture of fake antiquities; his construction of a museum at Teotihuacan, the planting of trees there, the construction of a wall round the site, and his vigour in travelling widely through the republic to distant ruins. But the enormous task he was charged with by President Porfirio Díaz – that of refurbishing the Temple of the Sun at Teotihuacan for the centenary celebrations of Mexico's Independence in 1810 – this Batres accomplished by a method denounced by many critics, as related below.

With Maudslay's hopes of working at Monte Albán now at an end, he and Annie sold Zavaleta, and chose as their quarters for the following winter a house in San Angel, then a charming little colonial town still quite separate from Mexico City. Here, Maudslay would pursue researches in Mexican archives. His interests, apart from Bernal Díaz, included Tenochtitlán (the Aztec capital) at the time of the Conquest, and, in particular, the precise location of Moctezuma's *Teocalli* and surrounding precinct. This was the subject of great debate at the time, because Hernán Cortés had taken pains to obliterate every trace of the temple, since he knew it was sacred, and the centre of the Aztec universe. Maudslay, therefore, studied closely all the early documents that were available, and also the ground in question.

Then at last, in May or June 1907, Maudslay and Annie left the shores of Mexico and the New World, never to return. Before leaving, Alfred presented to the National Museum two pottery figures from Cuilapan, and a large pottery vase embellished with a figure, described as Mixtec-Zapotec.[16] It was later in the year that he was informed of the appointment that Batres found so outrageous: his Honorary Professorship at the National Museum. In his letter of thanks to Chávez, written from London, Maudslay expressed his gratitude for the delicate and agreeable consideration he had always received from the Mexican government.

Chapter 17

Biologia Centrali-Americana

The 1894 expedition to Copán was Maudslay's seventh to the Maya area, and would be his last. This time, of course, he brought back no sculpture or other artefacts, but since his first venture in 1881 he had shipped back to London about twenty pieces of original sculpture, several tons of plaster and about 400 paper moulds, and had accumulated a large quantity of photographic negatives, maps, detailed plans and notebooks, and some Mesoamerican textiles, too. What use, then, was he planning to make of these materials?

A possible plan might have been to store everything until his career of active fieldwork was over, and only then begin studying the collection as a whole, with the eventual purpose of publishing a full report. Nowadays, it is common practice for much of the analysis and writing-up of work at an archaeological site to be performed after excavations have ended. But Maudslay's situation was peculiar. Instead of working for an institution, as archaeologists, with very few exceptions, do today, he was working alone. Under these circumstances he must sometimes have worried that for lack of a professional colleague to fall back upon, an illness or other misfortune might frustrate the central goal of all his work, the publication of a full and abundantly illustrated report.

Indeed, he wasted no time in working towards this goal. Casting from the moulds had begun immediately, and by 1884 Maudslay was able to present a number of casts of Quiriguá monuments to the Cambridge University Archaeological Museum in return for the grant he had received from the University.

But as the casting proceeded, a difficulty arose: the casts were bulky, and the expense of storing them in London considerable. Cambridge was offered the Copán casts too, but declined to accept them for lack of space. Early in August 1885, therefore, Maudslay made arrangements with the South Kensington Museum (after 1899 known as the Victoria and Albert Museum) for exhibition of the Yaxchilán lintels, together with photographs of the ruins and a plan of the site. These he seems to have dangled as bait, hoping the museum would soon swallow the entire plaster-cast collection.

At the end of the same month he wrote to the museum authorities from Armadale Castle, Skye (where he was staying with his brother Charles), making use in this letter, for greater persuasive effect, of a tone slightly less reticent than usual. He describes the high level of the Maya civilization and the importance he attaches to its study; mentions other museums containing similar materials, and states that the originals and casts in his collection are finer and more comprehensive than any of these. He proposes therefore, for the museum's consideration, the gift of the whole collection on two conditions: that the casts and originals be exhibited together for the benefit of students, and that the museum take over the services of Giuntini, paying his salary and relieving Maudslay of all further expense.[1]

In November, after an official had been to Cambridge to look at the Quiriguá casts, Maudslay was informed by the South Kensington Museum that his collection (with the exception only of those pieces already on display in Cambridge) could indeed be accepted for exhibition in the East Architectural Court; and they would for a time take over the employment of Giuntini. So in January 1886 the casts and moulds were delivered to the museum.

It would be tedious to follow in detail the negotiations over the destiny of the casts, which continued for many years. One can understand the growing alarm of the Museum administrators as more and more crates of moulds arrived every second year, and the need to employ Giuntini continued. In 1891 they told Maudslay that Giuntini's services would have to be dispensed with, but Maudslay succeeded in obtaining an extension with the plea that one Quiriguá monument (Stela J) still remained to be cast from paper moulds. Two years later they suggested that the whole collection might be transferred to the British Museum, but the trustees of that museum were willing to display only the original sculpture; the casts would have to be stored away in the basement. On hearing this, Maudslay revealed that his own first inclination had been to offer the collection to the British Museum, but he had not done so on learning that this very condition would be imposed.

His principal reason for opposing any move to store the casts (especially in the British Museum basement, where in those days everything soon became covered in greasy soot) was that he needed access to the casts himself. Artists were at work making careful renderings of the sculpture on a daily basis, with Maudslay sometimes visiting them for discussions about the way certain details should be drawn.

The professional artists employed by Maudslay were Edwin J. Lambert and Annie G. Hunter. In drawing the monuments of Copán, the site they began on, their contributions were nearly equal; for Quiriguá monuments, Lambert did one-third of the work and Annie Hunter the rest; and then she was entrusted with all the drawing of sculpture from

Chichén Itzá, Palenque, and other sites.

Very little about Lambert has come to light beyond the bare facts that he lived in Hampstead, exhibited paintings at the Royal Academy, and died in 1932. Maudslay refers to his having 'done some of the first drawings from the casts, when the style of work was unfamiliar and consequently presented many difficulties'. 'Style of work' can be taken, I think, to cover two distinct problems.[2]

One was the manner in which an image carved in relief should be rendered in two dimensions. Should there be shading to suggest the relief? If not, then how for example should a groove carved in the stone be represented: by two parallel lines, as is often done, or a single line? How should features weathered into vague outlines be shown? On these questions and many others a policy had to be established.

The second problem hinged on the artist's understanding of what he or she was attempting to draw, since a misunderstood element is likely to be misdrawn, or wrongly articulated with adjoining elements. A line drawing is necessarily a simplification, and thus to some extent an interpretation; as such, its success depends on the interpretation being soundly based on knowledge. As Catherwood found, Maya reliefs can be highly confusing on first acquaintance; one has to study the component parts of Maya iconography and become familiar with them as presented in various degrees of stylization, before one can 'read' a sculpture well. More will be said in a later chapter about the contribution made by Maudslay and his artists to this aspect of Maya studies; here my intention is simply to recognize the important role played by Lambert as he began work on the Copán monuments in establishing the style and standards that would guide his and Annie Hunter's work throughout its course. It is indeed a tribute to the professional skill of both artists that the work of one can scarcely be distinguished from that of the other.

More is known about Annie Hunter, since she gained some renown as the person who in the end executed the majority of the drawings for Maudslay, and as a result was later employed by other archaeologists and museums. She was born in Cheshire in 1860, the daughter of a certain John Hunter, described on Annie's birth certificate as a 'commercial traveller – grocer and draper,' and his Irish wife Annie, formerly Groom (four years later when another daughter, Blanche, was born, the Hunters had moved to Kensington, and John gave his occupation as 'civil engineer'). Blanche and another sister, Ada, also became artists and did some work for Maudslay. All three had pictures accepted for exhibition at the Royal Academy, Ada's entry for 1886 being a portrait of Annie (long lost, it seems). Annie never married, and after her eighteen years of work for Maudslay is known to have made watercolour copies (practically facsimiles) of Mexican pictorial manuscripts and other originals for various patrons, among them Charles P. Bowditch of Boston.

A few surviving letters of hers to Bowditch, extremely modest in tone but also showing determination, give a glimpse of her character: 'Kingsborough I must confess I am a little exasperated with, and I will tell you why [she had traced thirty-five plates of his published reproductions of copies made by Agostino Aglio, thinking she would have only to correct details]. Not one of the Kingsborough tracings would fit the original MS. I worried and fumed with them for a whole day, then gave them up.' So she was obliged to make fresh tracings from the original in the British Museum, through a sheet of protective celluloid. In December 1918 she was telling Bowditch about the first election in which women could vote. She thought voters were ignorant: 'I could not persuade one man that the British Isles were only a small part of Europe; he was contemptuous and incredulous. I brought an Atlas to convince him, but he was quite triumphant, "The map of England is as big as any of the others" he said scornfully. I explained that it was drawn to a larger scale. "Oh, you can account for anything if you like, of course," he said, and declined to hear anything more.'

More illuminating in the present context is a sentence from a letter she wrote Bowditch in reply to one in which he evidently suggested changes to a drawing: 'You are not a bit over-critical; Mr. Maudslay and I used to correct over and over again.'[3] Her drawings could indeed always be corrected as they were done in pencil, yet they are remarkably clean-looking in spite of corrections. Whereas most illustrators make their drawings at a scale that allows reduction to half size or less when printed, thus rendering less conspicuous any blemishes or shakes in the line, Maudslay's artists drew at actual reproduction scale, yet no blemishes are detectable.

After the First World War, Annie Hunter was engaged by George Byron Gordon (who was then director of the University Museum of the University of Pennsylvania) to prepare watercolour and line drawings of some of the finest examples of Maya pottery in English collections. She contributed fifteen of the sixty-six splendid illustrations in colour that were later published as a portfolio by the Museum.[4] Her home for many years was a flat in Kensington which she shared with her sisters, and there her life came to an end in May 1927.

While the drawings, maps, and photographs were being prepared, Maudslay was evidently at work on the text to go with them, for it is clear from the Introduction to his work that it was written before the plaster-casting had progressed very far. Since he regarded his record of monuments at Copán as more nearly complete than that at Quiriguá (which he intended to revisit before long, to improve the coverage) Maudslay decided that Copán should be dealt with first in the publication. Once he had listed all the illustrations that would be available when Giuntini and the artists had finished their work, he began to plan the form the publication should take.

In making these plans, Maudslay didn't have a completely free hand; or perhaps it would be fairer to say that he had the advantage of an already established framework of style and format within which to work. This was because he had, as we have seen, accepted the extremely generous offer of Godman and Salvin to publish his work as a special section of their monumental series of volumes, the *Biologia Centrali-Americana*. Naturally his section would be expected to conform as far as possible with the main body of the work in respect of typeface, quality of paper, format, arrangements for issuing the constituent parts of a progressive series, and so forth.

Something must be now said about these two collaborators of Maudslay's, without whose help the resulting publication would undoubtedly have been far less splendidly presented. They were both remarkable men.

Frederick DuCane Godman was born in 1834, the third of seven sons and six daughters of a Sussex squire. His father, a partner in Whitbread's brewery, had prospered exceedingly, but it is puzzling that Frederick should have been so very rich – a multimillionaire in today's term – since his father's fortune was presumably divided between his thirteen children. Frederick was sent to Eton College at the tender age of ten, but was taken away three years later because of illness, and thereafter educated by tutors. During those next years spent at home he interested himself in natural history, taking a special interest in mosses and ferns, and making a good collection of them.[5]

Shortly before going up to Trinity College, Cambridge, in 1853, Godman showed his love of travel, and youthful mettle, when faced with an awkward predicament during a tour of Mediterranean countries with a tutor. As a friend later told the story,

> On the afternoon of arrival in Constantinople, for no other reason than that he heard of a homeward-bound vessel, the tutor suddenly announced his intention of returning to England at once, a proceeding which he carried out, leaving his pupil, who declined to accompany him, without letters of introduction, and with only a single sovereign in his pocket. Being thus stranded, Godman sought the assistance of Misseri, the hotel-keeper, who accompanied him to the Bank and initiated him in the art of 'drawing a bill' in order to provide for his maintenance while at Constantinople. Then he fortunately made the acquaintance of the British Consul at Trebizond, who was staying at the hotel, and accompanied him in a steamer on an expedition to various places in the Black Sea.

At Cambridge, we are told, 'he took his ordinary studies lightly and gave free bent to a taste for Natural History, especially ornithology'. In fact he never graduated. It was through interest in birds that he came to

1 Loading a launch at
Champerico, Guatemala
(photo by Eadweard
Muybridge, c. 1875,
reproduced courtesy of the
Boston Atheneum).

2 Landing at San José
(drawing by Ada Hunter
from a photo, A. C. and
A. P. Maudslay 1899, p. 8).

3 Maudslay's pencil sketch of San José, inked over (author's collection).
4 Charles and Alfred Maudslay with Minnie and Annie Morris in San Francisco, California; Annie is on the right (author's collection).

5 Birthplace of Henry Maudslay (the farther, two-roomed half of this house) in Salutation Alley, Woolwich.

6 Cast-iron tomb of Henry Maudslay at Woolwich (now demolished).

7 Henry Maudslay in the last year of his life (previously unpublished 'Physionotrace' by Kennedy, collection of Margaret Whittingdale).

8 Maudslay's father, Joseph (author's collection).

9 Maudslay's mother, Anna Maria, née Johnson (author's collection).

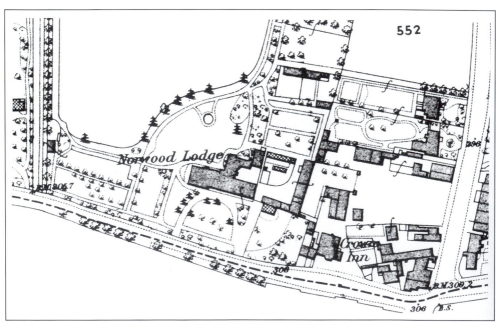

10 Map showing Norwood Lodge, Maudslay's birthplace and childhood home.

11 Alfred Maudslay at the age of about fourteen (author's collection).

12 Alfred Maudslay aged thirteen.

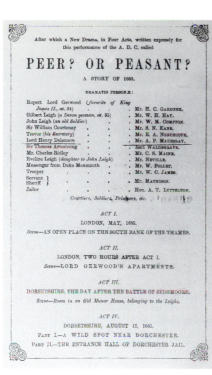

After which a New Drama, in Four Acts, written expressly for
this performance of the A. D. C. called

PEER? OR PEASANT?

A STORY OF 1685.

DRAMATIS PERSONÆ:

Rupert Lord Gerwood (*favorite of King James II., æt. 34*) . .	Mr. H. C. GARDNER.
Gilbert Leigh (*a Devon yeoman, æt. 55*)	Mr. W. H. HAY.
John Leigh (*an old Soldier*) .	Mr. W. M. COMPTON.
Sir William Courtenay . .	Mr. S. N. KANE.
Trevor (*his Secretary*) . .	Mr. E. A. NORTHCOTE.
Lord Henry Delamere . .	Mr. A. P. MAUDSLAY.
Sir Thomas Armstrong . .	Earl WALDEGRAVE.
Mr. Charles Ridley . .	Mr. C. S. MAINE.
Eveline Leigh (*daughter to John Leigh*)	Mr. NEVILLE.
Messenger from Duke Monmouth .	Mr. W. FOLLET.
Trooper . . .	Mr. W. C. JAMES.
Servant } . . .	Mr. MATHISON.
Sheriff }	
Jailor . . .	Hon. A. T. LYTTELTON.

Courtiers, Soldiers, Prisoners, &c.

ACT I.

LONDON, MAY, 1685.

Scene—AN OPEN PLACE ON THE SOUTH BANK OF THE THAMES.

ACT II.

LONDON, TWO HOURS AFTER ACT I.

Scene—LORD GERWOOD'S APARTMENTS.

ACT III.

DORSETSHIRE, THE DAY AFTER THE BATTLE OF SEDGMOORE.

Scene—Room in an Old Manor House, belonging to the Leighs.

ACT IV.

DORSETSHIRE, AUGUST 15, 1685.

PART I.—A WILD SPOT NEAR DORCHESTER.
PART II.—THE ENTRANCE HALL OF DORCHESTER JAIL.

To conclude with the original Burlesque by F. C. BURNAND, Esq.,
entitled

PARIS.

DRAMATIS PERSONÆ:

Jupiter . . .	Mr. S. N. KANE.
Juno . . .	Mr. F. H. HODGSON.
Venus . . .	Mr. A. P. MAUDSLAY.
Minerva . . .	Mr. C. G. KELLNER.
Cupid . . .	Hon. A. T. LYTTELTON.
Psyche . . .	Mr. C. E. LYON.
Mercury . . .	Mr. C. G. WALPOLE.
Castor . . .	Mr. C. R. ALEXANDER.
Pollux . . .	Mr. W. H. HAY.
Ganymede . . .	Mr. NEVILLE.
Paris . . .	Mr. H. C. GARDNER.
Œnone . . .	Mr. N. A. HUNT.

Pleasures, Deities, &c., by Messrs. Agnew, Jekyll, Hon. J. B. Roche,
Thornhill, James, Baker, Mathison, &c.

SCENE I.

CUPID'S TEA-ROSE GARDENS.

Psyche at Home.

How the Apple falls in and the Goddesses fall out.

PARIS AND BACK FOR £5.

SCENE II.

ŒNONE'S COTTAGE.

HEARTLESS DESERTION !

TRIUMPH OF INIQUITY !

SCENE III.

A VALLEY ON MOUNT IDA.

THE GODS AT A PIC-NIC.

JUDGMENT OF PARIS.

---

13 Cambridge ADC
programme, 31 May 1871.
Maudslay appeared in two of
the three plays performed that
evening (author's collection).

14 Alfred as 'Venus' (author's
collection).

15 Alfred Maudslay at Cambridge (photo courtesy of the Cambridge University Museum of Archaeology and Anthropology).

16 Government House,
Fiji, in the 1870s (photo
courtesy of the Cambridge
University Museum of
Archaeology and
Anthropology).

17 Alfred Maudslay in Fiji
(photographer unknown;
reproduced with the kind
permission of the Fiji
Museum, Suva).

18 Sir William Cairns
(*Illustrated Sydney News*).

19 Maudslay's house in Tonga (author's collection, which also includes a stereogram of the same view).

made some progress – He excites me by an
account of a newly discovered & undescribed
ruined city near Flores which is said to be
as fine as Palenque – Guatemala has
become, you will be pleased to hear, quite
civilized now – a strong government & no
revolution for eight years – Regular posts
& telegra... ... all ... the country ...
& not ... ...
a... ...
... ...
... ...
... ...
white ... ... some
Gulf weed ...ed up in the middle of the
Atlantic, & you must give a bit to Cousin
Anne with my love. We get off again to:

20 Letter from Maudslay to his
sister Isabel, dated 27 December
1880, with the sample of Sargasso
weed included in it (author's
collection).

21 Frank Sarg (photo courtesy of
Sr Francisco Sarg).

22 Otto Stoll, seated on Maudslay's camp-bed. Maudslay used this photo in *A Glimpse at Guatemala*, but since he was less interested in portraying Stoll than the men he had engaged for the ascent of Volcán de Fuego, he blocked out Stoll entirely, using the space for the chapter-heading. In the process, the top of Stoll's head was touched out.

23 View of Kaminal-Juyu, an important Preclassic site, which in Maudslay's time lay well beyond the western limits of Guatemala City. With later growth of the city, most of the site now lies beneath streets and buildings.

24 Maudslay's men encamped at Yaxchilán. The stone mound or pier that drew Rockstroh's attention to the site is visible, the water level being very low at that time.

25 Yaxchilán: Structure 33, north end.

26 Yaxchilán, 'Labyrinth' with Charnay's secretary.

27 The sleeping arrangements of Maudslay's men at Tikal.

28 Tikal: View from Temple V, looking east.

29 Tikal: Front view of Temple I.

30 Tikal: Temple V.

31 Tikal: Temples II, III, and IV, from Temple I.

32 The stern-wheeler *Esperanza* (from Anon. 1938, p. 44).

33 Lorenzo Giuntini, a few years before he began working for Maudslay (photo courtesy of Mr and Mrs Max Emmons).

34 Quiriguá:
Lorenzo Giuntini
making his mould
of Zoomorph P.

35 Quiriguá:
Stela D, viewed
from the
northeast.

36 Quiriguá: Zoomorph B.

37 Quiriguá, Zoomorph P.

38 Copán: Stela D. In this drawing, Annie Hunter has rendered intelligible the welter of intertwined elements visible in the photograph. This she was able to do only because she had a plaster cast to work from, as well as guidance from Maudslay. In this drawing as published, various iconographic elements are identified by means of coloured washes.

39 Copán: Stela D, east side.

40 Copán: Covered stairway in Structure 20, on the east side of the Eastern
Court of the Acropolis.

41 Copán: Altar Q, west side. All four sides carry images of former rulers of the city.

42 Copán: Stela 6.

43 Important visitors to Copán.

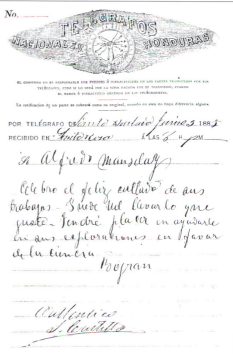

44 Telegram from President Bográn
of Honduras (by kind permission of
the Royal Geographical Society).

45 Ruins at
Chuitinamit.

46 Ixkún, Stela 1.

47 Chichén Itzá: View from the terrace of the Casa de Monjas, looking north. The Castillo is visible beyond the Caracol, with the Casa Colorada to the left (photo: H. Sweet).

48 Maudslay at Chichén Itzá (detail of photo by H. Sweet).

49 Chichén Itzá: Maudslay at work in one of the chambers of Las Monjas, 1889 (photo: H. Sweet).

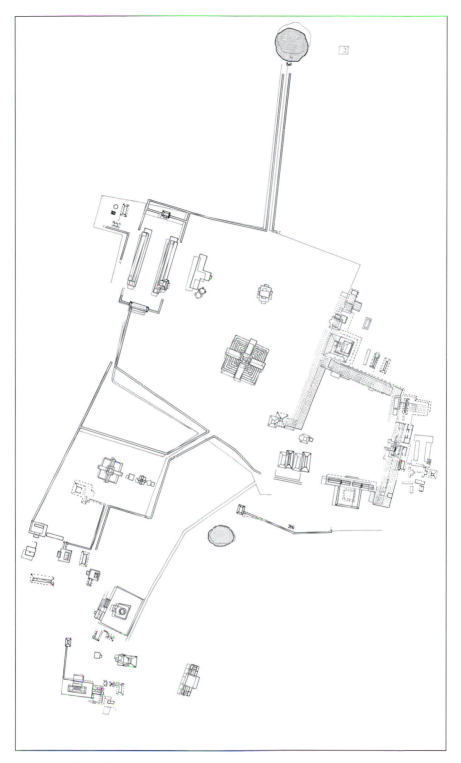

50 Two plans of the ruins of Chichén Itzá, the one drawn by Kilmartin here
superimposed (in grey) over the drawing by Maudslay.

51 At a rented castle in Scotland: Alfred at left, Violet (Walter's wife), Isabel and Clara Field.

52 Gorgonio López at Palenque (from A. C. and A. P. Maudslay 1899, p. 224).

53 Palenque: The Temple of the Sun.

54 and 55 Palenque: Eastern side of House C of the Palace, which Maudslay, Price, and Gorgonio López adopted as their quarters. In the photograph below, Price has carelessly propped the tripod of his surveying instrument against the portrait of the mysterious lady.

56 and 57
The mysterious lady.

58 Palenque: Pier F, in the western court of the Palace, which like many others in the complex retains much of its stucco embellishment.

59 Palenque: House D, Pier F.

60 Palenque: Temple of the Inscriptions, in the foreground two platforms built to allow a camera to be set up at a sufficient distance for photographing the stuccoed piers.

61 Maudslay on muleback.

62 Annie Maudslay in Guatemala, riding her cherished mule.

63 Maudslay in his garden at Zavaleta (photo perhaps by Arthur Laughton).

64 Zavaleta, with corrugated iron roof of ore-crusher in the foreground, and offices, presumably, at left (negative in author's collection).

65 Annie Maudslay in the hammock at Zavaleta (author's collection).

66 and 67 Annie Maudslay in the kitchen (above) and the *sala* (below) at Zavaleta (after Graham 1977).

68 Fiesta in Oaxaca.

69 Osbert Salvin
(original print in author's
collection).

70 Frederick DuCane Godman c. 1865 (duplicated from a photograph in the possession of his daughter, the late Edith Godman).

71 Tikal, Lintel 3 of Temple IV. Pencil drawing on card by Annie Hunter – probably her finest. The lithographic copy at the same scale by W. Purkiss, published in *Biologia Centrali-Americana*, is also remarkable for its fidelity (photograph of the drawing in its collection kindly provided by the University Museum, University of Pennsylvania).

72 Drawing by Leopoldo Batres showing his conception of the process by which Mesoamerican pyramids were built up in a single operation by stages, so that structurally they resembled an onion (after Batres 1902, p. 12).

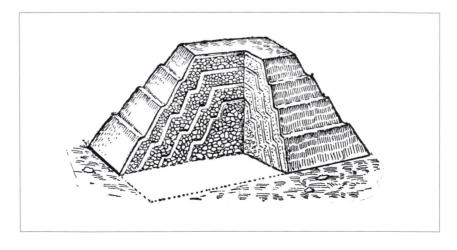

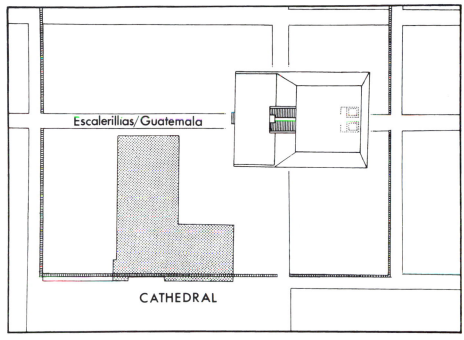

Escalerillas/Guatemala

CATHEDRAL

73 and 74
Two plans of the Great Temple, Mexico City.

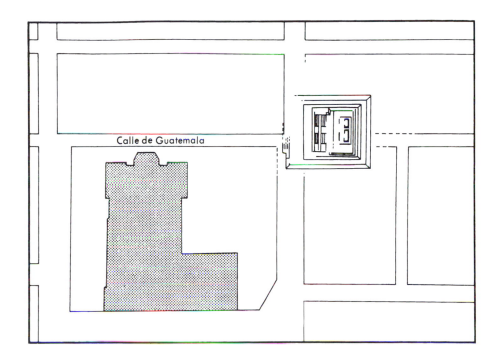

Calle de Guatemala

75   Alfred Maudslay with salmon at Aasleagh, 1919 (author's collection).

76   Petroglyph at Cerro Cuailama, Mexico.

77 Maudslay and chauffeur with Maudslay Motors tourer at Stavordale.

78 Morney Cross (photo by author).

79 Alfred Maudslay, studio portrait c. 1920 (duplicated from a print in the collection of the late Edith Godman).

80 Alfred and Annie Maudslay with family c. 1922.

81 Alfred and
Annie Maudslay
with a niece,
c. 1925 (detail
from a family
group, author's
collection).

82 Alfred and
Alice Maudslay,
1930.

know Osbert Salvin, a mathematical Scholar (and later Fellow) of Trinity Hall, who was a year younger than himself. Salvin was a son of Anthony Salvin, a well-known architect, the last practitioner of the Gothic Revival style, and designer of such mansions as Peckforton and Keele, and of the keep added by the Duke of Northumberland to his castle at Alnwick. With similar interests in Natural History and travelling, Godman and Salvin became firm friends for life. Meetings in their rooms, and those of a few friends, led to formation in 1858 of the Ornithological Union, with its still flourishing journal *The Ibis*.[6]

Late in 1857 Salvin set out on his first journey to Guatemala, made under the patronage of the manufacturers of Price's Patent Candles. He was to report on the nuts of a certain palm, the oil from which they hoped to use in the manufacture of candles. But he was obliged to describe it as 'useless for practical purposes' (the palm may have been *corozo*, known in Belize as *cohune*, one of the toughest of nuts to crack). Salvin then found himself free to devote the rest of his stay to the collection of birds and insects. A year later he returned to England, but so exciting had this experience been for an ornithologist that he was soon off to Guatemala for a further twelve months of collecting.

As it happened, the famous paper by Darwin and Wallace on natural selection was read during Salvin's first visit to Guatemala, and in the following year, while Salvin was in England between these two journeys, Darwin published *On the Origin of Species*. Soon (and perhaps encouraged by advice from Spencer Baird, of the Smithsonian Institution) Godman and Salvin concluded that, on the basis of the latter's observations and collections in Guatemala, a complete examination of the fauna and flora of Central America might throw light on the currently much-discussed subject of the distribution of species and its bearing on evolution, since at that time no exotic fauna had yet been studied as a whole with any degree of thoroughness.[7]

Partly with this idea in mind, and partly for sheer love of travel, Godman joined Salvin on his third visit to Central America and southern Mexico. They landed at Yzabal in 1861, and from there made a visit to the ruins at Quiriguá. For photography Salvin had brought a stereoscopic camera and dry (tanning) plates which did not have to be developed immediately, thereby avoiding both the need to bring right to the scene the bulky paraphernalia and the difficult procedures required by the wet-plate process, then in almost universal use. Instead, the developing could be done in the evening.

He was unprepared, however, for the extremely dim light that filtered through the forest cover. When exposures of twenty minutes produced no image at all, they had to have trees cut down to achieve success. Later, both men visited Copán, separately, Salvin taking numerous stereoscopic photographs, prints of which, with a descriptive booklet, were published in a small edition after his return to London.[8] In 1873, a few years after getting married, Salvin made a fourth and final visit to Guatemala with his wife. They stayed for a year, spending much of that time in collecting. Godman, for his part, also made another collecting trip, mostly in southern Mexico.

Their ornithological and other collections were kept in Salvin's London house, until he and Godman bought another house for exclusive use as their private museum and library. Not only was it to contain their own collections, but soon other large collections would be added to them by purchase. Eventually, towards the end of Godman's life, the whole of the collections were made over to the Natural History Museum (a department of the British Museum). To give an idea of their size, one statistic will do: Godman's *personal* collection of butterflies numbered 107,000.

The almost absurdly ambitious idea of describing the fauna and flora of Central America remained in abeyance for several years. Perhaps the disturbed conditions in Guatemala following the outbreak of war with El Salvador in 1863 were partly responsible. But whatever may have been the cause of the long dormancy, Godman and Salvin did eventually decide in 1876 upon a plan for the production of a work to be called the *Biologia Centrali-Americana*, and soon began commissioning collectors who specialized in various zoological and botanical orders to go out to Guatemala and other parts of Central America and Mexico to supplement their own collections, which were centred on birds and butterflies.

Their publication plans, according to Godman, were to 'bring out six quarto parts a year; each to be made up of various subjects with six coloured plates, the plates and letterpress so numbered and paged that the parts might ultimately be broken up and bound together in their respective volumes when completed. In this way it was possible to keep several subjects in progress at once, and the plan answered well.' In their original scheme they envisioned a section on zoology made up of sixty parts (equivalent to twelve volumes), and one on botany of twenty parts, but the amount of material received from their collectors was so abundant that the zoology section grew to three-and-a-half times the size originally estimated, and the span of time occupied in producing the work extended to thirty-seven years.

The coverage of the fifty-one volumes devoted to zoology may be summarized as follows (in non-technical terminology): one volume on mammals, four on birds, one on reptiles and frogs, one on fish, one on molluscs, four on spiders and scorpions, one on centipedes and millipedes, eighteen on beetles, three on wasps, ants, etc., seven on butterflies, three on flies, etc., two on rhyncota (a difficult group of snouted insects), two on cicadas, chinch bugs, etc., and two on grasshoppers, cockroaches, etc. Taking into account also the five volumes on botany, the work contains 1677 plates, more than half of them in colour, depicting 18,587 subjects. About fifty thousand species are enumerated, over nineteen thousand of them described for the first time. Godman himself was largely responsible for the seven volumes on butterflies, and Salvin was to have been for the four on birds, but preparation of these was still in progress when he died in 1898, and the work was completed by Godman.

Godman had wisely abstained from commencing the series with an introductory volume; instead he postponed writing it until after the body of the work was complete, when the dimensions of what he was 'intro-ducing' would be known. By the time this last volume was out, in 1917, he only had two more years to live. But the work was finished, and what a truly monumental work it is! In the nineteenth century there had been a few other undertakings by private individuals in the field of scholarly publishing on a grand scale, such as Lord Kingsborough's *Antiquities of Mexico* and Sibthorp's *Flora Graeca*, but these had been left unfinished. The joint editors of the *Biologia Centrali-Americana* brought theirs to a triumphant conclusion.[9]

A work published in many small parts, which later have to be collected and bound, can hardly be sold in any other way than by subscription, and that is how the *Biologia* was sold, but the disbinding, sorting, and rebinding of the parts must have been very troublesome for subscribers. They ended by paying a little under £300 for the whole run of sixty-seven volumes, a sum which would then have allowed a person to live in comfortable idleness for a whole year. The work was never advertised to the public. But shortly before Godman died he disposed of the unsold copies to the bookseller Bernard Quaritch, who then adver-tised complete sets of the zoology, botany, and archaeology volumes, bound in boards, at a bargain price of £180.[10]

This, then, was the publication into which Maudslay's Archaeology section was to be incorporated. The title page of his first volume of text reads: Biologia Centrali-Americana; / or, / Contributions to the knowl-edge / of the / Fauna and Flora / of / Mexico and Central America. / Edited by / F. Ducane Godman and Osbert Salvin/ Archaeology / Volume I / (Plates) / By A. P. Maudslay / London: / Published for the Editors by / R. H. Porter, 7 Princes Street, Cavendish Square, W. , / and / Dulau and Co., Soho Square, W. / 1889–1902.

Most copies of the text were printed on the serviceable paper used for the text of the other *Biologia* volumes, but some are on a Whatman paper, which is fifty percent thicker and more durable. The four volumes of text, usually bound into one volume (a title page for that purpose being pro-vided), were issued in paper-bound fascicles of as many as thirty-two pages, or as few as four. The Appendix, of about 270 pages, is a study by J. T. Goodman of the hieroglyphic inscriptions, with tables drawn up by him covering the entire Maya calendar.

The four volumes of plates departed from the large-quarto format of the rest of the *Biologia*. Drawings, photographs and maps all required pages of larger size to do them justice. The simple expedient adopted was to keep the page height unaltered, and to double its width. For a few subjects, such as stelae and wall-paintings, this unusual format has an obvious advantage, but it does have the serious disadvantage that the heavy pages are bound along their narrow edges, so that even with careful handling the binding is strained, and in time becomes loose. This weakness is exacerbated by the different kind of paper chosen for these illustrated volumes; perhaps it was more suitable for gravure printing, but it tends to fail at the hinge.

The photographs, all of them taken by Maudslay except for those of Chichén Itzá, taken by Henry Sweet, were beautifully reproduced in gravure by the Autotype Company.[11] Annie Hunter's and Lambert's drawings were reproduced by lithography, the redrawing on stone being the work of a man named Purkiss, who did much of the lithography also for the zoology section. Lithography was also used for the considerable number of plans and sections of buildings, and plans of ruined cities. Many of these were drawn by Maudslay himself, who was putting to good use the experience gained at Harrow of drawing maps, and putting in 'lats. and longs. and outsiders'. Some of them, like his schoolboy efforts, are even tinted with coloured washes.

The four volumes present information on the following sites (the asterisks mark sites only briefly described):

Volume I	Copán
Volume II	Quiriguá
	Ixkún
	Yaxché *
	Rabinal *
	Chacujal *
	Utatlán and Iximché *
	Guatemala (Kaminaljuyu) *
Volume III	Chichén Itzá
	Tikal
Volume IV	Palenque

We have already glimpsed Alfred and Annie Maudslay spending some time in San Francisco on their way to Guatemala in 1893. While there Maudslay intended to call on a man he hoped might contribute a commentary on the Maya calendar to his 'Archaeology'. This was Dr. Gustav A. Eisen, a Swedish biologist, and a man of varied interests whom he had very likely met in Guatemala in 1882, since he was a friend of Edwin Rockstroh.[12]

In that year, Eisen, who had become interested in Maya archaeology, spent some time travelling in Guatemala, Honduras and El Salvador, visiting, among other sites, Copán, Quiriguá, Pantaleón, and Santa Lucía Cotzumalguapa. A few years later he would publish drawings of sculpture from the latter sites, some of them entirely his own work, others based on drawings by C. H. Berendt.[13]

In a letter sent to Bowditch from Guatemala, Maudslay wrote:

> I think I told you that for some years I have been corresponding with a Mr. Eisen in San Francisco. He was away in Mexico when I first arrived, but I saw a good deal of his partner Mr. Goodman, and it is he apparently who has done most of the work at the inscriptions & not Mr. Eisen.

Maudslay himself had made one small but significant contribution to deciphering the dates in an informal note sent from Mérida in 1889 to some official of the Royal Geographical Society, who published it:

> I think I ought to put on record a little discovery I made some months ago. This is regarding the sign which occurs frequently in the Palenque Tablets and other Central American inscriptions, as well as in some of the Maya and Aztec MSS. I believe it to be the numeral 20; although I cannot give my reasons just now, as it would necessitate sending copies of many inscriptions, which I will do later on, but the statement may be of use to any one who may be working on the subject.[14]

In his letter to Bowditch, Maudslay goes on to comment:

> It seems to me that he [Goodman] has really made some advance, & it is principally in the direction in which I anticipated that discoveries would be made, that is in the comparative study of the 'Initial Series' which he finds gives him a date. I was not able to make any careful investigation of his system, but from what I can see it appeared to work out correctly & I have done my best to get him to publish his method & the calendars which he has worked out, & I hope we shall have it in our hands next year.[15]

Goodman, a New Yorker by birth, had moved to California in his late teens, and soon became the owner and editor of the *Territorial Enterprise*, of Virginia, Nevada. As such, he was percipient enough to hire an obscure reporter named Samuel Langhorne Clemens, who would become known as 'Mark Twain'. Later, his investments in mining companies enabled him to buy a large raisin vineyard.

At about the time of his meeting with Maudslay he wrote a brief manuscript account of how he became interested in Maya writing:[16]

> In 1883 I owned a raisin vineyard in Fresno County, California. While

in town one day I called upon Dr Gustav Eisen, a former neighbor, who had just returned from a visit to Guatemala and Honduras. I found him poring over a lot of photographs of Quirigua and Copan stelae, a study of the ruins of those places having been the object of his trip to Central America.

[After waxing enthusiastic about the sculptures] Eisen concluded with this remark: 'What a pity the glyphs can never be read!' 'Why can't they?' I inquired. 'Because the key to them is lost.'

Goodman rose to the challenge, and the two of them set to work.

The manuscript table of contents of their intended work begins: *The Archaic Writing of the Maya. Their Hieroglyphs and Sculptures. By Gustav Eisen* [*and*] *J. T. Goodman   October 8, 1888.* Contents. I. Introduction II. Nature of the Glyphs III. Nature of Symbols IV. Numerals [etc.] Having considered likely topics for the hieroglyphic texts, they asked themselves: 'Were they memorial or historical records? No, because their scarceness and variability precluded the supposition. . . . Did they relate to chronology, mythology, astronomy, prophecy, divination, or any of the sciences and superstitions which it was known the Maya cultivated?' These, too, were rejected as possibilities, until they settled at last on tribute rolls: they decided that the large initial glyph found on stelae could be easily be construed as 'tribute'. After a great deal of work, 'every glyph was catalogued and my reading of the glyphs finished. . . . So satisfied was Dr Eisen with the solution, so eager the world should know its result, that he urged its immediate publication. But it was not to be. Fortune kindly remitted it to blush unseen.'

Reluctantly, he discarded taxes and tribute. Now, though, he was 'also paying attention in a desultory way to the Maya Calendar'. Both Juan Pio Pérez, whose description of it had been published by John Lloyd Stephens, and Bishop Diego de Landa had furnished examples. 'I had encountered the inevitable; there was nothing left to do but yield. Dr. Eisen was not so readily submissive.'

Goodman, now apparently working alone, put a tremendous amount of effort into elucidation of the calendar (registering, by the way, his annoyance with Pio Pérez for providing incorrect information: 'No wrecker ever caused more disaster by kindling false beacons upon a dangerous shore than did Señor Pérez by his purported ancient Maya Chronological system.')

Several years later, perhaps in the late 1890s, Goodman wrote another brief manuscript account of his attack on Maya hieroglyphs – apparently an outline for a larger work, never completed. The chapter headings are:

1. The Quest, and How I Happened to Engage in It (pp. 25)
2. An Enthusiastic Onset and its Discouraging Failure (pp. 32)

3. A Renewed Attack that Succeeds (pp., say 32)
4. On the High Road of Discovery (pp. 25)
5. Groping after the Meaning of Glyphs (pp. 25)
6. An Incursion into the Fastness of Cakchiquel Chronology (pp. 31)
7. A visit to England and the Publication of 'The Archaic Maya Inscriptions' (pp.)
8. Confirmation of My Belief that the Maya Graphic System was Merely a Cipher Code (pp.)
9. The Initial Directive Series [now known as the Supplementary Series]
10. The Reckoning by Different Chronological Counts
11. An Outline of the Purport of the Inscriptions

Chapter 7 begins:

By the beginning of 1895 I had come practically to a stand-still in my studies. I had gone over and over the material in my possession until my mind seemed to have got into a rut which it could not get out of. . . . I began to apprehend that Dr. Eisen's prediction that I had gone as far as I could would prove true.

While in this depressing state, I received from Mr Maudslay in London an urgent appeal to come to London, that I might have the advantage of studying his collection of unissued material, and also to put the result of my studies up to that time in shape for publication.

Thus encouraged, Goodman drew up a set of tables displaying the rotation of twenty day-names with thirteen day-numbers (forming the Tzolkin, or Sacred Round of 260 days), as they run simultaneously through eighteen twenty-day months plus one month of five days (constituting a 365-day year). With these two counts running concurrently, any given day specified in terms of these two calendars will not recur for fifty-two years. This period is known as a Calendar Round. The tables that Goodman compiled, which run through an entire Calendar Round, form an important part of the Appendix to Maudslay's *Archaeology*; in fact the tables are the one portion of the Appendix that retains its usefulness today.

Then there is the Long Count. This is a statement of time elapsed since some fixed, conventional date, far in the past. It is expressed in units of four hundred years, twenty years, single years, months, and days. A date given in this form is almost always preceded by a distinctive glyph, called by Maudslay the 'Initial Glyph'. This is usually twice or four times the size of other glyphs, and is nowadays known as the Initial Series Introducing Glyph. The full expression of a date in the Long Count, ending with its Calendar Round position, Maudslay called an Initial Series date.

Now, in most of the stelae recorded by Maudslay the numerals are represented by an easily read bar-and-dot notation, with a bar standing for 5, and a dot for 1 – thus, three bars and two dots signify 17. There is also a sign for zero – or, more properly, completion of the count in the unit of time to which it refers. On many stelae, however – among them several at Copán – the usual bar-and-dot numerals are not found; instead there are profile heads of generally human aspect. These represent, broadly speaking, gods associated with numbers, their presence adding certain mystic overtones to the statement that plain bars and dots could not convey. Although Maudslay had recognized that heads could replace bars-and-dots, he never attempted to identify the numerical value of the various 'head-variant' numerals, each of them characterised by particular facial features or adornments. It was in fact Goodman who would later achieve this for most of them.[17]

Some other decipherments can be credited to Goodman, but there is undeniable evidence that in certain important matters he made unacknowledged use of discoveries made by Ernst Förstemann. In 1880, at the age of fifty-eight, this great German scholar, and Librarian of the Royal Library in Dresden, turned his attention to the study of the Maya codex in that library. Over the next twenty-five years he was to publish two or three papers each year on Maya hieroglyphs and related topics. Naturally, the principal focus of his work was on Maya codices, and since the Dresden Codex is full of calendric matter, this brilliant and methodical scholar soon achieved a remarkable mastery of it.

Goodman may not have been able to read German. But among his papers preserved in the Peabody Museum is an original typescript translation from German into English of a paper by another eminent student of the Maya, Paul Schellhas. So Goodman should have had no difficulty in obtaining a translation of an 1886 paper of Förstemann's, the first few pages of which would have revealed the author's identification of the shell-like symbol for zero, and the fact that this had enabled him to work out the units of time constituting the Maya Long Count. As the late Sir Eric Thompson has pointed out, irrefutable evidence that Goodman had read Förstemann comes from his own pen. In discussing the chronological calendar, Goodman writes, 'It has been known that the Mayas reckoned time by ahaus (i.e. tuns), katuns, cycles (i.e. baktuns) and great cycles (i.e. pictuns).'[18] That information is in none of the early sources, but was brought to light only through the studies of Förstemann.

Goodman's Chapter 9, listed above, indicated the unfortunate direction that his epigraphic efforts were beginning to take: the notion that the inscriptions were no more than a recitation of numbers – that is, just an arid numerological desert. Even Maudslay, in his Preface to *Archaeology*, hinted at his doubts about the statement by Goodman in the Introduction to his Appendix to *Archaeology* that 'all the inscriptions so far brought to light are of a purely chronological character, destitute of any real historical importance'. Maudslay commented, diplomatically: 'This is not the place to uphold the merits of Mr. Goodman's work, but I think the continual use made of his calendars by students of the inscriptions will reconcile him to any exception taken to some of his theories.'[19]

Goodman did, however, have one more useful contribution to make, namely a correlation of the Long Count with the Gregorian calendar. With very slight revisions this, the Goodman–Martínez–Thompson correlation, still stands as the most widely accepted of several rival correlations. As he pointed out, this placed the heyday of Copán, Quiriguá, Tikal, and some other sites between the sixth and ninth centuries AD – still the generally agreed period – but the inscriptions of Palenque betrayed him. He insisted, in spite of objections, in dating them to the thirty-second century BC.

In the midst of his work on *Archaeology*, Alfred Maudslay, jointly with Annie, embarked on the production of another book. For some time past Maudslay seems to have wanted to write a book for ordinary readers about his experiences and discoveries, but, as he confesses in the preface to the book that resulted, *A Glimpse at Guatemala*, he had never been able to keep a proper journal while in the field. (One man who did somehow manage to do this was Sylvanus Morley, although perhaps he was working under easier conditions.)

Notebooks of his that have survived[20] are certainly quite scrappy, and he seems to have given up writing the long letters home, full of anecdotes and descriptions of people and places, that he used to write from Oceania. The death of his mother cannot entirely account for this, because he also used to write to his sister Isabel, with whom he remained on very close terms; of course, those letters may simply have disappeared. But it is hard to write long letters when postal services are non-existent or known to be extremely unreliable, or to keep a journal while enduring difficult conditions in the field.

Maudslay goes on to say, in this preface:

When, in 1894, my wife accompanied me to Central America, a splendid opportunity offered of avoiding all responsibility in the matter of keeping a diary. She should keep a diary and write a book, and I would add some archaeological notes! It was to be a small book with a few illustrations, and was of course to be published within six months of our return home. However, when we did get back to England there were other matters which called for our attention, and the notes had perforce to be laid aside. During the following winter a fair start was made, and some experimental illustrations were prepared; but each of us discovered in the other a deeply-rooted objection to process-blocks and shiny paper, so we began to dabble in photogravure and typo-etching. Then the archaeological notes began to expand, and as we had no publisher to put a proper curb on our whims and fancies, the book continued to grow on a soil of hand-made paper and to blossom with coloured plans, chromo-lithographs, and photogravures.

The full title of the book is *A Glimpse at Guatemala, with some Notes on the Ancient Monuments of Central America*. The main title was probably Annie Maudslay's suggestion, since she had contributed an article on her grandfather to the very first issue of *Scribner's Magazine* under the title 'A Glimpse . . . at Gouverneur Morris'. Between them the Maudslays produced a charming and extremely beautiful book, with Alfred's contribution amounting to slightly more than half of it. But it should come as no surprise, in view of the quotation above, that it was also a very expensive book. Printed on handmade Whatman paper and published in 1899 by John Murray, it sold for four guineas (that is, £4 4s, or $21) – about twenty times the price of most books. Hardly a book for the mass-market, then; and the print run was small. Today copies are very scarce and correspondingly expensive, and a facsimile edition published twenty years ago sold out long ago. It should be re-issued.

Since many passages from *A Glimpse at Guatemala* have been quoted in this biography, there is no need to draw attention to the pleasant and informal style of writing, or to the contents of the book. It has enduring value. Many photographs are beautifully reproduced in gravure; others were used as the basis for etchings by Ada and Blanche Hunter, these being printed on tissue which was then laid down on the page with a light wash of adhesive.

Further on in the book's preface we find Maudslay acknowledging his debt to Francis Sarg and others, and to Osbert Salvin, who had recently died. With characteristic generosity he ends by offering

> sincere thanks to Miss Annie Hunter and her sisters . . . and my acknowledgments for the good services rendered to me by the companions in my travels, the men of the Lopez family, and especially my friend Gorgonio, whose gentle manners and sweet disposition helped to smooth over many a bad half-hour during my earlier expeditions, and whose ceaseless vigilance over the welfare of my wife during our last journey did so much to lessen for her the discomforts of camp-life.

Maudslay showed his affection for Gorgonio in a more tangible way, and his gratitude, by bringing him over to England in the autumn of 1891 to stay with him and Annie as their guest for some months, during which time Gorgonio may also have helped him make casts from paper moulds, since Giuntini was probably working just then at Persepolis.

Chapter 18

The end of Maudslay, Sons and Field

After the death of Henry Maudslay in 1831, the company he founded, Maudslay, Sons and Field, was carried on by the remaining partners, Joshua Field and Maudslay's two surviving sons, Thomas Henry and Joseph. By the mid-1860s these had died too, and the partners were now Henry Maudslay's grandchildren, among them Alfred's two eldest brothers, Herbert Charles and Walter, and a son of Joshua Field.

By 1889 the retirement of three partners at various times had reduced their number to two: Walter Maudslay and Joshua Field the younger. No other family members appear to have been interested in working for the company. The fact that out of Henry Maudslay's eight male grandchildren only one had stayed with the family business may be regarded as something of a defection from responsibility towards the family firm, and this can't be explained entirely by lack of mechanical ability among the seven others.

For one thing, Alfred's brother Walter, who appears not to have been especially gifted technically, proved himself quite able to contribute managerial and entrepreneurial skill to the company;[1] for another, there was at least one member of that generation who did have technical ability, his cousin Henry. He had become a partner when quite young, and is known to have made apparently successful experiments with a novel technology, glass-working with the use of hydrofluoric acid. But after a few years Henry abandoned industrial for antiquarian pursuits, and in doing so exemplified a trend that began to be evident in England around the middle of the century.

It's a notorious paradox that Britain, having pioneered the Industrial Revolution and thus become more dependent than other countries on its benefits, nevertheless accorded little recognition to its engineers. Bankers, brewers, philanthropists, and of course politicians and proconsuls of empire, all these and notables in other fields had a fair chance of their efforts being rewarded by a knighthood. But mechanical engineers?

In early Victorian times only two received such a distinction: Marc Isambard Brunel and Robert Stephenson.

Philosophically, engineers were inclined to avoid extravagance of manner and speech, just as in design they avoided extravagant use of materials. Though some lacked social polish, they tended to be outdoor, practical, and yet reflective men, many of them comparable in creativity and intelligence to scientists, a group that did command respect. Painters and musicians were recognized with civil honours (in 1877, for instance, there were ten knights among them), so were lawyers and doctors, yet in that year there was but one living mechanical engineer with a knighthood, Sir William Armstrong, and he, significantly, was an armaments king. Perhaps if Prince Albert had lived longer, more mechanical engineers might have been honoured, and the profession as a whole might have risen in public esteem.

In Henry Maudslay's use of Gothic Revival ornamentation in the framework of one of his last engines (those for HMS *Dee*) an unconscious irony may be discerned, for social historians see the Gothic Revival movement as expressing a reaction to the Industrial Revolution. One such historian has suggested two metaphors for the nation in late nineteenth-century England, labelling them 'northern' and 'southern'.[2] The northern was pragmatic, empirical, calculating, puritan, bourgeois, enterprising, competitive and scientific; the southern romantic, muddled, aristocratic, traditional, and frivolous. The southern became dominant, with an elite that separated itself from the sources of dynamism in the existing society and attached itself to an older way of life; they did as William Morris bade them do: 'Forget the snorting steam and piston stroke / Forget the spreading of the hideous town / Think rather of the pack-horse and the down.'

In the north, indeed, the typically hard-headed, plain-living, low-church folk did prove less susceptible to Romantic blandishments, and it was northern engineers, single-minded, competitive, and undistracted by frivolous pastimes and ambitions, who eventually captured business from the Maudslay company.

In transmitting this bias against careers in industry, and fostering the gentlemanly ideal, the fee-paying public schools must bear some of the blame. As G. K. Chesterton remarked, such schools were created not for the sons of gentlemen, but for the fathers of gentlemen. . . .

At such schools (and at home) most boys quickly learnt what careers were compatible with living the life of a gentleman. Broadly speaking these were management of one's own estate, the armed services, the church, government service, certain professions, and, most effective (if one could afford it), avoidance of any career at all. On the other hand, there were occupations, indeed nascent professions, that scarcely merited consideration, among them engineering.

The Maudslay cousins may not have been deeply imbued with such snobbery, for Henry and Herbert Charles did, as we have seen, enter the firm and stay awhile, and Charles dabbled a little with engineering projects. But they left the field, suborned by pleasant pursuits and abundant incomes, while giving little thought to the possible impermanence of prosperity.

In view of this lack of family interest or involvement in the business, it was decided in 1889 to register the business as a limited liability company, with a share-offering to the public of £450,000. In the prospectus it was stated that at the time the annual net profit was £35,000.[3]

The new company soon found its prospects turning bleak. For one thing, the British economy, so buoyant in the early 1870s, had relapsed into a long depression, with the annual growth rate sinking by 1890 almost to zero.

In June 1897 a naval review was held at Spithead to celebrate Queen Victoria's Diamond Jubilee. In the course of it there occurred a startling event, with implications for Maudslays that no one then could have foreseen, but which soon would portend the eclipse of both Maudslays' and Penn's engineering works.

On that day, during the stately procession of battleships and cruisers in line astern, and before the Queen's very eyes, Charles Parsons put on an uninvited demonstration of his speedboat *Turbinia*. Parsons, inventor of the multi-stage steam turbine, had fitted his 100-foot boat with turbines of 2100 horsepower, capable of driving her at 34.5 knots, an unheard-of speed.

Just before the Royal Yacht *Victoria and Albert* was due to pass between the lines of British and foreign warships, Parsons drove *Turbinia* down the same course, with a loud rushing sound coming from the turbines and a plume of flames blazing from a red-hot funnel. Admirals must have blustered and signalled furiously, but the fastest patrol boats were powerless to head her off. Next day *The Times* gave its weighty editorial opinion that perhaps *Turbinia*'s lawlessness might be excused by the novelty and importance of the invention embodied in her, but it was well to remember that ten years earlier, at the Golden Jubilee Naval Review, the Nordenfeld submarine had made its appearance, and nothing more had been heard of that. . . .

Within a year, however, the Admiralty ordered a turbine-driven destroyer, the *Viper*, and, from then on, development of the Parsons marine turbine progressed at astonishing speed. Only eight years later the turbine-engined battleship *Dreadnaught* was launched, and the liner *Mauretania* was under construction with engines of 70,000 horsepower, a figure scarcely imaginable for reciprocating engines. For large vessels intended to have high speed, the turbine quickly became supreme, rendering obsolete the kind of engine that had so long been the mainstay of Maudslays. This did not mean that less powerful steam engines of the ordinary kind were completely outmoded, since they remained more economical for slower vessels such as cargo ships. Those engines, however, were now furnished by northern builders.

Another obvious handicap for a heavy-engineering firm with its main works in Lambeth was the high rent and rates (property taxes) that had to be paid for its premises. The importance of this factor was shown a few years later when Yarrow's, notable constructors of boilers and of small naval vessels, decided to move from premises in Poplar (on the Thames, but far less central than Lambeth, and therefore less expensive) to Scotstoun on the Clyde, where the rent, rates, and wages would all be much lower.

There was another important factor leading to the firm's failure, and this had to do with boilers rather than engines. From the early 1880s interest had been growing in water-tube boilers for ships, which had been pioneered in France by Bellevilles. Boilers of this kind weigh less, and steam can be raised in them far more quickly, both of these important advantages for naval use. Equally important, this design made possible much higher steam pressures, leading to increased engine efficiency and power.

Having formed a high opinion of them, Walter Maudslay decided that this new technology might be the salvation of his company. When the opportunity came, he obtained from Belleville's the exclusive British manufacturing rights, then had the former Maudslay shipyard in East Greenwich laid out at great expense for the manufacture of these boilers.[4]

Perhaps this move by Walter Maudslay was a gamble, but it is unlikely that anyone in possession of the facts could have expected that an Admiralty committee, swayed by the campaign of one member of Parliament (in whose constituency a manufacturer of 'scotch' boilers could be found), would soon announce that no more Bellevilles would be ordered for ships of the Royal Navy.[5] That hasty and mistaken decision came as a terrible blow. It was no satisfaction, but only a bitter irony for Walter and others concerned, when later – too late, though, to benefit Maudslays – the Admiralty reversed its decision and specified Bellevilles for most of its new warships.

When Maudslay, Sons and Field was declared bankrupt in 1899, it was Alfred Maudslay who applied to the Court of Chancery, on behalf of himself and all other holders of the 1889 mortgage debenture stock, for a Receiver to be appointed for the safeguarding of their interests.[6] His counsel emphasized the importance of trying to keep the workshops going in view of the uncompleted Admiralty contracts, but conceded that the company was hopelessly insolvent, with mortgages and first and second debentures totalling a quarter of a million pounds, a payroll of £2000 a week, and very little coming in. In the event, the Lambeth works were soon closed down; the East Greenwich branch lingered on for two or three years, finishing current contracts, then it was closed too. A faint reminder of its former existence survives in the name 'Maudslay's Bight', still attached to an indentation in the riverbank where the shipyard used to be.

And yet, with the disappearance of the long-established company, the family's involvement in engineering had not ended altogether. This becomes apparent if one searches for British patent applications made after 1900 by inventors named Maudslay. A great resurgence is seen.

This was not just the consequence of Athol continuing to devise new forms of sleeping-bag, railway porter's barrows, and 'Naval, etc. caps', though he went on doing so until the First World War; rather, it was a stream of patent applications from Reginald W. Maudslay, Athol's son. Beginning in 1897 with 'Vehicle mudguards', then slipping for a moment into an Athol-like genre with 'Picking up tennis balls' (an invention for ever mysterious, because never registered or described), Reginald soon gets into his stride with 'Motor vehicle fluid circulating systems', 'Internal combustion engines', 'Road wheels', 'Spring shackles', and so on, racking up a total of fifty-six patents. The last was in 1934, the year of his death.

Reginald Maudslay – known as Dick – was no dilettante, since he had been apprenticed to a civil engineering firm before founding, in 1902, a car manufacturing company of his own in Coventry: the Standard Motor Company. From modest beginnings the company grew to the point of requiring a much larger factory, and in 1915 they were able to build it on a 100-acre site. Standard Motors was well known as an independent marque until the 1960s, when it was absorbed into British Leyland as their Standard-Triumph Division.[7]

Dick was able to found his own company, despite the recent severe setback to family finances, because he had inherited a fortune from his mother. She had been Kate Lucas, a daughter of Sir Thomas Lucas, baronet, who was a founder of the great civil engineering contractors Lucas and Aird, builders of the Albert Hall, the Metropolitan Underground Railway, Cliveden House, and numerous docks, railways, and the like.

As for Athol himself, he had soon been divorced by Kate Lucas, and went on to occupy his days, when not busy with inventions, in writing little books on diverse subjects. One consisted of reflections evidently based on first-hand experience gained in selling his house, with comic pen-portraits of the people who came with an 'order to view' from the agents. He did at least show discretion in ascribing the authorship of this negligible work to 'Lohta Yalsduam'.

Curiously, in two respects the story of Athol Maudslay and Dick is repeated in that of his brother Walter and his son; for Walter, too, married

a Lucas – Kate's first cousin Emily – and their son Cyril started a car manufacturing company in the same year. Emily died young, leaving Cyril as
her only surviving child, and from her Cyril inherited a substantial fortune, although part of it was soon lost through an investment the family
encouraged him to make in Maudslay, Sons and Field in an effort to stave
off collapse. Even so, enough remained for him to establish, at the age of
twenty-six, the Maudslay Motor Company, with the initial objective of
producing silent, reliable cars as well as heavier chassis suitable for vans,
buses, and so on.[8] Although he was not one to have frequent recourse to
the Patent Office, Cyril did make contributions to automobile engineering, most notably by pioneering overhead valves – indeed, overhead
camshafts as well.

During the First World War, Cyril decided to concentrate on the manufacture of heavy commercial vehicles, and to give up the manufacture
of cars. His company survived the Depression, but passed out of Cyril's
ownership before his death. Eventually it, too, became part of the ill-
fated British Leyland combine. With Dick and Cyril the line of Maudslay
engineers comes to an end. Since 1798, when Henry Maudslay first set up
in business on his own account, there had been continuous Maudslay
involvement in high-class engineering for nearly a century and a half.

Alfred Maudslay had five brothers and two sisters. Of these, Eustace, the
youngest, was the first to die, in 1916, and by then poor feckless Eustace
was heavily in debt.[9] Herbert Charles, the eldest, continued to ride to
hounds and sail his own yacht beyond the age of eighty, his expensive
recreations sometimes requiring a little financial help from other members of the family. Charles Edward, his former partner in business, lived
out his days quietly and comfortably with his sister Isabel who, like him,
never married. The others, Clara Rose (Field), Athol, and Walter all died
in the 1920s, leaving Alfred to outlive them by a few years.

It would be interesting to know how Alfred Maudslay's own financial
situation fared during the 1880s and 1890s: that is, how seriously his
fortune was reduced by the failure of the family firm, and how much it
had already been reduced by expenditure on his forays into the Maya
area. While the information available is sparse, some very rough estimates can be attempted.

His father's will, beautifully engrossed on many pages of vellum, and
couched in language that allows the layman only the merest glimmers of
comprehension, assigns his one-third share of the partnership to Herbert
Charles and Walter, equally divided; Clara Rose was bequeathed £10,000
(she was about to marry Joshua Field's son Telford); the remainder of the
estate, probated at 'under £300,000', seems to have been left to his widow
in trust for the children. This was apparently only a category for estimat-
ing the newly introduced 'death duties', but it enables us to reckon the

eventual inheritance of each to have been something less than £40,000. Such a sum, invested at the then usual rate of three to four per cent, would have yielded between £1000 and £1500 per annum, even the lower figure being quite enough in those days to enable a bachelor to lead a life of ease in London, attended by three ot four servants. In the context of the English upper-middle class of the time, a man with such an income would have been considered 'comfortably off', although not rich (a discussion conducted not long before in the correspondence columns of *The Times* had established that a man with less than £150 a year could hardly be a gentleman, but, if married, his income would have to reach £250 before his wife could be considered a lady).

What proportion of his fortune Alfred Maudslay invested in the family firm when it went public is unknown, but the fact that it was he who instigated the suit in Chancery on behalf of stockholders suggests that his holdings were considerable. Equally unknown is what fraction of their investment the debenture holders eventually recovered. But if one is to hazard a guess, then Alfred Maudslay's losses may be put in the neighbourhood of £10,000. And besides, in the years of decline preceding the collapse, his income would have been affected by the reduction and then cessation of dividends.

His capital must also have been eroded by the mounting of seven expeditions between 1881 and 1891 at his own expense. As he himself once revealed, he spent over £10,000 on them, or an average of £1,600 on six of them (assuming that the last one to Copán cost less). They were mounted in alternate years, thus spreading the cost, but there were annual expenses too, notably the salaries paid to artists and in some years to Giuntini. In view of this, it can scarcely be doubted that Maudslay had to dip into capital, perhaps to the extent of £500 a year.

In connection with these figures, there's no single conversion factor one can give to express accurately the purchasing power of the late-nine-teenth century pound in terms of today's much devalued currency. Regarding the ordinary goods and services of daily life – including some that were considered indispensable at that time by the middle classes, but now almost unknown, such as domestic servants – the costs of these have not risen uniformly; another complicating factor is the very differ-ent impact of taxes. If a multiplier of seventy-five be taken as a guide, Maudslay would have spent on his explorations, in today's money, over three-quarters of a million pounds (roughly $1.1 million).

It would be vain to speculate whether Maudslay, had he remained single, would have mounted further expeditions in the Maya area – one to Uxmal, or perhaps to Benque Viejo (now known as Xunantunich). Energy and enthusiasm were not failing him; quite the reverse, for we know that for another twelve years he remained keen to get back into the field. The real question was whether he could afford it. It may be that he would have soldiered on, perhaps giving up the making of plaster casts.

Once married, he had to conserve his capital, if only to avoid depending on his wife's money, for Annie had some private income and could certainly take care of her own expenses – and it is likely she insisted on bearing some of their joint expenses, too.

As mentioned already, the southern part of Westchester County, which then extended down to the Harlem River's north bank, had been largely occupied by large estates: Morrisania, belonging to the Gouverneur Morris family; the Mount Fordham estate on Morris Heights, belonging to their cousins the Lewis Gouverneur Morrises; and then there was the property of the Lorillards, the site of whose house can still be perceived today in the New York Botanical Gardens (the old snuff mill still stands nearby on the banks of the Bronx River, originally its source of power).

But by the end of the nineteenth century, when Manhattan Island was already completely built up, apart from Central Park, it became plain that the still-rural land across the river to the north would have to succumb to urbanization. Furthermore, within both lines of the Morris family one generation was about to succeed another, with the second Gouverneur dying in 1888 and his cousin Lewis dying at a great age not many years later. The Morrises and Lorillards bowed to the inevitable, and when the Borough of the Bronx was incorporated in 1898, the third Gouverneur, Annie's brother, moved away to a farm at Bedford, New York, naming that Morrisania instead. Old Anna Morris, the second wife and widow of Gouverneur II, remained in the house until she died, and then, in 1905, the property was sold.[10]

The buyer, for $400,000 in cash, was the New Haven Railroad. Apportionment of this among the family gave Annie $59,000; to that sum was added another $29,000 from her share in other Port Morris property, plus a direct bequest from her father. But it was not until 1905 that these affairs were all settled.

Prior to its sale, the house that Annie's grandfather had built in about 1789 – its wooden staircase still showing marks made by his wooden leg – had been demolished. Before its demolition, Annie inherited a generous portion of the superb French furniture that had graced it for a century; and prior to this, on her father's death, she had also inherited the diaries and papers of Gouverneur Morris, and among other relics the wooden leg itself.

Chapter 19

Bernal Díaz and other works

T he Maudslays had torn themselves away from their winter refuge, Zavaleta, and from San Angel, and now we can imagine them on the deck of a steamer (unless they went north by train), watching for the last time Mexico's shoreline as it slowly disappeared over the horizon. Then, resolutely, they would have turned their minds to the new pattern of life that awaited them on English soil.

They were already comfortably enough established in London, but both of them were lovers of the countryside, of gardens and birds and a quiet life. So they decided to look for a suitable country house, preferably one in the southwest, where other members of the family had settled. Fortunately, the purchase of such a house had lately been made a little easier by virtue of Annie's receipt of her share of her father's bequest, and immediately she arranged for $5,000, half of the cash component, to be paid into Alfred's bank account.

To secure a temporary rural base they leased Stavordale Priory, near Wincanton, Somerset, the surviving portion of an Augustinian priory founded in the reign of King Henry III. By 1800 this had decayed into a run-down farmhouse and barn, but out of these, long before the Maudslays moved in, a comfortable house had been made.

Then they bought a touring car – a proud product of Maudslay Motors, the company Alfred's nephew Cyril had started. With this powerful tourer he and Annie would be able to roam far afield in their search for a house to buy, and for one of these excursions they invited Dorothy Fleming, a great-niece of Alfred's, to accompany them.[1]

Known always as Dolly, and then aged about eight, she was to become an even closer relative some seventeen years later when she married Cyril, her senior by about twenty-five years. In view of the fact that Cyril was Alfred's favourite nephew (and would later be named chief executor of his will) it was for this biographer the greatest good fortune to have tracked his widow down in 1974, at a very early stage of gathering material for this book, for she had in her possession a mass of material of the greatest interest, and a fund of recollections. She, in turn, was so delighted at meeting someone interested in her greatly revered relative that she made available everything she could find, and willingly presented me with much of it.

So it was some sixty-five years after the event when Dolly told me about her participation in one of the house-hunting expeditions. Regrettably I took no notes, but one detail of her account remains very clear in my memory simply because she asked me then to keep it private, as it had to do with a discovery she had made concerning her august relatives' intimate lives together. But shamelessly, despite her plea and aware of the charges of faithlessness that may be raised against me, I've decided with due deliberation to ignore her request and reveal the secret. My chief grounds for doing so are that she told me later of a far more delicate matter concerning her uncle, without on that occasion making any prior request for confidentiality.

Here I should declare that I became fond of Dolly as well as grateful to her, and would never impute any baseness to her, but I do wonder whether she may not have made this particular request, not so much out of concern about protecting the privacy of her aunt and uncle, as from concern that anyone hearing the story might suspect a little girl of having spied through a peep-hole, thus allowing her to view an unusual scene.

The chance occurred when they passed a night in a pair of hotel rooms provided with a communicating door. This door either had a knot-hole in it, or didn't close properly – I forget which. What, then, did little Dolly discover? She learnt that, on getting into bed, Aunt Annie liked to lay her head on the pillow and go to sleep as soon as possible. Uncle Alfred, on the other hand, liked to read awhile, and out of concern that the light might keep her awake he had taken to putting up his umbrella and laying it over her head as a shade. . . .

At last the Maudslays found the house they liked. One day their chauffeur, having driven them to look at a house that was for sale about 6 miles from Hereford on the road to Ross-on-Wye, remarked upon arrival that they were not likely to find a sweeter air or a finer view than there. And they agreed.[2]

The house was called Morney Cross, standing by itself outside the village of Fownhope. Built near the foot of a gentle hill and flanking a then little-used road passing just below it, the house commands a view across meadows dotted with short and very sturdy oak trees in the Wye valley. Beyond, the Black Mountains can be seen in the distance between nearer hills, while, to the right, Hereford and its cathedral are just within view.

Of Jacobean origin, the house was finished in rough-cast with courses of rusticated stonework and mullion windows, and with dormer windows in the roof. The Maudslays added a drawing room, entrance hall and porch in red sandstone with Caen-stone quoins. Inside, the drawing room walls were given polished birch panelling, and at the back of the house a somewhat narrow and rather peculiar dining-room was built with a pitched wooden roof and ceiling. This was where much of the remaining Fijian collection was displayed.

In front of the porch a copper beech stands in the centre of the gravel sweep, with a low stone wall isolating this from the road. Along this wall Annie's pack of Pekinese, when aroused by an arrival, used to flow like a silky serpent, yapping excitedly. At the back of the house a paved way nearly 200 yards long leads up the hill, with detours among rare trees, to rockeries constructed by Maudslay, and a sunken garden. The kitchen garden had been higher up; but this location was inconvenient, especially for bringing up manure from the cow sheds below the road, so a new one was laid out down there, on the other side of the road. There the Maudslays' land ran down to the river, providing 90 acres of pasture for cows – and fishing for him. When I visited Fownhope, his old cowman, John Williams, was still alive to describe for me the formidable cook/housekeeper, Mrs Mathews, and the disagreeable gardener whose bad language 'was not fit for a gypsy to hear'.

Maudslay himself was described by Mr Williams as a man of few words. Besides gardening, he was given to spending days on end out with a rucksack, 'stone-tapping'. The purpose of this activity he was unable to explain, but probably it was connected with the very unusual geological formation of the valley, a stratum of Old Red Sandstone broken through by uplifted Upper Silurian strata. Examination of this was a principal activity of the Woolhope Naturalists Field Club, of which Maudslay was a member.

After moving in and making a few improvements to the garden, Maudslay must have settled down to resume work on his translation of *The Conquest of Mexico* by Bernal Díaz. Almost from the moment he had first taken an interest in the Maya, he had been aware of the contribution that early Colonial documents could make to understanding pre-Columbian life and religious beliefs. This is clear from the long passages from Villagutierre's *Historia de la Conquista de la Provincia de el Itza* copied by him into notebooks early in his career, and again when, having taken refuge one winter in Spain, he learnt from Dr Marimón, librarian of the Archives of the Indies in Seville, that he had found a *Relación* of Valladolíd, Yucatán. This town had been established on the site of a Maya provincial ruler's capital, and this early account contained a chapter on Chichén Itzá, the ruined city at which Maudslay was then thinking of attempting a season's work. So he copied relevant passages from that document, too.[3]

Most Mayanists would, I believe, name the *Popol Vuh* (a traditional work), Bishop Diego de Landa's *Relación de las Cosas de Yucatán*, and

Bernal Díaz del Castillo's *Historia Verdadera de la Conquista de Nueva España* as the three post-Conquest documents most valuable for their studies.

The *Popol Vuh* is accepted by most scholars as the greatest literary production of native America. It is important not only as a history of the Quiché Maya of highland Guatemala in their own language, but also because it presents the creation myth that appears to underlie all Maya mythology. This text, undoubtedly of pre-Columbian origin, may originally have been written down on bark-fibre paper in some highland script, perhaps in several copies. The text, however, in Quiché Maya was preserved by oral transmission long enough to be set down phonetically in European script at an early date.

In about 1700 this manuscript was found in Chichicastenango by a Spanish friar, who made a copy and translated it into Spanish. Since the first publication of this translation in 1857, many other editions and translations have appeared; in Maudslay's day, however, the potential value of this text in explicating Maya mythology, iconography, and hieroglyphic writing was scarcely imagined.

The second of the three documents, Landa's *Relación*, was discovered and promptly published in 1864, but did not become available in English translation until several years after Maudslay's death – but of this more will be said later.

Bernal Díaz del Castillo's great work had quite a different history. It had never been lost, and had long been in print, not only in Spanish but in English and other languages. Its author, an old warrior who had taken part in two expeditions to the Mexican coast before serving under Cortés in his fateful campaign, had retired to the original Guatemalan capital, now known as Antigua. There, in 1568, when Díaz was well over seventy, he completed his *True History*. There are reasons, however, for believing that he had started writing it long before, and began it not as a history but as an autobiography.[4]

In old age, having read accounts published in the 1550s and 1560s, he first became annoyed by errors in them, and then grew indignant at Cortés for failing, in his letters, to give his soldiers proper credit for his successes. Díaz himself was a common soldier, and one who bore considerable resentment over his failure to receive any tangible recompense for loyal service. But despite his lowly status and rough education, his work is a masterpiece of vivid narrative. And for Maudslay and others interested in indigenous cultures at the time of contact with Europeans, it is not only a history of the Conquest but a mine of ethnographic detail as well.

By 1904 the two manuscript versions of the work then known had been transcribed and published, both somewhat corrupted by later alterations and additions. The original, inherited by his son Francisco, has never left Guatemala, while the other was sent by Díaz himself to Madrid for publication (a useful third version came to light in Murcia after Maudslay's death). The Madrid version was published there in 1632 by a Mercedarian friar, but not before the friar had made some changes, such as making Díaz speak highly of his Order's charitable works in Guatemala. The first English translation of this version appeared in 1800.

The original manuscript on the other hand, the one inherited by Francisco Díaz, contains material added by his father after the copy had been made and sent to Spain. Later, Francisco took it upon himself to suppress certain passages, and add others designed to magnify his father's fame. Nearly 350 years then passed without this version being put into print.

By the 1890s Mexican scholars were beginning to make requests for a photostat or faithful copy of this important work, and in 1895 they were able to secure a photographic copy, sent from Guatemala, but this, it was stressed, was not for publication. Finally, in 1901, President Estrada Cabrera of Guatemala sent a copy to the Mexican historian Genaro García for his unrestricted use. And good use he did make of it: he transcribed the text with scrupulous accuracy, and his work was published without delay in 1904.

Maudslay now undertook to translate this into English, but exactly when he was able to begin this tremendous task is unclear. He would almost certainly have known Genaro García in Mexico, so one wonders whether they may have come to some arrangement whereby García would provide him from time to time with photostats or carbon copies of completed sections of his work, so that he could busy himself with translation during the months – and, as it turned out, years – of waiting for a favourable decision on funding for the research he hoped to do at Monte Albán. If, in fact, he did not have García's text to work on, time must have hung heavy on his hands between 1902 and 1904, especially during winters spent at Zavaleta.

And if no such arrangement existed, then Maudslay must have worked extremely hard from the very moment García's work was published in 1904, for – in spite of the distractions of quitting Zavaleta and moving to Mexico City (where in any case he had other researches to make), and then moving to England, and settling first into one house and then another – he managed to have the first volume of 450 pages published in 1908.

One may suppose that work on the next volume was already well advanced when it began to be interrupted by Maudslay's need to visit London for meetings or other business at learned societies. In 1900 he had been elected to the new Council of the Royal Geographical Society, and then was elected President of the Royal Anthropological Institute for the years 1911 and 1912, a position he accepted with considerable misgivings (as he said with characteristic modesty) since he was not a trained anthropologist.

Still more of his time was consumed in the work of planning for the 18th International Congress of Americanists, scheduled for the summer of 1912 – the first of these Congresses to be held in England. Sir Clements Markham was elected President of the Organizing Committee and Maudslay its Chairman, with Francis Sarg as Secretary and Adela Breton as Assistant Secretary. The committee of eleven included J. Cooper-Clark and Anatole von Hügel, also C. L. Fleischmann, a friend of Maudslay's who had been a coffee-grower in Guatemala, British Vice-Consul there, and a collector of Maya antiquities.[5] To Maudslay would fall not only delivery of a short address at the opening ceremony – that would be the least of his labours – but also regular attendance at committee meetings in London, and participation in efforts to drum up international and local interest in the congress itself.

In replying to a letter from Bowditch, which evidently contained a passing comment on Maudslay's character, Adela Breton described a little difficulty she had had with him:

> Maudslay is much too modest or proud to assert himself in any way. I reproached him about Who's Who because when I was trying to interest people in the Americanist Congress, they wanted to know 'who is this Mr. Maudslay,' as Chairman and promoter. He said he would not send his description to Who's Who, (which most people do), and I have been intending to write to the Editor to ask him to write and request it.[6]

In addition Maudslay had set himself to complete in time for the Congress some researches which had originated in his close reading of Bernal Díaz's *True History*. This work bears the title 'A Note on the Position and Extent of the Great Temple Enclosure of Tenochtitlan, and the Position, Structure and Orientation of the Teocalli of Huitzilopochtli'. It was, of course, another fruit of the months he spent in San Angel, and incorporates evidence from such early sources as Motolinia, Sahagún, Torquemada, 'Anonymous Conqueror, companion of Cortés', Diego Durán, Hernando Tezozomoc, and Ixtlilxochitl; and, of course, the views of nineteenth-century scholars. As he says,

> the positions of the palace of Montezuma, the palace of Tlillancalqui, the Dance House, and Old Palace of Montezuma have been well defined by various writers and are now generally accepted. The principal difficulty arises in defining the area of the Temple Enclosure and the orientation of the Teocalli of Huitzilopochtli.[7]

Maudslay decided to publish this work in the form of a slim volume of large quarto format, with his conclusions graphically presented in a series of unbound translucent overlays, any of which could be placed over a contemporary map of the streets (also included). When drainage pipes were being laid in 1900, Leopoldo Batres had been watching the excavations on behalf of the Government. Two sets of steps were found, crossing the Calle de Escalerillas, but as Maudslay wrote, 'unfortunately Batres was already fully convinced that the Great Teocalli faced the south and occupied more or less the position of the present Cathedral'.[8]

Confirmation of Maudslay's conclusion that the temples and enclosure faced west was soon to be provided by Manuel Gamio's excavations in 1914, which revealed a corner and an identifying pair of stairways leading to the temples. More recent excavations also support Maudslay's conclusions. The cost of printing this work was borne by Maudslay, and with those translucent overlays it must have been considerable. (A three-page abstract of this work was published in the *Proceedings* of the Congress.)[9]

Two years later Charles P. Bowditch, writing to Adela Breton on another topic, apparently took the opportunity to enquire how he could obtain a copy of Maudslay's paper on the Temple Enclosure.[10] She replied:

Mr. Maudslay probably thought he sent you his book when he only intended to do so. His memory fails in the matter of letters, etc. He would certainly wish you to have it. It is however disastrous that only 75 copies were made when double the number would have cost scarcely more, and not even the blocks were saved I fear, for the man who did them died and his things were dispersed. If I had had time to think I would have rescued them.[11]

In his brief opening address to the Congress as Chairman of the Organizing Committee, Maudslay emphasized the need for exploration in America:

Europe, Asia and Africa have monopolized all the attention. . . . All forms of anthropological investigation have the same end in view, that is, the acquiring of knowledge concerning the origin, development, and history of the human race, and the task cannot be satisfactorily accomplished if we leave out of account that branch of the human race which inhabited the continent of America before the end of the fifteenth century. Especially in America we have the chance of studying human development, unaffected by the cross currents of the ancient civilisations with which we are best acquainted.[12]

Invitations had been sent out for each country to send four delegates to the Congress. When, six weeks later, the Mexican Secretariat of Public Instruction requested permission to add Alfonso Pruneda to their delegation, Adela Breton had to explain that the sheer number of the delegates from twenty-four governments and forty universities ruled out any additions. Later, however, he was accepted, perhaps because Nicolás León had dropped out – but Franz Boas was now added, to represent the newly founded Escuela Internacional de Arqueología y Etnología Americanas.[13]

Very late in the day Martínez Hernández lobbied for the inclusion of Teobert Maler, and only a month before the congress was due to open the Mexican government issued $1200 for Maler's expenses. Then, for some reason, Martínez himself also backed out, but as Pruneda reported,

> It should be noted that Sr. Don Teoberto Maler, a resident of Mérida, was present at the Congress, who told me that he had been named a delegate in the place of Martínez Hernández; but he had not received official notice of this appointment [probably because the appointment could not be approved in time], and I understand that neither had the Secretary of the Congress [been informed], so he was not recognised as an official delegate.

Maler had brought with him a large number of photographs for exhibition, as noted in the *Proceedings* (p. lxxvii): 'Lent by Teobert Maler. Several sets of photographs by him, which were shown 150 at a time, of the ruins and sculptures in Yucatan and Central America, mostly unknown previous to his discovery of the places.'

No record exists of conversation between Maler and Maudslay during the congress, as must surely have occurred; nor, to the best of my knowledge, is there any surviving correspondence between them from any period, although it is known that some years earlier Maler did send Maudslay a photograph of a stela he had found at Piedras Negras. It is also known that they once met in Mexico City in 1903, but again there is only the briefest record of what passed between them.

Maler was a man of choleric temperament, and there are clear signs that he felt jealous of Maudslay. But well aware of the high esteem in which Maudslay was held, he stifled direct criticism of him in print, directing his barbs instead at poor Gorgonio López, with accusations that he damaged monuments by lighting fires (as was normal practice in damp climates) to dry the paper while taking moulds. After raising the matter with Maudslay during their single known encounter, and having received his assurance that Gorgonio never caused such damage, Maler did retract his accusations in print.[14]

One great disappointment at the Congress must have been the failure of the Victoria and Albert Museum to respond to Adela Breton's request for the loan of some Maudslay casts to exhibit during the meetings. 'It is extremely unfortunate', she wrote to the Director, 'that your department has been able to do nothing since I wrote about the matter last autumn, for Mr. Maudslay's work is world-known & foreign members will be astonished that so little regard is paid to it.'[15] She also expressed her vexation in a letter to Bowditch: 'He [Maudslay] has been so disgusted with the treatment of his invaluable casts and paper moulds at S. Kensington that I only wonder he does not give up Americanist studies altogether.'[16]

Visits to Oxford and Cambridge formed part of the programme of the Congress. At Cambridge the Director of the newly inaugurated Museum of Archaeology, Maudslay's old friend Anatole von Hügel, showed them round, while at Oxford the Mexican manuscripts in the Bodleian Library were the centre of attraction. Then as a special gesture to honour their visit, the University called a Convocation on that day (4 June 1912) so that Honorary Doctorates of Science could be conferred upon Maudslay and Franz Boas.

As for Maler, on leaving London, he went on to Paris and there presented some superb large-format photographs to the Bibliothèque Nationale, where they remain today in perfect condition. Then he returned to Mexico.

In his Presidential Address to the Royal Anthropological Institute for the second year of his tenure, Maudslay reviewed the papers on Mesoamerican topics that had been read at the International Congress of Americanists, especially those referring to the Valley of Mexico.[17] A paper soon to be recognized as being by far the most important of all was that given by a young Mexican archaeologist, Manuel Gamio, who had studied under Franz Boas at Columbia University, and under him again at the Escuela Internacional de Arqueología y Antropología Americanas.[18]

Gamio had dug a test-pit 18 feet deep in refuse at Azcapotzalco in the Valley of Mexico. This revealed three distinct types of pottery: Aztec on or near the surface; then a band of mixed Aztec and Teotihuacan sherds; below that, Teotihuacan pottery in a layer about 9 feet deep, and, below that again, a gradual transition to sherds of unknown affiliation, soon to be called 'Archaic'. In revealing occupations of the valley by three sequent groups, over the course of a long period, Gamio heralded a revolution in archaeological practice in Mexico – but this was long overdue because, as Joan Mark has pointed out, W. H. Holmes had demonstrated and published a similar stratigraphy on the outskirts of Mexico City twenty-three years earlier.[19] In any case, Maudslay, by reproducing Gamio's drawing of the pit in cross-section, signalled his recognition of this technique's importance.

Among other papers presented was one by Leopoldo Batres describing his work at Teotihuacan, in the course of which he stated:

I removed the earth at the level of the base of the Pyramid of the Sun, at the south-west angle, and beneath the accumulated soil and one structural layer, 4 metres thick, already in ruin, there appeared a fragment of facing formed of stones whose regular and level surfaces faced outwards. . . . I became firmly convinced that the Monument could be revealed in all its majesty. . . because its construction must have been by superimposition of layers. . . . The inner construction was the leitmotiv for the rest; all were equal and each completely finished with a stairway to ascend to the shrine . . . so that one may feel certain that by removing, so to speak, the outer layer, the under layer would reproduce in its entirety the arrangement of the former as do the underlying leaves of an onion.[20]

So it is clear that, in his opinion, these layers represented no more than stages in a continuous process of construction.

Removing the outer skin of this onion proved to be a colossal task, and eventually a narrow-gauge railway 4 miles long had to be built, so that four steam locomotives could haul away about a million tons of rubble (for which there was a ready market in the capital). Only in this fashion could the work be completed in time for display of the pyramid in celebrations of the centenary of Mexican independence.

Maudslay was unable to conceal his indignation.

The cement facing on the Pyramid of the Sun at Teotihuacan was certainly intact in some places when I examined it not many years ago; it may only have been in patches, it is true, but enough remained to form some idea of the finished appearance of the building. Whether Señor Batres removed a thickness of 4 metres, as he states in one paragraph, or 15 metres as he states in another, there can be little doubt that he has destroyed the value of one of the most interesting structures of the ancient Americans, and left in its place a stupendous monument of self-assertion and incompetence. This is all the more to be deplored as the culture associated with Teotihuacan is every day becoming a matter of greater interest to the archaeologist and ethnologist.

In a passing reference to the ruins of Monte Albán, Maudslay felt obliged to deplore another of Batres's interventions: he had removed a set of carved panels from their original positions at that site, where in Maudslay's opinion 'there was no damage from forest growth to contend against, and they could have been easily protected had they remained at the site' (Batres had taken them to Mexico City).[21]

Maudslay must have felt relieved when all these public activities were over. Perhaps he and Annie escaped to Galway to recover from the strain, but they seem to have remained in England during the next winter, since Adela Breton mentioned in a letter to Bowditch dated 12 March 1913: 'I am sorry to say he [Maudslay] has been rather out of health lately – lungs – and the specialist has ordered him to be out of doors as much as possible.' (His smoking can't have helped the lung trouble which had bothered him since his teens, for in several snapshots, right to the end of his life, he is seen holding a cigarette.)

By this time one may imagine that Maudslay was eagerly awaiting the arrival of a certain scholarly work, the publication of which he knew was imminent. This, *A Study of Maya Art: Its Subject Matter & Historical Development*, by Herbert J. Spinden, was based on the author's Ph.D. dissertation, originally delivered to Harvard University in 1909, and then expanded by its author for publication by the Peabody Museum in 1913. A principal adviser of Spinden's had been Frederick Putnam, who was of course well known to Maudslay.

This was a pioneering work that sought to explicate Maya art, many features of which had previously been difficult or impossible to interpret because the original and probably more literal representations had been so thoroughly stylized as to be almost unrecognizable. Spinden's great contribution was to demonstrate how the ancient Mayas transformed graphic elements such as serpents' heads through several stages into iconic elements; in other words, he identified the basic vocabulary of motifs, analysed their design, and interpreted them. Naturally, in illustrating his book, Spinden made great use of images published in Maudslay's *Archaeology* volumes – although he chose to redraw everything himself, in order to maintain a consistent style in his line illustrations, regardless of their sources. So here was the first scholarly analysis built to a considerable extent on a data-base provided by Maudslay and Annie Hunter. It must have given both of them considerable satisfaction.

A review of the book by Maudslay and T. A. Joyce in the same year begins: 'In a field which has afforded material for the wildest speculation, it is a treat to meet with such an eminently sane book as Dr. Spinden's work on Maya Art.' (It is, by the way, interesting to find among the many comments offered by Maudslay and Joyce this suggestion: 'the extraordinarily thick walls and small cells of the Tikal temples might imply an architectural survival of a primitive sacred cave' – possibly the first expression of a notion now widely accepted.)

By the following December Breton was informing Bowditch that Maudslay had been in Florence, without giving further details. And now, at last, the tremendous task of translating Bernal Díaz was completed, and in 1916, within a few days of the tercentenary of Richard Hakluyt's death, the fifth and last volume was published by the Hakluyt Society. How Maudslay and Annie celebrated his liberation from the desk at long last can only be guessed. Since the war was at its height, no relaxation in a southern clime could be contemplated, but perhaps they went to Ireland. It had by no means been an easy row to hoe. As was desirable, García had copied Bernal Díaz's text letter for letter, preserving the archaic orthography, and abstaining from spelling out any of Díaz's idiosyncratic abbreviations. Since there is scarcely any punctuation, one sentence runs into the next, and each chapter consists of one long paragraph. An example, taken almost at random from the opening page, may illustrate the skill with which Maudslay turned the original into readable English without loss of fidelity:

> la nueva españa que es vna de las buenas partes descubiertas del nuevo mundo, lo cual descubrimos a nra. costa sin ser sabedor de ello su mag. y ablando aqui en rrespuesta de lo q an dho. y escripto personas que no lo alcançaron a saber ni lo uieron ni tener noticia verdadera de lo que sobre esta materia ay, propusieron salbo hablar al sabor de su paladar.

This Maudslay renders as:

> that [New Spain] is one of the best countries yet discovered in the New World we found out by our own efforts without His Majesty knowing anything about it.
>
> I also speak here in reply to all that has been said and written by persons who themselves knowing nothing, have received no true account of what really took place, but who nevertheless now put forward any statements that happen to suit their fancy.

When completed, Maudslay's translation would fill five quarto volumes, each containing about 110,000 words of text, plus notes and other matter. In the first volume there is an appendix in which Maudslay attempts to trace the fate of the gifts Moctezuma gave to Cortés, and those sent by Cortés to Charles V. A rather full bibliography is also provided, and, on the otherwise blank page facing the beginning of this, Maudslay placed a quotation from Anthony à Wood's *History of Oxford*, as a sort of *cri de coeur*: 'A painfull work it is I'll assure you, and more than difficult; wherein what toyle hath been taken, as no man thinketh, so no man believeth, but he that hath made the triall.'

These words were clearly appropriate for the labour of making the translation, but the toyle resulted in a masterpiece. Even with the passage of a century Maudslay's language – or more justly, the Maudslays', since Annie had helped in the work – remains effortless to read, while at the same time preserving an old-fashioned air, as was only fitting in rendering the unliterary narrative of an old soldier, written four-and-a-half centuries ago.

The most intelligent review of Maudslay's work was that of Basil Thompson, who gave his opinion that

> Those who have formed an impression of Bernal Díaz from the quotations given by Prescott will have a pleasant shock of surprise when they turn to Mr. Maudslay's translation. . . . Prescott, who consulted him very freely, accused him of 'vulgar vanity which breaks out with a truly comic ostentation on every page', but he admitted the charm of the work. [As Thompson remarked,] despite Díaz's lack of instinct

for the picturesque and skill in literary expression, we know every conquistador as well as we know the neighbours of Samuel Pepys . . . but this feeling is very largely due to the excellence of the translation, which preserves the rude idiom of the original without sacrificing any of its charm.

Some of the conquistadores do, indeed, come alive for us through the pen-portraits of them provided by Bernal Díaz: Juan Velázquez de León, for example, aged thirty-six: 'His countenance was a strong one and his beard was somewhat curly and well kept, his voice was harsh and coarse and he stuttered a little; he was very spirited and a good talker'; or Captain Luis Marin: he was 'of fair size, robust and vigorous; he was bow-legged and his beard was reddish and his face long and pleasing, except that he had scars as though he had smallpox'.

A further point worth making is that Maudslay's edition is much more than simply a translation: it is also an examination of the document in the light of other sources capable of providing comparison and elucidation. An example of this is his 'Map of part of Mexico showing the route of the Spaniards from Vera Cruz to the City of Mexico'. Next to Lake Texcoco in his delineation of it, one finds a little note: 'The water in the lake is restored as nearly as possible to its level at the time of arrival of the Spaniards.' This small detail of the map, which must have cost him a good deal of field and library research, accords well with recent research.

Not long after completing Bernal Díaz, Maudslay agreed to the Royal Geographical Society's request for a lecture – doing so, perhaps, as light relief after that prolonged labour. The topic of the lecture, illustrated with lantern slides, was the Valley of Mexico, and the printed account of it is well worth reading.[22]

Whereas a number of tentative reconstructions of Mesoamerican prehistory had been proposed by others since Maudslay began his studies of that area, he himself, ever conscious of the shaky foundations for such efforts, refrained for twenty-five years from venturing any opinions of his own on the matter. But at last, in the introduction to his edition of *The Conquest of Mexico* he did devote three pages to it.

Maudslay begins by summarizing the commonly accepted story that

the Toltecs, whose capital was Tula, were a people of considerable civilisation, who, after imparting something of their culture to the ruder Nahua hordes that followed them from the North, themselves migrated to Guatemala and Yucatan, where they built great temples and carved the monuments which have so often been described by modern travellers. I am not, however, myself able to accept this explanation of the facts known to me. The monuments and architectural remains of Guatemala and Yucatan are undoubtedly the work of the Maya, who, although nearly related to the Nahuas, are admitted to be a distinct race, speaking a different language; and I am inclined to believe that the Maya race formerly inhabited a considerable portion of Central and Southern Mexico, and it is to it that we must give credit for Tula, Cholula and, possibly, Teotihuacan. . . . [Then,] driven from their Mexican homes by the pressure of Nahua immigrants, they doubtless took refuge in the highlands of Chiapas and Guatemala, and along the banks of the Rivers Usumacinta and Motagua, and pressed on as far as the present frontier of Guatemala and Honduras; but it must be admitted that, so far, no account of this migration and settlement is known to us.

[Maudslay was] further inclined to believe that, after some centuries of peaceful development had elapsed, the Maya defence failed, and that the people were again driven from their homes by invaders from the North West, and leaving Chiapas and Guatemala, took refuge in Yucatan, where they founded Chichen and Uxmal. . . .

It is worthy of note that weapons of war are almost entirely absent from the Central American sculptures, and at Copan one of the most important sculptures is that of a woman, whereas in Yucatan every man is depicted as a warrior with arms in his hands. . . .

At the time of the Spanish conquest the highlands of Guatemala were held by tribes of the Maya Quiché race, who were probably descendants of the Mayas and their Nahua conquerors.[23]

He goes on to speculate that the Huastecs (who are settled around the mouth of the River Pánuco and whose language is related to Mayan) were remnants of the Maya race left behind when the main body of them was driven to the southeast, and he suggested that the Huastecs had no hieroglyphic writing because the Mayas, at the time of the migration, had not yet developed their writing.

A few years later, in 1913, when T. A. Joyce was making a study, both more wide-ranging and more detailed, of relations between Toltecs, Mayas, Zapotecs, Chichimecs, etc., and trying to trace possible migrations, he is likely to have consulted Maudslay, a man he greatly admired, but his eventual conclusions differed from his. Although both men made valiant attempts to solve the conundrum, neither of them, as can scarcely be wondered at for such early attempts, bears any resemblance to the near-consensus of opinion more recently achieved.

It is the study of linguistics that best illuminates this question of ancient migrations. Numerous languages of the Maya family are still spoken (twenty-eight being the usual reckoning), all of these presumably developments from one ancestral language in the not very remote past. Although the time necessary for such diversification can't be estimated with any precision, it is likely have been about three millennia. But whatever the time span, a mass migration of the Maya within that period has to be very unlikely – unless one can imagine all the members of each language group marching forth in good order, as if from the Ark, to their designated areas in the new territory, without commingling along the way with those of related tongues!

Furthermore, the striking abundance of distinct but related Maya languages found in the highlands of Guatemala and Chiapas does argue for this region having been the original homeland of the Maya, because a diversification of languages such this is more like to have occurred in mountainous country with poor communication between valleys.

This theory also receives some support from the typical features of Lowland ceremonial centres: tall pyramids, temples built upon them containing small cells within massive walls (just as Joyce and Maudslay described them), and the stela cult, since the creators of these may have been Highland Maya who had moved down to the lowlands, and needed to create substitutes for the sacred caves and the stalagamites often found within them.

That some migrations did take place is certain, one of them being that of the Itzas who dominated Chichén Itzá from the ninth century, for they seem to have come from the centre of the Guatemalan Petén, whither they would later return. But the difficult question of Toltec influence at Chichén Itzá has not been clarified; nor has that of the Maya–Huastec relationship.

In the wider field of cultural diffusion between the Old World and the New, Maudslay rejected outright – as we shall see – the extreme diffusionist notions of Sir Grafton Elliot Smith. But thirty years earlier, in about 1895, he had told a certain Mr Pratt about Cyclopean breakwaters and other stone structures on a Pacific island that he had heard about, apparently suggesting that they might possibly have served as a link in a hypothetical chain of cultural diffusion from Asia to the Americas.[24]

Quite likely, during his years of service in the Pacific, he had been told of great stone ruins at Metalanim on Ponapé, one of the Caroline Islands (a scattered group lying about a thousand miles north of New Guinea and the Solomon Islands), and soon, in 1886, he was to hear more about that extraordinary and extensive complex of structures from a lecture given by a naval captain at the Royal Geographical Society.[25]

But in 1899, a few years after his conversation with Mr Pratt, he would see photographs of those structures at another Royal Geographical Society lecture, and these decided him against accepting any such theory. The hexagonal basaltic prisms, brought down the coast from about 30 miles away, and then laid horizontally, criss-cross in alternating layers like logs of wood, bore no relation to stone constructions in Mexico or Central America, nor did they appear to bear any sign of masons' toolmarks. And besides, he thought the bones found in a grave by the lecturer were another nail in the coffin of that hypothesis, for they appeared to be of no great age.[26]

Chapter 20

Last years

In 1918 a new and extremely virulent strain of influenza struck the world, killing uncounted millions, and in February of the following year Annie succumbed to the dreaded virus. When her condition became serious, Alfred spent three days looking for a nurse, but owing to the multitude of flu cases throughout the country, and the fact that many nurses were themselves stricken with it, none could be found. He searched in Hereford, Malvern, Cheltenham, Gloucester, and Worcester, until at last one was found in London. Then a niece of Annie's who had spent some years working in a hospital also came to help, and Annie survived, but her health thereafter seemed precarious.[1]

That July, the Maudslays returned once more to Aasleagh Lodge (pronounced 'Ashleah'), near Lenane in County Galway. This is a large fishing lodge standing above a river about half-way between the river's well-known falls and its mouth, where it empties into Ireland's only fjord. Annie's doctor had probably approved the Atlantic coast as having a summer climate likely to promote Annie's recovery, and she herself must have loved the place for its beauty.[2] Walter Maudslay had held this lodge on a long lease for the past thirty years or so, perhaps in partnership with his brother Alfred, for both of them were keen fishermen. For his part, then, Alfred must have been glad of the opportunity to flog once more those waters so full of salmon and trout – and as it happened, he was to catch a 35-pound salmon, supposedly the largest fish ever taken out of that river.

Two years later Maudslay seems to have decided that the time had come to make one last onslaught against the entrenched positions of both the British Museum and the Victoria and Albert. He was determined to get his collections housed under one roof, and suitably displayed, knowing well that the time remaining for taking up the cudgels was getting short. By then, three years had passed since the end of the war, the national situation was apparently recuperating (although fated soon to deteriorate), and in Thomas Atholl Joyce, now a Deputy Keeper in the Department of British and Mediaeval Antiquities at the British Museum, he knew that he had a firm ally.[3]

So on 6 December 1921 he took up his pen and indited a four-page missive directed to the President of the Board of Trade (the Cabinet Member responsible for the V&A), uncharacteristically emphasizing points in his argument with underlining: 'Sir, As early as the year 1885 *I presented some of the results* of my expeditions to Central America to the South Kensington Museum & *placed some original sculptures on loan*. During the following years *I added to the collection of moulds, & made a gift* of the original sculptures to the Museum, on condition that casts should be made from the moulds & that they should be exhibited as far as space would allow.' He then reminded the minister that in 1893, much to his regret, the casts had been moved to a gallery, and he had been obliged to consent to the original sculptures being removed to the British Museum.[4]

> Then, the space allotted to me [for the casts] was reduced by half, and finally, during my absence in America, the casts were taken to pieces & stored in the basement . . . where they have remained ever since [and, as he might truthfully have added, falling apart and being eaten by rats.][5]
>
> I am now in my seventy second year, & I should like to know, before I die, what is to become of the collection? [Then in a strenuous effort to suppress his natural modesty, Maudslay ended his letter thus:] A Spanish proverb says that 'one cannot ring the bells & walk in the procession' and as there is so little interest shown in American Archaeology in my own country I must get my bells rung by an American, & end this letter by a quotation from Mr. Morley's great work on the inscriptions from Copan (one of the four principal sites which I explored). . . . Yours faithfully, etc.

The passage he copied into this letter ends by describing his work as 'the greatest archaeological investigation ever accomplished in the field, and the most important publication by which the science has been enriched'.

Frederick Godman had been a trustee of the British Museum, and he would very likely have urged the Museum's acceptance of the entire Maudslay collection, and if so his advocacy would have been heard with respect, but unfortunately he had died in 1919. What, in the end, really made this step more feasible was a redrawing of the Museum's departmental boundaries in 1921, for this resulted in the creation of a new Department of Ceramics and Ethnography (hived off from the Department of British and Mediaeval Antiquities and Ethnography). Joyce was appointed Deputy Keeper of Ethnography, and in 1922 an agreement over the Maudslay collections was reached.

The casts were brought over from South Kensington, and then all the original sculptures, together with some of the best casts, were displayed in a gallery at the head of a stairway. This was opened to the public on

1 January 1923, and dedicated as the Maudslay Room – the only gallery within the Museum ever to have been named for a living person. A well-illustrated ninety-three-page *Guide to the Maudslay Collections* was written by Joyce and printed in time for the opening.[6]

The resolution of this long-standing and deeply felt concern gave Maudslay tremendous satisfaction, but, even as the new gallery was being installed, it was becoming clear that Annie's health had become precarious; and he, too, was laid low more frequently than ever by colds and other maladies. In notes sent to his friend Keltie[7] at the Royal Geographic Society, Maudslay sometimes included reports on Annie's health, or his own. Some examples – 1920: APM, streaming cold. 1921: APM, doctors forbid travel. 7 March 1924: Annie seriously ill, too weak to be told of her sister Mrs Davenport's death. 3 May 1924: Visit to Cornwall has done Annie good. 26 May 1926: Annie has German Measles. 7 September 1926: APM cannot go to the International Congress of Americanists at Rome because his wife is seriously ill. (He had attended the 1924 Congress at Gothenburg.)

A few days after this, on 12 September 1926, Annie died.[8] She was cremated, and her ashes were interred in the crypt of Hereford Cathedral. Her last years had been made miserable by shingles in the face, and sores upon it continually distressed her; she also had a facial tic severe enough occasionally to unseat her pince-nez. When out of doors she often hooded her face to protect it from wind and sun – and probably from view, because she had indeed become a sorry sight.[9]

Needing to get away, Maudslay went to Egypt, taking Annie's niece Beatrix with him. They went upriver to Luxor, then took a steamer to Aswan for a stay of three weeks, and from there visited Abu Simbel. While still in Cairo, Maudslay had written to Arthur Hinks, Keltie's successor as Secretary of the Royal Geographical Society: 'I have had some cuttings from the Times sent to me in which Elliot Smith has been putting his foot in it again – Waldeck's drawings are worthless & just fancy pictures.' Then on the same day he received another article by Elliot Smith, published in the *Illustrated London News*.

It is probably true to say that only two people ever really upset Maudslay's equanimity, Leopoldo Batres being one, and, to a lesser degree, Professor Sir Grafton Elliot Smith,[10] FRS, the other. Elliot Smith had made his reputation as an anatomist, notably of the brain, but he also had a strong interest in archaeology, especially Egyptology. Having developed some idiosyncratic theories, he became a thorn in the flesh to colleagues of more sober judgment. In fact he was an outstanding example of a curious phenomenon: the respected expert in one field of science who airily abandons his critical faculties while engaging in vigorous advocacy of barmy ideas in another field – as often as not prehistory.[11]

Elliot Smith, in his book *Elephants and Ethnologists* and in an article in

Nature, strained mightily to prove that American civilizations were largely derived from the Old World. He was, of course, neither the first nor the
last to espouse this view, but his eminence in another branch of science
lent weight to his ideas. His adversarial style may be termed forthright,
as shown by a paragraph from a letter he sent to *Nature* rebutting criticisms that Alfred Tozzer and Herbert Spinden, both from Harvard, had
made of a previous article of his.[12]

> The account given in my memoir sheds a remarkable light upon the
> psychology of Americans, both ancient and modern, and especially
> upon the ethnological 'Munroe Doctrine,' which demands that every-
> thing American belongs to America, and must have been wholly
> invented there. The Maya civilisation was American in origin only in
> the same sense that Harvard University is – immigrants from the Old
> World supplied the ideas and the technical knowledge, which
> enabled an institution to be built up, no doubt with certain modifica-
> tions prompted by local conditions and the contact of a variety of
> cultural influences.

Elliot Smith had now seen photos of Frédéric Waldeck's watercolour
renderings of sculptured panels at Palenque and Copán, lately brought
to light by Eric Thompson. In them Elliot Smith found what he was sure
were representations of elephant's heads, and seized eagerly upon them
as supporting his theory of Indo-Chinese culture having diffused to
Central America in the eighth century AD.

In his *Times* article Elliot Smith wrote: 'If the animal represented by
the ancient Maya artists is really a conventionalised Indian elephant, and
the scenes in which it appears in the Maya and Aztec codices represent
the exploits of the Vedic god Indra, then the Asiatic inspiration of the earliest civilisation of the New World is established.'[13]

Reacting to this, Sir Hercules Read of the British Museum wrote, in an
internal note, 'Of course Maudslay is the proper person to fight Elliot
Smith, but he is too old and too much of a gentleman.' Maudslay was,
indeed, extremely reluctant to be dragged into controversy (in fact, Elliot
Smith had once tried to do this himself by attacking him at a meeting of
the Royal Anthropological Institute),[14] but on this issue he needed no
prompting. He wrote to *The Times* from Luxor inviting comparison of
Waldeck's drawings with drawings and photographs published in his
Archaeology, or with his plaster casts. 'I have no doubt that [readers of *The
Times*] will be convinced of Waldeck's inaccuracy and the worthlessness
of his drawings in support of Professor Elliot Smith's views.'

The near certainty (then unknown) that Waldeck never had, in fact,
visited Copán would surely have amused Maudslay. His drawings were
obviously based on those of Catherwood – and freely embellished, to
boot.

Maudslay did take the trouble to reply to Elliot Smith in a long personal letter, which includes a statement that some of the crazier diffusionists would do well to bear in mind: 'We are so much in the dark about the origin of Maya culture that one does not wish to put any theory aside, but it always seems to me that the absence of Asiatic food grains and the development of the maize plant is a strong argument in favour of the long isolation of America. Drifts across the ocean there may have been, but unless survivors had been reduced to their "last split pea" some grain would surely have come with them.'

At about this time Maudslay appears to have been working on two books concurrently. He had agreed to prepare an abridged version of his translation of Bernal Díaz's *History* for the 'Broadway Travellers' series of Routledge, the publishers, and was at work on this in 1927 (rather oddly writing draft versions of the introduction to it on blank pages in his old Chichén Itzá field notebook). For this edition, not only was the text of *The Discovery and Conquest of Mexico* abridged, but it also ended with the fall of Tenochtitlan, since the march to Honduras was, as Maudslay put it, another story. The book was published in the following year, and has been reprinted several times – most recently, and with further abridgement, in 1953 and 1996.[15]

The other work he was engaged on is known to have been ready in typescript form by October 1928, and was published in 1930. This was a book of reminiscences, *Life in the Pacific Fifty years Ago*, covering his life from childhood up to his resignation from government service. Its completion so soon after *The Conquest of Mexico* suggests his having worked on it at odd moments for some time.[16]

The source for much of its text was letters he had sent home to his mother or sister, these often being quoted directly. The narrative is therefore fresh and vivid, and told with his usual gentle humour. Critical remarks, however, are not lacking, although a few were eliminated on the advice of friends to whom he had sent his typescript for review.[17] Altogether, it is a charming and interesting book, and I have made extensive use of it in writing the early chapters of this biography.

In a roughly chronological account of Maudslay's last years, this may be about the right place to introduce a short, undated manuscript in Maudslay's hand which I found loosely inserted in one of field notebooks of his that are now preserved in the library of the Royal Geographical Society. It bears the title 'The end of Frederick Catherwood', and consists of three sheets of notepaper folded across the middle and stitched together. There is no clue to its date except for the quality of the handwriting and some internal evidence. These suggest it was written in about 1925–9.

Some background needs to be sketched in first. Sir Charles Lennox

Wyke was born in 1815, ostensibly the son of a certain Captain George Wyke, of Rubbleston, Pembrokeshire, but widely regarded as being the natural son of Ernest Augustus, Duke of Cumberland, a son of George III. During his youth and middle years in England as Duke of Cumberland, Ernest Augustus gained a terrible reputation, but on inheriting the kingdom of Hanover upon the death of William IV he became a well-respected monarch. We know that Wyke's father was tutor to Ernest Augustus's legitimate son and heir, and that young Wyke was educated as his fellow pupil. Later, some possibly jealous persons ascribed Wyke's rapid promotion in the diplomatic service to 'Royal Interest', but in fact he proved himself very capable. Some support for his supposed parentage is also provided by the striking likeness of Wyke, as portrayed by the cartoonist 'Ape' in *Vanity Fair*, to the Hanoverian king as he appears in paintings displayed in Hanover.

Charles Wyke was appointed Consul-General to Central America in 1852, and later, as British Minister in Mexico, he won praise for not removing his mission when France and England broke off diplomatic relations with Mexico in 1861. He died in 1897.[18]

Here, then, is Maudslay's tale:

THE END OF FREDERICK CATHERWOOD.

There must be still many who remember that beautifully turned out old dandy, Sir Charles Wyke, taking his morning ride on his black cob in Rotten Row. I forget when I first met him, it must be forty years ago, but I attracted him because I knew Guatemala, & would often dine with him in his charming house in Cheyne Walk, Chelsea, where I was welcomed by his Guatemalan servant who acted as butler.

Sir Charles was, I believe, a natural son of the King of Hanover. He entered the diplomatic service in [left blank by Maudslay; the year was 1845] and was appointed consul in Panama, in [1852] he was moved on to act as chargé d'affaires in Guatemala. Later on he was moved to Mexico where he did good service by, on his own responsibility, ordering the British troops to re-embark at Vera Cruz [in 1861], thus saving us from being mixed up in Napoleon III's scheme of establishing the unlucky Mexican Empire of the unfortunate Maximilian.

Sir Charles was always delighted to talk about Guatemala, especially expatiating on the charms of certain Guatemalan ladies, adding 'of course you know the family of so-and-so' entirely forgetting that these charmers were flourishing nearly ten years before I was born.

One evening he told me the following story: When he was in England packing up for his voyage to Guatemala, a card was sent up to him bearing the name of Frederick Catherwood; he did not know the name, but asked the gentleman to come in. Catherwood said to him 'Mr. Wyke, I hear you are going to Guatemala, it is a country I know fairly well, as I have been travelling there with my friend Mr. Stephens who is U.S. Minister to Central America, & I am now in London preparing the plates for our book of travels which is being published by Mr. Murray, and I intend shortly to return to Guatemala.' (This must have been 1842–3 when the second book "Travels in Yucatan" was published.) He went on to say: 'When we were travelling among the mountains between Guatemala City and the ruins of Palenque, halting one day for lunch [probably in the Sierra Madre] I began as usual to examine the rocks and chip off spec-imens. Stephens called out to me, hurrying me off, saying "leave that stuff alone Catherwood, you have seen plenty of it before, it is only pyrites, and we shall not get to our destination before dark if we don't hurry up" – I put the specimens in my saddle bag, & that night put them in my travelling box, & thought nothing more about them until I unpacked the box in New York.

'I happened to have a friend in the Assay Office, & thought I might as well take the specimens to him & find out what they were. A few days later my friend came rushing into my room in a state of excite-ment, saying "Catherwood where did you find those specimens you gave me – Why, man, it is the richest gold ore I have ever seen in my life!"

'I told him I could not show him the place on the map, as it was a wild unmapped country, but that I had no doubt I could find the place again myself; this he urged me to do.

'That, Mr. Wyke, is my story, and my reason for coming to you, for I am ready to return to Guatemala as soon as our book is through the press. Meanwhile, if you can do anything to smooth the way for me when you are in Guatemala, I shall be very grateful.'

After Sir Charles Wyke arrived in Guatemala he became on very good terms with Carrera, the Indian President, and used to invite him to dinner. One evening when chatting after dinner he told the President the story he had heard from Catherwood. Carrera got very excited & said 'I always knew there was gold in that district, but no one could tell me where; write to your friend & tell him to come out here at once.'

First of all, said Sir Charles, we must have some agreement on the matter, as to Mr. Catherwood's share in the matter. Well, tell Mr. Catherwood, said the President, that I will find the labourers & bear all the expense, & and he shall have half the profits; is that good enough? Certainly, said Sir Charles, & then & there sat down and wrote out the Agreement, which Carrera signed.

Sir Charles at once sent the good news to Catherwood, & heard in reply that he was just about to leave England & would write again when he reached New Orleans. This he did sending the letter by sailing schooner which carried the mail between New Orleans and Belize, but adding that a steamer was leaving for Belize in a few days & he had taken passage in her, & might possibly arrive before the letter. However, the letter arrived, but there was no sign of Catherwood.

Carrera sent messengers post haste to Yzabal, but there was no news. At last the mail schooner on her return voyage brought a letter to Sir Charles, stating that the steamer in which Catherwood had taken passage had actually started from New Orleans & had never been heard of again.

When Sir Charles gave this news to Carrera, he said that the President in his excitement raved like a lunatic, stamping round the room, & actually tearing out his hair by the roots, shouting 'I will have that gold! I will have that gold.' He sent officers to the district & had the country divided into sections & had each section scoured by Indians & Mestizos, but no trace of gold was ever found.

(signed) Alfred P. Maudslay

A couple of mistakes are apparent in this story, as is hardly surprising in a tale twice told, both times after forty-year intervals; neither of them, though, is important in this restricted context. One concerns the date Maudslay suggested parenthetically for Catherwood's visit to Wyke on the basis of his having then been busy with the publication of Incidents of *Travel in Yucatan*; instead, the edition he was busy with was clearly that of 1856, which contained additional engravings. The second concerns the voyage on which Catherwood perished. He had not, in fact, reached New Orleans; far from it, he was bound for New York out of Liverpool when the SS *Arctic* sank as the result of a collision in fog on 27 September 1854. Only a few of the more than three hundred passengers survived, and for ten days the New York newspapers were full of obituaries of those lost in that disaster. But, as a biographer of Catherwood has written,

> there was not a word of the friend of Keats, Severn, [and] Shelley . . . the pioneer of Egyptology, co-discoverer of the Mayan culture. The New York newspapers, which over a period of fifteen years had pursued many news releases on one of the greatest archaeological explorers that ever lived did not even print his name . . . until many days had passed. Then, as a sort of afterthought, Catherwood appeared in a single line under the heading 'The Saved and the Lost': 'Mr. Catherwood is also missing.'[19]

On 9 June 1925 the University of Cambridge at last followed the example of Oxford in conferring upon Maudslay an honorary degree of Doctor of Science.[20] At a Congregation assembled in the Senate House that morning the Public Orator delivered a speech in Latin as he presented each recipient to the Chancellor. In presenting Maudslay, his words were as follows, freely translated:

There are some who delight in European antiquities, others in Asiatic, and a few, I concede, who delight in those of the Americas. Who has not heard of those conquered by the Spaniards – the Aztecs and the Incas? Indeed a third tribe among them in ancient times has left us Mayan writing, palaces, temples, monuments full of astonishing art and mystery. The Spanish priests burnt the annals of this people; John Lloyd Stephens came upon their deserted buildings; our alumnus recorded images of their gods or kings with the help of Phoebus [the sun-god], and furthermore reproduced them precisely in plaster so that in the British Museum and in our Museum we can almost believe we are seeing the same images. Meanwhile, he described all the wildness in those regions, returning there again and again. If you should want all the American history which surpasses the rest in the greatness of achievements and the excellence of victories and the strangeness of the enemies, seek out that honest work which Bernal Díaz wrote, and Alfred Maudslay translated.

The recipients of honorary degrees then repaired to Downing College, where the Vice-Chancellor entertained them and other guests with a lunch of salmon cutlets, lobster in aspic, tongue, roast lamb, pineapple ices, and so forth. And in the evening it was the turn of the Master and Fellows of Trinity College to entertain them, undoubtedly with no less lavish a feast, in the Great Hall of Trinity College.

A year later the Royal Anthropological Institute awarded Maudslay the Rivers Memorial Medal for Anthropological Work in the Field. He was, and would remain for many years, the only recipient to have been given this medal for archaeological work, the others all having been ethnologists.

In January 1928 Maudslay married (Louisa) Alice Purdon, widow of John M. Purdon, and daughter of Edward M. Clissold. She had been living at Rock House (once a small brew-house), which stands by the road next to the Morney Cross garden fence. According to Dolly Maudslay, she was a fine, plucky old lady, and a comforting companion for Alfred. The daughter of a Ceylon tea-planter, she always wore white gloves and carried a parasol when she came over for her daily visit to the Maudslays next door, as had been the custom in Ceylon. On marrying Maudslay she simply trundled her belongings over to Morney Cross in a wheelbarrow.

The last task Maudslay set himself was to produce a translation of Bishop Diego de Landa's *Relación de las Cosas de Yucatán*. It has been suggested that this work was undertaken at the request of the Hakluyt Society, but no confirmation of this story has been obtained. The task was a formidable one for a man who was approaching eighty years of age and in poor health, but he did succeed in completing a draft version, and had it typed up.[21] As Maudslay's health worsened, T. A. Joyce took steps to prevent the translation disappearing into limbo at his death, and this he did by persuading Maudslay's old friend Charles Fenton, who had an almost perfect command of Spanish, to revise it.[22]

Maudslay's typescript draft of Landa shows many alterations in what is probably Fenton's hand (a beautifully legible, rounded, Germanic hand, similar to Teobert Maler's), together with a few that may be Maudslay's, or perhaps Joyce's. There is an introduction by Fenton, which has some interesting passages, but these provide more of a 'Relation of the Things of Alta Verapaz' than of Yucatán.

The translation itself is good, but unfortunately Fenton outlived Maudslay by only one year, so the work was never published. It would, nevertheless, have been eclipsed within a decade by Alfred Tozzer's edition. Evidently Maudslay had not heard that this was in preparation, any more than had William Gates, who produced his own translation in 1937.

For Tozzer's edition, published in 1941, the translation was revised by various colleagues, and checked against the original.[23] The great value of his work lies in the notes, syllabus, and appendices. The 1154 notes constitute in themselves a most valuable contribution to ethnography. (A more recent translation has been published, the work of A. R. Pagden; this is less literal and more readable, but unreliable.)[24] And now, very lately, Landa's original – and much longer – manuscript has reportedly come to light in Spain.

In June 1930 Maudslay paid his last visit to the Royal Geographical Society, the society that he valued so highly, and had served as a member of its Council, as Honorary Secretary and as Vice-President. The Society was moving out of cramped quarters in Saville Row into splendid new premises overlooking Hyde Park; this was Lowther Lodge, formerly the mansion of Lord Lonsdale.[25] The necessary additions and alterations were nearing readiness, and Maudslay inspected them resolutely, but felt that he would not see them finished.

On 9 October, having been invited to the celebration of its completion, he wrote to Hinks: 'I put off writing to you in the hope I might be able to say that I would come up to town for the celebration – but alas! I doubt if I shall be able to come up to town again – I am played out – anyhow crowded meetings would be out of the question.' Two days later Alice reported to Hinks: 'Alfred is better some days, but his memory is so bad and he is failing. He gets up daily and walks in the garden. But any effort about writing, etc. is very hard for him now.'

On 22 January 1931 Alice Maudslay wrote to Hinks: 'Alfred was taken ill last week with a heart attack & he has been lying unconscious ever since & I fear there is very little chance.' In fact he died the next day, the death certificate giving three causes of death: heart failure, cerebral thrombosis, and arteriosclerosis.

His ashes were buried next to Annie's in the crypt of Hereford Cathedral.

Chapter 21

Tributes

S everal obituaries of Maudslay were published in newspapers and professional journals within a year of his death.[1] The *Times* obituary (its authorship anonymous, as usual) was admiring and quite comprehensive, but offered no personal insights. In March James Cooper Clark contributed a memoir to *Nature* in which he summed up Maudslay's character in these words:

> Throughout all his Central American travels, Maudslay seems to have been endowed with extraordinary patience and perseverance, and this, together with his charm of manner and personality, enabled him to overcome all obstacles, whether of local politics, native prejudice, lack of guides, transport or labour. Maudslay always gained his point and got his way. To the young archaeologist he was always ready with help, advice, or encouragement, especially in the study of Maya glyphs, and it is difficult to speak in measured terms of his loss to the Mexican and Mayan student of archaeology. Those whose privilege it was to be numbered among his personal friends will perhaps best remember him for his kind and gracious disposition, his keen and sparkling eye, and his blameless life. He was the type of the true English gentleman. We shall not look on his like again.

The unsigned obituary in *The Geographical Journal* may have been written by Arthur Hinks of the Royal Geographical Society, or if not perhaps by Hermann J. Braunholtz of the British Museum. In addition to a quite thorough listing of Maudslay's works, it describes the irritating, if perhaps unavoidable, way in which the *Archaeology* volumes were published. The author, clearly writing from first-hand experience, mentions the subscriber's chore of disbinding the slender fascicles of *Biologia Centrali-Americana* that arrived at frequent intervals, and distributing the leaves among the folders representing parts of works that eventually, when complete, would all be bound up in their respective volumes. Thus, one fascicle, issued in September 1893, consisted only of pages 55–64 of Part IV of the *Archaeology* volumes. For these, the process was troublesome enough, but how much worse it must have been for purchasers of the other fifty-nine natural history volumes!

We have gone into the form of the publication in some detail, [the author continued] because it seems to explain what would otherwise be difficult to understand: the considerable neglect for many years of what to a few scholars was the foundation of accurate knowledge in this field. An irregular issue of awkward fragments of the greater work must have been the despair of librarians, while the formidable cost, and to some extent the mere weight of the volume designed for the public defeated the object of the publication.

Four pages are devoted to a description of the Maya calendar, and the obituary ends with warm appreciation of the donations Maudslay made to the Royal Geographical Society during his lifetime, and then by bequest.

Next, Professor Alfred M. Tozzer wrote an eleven-page tribute for the journal *American Anthropologist*. Its concluding paragraphs (based large- ly on material supplied by Nadine Laughton) are well worth quoting:

Mr. Maudslay was a man who was fond of simple things. He sur- rounded himself with a garden wherever he happened to live – in Fiji, at Zavaleta, and at Morney Cross, where, during the last years of his life, he spent hours planning and planting, weeding and pruning his flowering terraces. His wide interests included a knowledge of embroideries and of old furniture; he was an excellent photographer, and a keen fisherman. Without exception, Mr. Maudslay's pioneer work in Maya archaeology is the single greatest contribution to this study. Inspired by Stephens, he, in turn, inspired many others to select the Maya field for research and exploration.

His aim was perfection, and his published scientific works show that his ideal was accomplished. As a scholar, he refused to be satis- fied with hazy generalizations, and sought the truth. His gentle nature, retiring disposition, and great modesty were outstanding characteristics. He was without guile. One can often wonder as to his reactions to the modern scientific expeditions with their aeroplanes and motors, their staff secretaries, moving picture operators, and, most necessary of all, publicity agents. His own splendid accom- plishments were unrecognized except by a few faithful friends and fellow archaeologists until toward the last twenty years of his life. Mr. Maudslay's work can never be equaled. During the last forty years, time and man have worked havoc with the Maya ruins. Priceless records have now disappeared, but many of them are permanently recorded in the monumental volumes of the Biologia Centrali–Americana. And Maudslay's schoolmates at Harrow [in fact, one of his schoolmasters] called him 'a barren tree!'

On his return from taking part in excavations in British Honduras, T. A. Joyce wrote a tribute for the journal *Man*. Having reviewed his life and work, Joyce comments that 'for all his work and services to the Nation, Maudslay received little adequate recognition from his own country'. This may be interpreted as regret that he had never been given a knighthood, as might have been expected; indeed Sylvanus Morley and some other colleagues assumed that he had received that honour.[2]

Joyce closed with this paragraph:

> I personally had the great privilege of Maudslay's intimacy over near-ly thirty years. He belonged to a class of mankind which seems to be passing. He had the gentlest manner, but behind that lay the most rigid determination. I have never known him say an unkind word about anyone. In any society he was just himself, and in anything he did he aimed at perfection as far as can be attained. Possessing that perfect security of poise which belongs to a 'chief', 'sahib', or 'gentle-man' (it does not matter what the word is) and a great human sympathy, he had the instinct of handling primitive peoples. That sympathy inhibited any form of jealousy in his mental outlook, and to the humblest of the younger enquirers he gave freely of his advice, his notes and his photographs. A great gentleman who died amongst his flowers in the terraced garden that he had created, who had enjoyed life, and, as the perfect host, stinted neither hospitality nor information, in an atmosphere of modest security.

Maudslay had named his nephew Cyril as chief executor, and another nephew, Joseph, as co-executor. Almost immediately Cyril and his wife Dolly moved in at Morney Cross; they came not only because Cyril had this duty to fulfil but also to enable Dolly to care for Alice, who had fall-en ill. In May, when it was warmer and she was well again, the gardener trundled her possessions back to Rock House by wheelbarrow, and there she stayed until her death on 8 June 1939. Modestly, she had arranged for her remains not to join Alfred and Annie in Hereford Cathedral but to be buried in Ireland.

In his Will Alfred left Alice £3000 (equivalent to about £220,000 today). Bequests to nephews and nieces were made, and trusts set up for other members of the family. Beatrix and Hetty, the daughters of Annie's sister, Mary Morris Davenport, were left the gorgeous furniture bought by their great-grandfather from Marie-Antoinette's Cabinet Intérieur at Versailles, and Beatrix, who was passionately interested in everything to do with her great-grandfather, was bequeathed his wooden leg.[3] All of Maudslay's photographs, prints, papers and maps (his collection of old maps of Mexico being probably the finest in private hands) were left to T. A. Joyce, presumably for him to apportion between the British Museum and the Royal Geographical Society. His collection of Guatemalan and Mexican textiles, the earliest of its kind, went to the

Victoria and Albert Museum, his lantern slides to the Royal Anthropological Institute, and the remainder of his Fijian collections to Cambridge. His stuffed quetzal and parras – charming little chocolate-brown rails that run daintily across the waterlilies on the shores of Lake Petén-Itzá, showing a flash of yellow under their wings as they are folded – these were willed to the Hereford Museum, but the glass case they were in, measuring 8 by 8 by 5 feet, was too large to be accepted, and its fate is unknown.

Then Morney Cross was sold.

And now the author must again emerge from the shadows in order to tell an interesting story.

Some forty-four years after Alfred Maudslay's death, I was staying with Dolly in Somerset, and one afternoon was listening with interest to her reminiscences, when of a sudden she imparted an astonishing piece of information – quite freely this time, and without any request for confidentiality. We were talking about Maudslay's bequests, and she told me that the Will had provoked considerable murmuring among some of the nephews and nieces. They felt aggrieved that her husband, Cyril, had been left the same sum of money as they had, when it was well known in the family that he was far better off than they were, having inherited a fortune from his Lucas mother. 'What Cyril was unable to explain to them', Dolly went on, 'was that Uncle Alfred had spoken to him about his Will a year or so before his death, and about the bequest he would receive; and instructed him that he wished that money to be passed on to the mother of his illegitimate child.'

Well! This was a bolt from the blue! . . . Could she tell me anything more? Only that the child was male, and that by the time of Uncle Alfred's death he was a grown man. She didn't think she'd ever been told his name, or anything about the mother.

If I may obtrude a recollection of my own feelings upon hearing this revelation, I have to confess that in my ambitiously assumed role of biographer I felt first of all simple frustration at this obstacle – at the impossibility of ever discovering where and when this liaison had taken place, and whether the offspring were still alive. Cyril would certainly have destroyed any papers relating to the matter as soon as he had done his duty; and with the passage of forty years even the most ingenious and dogged investigator could scarcely hope to learn anything more. But my reaction of selfish inquisitiveness soon passed, and was replaced by a feeling of relief at the banishing of a barely felt unease.

In so far as Maudslay has been written about since his death, he has always been portrayed as entirely admirable: a perfect human being, in fact. But we have become cynical, and others besides myself must occasionally have wondered if this picture of him were not too good to be

true. Since Lytton Strachey shook the foundations of traditional, lauda-
tory biography, those following him in that field have scrutinized their
subjects more searchingly, and have seldom failed to discover in them
flaws.

Thus it has become difficult to believe that anyone famous for talent
and accomplishment could ever be innocent of lapses, or at least minor
infractions, of good behaviour, morality, or the law. And yet my initial
examination of Maudslay's history hadn't revealed anything of the sort;
and for a man who was energetic, handsome, rich, much travelled, and
unmarried until the age of forty-two, this blameless record did seem altogether exceptional. I was put in mind of Max Beerbohm's (actually
groundless) complaint about Goethe: that he was simply too perfect.

With the revelation that at least once in his life he encountered temptation too strong to resist, and had had a 'relationship' which may have
lasted for some years, Maudslay became for me at once more human: a
man who was not quite so impossibly steady and faultless as he might
otherwise appear. One can only rejoice for his sake that he had known
passionate love and the joy of fatherhood – for as regards his marriage,
hot blood probably played little part, or none (remembering Dolly's
opinion, that Annie had chased him to the altar). So now one could feel
sure that his otherwise blameless life had not been lived as a cold fish,
immune to all temptations of the flesh, and deprived of its pleasures.

Then, of course, another question arose: how much had social,
geographical and matrimonial constraints hindered the growth of famil-
iarity and affection between father and son, and its expression? This was
a topic less heartening to consider. But one thing does seem certain: as his
instructions to Cyril indicate, Maudslay would always have provided
generous financial support for mother and son, no matter in what corner
of the world they were living.

I once told a friend of mine, an eminent historian, about Dolly's revelation. 'My dear fellow!' he exclaimed, 'but this is hearsay, you can't use
that. None of us professional historians would ever *dream* of using it.'
'But look', I replied, 'this story was told me by an old lady who adored
her uncle and revered his memory; she would never have invented anything derogatory about him. No, I'm sorry, I believe her story implicitly.'
(And I almost added that I, having no pretensions to professional status
in his field, felt myself exempt from this rule!)[4]

Since then, as I was making contact prints from some of Maudslay's
glass plates preserved at the Museum of Mankind, it occurred to me to
enlarge a portion of a negative showing the east side of House C in the
Palace at Palenque, the corridor chosen by Maudslay upon arrival to
serve as dormitory and office because it was the driest (or rather, the least
wet). I adjusted the exposure to bring up detail within the shadowed
interior of the building – and with astonishing clarity there sprang into

view, affixed to the back wall, a framed portrait of a well-dressed woman! Well, she is certainly not his mother, nor does she resemble Annie. Could she then be the mother of his child? We shall never know.

Maudslay returned to England from Palenque in mid-June 1891, eleven months before his marriage. This much we know. But can we imagine a scenario for the ensuing eleven months? Frankly, no; not without piling speculation upon hearsay. But one matter of possible relevance may be mentioned. The transfer of affection (if it occurred) may explain a minor mystery. Whereas a certain amount of Alfred Maudslay's family correspondence dating from the 1870s and early 1880s has survived, none has from the next few years.

It wasn't long after Maudslay's death that Cyril received a letter from Beatrix Davenport. In it she requested him

> not to allow anyone to see the Morris papers, should they ask to. I have already been applied to by a Mr Harold Landin who says he is a professor of History in a University in Ohio. . . . If he had applied to Uncle Alfred I know he would have refused, for he was so interested in my copying and editing these papers. . . .
>
> After we came back from Egypt he and I both thought it was a pity there should not be a pretty full copying of these papers in case anything should happen to them, and he thought I was the person to do it. So I used to work for long hours at them at Morney Cross while Uncle Alfred was sitting at another table writing his book about Life in the Pacific. . . . Added to my interest in the subject matter . . . is the fact that I was born and spent my childhood up to fourteen in the house which he built, and am writing at the french desk at which he must have written a great part of them.[5]

Arrangements were therefore made for the papers to remain temporarily in Beatrix Davenport's custody, allowing her to bring her task to completion. And this she did very successfully: the two volumes of *A Diary of the French Revolution, by Gouverneur Morris, 1752–1816* were published in Boston in 1939. Then, as the Maudslays had directed, she delivered the diary and letters to the Library of Congress (and the wooden leg eventually came to rest in the New York Historical Society).

Her edition is excellent – almost as much an improvement over Annie's as hers had been over the use Jared Sparks made of them in his biography of Morris, written in the 1830s. Beatrix Davenport's transcription is straightforward, with the addition of a few letters, and it is complete. Therein lies its importance. By contrast, Annie, in her desire to produce a readable work, had used the scissors freely, cutting out as much as two-thirds of the text in some passages. And, since it was her own grandfather she was writing about, and she was doing so for the edification of late Victorian readers, she spared them from suspecting that her grandfather might have engaged in amours. From it, one would never know that Morris and the Comtesse de Flahaut, who was formerly (and for a time concurrently) Talleyrand's mistress, were long-time lovers.[6] Beatrix Davenport's edition focuses almost exclusively on the Diary (which Morris ended before he left Paris during the Terror, for fear of compromising those mentioned in it), whereas Annie Maudslay wove his letters and other documents into a narrative continuing up to his death in 1816. This gives the latter a continuing usefulness, although the serious historian now has access to all Morris's papers on Library of Congress microfilms.

Chapter 22

A backward glance

It might be interesting to pose this question to a random sample of active Mesoamerican archaeologists: 'What single published work on a topic relevant to your field do you most regret not having in your own working library?'

To an observer outside this field of study, the possibility that any would name a set of the *Archaeology* volumes from the *Biologia Centrali-Americana* as more desirable than all other publications might seem bizarre, for it would seem unlikely that any scholar at the forefront of research would need to own a set of six tomes, awkward to shelve, weighing fifty pounds, and published a full century ago – in an epoch, as is well known, prior to the adoption of scientific methodology in this field.[1]

Yet I suppose that some, or even many, of those archaeologists might indeed make that choice. Of these, a few might be antiquarian bibliophiles, but the others could only want to own this late Victorian magnum opus because of its continuing value as a basic reference work. Proof of this may be found in research libraries that are commonly used by active Mesoamerican archaeologists and their students, for the bindings and pages of the facsimile edition of the work that would be available to them are likely to show unmistakable signs of wear and tear.

Whilst utilitarian considerations provide reason enough for a Mayanist to obtain a set of these volumes, it's possible that the actual placing of those tomes in the fortunate acquirer's hands may be accompanied by perceptible emotion – for acquisition pays tribute to a tangible element of the pioneer's achievement, and establishes some kind of connection. But a more durable sentiment provoked by those volumes might be a sense of awe and astonishment at the extraordinary benefaction bestowed upon Mayanists long ago, when out of happy chance, or historical necessity – or both – there landed on a distant shore the one person in the world equipped with the inspiration, will, ability and money – all four of them being necessary – to venture upon this important undertaking.[2] And again by good fortune, this person had arrived at the very moment in history most favourable for the purpose, both from a technical standpoint (the recent crucial advance in photographic technique), and from a political one (a period of calm between turbulent times in Mexico and Guatemala).

While the works of Alfred Maudslay have long been showered with praise, criticisms of his *Archaeology* volumes have been mild. Some have regretted the oblong format of the four volumes of plates, which certainly makes them awkward to handle and to shelve – but that, surely, is a price worth paying, since it allows tall monuments, such as the Quiriguá stelae, to be reproduced at a suitable scale. The other objection often heard concerns their cost. Certainly, the set was extremely expensive to begin with, and since the edition was, reputedly, of a mere three hundred copies, and the demand for it, far from dying out, rose instead, the price for a complete set in good condition had reached thousands of pounds, and correspondingly more dollars, by the 1960s, placing it beyond the resources of most scholars.

So it was an admirable service that was rendered by an American surgeon and Maya enthusiast when he arranged for the production of a facsimile edition, somewhat reduced in size, but serviceable. This appeared in 1974, in time to satisfy a new wave of demand caused by the burgeoning interest in Maya studies then spreading among amateurs as well as professionals.

As with almost every work from the hand of man, the *Archaeology* volumes are not entirely free from small errors. Adela Breton, for example, pasted a note into her copy drawing attention to a mistake in a caption,[3] and the late Sir Eric Thompson did the same with a note written in Teobert Maler's unmistakable handwriting correcting another caption. Proportionately, however, these blemishes are mere fly-specks.[4]

Regarding the drawings of inscriptions, these too are not quite one hundred per cent reliable, as is hardly surprising. Sometimes errors can be attributed to damage suffered by the moulds in transit, notably those from Quiriguá that mysteriously went astray for months before arriving damaged by water, or to the damage (fortunately less serious) suffered by some Palenque moulds. Occasionally another kind of mistake has resulted from the artist–transcriber making a slightly incautious restoration of a certain sequence of weathered glyphs, basing this upon its perceived near–identity with a similar, but better preserved, sequence from the same site, or perhaps from the same inscription. Today, with much greater understanding of the script, we can sometimes see that the two groups of glyphs in such cases differ in small but significant respects.

And then, long ago, the archaeologist Sylvanus Morley mildly criticized another aspect of Annie Hunter's drawings:

Her delineations of the glyphs are extremely accurate, and with few exceptions . . . they may be trusted, so far as glyphic details are con-cerned, with the same degree of confidence as the originals them-selves. Their chief fault is that in many cases they are over-drawn, made more beautiful than the originals really are. This is particularly true of her drawings of texts from the Early and Middle Periods, when Maya delineation had not yet reached the degree of perfection which it attained in the Great Period [the Late Classic]. Miss Hunter's drawings are standardized to the best period of Maya art, and conse-quently those of the earlier texts have been somewhat overestheti-cized. So far as the subject-matter is concerned – that is, where the dates are perfectly clear – this makes little difference, but when it is necessary to depend upon the stylistic criteria for accurate dating, the style of the carving must be portrayed as well. With this single reservation, Miss Hunter's drawings are as serviceable for study as the originals or casts.[5]

These occasional minor defects in the *Archaeology* volumes are mas-sively outweighed by the vast amount of productive use made of them over the decades that have passed since their publication. In addition, useful amounts of previously unavailable data are still being extracted from Maudslay's legacy in other ways. The casts from papier–mâché and plaster moulds, stored by the British Museum at the time of writing in a warehouse, will soon, according to reports, be more readily accessible for study than in the past. They are currently set up leaning at an angle of about sixty-five degrees against double-sided wooden racks, these being arranged in rows with alleys between them wide enough to allow inspec-tion. The casts occupy an area of approximately 5000 square feet. Another resource not yet fully exploited is the collection, stored at present in the Museum of Mankind, of Maudslay's photographic negatives. These are glass plates exclusively of archaeological subjects, and they seem to represent a large proportion of those taken originally.[6]

In assessing Maudslay's contributions to Mesoamerican archaeology other than his work in recording sculpture, the site plans that he and Hugh Price surveyed should not be overlooked, for they were a vast improvement upon the plans made by other workers active in the area at the time, or for many years to come. Incidentally, Maudslay may also be credited with pioneering on some of his site-plans (those of Ixkún and Yaxchilán, for example) the method, now conventional, of representing mounds of indistinct shape by means of a simplified geometrical form. This convention is often, and perhaps erroneously, attributed to Teobert Maler. As regards precision, Maudslay's plans cannot of course compete with those made in Egypt during the same period by Sir Flinders Petrie, since the conditions of work were entirely different (rubble and other obstacles on the ground not being conducive to precise surveying). But Maudslay's plan of Chichén Itzá was not to be improved upon for another thirty-five years, and, when it was, the survey was made as part of long-term and well-funded research supported by the the the Carnegie Institution of Washington. By then, the whole central area of the ruins had been cleaned up, the surveyor had the luxury of being able to work without haste, and he was a professional, J. O. Kilmartin of the US Geological Survey.

In the history of exploration in the Maya lowlands, there is another technique that Maudslay pioneered: his use of celestial navigation. Here, again, decades were to pass before another Maya archaeologist would attempt to determine the geographical co-ordinates of ruins by this method, the only one available until the Global Positioning System became available in the 1990s. It was Karl Ruppert of the Carnegie Institution who revived this technique, enabling him to establish the location of many previously unknown sites during his explorations in southern Campeche in 1932–3. But he, too, was favoured by a technology unavailable in Maudslay's day – portable radio receivers able to pick up time signals broadcast from Washington. These allowed him to determine the longitude of sites with a precision that Maudslay, relying on half-chronometer watches, could never have dreamt of.

Yet another aspect of Maya research pioneered by Maudslay was his reconnaissance of ruined towns dating from the period between the collapse of the great Maya cities and the arrival of the Spaniards – the Postclassic and Contact periods, as they are now called. No one else was then taking much interest in sites in the Maya highlands, such as those he explored in Quiché and Cakchiquel territory, or those he had hoped to find in 1885 (but did not) in the Kekchi country of eastern Alta Verapaz. Nor would it have occurred to others to search for Chacujal, the town raided by Cortés during his march to Honduras. By means of investigations such as these, and the study of early post-Conquest documents, Maudslay was hoping to form some idea of the prehistory and migrations of the Maya and other peoples, a topic he was to treat tentatively in the introduction to his translation of *The Conquest of Mexico*. In this connection, Harry Pollock, director of the Carnegie Institution's Department of Archaeology in the 1950s, gave his opinion that 'Maudslay was entirely modern in his approach to the historical problem, appreciating the value of combining early documentary material, geography, ethnology, linguistics, mythology, and archaeology in the recovery of history'.[7]

Maudslay shied away, however, from formulating grand theories concerning the rise and fall of civilizations, or the peopling of the New World, or anything else of that nature. He would have given two reasons for disqualifying himself: the inadequacy then of data bearing on the question, and his lack of training as an anthropologist – as he humbly confessed when assuming the Presidency of the Royal Anthropological Institute. (A third factor, of course, was that constitutional impediment, his modesty.)

To this brief listing of Maudslay's contributions to anthropology three others already mentioned may be added. One was his part in establishing the Cambridge University Museum of Archaeology and Anthropology with the gift of his collections from the Western Pacific; the second, his translation of the *Historia de la Conquista*, by Bernal Díaz, a version certain to endure; and the third, his collection of textiles from Guatemala and Mexico, now in the Victoria and Albert Museum.

Regarding Maudslay's mentality, it would presumptuous to attempt any analysis, beyond suggesting that two of his characteritics – respect for precision and reluctance to draw grand conclusions from sparse data – can probably attributed to his education at Cambridge, but also, perhaps, from the engineering background of his family. Engineers, and his grandfather above all others of his time, value exactitude, simplicity, logic, and avoidance of excessive extrapolation, so that Maudslay in his youth may unconsciously have been inoculated against woolly thought and the building of theories upon unstable foundations. But woolliness is not the only corrupter of thinking; excessively rigid theorizing is another, and from this fault, too, Maudslay was free. He, surely, would never have taken it upon himself to dictate the menu, or the tableware, for Moctezuma's breakfast.

It may be asked whether the field techniques employed by Maudslay remained in use on later expeditions in the Maya area. The truth is, they did not. It was only the Peabody Museum that retained his methods while working at Copán, alhough Saville also planned to do so on that abortive expedition to Yaxchilán. Mould-making was too expensive for general use, but, although seldom used, it was never given up entirely.

The use of large-format cameras would be abandoned in favour of 4 by 5 inch or 9 by 12 cm negatives, formats adequate for most purposes; but it was when field archaeologists ceased developing their negatives on the spot that the photographic record of sculpture suffered its really abysmal decline in quality.

Responsibility for this rests principally, it must be said, upon the shoulders of George Eastman. The roll-film was a wonderful invention, but Kodak's motto, 'you press the button and we do the rest' rang the death-knell for successful expeditionary photography as practised in the late nineteenth century and the early twentieth. Since exposure meters would not be available until the 1930s, the correct exposure for any photograph – especially those taken in the shade – was a matter of guess-work. Consequently, from all the roll-films and filmpacks that were sent for professional development in the US upon return from the field a good proportion were found to be seriously under- or over-exposed, or else badly focused. In earlier times, of course, the negatives would have been developed the same day during the evening, so that sub-standard shots could be repeated immediately with little trouble.

Until the beginning of the 1960s the only intelligible portions of the hieroglyphic texts carved on monuments had been those registering dates, the naming of dieties in charge on those dates, and the phases of the moon. As for the remainder, there was almost total incomprehension. But then three scholars, Yuri Knorosov, Heinrich Berlin, and Tatiana Proskouriakoff, using complementary approaches, between them cleared the way for an extraordinary and most exciting process of gradual and continuing decipherment, which since then has been yielding astonishing amounts of information of various kinds about the ancient Maya, much of it historical. This has been truly one of the greatest intellectual feats in any branch of the humanities in recent times.

In the 1920s and 1930s, the great popularizer and promoter of all things Maya was Sylvanus Griswold Morley. He was also an active epigrapher, and it was he who succeeded in obtaining from the Carnegie Institution of Washington a commitment to long-term support of Maya research, with emphasis on exploration of the whole area, excavation of certain ruins, and sometimes their restoration. Dozens of ruined cities were discovered and surveyed during the 1920s and 1930s, and of course photographs were taken of the numerous sculptured monuments found in them. The results were published by Morley in five large volumes.

The tragic aspect of this work was that, quite early in his career, he became convinced that, apart from the various dates that might be found in a typical text, nothing else would have been interesting, even had it been decipherable. All those texts, in his opinion, treated of nothing more than astrology and arcane religious matters. 'They tell no story', he wrote, 'of kingly conquests, recount no deeds of imperial achievement . . . indeed they are so utterly impersonal, so completely non-individualistic, that it is is even probable that the name-glyphs of specific men and women were never recorded upon Maya monuments.'[8]

Alas! he could not have been more mistaken. The names of rulers and records of their conquests and other events were among the first decipherments achieved by Tatiana Proskouriakoff, a dozen years after Morley's death. His failure to match this achievement himself would not have mattered if only he hadn't so completely discounted the possible value of the latter portions of monumental texts that he stopped taking the trouble to record them at all. Often, it was only the upper portion of the inscription on a stela that was photographed; and, almost equally frustrating, the quality of the photographs that were taken is generally disappointing.

In Maudslay's opinion, too, the chances of ever being able to read the glyphs seemed poor; it appeared to him 'doubtful if more than a mere trace of phoneticism has as yet been established, and more than doubtful if the inscriptions when fully deciphered will yield us much direct information of a historical nature'. But since, in stating this opinion, he was looking ahead to a time *when* they would be fully deciphered, and not *if*, he maintained a firm policy of recording every inscription in its entirety, and for this, all Maya epigraphers are thankful.

Mesoamericanists must be glad that Maudslay did not choose to pursue a career in the Colonial Service, nor opt for archaeological investigations in Sri Lanka, where he would have found a far less fruitful field, because, in either event, not only would the progress of Mesoamerican research have been greatly retarded in its early years, but the record of Maya inscriptions available to us now, more than a century later, from those ancient and steadily eroding monuments would be much less complete.[9] But what personal preferences, what chance events, what mysterious forces of history led Maudslay to take the path he did will never be fully understood.

As seems appropriate, a colleague has referred to Maudslay as 'the New World Pitt-Rivers', a reference to the British general who became a celebrated archaeologist, and left to posterity a unique museum filled with artefacts displayed on a system designed to show their evolution through time. Born twenty-three years before Maudslay but turning to archaeology relatively late in life, Pitt-Rivers is rightly honoured for introducing rigour into excavation techniques and for improving the documentation of excavations, particularly the cross-sections revealed in cuts. He is also praised for his careful description of the artefacts found in such excavations, and for deriving typologies demonstrating their evolution through time.

To compare Maudslay's achievement with that of Pitt-Rivers is difficult for several reasons, one of them being the limited amount of excavation that Maudslay actually performed; another is that archaeology in Mesoamerica, when he became engaged in it, was in a rather more primitive stage of development than it had been in the Old World when Pitt-Rivers began his work.

As a general rule it is probably true that any great advance in the the techniques of field archaeology has originated with some unusually intelligent person who has had the benefit of considerable experience in that occupation. But until the closing decades of the nineteenth century archaeologists or proto-archaeologists of any kind were relatively few in number, and the opportunities for gaining that long experience were rarer still, being essentially confined to those who had either Imperial Prussian patronage (for example) or else considerable personal wealth.

This was the case with Schliemann and Sir Arthur Evans, as well as Maudslay, Pitt-Rivers and a very few others (in view of which it is remarkable that from such a small pool of those suitably endowed two such outstanding practitioners in the field should have emerged).

From among this small group of pioneers in archaeological fieldwork it may be tendentious to present Pitt-Rivers and Maudslay as the exemplars of emerging scientific method in the 1880s on either side of the Atlantic, but good arguments could be made for such a view. Both of them, each in his own realm of activity, played a leading role in setting the professional standards so badly needed in what was then a nascent but undisciplined field of study, and as such deserve our attention and respect.

Notes

1 SS *Guatemala* Wrecked a year later on Senola Bar, near Tehuantepec, with the loss of several lives.

2 Panama – San Francisco direct service This called only at Mazatlán and Acapulco, sailing every ten days.

3 Ruins in other jungles beyond the volcanoes Many years later, Maudslay would visit one ruined city on the same side of that mountain range, namely Santa Lucía Cotzumalguapa.

4 J. L. Stephens Stephens died from a tropical fever caught while supervising construction of the railway being laid across the Isthmus of Panama. An obelisk was erected to his memory near the Episcopalian church in Colon, so perhaps the Maudslay brothers paid their respects to his memory while passing through.

5 Sir William Robertson See Robertson 1777, vol. II, p. lviii. A distinguished historian who had, for that time, an outstanding knowledge of Spanish colonial sources. Perhaps his most important achievement was the discovery in Vienna of Cortés's letters, including the previously unknown Fifth Letter of Relation and the Cabildo Letter of 1519. And yet he was called (admittedly a century after his birth) 'inexcusably ignorant of the existence of a *Codex Mexicanus* in the Bodleian Library at Oxford; insomuch that M. de Humboldt, hearing of its existence incidentally from a traveller, could scarcely give credence to the account, and remarked, how could this Oxford collection have remained unknown to the illustrious Scottish historian? And the same celebrated author [Humboldt] frequently betrays, in the course of his [own] work, a similar disbelief or ignorance in this respect; relying, probably, on the erroneous assertion of the historian that no other monuments of Mexican industry and civilization existed in England. . . . He at length learned . . . that no less than *five* Mexican manuscripts are preserved in the Bodleian' (Anon. 1832, p. 93).

1 Great-grandfather Maudsley In early records of the family in Yorkshire and Lancashire the commonest spelling of their name is 'Mawdesley.' One branch of the family then dropped the *d* and became Mosely or Mosley, while another opted for the spelling Maudsley. This was how the future wheelwright's name was spelt at his baptism, but years later his certificate of marriage shows inconsistency: 'Henry Maudsley, of this parish, and Margaret Laundy, of the same, by banns, 26th July, 1763. This marriage was solemnized between us, [signed] Henry Maudsley – Margaret Maudsley.' His descendants (without exception I believe) have ended their name with *-lay*. (See Vincent 1889–90.)

2 Slide-rest Earlier slide-rests had been made, but Maudslay's was the first to be designed and built properly. The modern version is a lineal descendant of Maudslay's (Roe 1926, p. 6).

3 Screw-cutting lathe Background and final achievement described in Holtzapffel 1847–84, vol. 2, pp. 581, 641.

4 Maudslay thread After modification by Joseph Whitworth, who had been one of Maudslay's apprentices and perhaps his favourite, the thread became known as the Maudslay-Whitworth; then simply as the Whitworth thread. This was widely employed in Britain until the 1960s, and remains in limited use (for attaching cameras to tripods, for example).

5 Block machinery Credit for the idea of constructing the machines belongs exclusively to Brunel (see Gilbert 1965), but the final design was likely to have been Maudslay's. For instance, the design for the mortising machine, the most complex item in Brunel's patent application (no. 2478, 10 Feb. 1801) differs greatly from the machine that Maudslay made.

6 Visitors to Portsmouth Maria Edgeworth to Mrs Ruxton, 10 Apr. 1822: 'And now for the Block machinery, you will say, but it is impossible to describe this in a letter of moderate or immoderate length. I will only say that the ingenuity and successful performance far surpassed my expectations. Machinery so perfect appears to act with the happy certainty of instinct and the foresight of reason combined' (Barry 1931, p. 322).

7 Knight's Hill Until about 1810, when the large Norwood estate of the notorious former Lord Chancellor Thurlow was broken up and sold after his death, that area of south London had been completely rural. (Even as late as 1802 there had been a hermit living in the woods in a cave, or 'excavated residence'.). Several commodious houses with extensive grounds were then built on the hill, Henry Maudslay's being one of these.

8 Portrait of Henry Maudslay The chill leading to pneumonia from which Maudslay died was caught during a visit to Paris. While there, he sat for his portrait by 'physionotrace'. This process required the subject to sit within a wooden framework, to one side of which was fastened a sighting device connected to a pantograph. While the artist, peering through the sight, followed the sitter's profile, the other end of the pantograph recorded the profile at reduced scale, either in ink on paper, or with a stylus on an etching plate. Interior detail could then be added (see Vivarez 1906). This previously unpublished physionotrace portrait, by Kennedy, is in the collection of Mrs Cyril Maudslay's niece, Mrs Whittingdale.

9 Wages paid by Maudslay Mentioned in letter, Marc Brunel to Goodrich, 6 May 1807 (Marc I.

Brunel Letter-book, National Maritime Museum, Greenwich).

10 Feathering propeller: Thus sang the Poet Laureate of Steam:
Various devices great mechanics gave
T'impart his action to the crested wave
. . .
But Paucton's snake-like screw, behind the car
The best propeller for the CHIEFS OF WAR
Is safely placed beneath the rolling sea,
And thus preserved from scaith of gun-shot free.
. . .
While Seguin, Foulton, Cartwright, Shorter, Burns,
Their screws of various forms produced in turns;
Each pushed his project with unwonted zeal
Which all inventors are well known to feel.
But MAUDSLAY'S FEATHERING SCREW of triple blade
Threw these, and all the rest, into the shade!
(Baker 1857, p. 134)

11 Norwood Lodge This, known also as Lower Norwood Lodge, stood on the north side of Crown Lane, about 150 yards from its intersection with Knight's Hill Road. It is shown, and identified, on the 1:2,500 Ordnance Survey map of 1870, Sheet LXXXVIII. Henry Maudslay's house lay perhaps a mile to the north, while Joseph's brother Thomas lived even closer. That map shows there were still large areas of open fields nearby, and the closest railway station was at Croydon, 6 miles away. This rusticity would soon be lost as suburban railway lines were laid, and housing development took over. Alfred's family then moved to 21 Hyde Park Square, in London.

12 Spinnaker sail This sail was first used in races held in 1866 between two racing cutters of about 50 tons, Maudslay's *Sphinx* and the *Niobe* of another owner. According to an article in *The Field* (3 Jan. 1920), 'In the days before these cutters raced, the sail carried for running [that is, sailing downwind] was a square sail. After the square sail came a jib topsail, or a balloon foresail boomed out – or even both boomed out one above the other. Then in the same season Sphinx and Niobe both blossomed out with true spinnakers. The sailors wanted a name for the new sail, and they nicknamed it a "niobe" or a "spinxer", since Mr. Maudslay's yacht was generally called by dockside hands "the spinx". The name "niobe" soon dropped, and the sail was called a spinxer, from which came Spinnaker.'

13 Athol Maudslay His calendar 'ring' was advertised in *The Field* of Aug. 1883. He was a horse-lover, and his obituary tells that 'with the coming of mechanised means of locomotion, Mr Maudslay took to tricycling and was a very well-known figure in the district in his frequent jaunts around the country' (*Hampshire Chronicle*, 17 Nov. 1923).

14 Eustace Maudslay Cited as co-respondent in the divorce of Colonel and Mrs Whigham (*The Times*, 20 Apr. 1883).

15 Harrow's decline In the 1830s, during the eight-year tenure of one headmaster, numbers fell from 165 to 78, 'and those 78 were handed over to the next Headmaster in a state of vicious lawlessness which has probably never been surpassed in a public school'. This headmaster then became Bishop of London (Anon. 1879, p. 276). Mary Shelley, a child of the enlightenment and widow of the poet, was once told she should encourage her young son to think like his father. Recoiling in horror, she exclaimed: 'Oh God, teach him to think like other people!' – and sent him to Harrow. The treatment was successful.

16 Schooldays at Harrow Maudslay 1930, chapter 1; Harrow School Register. A boy who arrived at Harrow about two years after Maudslay, thus overlapping his time there, was Arthur (later Sir Arthur) Evans, the excavator of Knossos, but no record of their having met as grown men has come to light.

CHAPTER 3

1 Swinging a golf club Anon. 1928.

2 Cambridge years Maudslay 1930, chapter 2.

3 Cambridge ADC This was always suspected by the Proctors of being a resort for drinking and revelry (a visit by the Prince of Wales in 1861 having failed to quiet their fears). During Maudslay's last year, twenty-five College tutors resolved that the ADC's plays had 'become highly detrimental to the discipline and studies of the University', and they aimed to close it down altogether. It owed its continued existence to Maudslay's mentor, J. W. Clark, although under the new regime the performances were limited, and were to include no burlesques (Searby 1997, pp. 716, 717).

4 Playing women's parts The roles he played as a freshman were as Topcliffe (a policeman) in *Guy Fawkes*, and Matilda Jane in *A Regular Fix*, a farce. In his final year he appeared as Lord Henry Delamere in *Peer or Peasant*? and as Venus in *Paris*, a burlesque. (From programmes in author's collection; none has been found from the 1870 season.)

5 E. F. Knight A prolific author, best known for *The Voyage of the Alerte*, London, 1907 and later editions. His early adventure in Algeria is recorded in Arthur Ransome's introduction to the 1984 edition of *Alerte* (pp. ix–xiv). The photograph of him with Maudslay and Forster is in the author's collection.

6 Curriculum *The Student's Guide to Cambridge University*, 1874.

7 J. W. Clark See *Dictionary of National Biography, Supplement 1901–1911*, Oxford.

8 Visit to Guatemala Maudslay 1930, chapter 3.

9 Loading the launch, Champerico, 1875 The hauling system probably worked like this. A heavy line was led through that moored pulley-block, and run back to shore, with a float attached near its mid-point. When one of the lighters was to be sent out from shore to bring in passengers or freight, the line would be hauled in until the float attached to it came within reach of men on the beach; the lighter would then be made fast to the line at a point near the float. Men and mules would then haul on the other end of the cable – the one leading to the pulley – thus pulling the boat out through the breakers. Similarly, a returning lighter would be rowed back as far as the float attached to the line, made fast to it there, and then pulled in to shore. (The float attached to the mooring of the pulley-block served to indicate where a boat being pulled out from shore should be released from the line, so as not to over-ride the pulley.)

10 Iceland and Caribbean sources Maudslay 1930, chapters 4 and 5.

11 Cairns looking like unknown brother Maudslay to his mother, 22 Apr. 1874, Port of Spain (letter in author's collection).

12 The Cottage Charles Kingsley stayed there, Dec. 1869 to Jan. 1870. The cottage was actually within the garden.

13 P & O Line Properly, the Peninsular and Oriental Steamship Navigation Company.

14 Cairns like a Mute at a funeral *The Australian Dictionary of Biography* describes him as never popular, his delicate appearance not assisting him. He had no interest in country life, nor could he ride or shoot. An anonymous squatter is credited as source for the pithy description.

CHAPTER 4

1 Fiji sources Maudslay 1930, chapters 7–11; Derrick 1946; Grattan 1963; Morrell 1960.

2 Muskets According to Fijian tradition, that shipwrecked sailor obtained his protector's leave to sail back to the the wreck in order to bring back 'certain crooked things, which were wooden at one end and iron at the smaller end, and hollow. . . . These crooked things were useful in war' (Morrell 1960, p. 117). Since in Fijian warfare the slaying of a chief in battle brought about the immediate yielding or flight of his followers, muskets, although notoriously inaccurate, were still useful for this purpose – though much less satisfactory for the victorious chief than braining his adversary with an ironwood club.

3 Cannibalism in Fiji Since W. Arens and others have persuaded themselves that the existence of cannibalism was largely a myth and pretext for colonial expansion, the faulty logic of those social anthropologists (or anthro-apologists) needs to be accounted for. There is, in fact, trustworthy evidence for this practice having been rampant in the Pacific islands in the first half of the nineteenth century – although far less in the second, for it had been almost completely suppressed by the 1850s, thanks to the efforts of missionaries and colonial administrators.

Arens chooses to reject any account of cannibalism not given by anthropologists, declaring that 'despite an extensive review of highly recommended and generally accepted basic sources, it was not possible to isolate a single reliable complete first-hand account by an anthropologist of this purported conventional way of disposing of the dead' (Arens 1979, p. 181). But we may ask, were there any trained anthropologists at large in the Pacific before the closing decades of the nineteenth century? It seems unlikely, so his failure to find any account acceptable by his criteria of this 'method of disposing of the dead' comes as no surprise.

So: some anthropologists spurn all data on this topic from the early and middle nineteenth century; but what about archaeologists, who do have ways of retrieving the past? On this topic, they do, and Dirk Spenneman of Australian National University has made use of such data. He begins his informative article thus: 'Despite Professor W. Arens' naive and ethnocentric claims that anthropophagy – the eating of one's fellow human beings – only ever existed in the imagination of travellers, traders, and, especially, missionaries, there is firm evidence that cannibalism was established in Fiji as early as 2,500 years ago and that it became a widespread and lasting habit' (1987, p. 29).

Spenneman examined (and illustrated with photographs) the bones of cannibal victims displayed as trophies between tree-forks, these later becoming wedged there inextricably by tree-growth. The tree-forks were sawn out in 1876 by none other than Sir Arthur Gordon, who sent them, with others found by Anatole von Hügel, to the British Museum and the Universities of Cambridge and Aberdeen. (Those formerly in the British Museum are now in the Fiji Museum, where cannibalism-denial does not prevail.)

Those still doubtful should refer to two highly professional examinations of human remains excavated from middens in Fiji (Degusta 1999 and 2000).

It is worth adding that, *pace* Arens, reliable mid-nineteenth-century eye-witness accounts of cannibalism in Fiji do exist – none, perhaps, coming from a more credible witness than Berthold Seemann, a distinguished botanist, a Ph.D., and Fellow of the Linnean and Royal Geographical Societies (Seemann 1862, pp. 173–85).

4 Spelling of Thakombau and other Fijian names For simplicity, the abbreviated, but less phonetic, spelling devised by the Wesleyan missionaries in the interests of economy in type is not employed in this context.

5 Exactions of Williams against Thakombau Morrell 1960, pp. 129, 130.

6 Colonel Smythe's uniform Seemann tells us that one day he was wondering why Fijian flora was so wanting in gaily coloured flowers, being mostly green, yellow, or white, 'when lo! a look in the valley revealed bushes covered with a perfect mantle of scarlet and blue, thrown up to great advantage by the bright rays of the sun. I saw my travelling companions had made a halt near the very spot where nature had condescended to refute a deeply rooted generalisation. I clambered down the hill as fast as the conditions of the ground would admit and for a while lost sight of the gay display by intervening objects. A few more steps and I stood before a startling sight – Colonel Smythe's artillery uniform hung up to dry in the sun' (Seemann 1862, p. 156).

7 Slave trade in the South Seas While cannibalism had almost died out, another abominable practice had become a cause for great concern, namely 'blackbirding'. This was a method of recruiting labour (principally for Queensland sugar-growers) which often involved coercion or deception. 'From the 1840s to the end of the nineteenth century thousands of male Pacific Islanders were taken to Australia or South America as laborers to be returned home (though often they were not) after a period of years in service' (Hays 1991, p. 397). It was to stamp out this practice that the 'Kidnapping Act' was passed.

8 Maudslay bringing out a large camera The disappearance of all the numerous photographs that Maudslay would certainly have taken in the South Pacific (the only known survivors being two interior views of his house in Tonga) is a mystery, and a cause for great regret. One can only imagine they were lost during shipment to England. That he had also brought a magic lantern is apparent from a note in Fijian he received at Mbau, Fiji, after midnight one Sunday in 1876: addressed to 'Misa Mosile', it was written in Fijian by Ratu Timoci (Timothy), second son of Thakombau, who with his wife Josefa wanted to witness its wonders (author's collection).

9 Arthur Gordon was grandson of an illegitimate son of the 3rd Earl of Aberdeen. He was to marry a niece of Sir Arthur Gordon, who considered nominating him for Governor when he departed, but he went back to live in Scotland, dying in 1918.

10 Fijian society bound by unilinear evolutionary laws See France 1969, pp. 104–6.

11 Gordon unfamiliar with Morgan's theory See Heath 1974, pp. 84, 85.

12 Legend from Rotuma Island Public Record Office, London, CO 83/18.

13 Sir Arthur Gordon a collector Roth and Hooper 1990, p. 86.

14 Von Hügel For biographical notes see Roth and Hooper 1990, pp. xi–xix; see also Ebin and Swallow 1984, pp. 9–12.

15 Maudslay and von Hügel drinking *yangona* 'Connoisseurs declare with one voice that grated yangona is not comparable to that which has been chewed . . . . This statement was repeated so often that Dr. McGregor, curious to discover

a cause for so strange a fact, took the trouble to weigh six ounces of the root, which he gave to be chewed in the usual manner. When deposited in the bowl he weighed it again, and found it had increased to seventeen ounces! The inference is obvious, and needs no comment. After this, the drinking of Yangona . . . fell greatly out of favour with the gentlemen of the party.' Gordon Cumming 1881, p. 88.

16 Commissionerships Roth and Hooper 1990, pp. 427, 429, and 438. The last of these describes how Maudslay dined with Mr Solomon, the editor of the *Fiji Times*, 'and danced until 11 p.m. with the fat Miss Solomon, much to Lady Gordon's delight'. It was after this gorgeous entertainment that he and von Hügel had their talk about the prospects of island commissionerships.

CHAPTER 5

1 New Zealand Principal source: Maudslay 1930, chapter 12.

2 Maori ten-day week It resembled the French revolutionary calendar, introduced on 23 September 1794 (J. M. Thompson 1943). This also had thirty-six ten-day weeks, plus five days known as 'les sansculottides' (equivalent to the unlucky days of Wayeb in the Maya 'vague year'). Neither of these seems to have allowed for any kind of leap year.

3 Order to be sent by telegraph Cable service between London and Australia had been inaugurated in 1872 (Barty-King 1979, p. 38, 39), but its use was extremely expensive. For example, the Foreign Secretary enquired whether the Secretary of State for the Colonies would repay the cost of cabling a message concerning Baker to be forwarded to Maudslay: it was £26, equivalent to £1250 today (Public Record Office, London, CO 83/21).

4 Mission to London Maudslay 1930, pp. 178, 179.

5 Maudslay's breakfast with Gladstone Only a passing reference to 'Mr. Mawdsley' is found in Gladstone's diary (Matthew 1986, p. 238).

6 Maudslay's memorandum on deputy-commissionerships See Scarr 1967, p. 34.

7 'Harry the Jew' Seemann (1862, pp. 99–102) tells something of this man's extraordinary life.

8 Samoa Principal source: Maudslay 1930, chapter 15. Also Scarr 1967, pp. 53–64.

9 Godeffroy's Having suffered financial problems, it was reorganized as a public company: 'Die deutscher Handels-und-Plantagengesellschaft der Sudsee Inseln zu Hamburg' – known for convenience as The Long Handle Company. As an historian has written, 'The active brain of its agent, [Theodore] Weber, was already passing from merely commercial to political plans. Maudslay in Samoa shrewdly connected these with the critical condition of the Godeffroy firm: "The new German company must make its plantations pay, and to ensure this it must consolidate its hold on the outer islands with a view especially to labour supply. He [Weber] evidently thinks that he is going to make another sort of East India Company out of it with ultimate views of Empire." In New Britain, Maudslay thought, "the Germans mean business and may perhaps hoist their flag." Maudslay guessed right. For an agreed price in clothing, hatchets, and knives, Captain von Werner of HMIA *Ariadne* on December 19 "bought" the harbour of Makeda' (Morrell 1960, pp. 247, 248).

10 Godeffroy Museum Catalogue: *Die Ethnographische-Anthropologische Abteilung des Museum Godeffroy in Hamburg,* 1881. See also 14 vols of *Journal des Museum Godeffroy.* For the history of Godeffroy's and the Museum see Spoehr 1963.

11 Stevens As von Hügel commented, 'poor Capt. Stevens decidedly put his foot into it and does not like the idea of his interview with the Commodore. For all his blundering, bouncing, self-willed stupidity one can't help admiring his . . . dashing pluck.' Roth and Hooper 1990, p. 298.

12 Maudslay's plan Maudslay to A. H. Gordon, 11 Dec. 1876 (Stanmore 1897–1912, vol. 2, p. 241).

13 Cornwall's atrocities For background on Cornwall see Scarr 1967, p. 79. For Maudslay's unpublished report see Maudslay 1878.

CHAPTER 6

1 Sources Maudslay 1930, chapters 16, 17, 18; Scarr 1967, pp. 82–100.

2 Pembroke See Pembroke 1872. In their chapter 9 he and the doctor present generally unfavourable views of missionaries in the South Pacific.

3 Baker's call on Maudslay Noel Rutherford, an historian presenting a less negative account of Baker's role in Tongan history than is usually found, maintains that, when Baker went to welcome Maudslay on board the boat that brought him, he was coldly rebuffed, and commented: 'from the first it was apparent that his instructions were to snub us in every respect' (Rutherford 1971, p. 79). By Maudslay's account, however, the coolness was on Baker's part.

4 Consulate built in traditional style Rutherford blames Maudslay for 'ostentatious *fakatonga* [traditional Tongan] behaviour', and quotes him as having written 'I find myself becoming a rallying-point for conservative reaction' (Rutherford 1971, p. 82) – but he omits the next four quite significant words, 'much to my amusement' (Maudslay 1930, p. 221).

5 Tui Tonga tombs It now appears that some of the huge slabs of cut coral may have been quar-

ried locally, rather then imported from Uvea, for Barry Rolett (personal communication) reports that there are places on the Tongatapu coast where there are holes left by the removal of slabs.

6 Report of hearings of charges made against Baker Anon. n.d. (a work apparently compiled and printed at Baker's expense). Scarr (1967, p. 94 note) cites Maudslay as being 'horrified to find that he was called upon to substantiate several charges – especially that Baker was a pensioner of Godeffroys – which had been constructed from his private letters to Gordon, wherein he retailed the gossip of the beach' (that is, European traders).

7 Investment in bank 'S' 1897–1912, vol. 3, p. 109.

8 Cricket Symonds, the British Vice-Consul, observed that, since the general introduction of cricket, petty pilfering and stealing, which the Tongans did not consider crimes but merely exciting pastimes, had dwindled away. At a meeting to discuss the new law, one man exclaimed 'so we must give up cricket and take to stealing again!' (Chapman 1964, p. 287).

CHAPTER 7

1 Charles and Isabel in India Maudslay 1930, pp. 258, 259. The photograph, taken out of doors in Japan, is a quarter-plate albumen print (author's collection).

2 Alberta Four matted prints, 10 by 12 inches, in Hereford Public Library, Reference Division. They are (1) Mountain view, labelled in APM's hand: 'Sir Donald Banff, Alberta, British Columbia', (2) 'Hotel Banff, Alberta', (3) 'View, Banff', (4) Untitled view with river in foreground. Prints of three of them can be found also in the Royal Geographical Society's collections.

3 Salvin photographs Salvin's photos of Quiriguá were never published, and seem to be lost. The set of twenty-four stereograms of Copán, with booklet (O. Salvin 1863), is now an extremely rare item. Apart from a notice of it in the *Illustrated London News* of 16 Jan. 1864 (with four engravings done from the photographs), the only other known reference to them is Gustav Bernoulli's mention of 'die schönen stereoskopischen Bilder von Salvin' (Bernoulli 1875, p. 326).

4 Santa Lucía Cotzumalguapa Most of the best stelae were removed to Berlin soon after Caroline Salvin sketched them, with the loss of one accidentally dropped into the ocean while being loaded from the pier at San José. One of Caroline Salvin's watercolour sketches of the stelae has been published (C. Salvin 2000, p. 246).

5 Ruins in Ceylon Probably the 'Golden Age' (mid-first-millennium) ruins of Anuradhapura, or those of the later Pollonaruwa, both in north-central Sri Lanka. Maudslay mentions both of these in another context (Maudslay 1892, p. 621).

6 Henry Maudslay in Jerusalem See Conder 1875, pp. 81–9. Access to early levels could gained only by means of shafts and tunnels because excavation within the walls was prohibited. An issue of the *Illustrated London News* (115: 129, 29 July 1899, with portrait) records 'Some interesting pavement [that Henry Maudslay] discovered was presented by him to St. Paul's Cathedral'. As an engineer, he made apparently successful (if dangerous) use of hydrofluoric acid for working glass with common tools (see *Macmillan's Magazine*, May 1861).

7 Letter to Isabel From A. P. Maudslay, on board ship at St Thomas, Virgin Islands, 27 Dec. 1880 (in author's collection).

8 Sir Frederick Barlee See Maudslay's comments following a paper by a former Governor, E. Swayne: 'British Honduras', *The Geographical Journal*, vol. 50, no. 3, pp. 161–76, Sept. 1917, London. While in Australia, Barlee took an active part in exploration, and his name was given to a lake at 29° S, 119–120° E.

9 Briefing by Barlee The gist of it was set down by Maudslay in about 1300 words on the loose leaves of the diary he had just started ('Log, Guatemala, part 1, Feb.–March 1881', Archives of the Museum of Mankind, London).

10 Maya of Santa Cruz See, for example, Cal 1995.

11 Narrative, Belize to Guatemala City From Maudslay's Ms. 'Log/Guatemala, part 1, Feb.–March 1881', Archives of the Museum of Mankind, London.

12 Arrival at Yzabal List of passengers arriving, 'Francisco Sarg, Señora [y] Ayra, y tres niños, H. R. Dieseldorff, esposa e hija, J. P. Madusley' (*Diario de Central America*, 19 Jan. 1881, p. 2).

13 Catherwood at Quiriguá Stephens 1843, vol. 2, p. 123. He reported 'a colossal head two yards in diameter, almost buried by an enormous tree, and covered by moss'. Stephens entered into negotiations with one of the Payes brothers for personal purchase of the ruins, but they thought the US government was behind this offer, and demanded $20,000.

14 Scherzer at Quiriguá See Scherzer 1855 and 1937.

15 Plates underexposed Osbert Salvin had experienced the same disappointment at Quiriguá in 1861. Even with a twenty-minute exposure his much less sensitive plates registered nothing, so he had to send for men with axes to cut down trees to admit more light. At Copán, where the forest cover was much thinner, both Salvin and Maudslay over-exposed their first photos (Godman 1915, p. 4).

16 Ivory-backed hairbrush ruined Maudslay

and Maudslay 1899, p. 149.

17 Maudslay not travelling light For his travels in Iceland he had a train of eighteen ponies (Maudslay 1930, p. 47)

18 Maudslay's intentions For remark made to Santa Cruz chiefs: Maudslay and Maudslay 1899, p. 190. For Maudslay's statement that his decision to work in Central America, rather than in Ceylon, had been 'just a toss-up', see Cooper Clark 1931, p. 345. Clark is best remembered for *The Story of 'Eight Deer' in Codex Colombino* (Cooper Clark 1912); for his obituary see *Man*, Art. 15, Jan.–Feb. 1945.

19 Ride to Cotzumalguapa and Quezaltenango Maudslay's Ms. notes, Archives of the Museum of Mankind, London.

20 Francis Sarg His parents must have been, for those days, an oddly assorted couple. Johann Anton Sarg, the son of a waiter, had become an impecunious schoolmaster, while his brother had worked his way up to buying a hotel in Nuremberg. In that hotel Mary Ellen Best, the daughter of a doctor from a well-established Yorkshire family, met Johann Anton, and married him (see Davidson 1985). Their son, Francis (Frank or Franz), and his wife Mary Parker, also English, spent much of their early married life in Cobán. Frank had started working a lead mine at Finca San Joaquín, near San Cristóbal, Alta Verapaz, but, finding the mule transport of the product too expensive, opened a store, first in San Cristóbal, and then Cobán. He was appointed Consular Agent of the USA at Cobán in 1875 (Tony Sarg papers in the Peter Foulger Library of the Nantucket Historical Association); German Vice-Consul in Cobán in 1879; and German Consul in Guatemala in 1884, styled in both cases 'Francis Charles Sarg'. For his account (in German) of those years, and of some of the travellers such as Morelet, Bernoulli, Rockstroh, Berendt, and Maudslay who benefited from his help and hospitality as they passed through Cobán, see Sarg 1938, pp. 9–44 (a Spanish translation can be found in the Guatemalan newspaper *El Imparcial*, 12 Nov. 1946). Frank and his wife retired to Frankfurt, Germany. He published a study of Australian boomerangs (Sarg 1911); he and Adela Breton were appointed Secretaries of the International Congress of Americanists in London, 1912; and Maudslay dedicated his edition of Bernal Díaz to him, 'to mark 35 years of friendship and his untiring help'. The Sargs' son, Tony, an artist and puppeteer, originated the Macy's Thanksgiving Day parade.

21 Boddham-Whetham Those lintel fragments were presented by him to the British Museum, and are now in the Museum of Mankind.

22 Journey from Cobán to Tikal and Belize Maudslay notebook, Archives of the Museum of Mankind, London.

23 Zapote-wood lintels missing 'Also coming from Peten in the middle of the rainy season in 1877 was my friend from the Costa Grande, the physician Doctor Gustav Bernoulli. He arrived on foot after long months of deprivation while doing botanical research. The town [Cobán] seemed to him a small Paris. . . . From Flores he had visited the ruins of Tikal and he told me of the wonderful wooden sculptures he had found in the temples there and which he had for the most part broken off, but had not been able to cart away, as the weight of the Chicozapote beams of which they were made was too far too great. He had conceived the idea of hiring people to hew the beams in such a way that only the picture-sculpted side would remain in the thickness of the board, and that this would be easy to transport. He persuaded me to equip such an expedition and send it where I did in the interest of ethnological research. The execution of this project was accomplished under considerable difficulty and expense' (Sarg 1938, pp. 35, 36, from a typescript English translation by Olga Stalling Thompson in the author's collection). For another translation of this passage see King 1972. In fact, besides removing Lintel 3 of Temple I, Bernoulli also took lintels 2 and 3 of Temple IV (Coe and Shook 1961). Maudslay illustrated Boddham-Whetham's two fragments correctly placed in relation to the beams of Lintel 3 of Temple I, now in Basel (Maudslay 1889–1902, vol. III, pl. 71), but understandably he was mistaken about the source of another beam in this plate, and in his uncertain attribution of Lintel 3 of Temple IV.

24 Curasows different from birds seen before Apart from the magnificent blue-wattled turkey, there are two other turkey-sized birds native to Petén and their chicks are somewhat similar. They are the currasow (*crax rubra*), the adult male of which is black, sports a yellow knob above the bill and has curly feathers on its head; and the crested guan (*penelope purpurescens*) of tawny colour.

CHAPTER 8

1 Arrival at San José Source: Maudslay's notes, Archives of the Museum of Mankind.

2 Rockstroh Born in Marienberg, Saxony, in 1852. His first reconnaissance of the Río Usumacinta and its tributaries took him some way down the great river, but evidently not as far as Yaxchilán. He came back up the Río de la Pasión (Sandoval 1945, p. 15; see also Estrada/Monroy 1972). The first published notice of Yaxchilán is found in an account of his travels published in a German geographical journal: 'My next journey along the Usumacinta brought me an exceptional surprise, the discovery on the left bank, above Tenosique, of ruins (known by the Lacandons as Menche), admittedly second to Palenque in splendour, but better preserved. Also impressive was a two-storey building with numerous great window openings in the upper storey' (Rockstroh 1881, translated from the German).

3 Carl Hermann Berendt A notable linguist and collector of ancient texts. Maudslay never met him, but recorded this tribute in his notebook:

'Something must be said about Dr. Carl Hermann Berendt, whom, however, I regret to say I never had the good fortune to meet, but this quiet, good-humoured, lovable gentleman made friends wherever he went, and I was constantly hearing about him. He wandered about Central America for thirty years earning but little by his profession of doctor, always at work in his quiet plodding way copying MSS, collecting vocabularies and making notes on all matters touching the native races. Unfortunately he had no regard for time. Apparently he thought he would live for ever, for when he came across some old book which he could not afford to buy he would patiently set to work to copy the whole of it. After his death in Guatemala City from an overdose of chloral, his books and papers were, according to his written directions, offered for sale to the Smithsonian Institution at Washington' (Maudslay notebook, 22 Nov. 1886, Archives of the Museum of Mankind, London). (In fact they were bought by D. G. Brinton, and have come to rest in the library of the University Museum of the University of Pennsylvania.)

4 Guatemala ready to cede Soconusco to the USA C. A. Logan, US representative in Central America, reported this in May 1881 to J. G. Blaine, US Secretary of State, and three weeks later told him that, for lack of interest in the proposal shown by the USA, Guatemala would undoubtedly make this proposal to one of the European powers (Sensabaugh 1940, pp. 6, 7).

5 The first proposed border During preliminary talks held in 1880 the Mexican Foreign Minister, Ignacio Mariscal, in consultation with García Cubas, proposed a boundary defining the western flank of Guatemala that would consist of four straight lines touching three recognized key points: Ocos, Cerro Ixbul and 'Yaxchilán' – a stream said to flow into the Río San Pedro (with the mouth of that stream presumably serving as the relevant vertex). No affluent of the Río San Pedro is now known by that name, but the most probable identification is with the Arroyo Agua Dulce. If this is correct, then the ruins of Yaxchilán would have fallen within Guatemalan territory. (The other candidate would be the Río Peje Lagarto, but its mouth lies much farther east than the location of the 'Yaxchilan' or 'Yanchilan' as shown on maps of that time.)

The Guatemalan Foreign Minister, Herrera, would not agree to this proposal, as he believed it would result in Guatemala losing too much valuable agricultural land on the Pacific piedmont. When an alternative was suggested by his consultant, Ing. José Irungaray, Herrera adopted it as a counterproposal: in exchange for obtaining more rich agricultural land in the piedmont, he would yield a modest amount of territory in the Usumacinta drainage – or what he and Irungaray *thought* was a modest amount. This would be defined by a line running due east from Cerro Ixbul (or more precisely, from a point near it called the Santiago Vertex). Unfortunately, the map they relied on was that of Hermann Au, printed in 1875, which contained two colossal errors (among many others). One was the position he gave for Cerro Ixbul, placing it about 35 km too far north, and too far west by a similar amount. The other was his portrayal of the Usumacinta River's course: he depicted it swinging away from its source far to the west, almost in a semicircle. Thus, a line running either east or northeast from Vertice Santiago would soon intersect with 'his' Usumacinta. Very little territory would therefore be lost in the change. But in fact, the Usumacinta flows in an almost straight line towards Tenosique in a northwesterly direction, and the agreed frontier line running east from Vertice Santiago never even meets it, for the Usumacinta itself comes into being at a higher latitude, at the confluence of the Salinas and Pasión rivers. Thus, Guatemala lost a tremendous amount of territory to Mexico in exchange for a thin slice of Soconusco.

The loss would have been even more serious had Pastrana succeeded in persuading the Commission that, since the frontier line running east from Vertice Santiago didn't intersect with the Usumacinta, then it should be continued to the Río de la Pasión, choosing to regard this as the 'Alta Usumacinta' – and Maler does in fact call it the 'Uzumatsintla Superior' (Maler 1908, p. 51). This line was actually mapped and surveyed, and Mexican troops had reportedly been sent in to secure this territory before that aggressive move was rescinded. See Zorrilla 1984, p. 404 and *passim*; also Miles Rock's map showing various versions or proposals for the frontier line (Rock 1895); the 'Carta formada por los Ingenieros D. A. García Cubas y D. L. Fernández por disposición del Secretario de Relaciones Exteriores para el estudio de las diferentes líneas propuestas como divisorias entre México y Guatemala, enero de 1882'; and Anon. 1895, pp. 172–4.

6 Otto Stoll Naturalist, linguist, and doctor of medicine. Born in Switzerland in 1849, he came to Guatemala in 1878, and there practised as a doctor, first in the capital, then in Retalhuleu, but, for reasons of health, moved first to Antigua, then to the capital. For the *Biologia Centrali-Americana* he wrote the section on *Arachnida Acaridea*, illustrated with his own drawings. Having returned to Switzerland in 1892, he served as director of the Zurich museum until his death in 1922. A biography and bibliography compiled by Antonio Goubaud Carrera can be found in Stoll 1938, pp. vi–xxviii. His account of climbing Volcán de Fuego with Maudslay is in Stoll 1886, pp. 273–84.

7 Journey and work in Petén Source: Maudslay's field notes, Museum of Mankind, London.

8 Désiré Charnay Between the years 1880 and 1883 Charnay was investigating Mexican ruins (and actually excavating at two of them, Tula and Teotihuacan), with the joint support of the French Ministry of Education and a tobacco manufacturer, Pierre Lorillard. A journal of his travels was published first in serial form (Charnay 1880–1), and later in the form of edited and lavishly illustrated books: Charnay 1885 in French, and 1887 in English, the latter some-

what abbreviated.

9 Men sent ahead by Charnay to make canoe, and their difficulties Charnay 1880–81, vol. 134, p. 66 and vol. 135, p. 68.

10 'Menché' or 'Yaxchilán' Maudslay himself expressed doubts about the appropriateness of Rockstroh's name for these ruins: 'I shall still call [them] Menché, although I am by no means satisfied with that name' (Maudslay 1886a, p. 588). Rockstroh objected to Charnay renaming the site (Rockstroh 1882, p. 435). Teobert Maler rejected 'Menché Tinamit' with scorn (Maler 1901, p. 105), and an objection to his renaming of the site as 'Yaxchilán' was made by Maudslay and Joyce (1913, pp. 242, 243) – Joyce having presumably overcome his co-author's dislike of conflict.

11 'Yaxchilán' as often pronounced Amusingly, many of the tourists who nowadays pay brief visits to this ancient city unwittingly avenge themselves on Maler by mispronouncing the name: this is because – unless they are Russian – the 'sh-ch' sound is awkward, so they say 'Yashitlán', giving a good Nahua ending to the word!

12 Figure of a Spaniard on horseback Charnay 1880–1, vol. 134, pp. 411–12. For the only known drawing of this now lost mural see Rosny 1869, pl. 20.

13 'Charnay well off for provisions' Charnay published the following menu ostensibly served up at Palenque (1885, p. 209), although it's hard to believe that the whole lot was ever offered at one sitting:
Soupe purée de haricots noir au bouillon d'escargots [snails known as locally as *jutes*, found in streams in the lowlands]
Olives de Valence, saucisson d'Arles
Poulet de grain, sauté a l'ail et de piment rouge
Morue frite
Chives, coeurs de petits palmiers en branch d'asperges
Frijoles ou haricots noirs rissolés
Crêpes saupoudrées
Fromage américaine
Vins, Bordeaux et Aragon
Café, habanero et cigars de Tabasco.
'The items are perhaps not in correct order', Charnay noted, 'but that is the list, and the reader can be sure that in the deep forest, at Palenque, with good weather, etc, etc.'

14 Removal of lintels by Gorgonio Lopéz Maudslay's report on Menché (Maudslay 1883) includes a map drafted for him by the Royal Geographical Society; it shows 'Ruins' (obviously Yaxchilán) marked on Mexican soil. Where to place them on it must have caused him some perplexity, because the map, largely based on that of Hermann Au, shows the entire central belt of Guatemala grossly extended in latitude, while the northern portion is correspondingly compressed; in addition, Tenosique is placed about 30 km too far north. So, if Maudslay had asked Charnay, or one of his men, how far distant Tenosique lay, that might account for his

'Ruins' also being located too far north. In these areas, of course, Au's map was the result of guesswork, as Maudslay must soon have realized, assuming that he kept an eye on his compass while travelling downriver, for by doing so he would have realized that the great loop in its course shown by Au was imaginary. In any case Maudslay may have felt justified in removing loose sculptures from a totally abandoned site for the sake of preserving them. This would have been no specious pretext, for he could not have failed to notice the serious erosion suffered by sculptures at Yaxchilán that were lying face-up.

It may be worth adding that, from the purely legal point of view, no Mexican law prohibiting the extraction of antiquities would be passed until 1897, although in 1880 the Mexican Congress did refuse Charnay's request to export to the Musée de l'Homme artefacts that he had excavated at Tula. (See Diaz y de Ovando 1990, *passim*.)

15 Lintel 56 Oswaldo Chinchilla Mazariegos has found among the archives of the Museum für Völkerkunde, Berlin, a letter from Francis Sarg to Adolf Bastian (1996, pp. 340, 341). Dated 12 Mar. 1886, it reads, 'The enclosed photograph, unfortunately a poor one, shows a hieroglyphic tablet 164 cm long, 38 cm wide and 6 cm thick, which I have sent for the museum by the steamer "Ramses" of the Kosmos Line, as per bill of lading, enclosed.

'This tablet, before it could be transported, was sawn from the lintel of a doorway in the ruins of Menché on the Usumacinta. I don't know what name you have for this place. I wrote to you on the 7th of April '83 about Menché for which our compatriot Rockstroh already in September '81 published the correct name, and not as the Lorillard City of Charnay. Anyway, you know the place in question. Although it is not as beautiful a piece as the one removed by Maudslay, I believe it will interest you and be welcome as representing a contrast with those of Santa Lucía in the Berlin collections. Anyway, this stone must be the last that can be brought from the Usumacinta; the ruins belong to Mexico, and it was found there last year by my men.

'You will find that I have insured this stone, which is packed in sawdust as were the last ones from Santa Lucía (one of which, the eagle stone, was lost, to my great sorrow).'

Believing the lintel's presence in Berlin to be explained simply as a mistake in shipping, Maudslay requested the Berlin museum to make a plaster cast for him. This was duly delivered, photographed, drawn, and published in his *Archaeology* – as was fortunate, for the original seems to have been destroyed by bombing during the Second World War, unless, perhaps, it still lies in some forgotten cache of postwar loot.

16 Border as shown by García Cubas From the late 1850s Antonio García Cubas, the pre-eminent Mexican geographer of the time, published maps showing the border running from Cerro Ixbul (near the eventually agreed-upon Santiago Vertex) to a point on the Usumacinta

below Yaxchilán (as did reprints of those maps, published well into the 1880s). Evidence of an actual landmark on the Usumacinta for the termination of this line may exist in a manuscript map of Tabasco (undated but surely from the second half of the nineteenth century). This, the work of a certain F. Nemegyes M, shows the portion of the border between Mexico and Guatemala that was constituted, in his opinion, by the Usumacinta River: the border runs upstream from Tenosique for perhaps 40 km, then runs off to the southwest, in the general direction of the Santiago Vertex. (This map is in the collections of the Sociedad Mexicana de Geografía y Estadística in Mexico City. It has been reproduced in one of those volumes put out by departing state governors (Anon. 1982, pp. 90, 91). So it is interesting that on the current Guatemalan 1:250,000 map of the area, just below latitude 70°N, there is a point on the riverbank identified as 'Piedra de Nemeguey'. The rock appears to be located at about the point where the northeast–southwest boundary line shown on those earlier Mexican maps (García Cubas 1858, for example) meets the river, and it's hard to imagine what significance it could have had, other than serving as a prominent boundary mark.

17 The doubts of Batres regarding Yaxchilán 'En primer lugar tengo dudas de si las ruinas de Yaxchilan quedaron dentro de la paralela en el lindero de México y Guatemala, y por lo tanto mientras no téngamos en seguridad podríamos exponernos a dar concesiones en terreno extraño que nos acarrearían dificultades internacionales, como ya sucedió otra vez en que, si mal no recuerdo, la misma casa de Valenzuela, solicitando hoy, fue la causa de que México hubiese llegado casi con guerra con su vecina Republica de Guatemala por un asunto parecido a este' (INAH Archives, Mexico, ref: B/311.1 (73-3) 01).

CHAPTER 9

1 Lightly engraved details springing to the eye In the 1970s the author made latex moulds of the lintels in Yaxchilán Structure 33. When illuminated by raking light the casts clearly show that the faces of the persons represented were polished to a finer finish than is seen elsewhere in those superbly carved panels. Observers of the lintels in situ have never been able to notice this detail.

2 Brucciani's Gallery D. Brucciani's Galleria delle Belle Arti, 40 Great Russell Street, Covent Garden. It was taken over by the Victoria and Albert Museum in about 1920.

3 Lorenzo Giuntini 'Giuntini a good fellow . . .' See Graham 1982, p. 433. At almost the last moment in the preparation of this book, Valerie Emmons, the wife of a Giuntini great-grandson, made contact with Dr Colin McEwan, Curator of Latin American Collections at the Department of Ethnography of the British Museum. To her, then, I acknowledge my gratitude for the photograph of Giuntini, and permission to reproduce it; also for the dates of his birth and death (1845–1920), some details of his life, and the fact that not only Maudslay, but also some of his own family were unsure of the proper spelling of his name! Following his work for Maudslay, Giuntini and one of his sons were engaged as piece mould-makers by Herbert Weld for his 1891 expedition to Persepolis (Simpson 2000, p. 29).

4 Talk at Royal Geographical Society Reported in *The Times* and the *Morning Post*, 12 Dec. 1882.

5 Reading 'Gil Blas' aloud See Graham 1982, p. 435.

6 Old Forty Drops Gosling 1926, pp. 29, 30.

7 Journey to Cobán Sources: Maudslay's notes, formerly in author's collection, now in Museum of Mankind (see Graham 1882 for Spanish translation), and Maudslay 1889–1902, text vol. II, pp. 2–6.

8 Letter from Walter Heston Author's collection.

9 Cambridge Museum and J. W. Clark 'The Museum of Ethnology was very dear to JW's heart, in fact it was one of the many things he helped to start in the University. Writing on the 27th April in his Annual Report, JW records: "I have to mention that my friend A. P. Maudslay, M.A. of Trinity Hall, has deposited in my charge a portion of the large and important Collection of arms, dresses, ornaments, domestic utensils, pottery, and other objects which he made in Fiji and the adjacent islands. It is more than probable that he will present the whole Collection to the University at no distant date; and it will form the nucleus of a Museum of Ethnology, the importance of which in connection with biological studies is now generally recognized"' (Shipley, 1913, p. 340). See also pp. 139 and 341 for von Hügel's part in establishing the Museum.

10 Del Rio See Del Rio 1822.

11 Jean-Frédéric-Maximilien Waldeck See Cline 1947.

12 Bernal Bibliography See Bernal 1962.

13 Lord Kingsborough The voluminous text he provided for *Antiquities of Mexico* was immediately criticized in the same review cited in the notes to Chapter 1. Its author, clearly an excellent scholar, noted that the learned lucubrations of the noble annotator were intended to support his hypothesis that the Jews were the early colonists of America; 'we beg leave to observe, however, that . . . very close analogies between the institutions and habits of remote nations are not of themselves a proof of their identity of origin' (Anon. 1832, p. 121).

Kingsborough's family had been enormously rich, but when his father, the third Earl of Kingston, became mentally ill and began spending wildly, his affairs were put under court administration. The court-ordered allowance for his son, however, was insufficient for payment of bills resulting from publication of those extravagantly produced tomes. Kingsborough was committed to a debtors' prison in Dublin, where he caught 'jail fever' (typhus) and died aged thirty-seven.

The coloured reproductions of Maya codices illustrated in the nine huge volumes of this work – as also Dupaix's representations of Palenque – would have been of great interest to Maudslay, who must soon have seen the set in the British Museum Library, or the one in Frederick Godman's possession (existence of which his elder daughter, Eve Godman, confimed to the author in 1974).

14 Landa's *Relación de las Cosas de Yucatán* A version of this text was discovered by the abbé Brasseur de Bourbourg, and published by him in a French translation in 1864. The standard English version, which is accompanied by copious and valuable notes by Alfred Tozzer, is Landa 1941.

15 *Popol Vuh* First translated into Spanish by Francisco Ximénez, the *cura* (priest) of Chichicastenango, and first published by Carl Scherzer in 1857. Of many subsequent editions, that of Dennis Tedlock (1985) is probably the best.

16 Bancroft's historiography Cline 1973, p. 333.

17 *Native Races of the Pacific States* See Bancroft 1874–5.

18 Before the 'three-age system' A Danish professor, Rasmus Nyerup, described his difficulties in 1806. Finding himself unable to classify his collections in any significant way, he confessed that 'everything which has come down to us from heathendom is wrapped in a thick fog; it belongs to a space of time which we cannot measure. We know that it is older than Christendom, but whether by a couple of years or a couple of centuries, or even by more than a millennium, we can do no more than guess.'

19 1850s study of Moundbuilder sites See Squier and Davis 1848.

20 Cyrus Thomas See Thomas 1885 and 1894.

21 Augustus Le Plongeon See Chapter 12 and relevant notes.

22 Charnay's discoveries at Tula In a letter to a Mexican French-language newspaper, Charnay calls Tula the 'Indian Pompeii, smaller but no less interesting. . . . This Toltec habitation, exhumed today from lying buried for ten centuries, consists of 24 rooms, 2 cisterns, 12 corridors, and 15 small stairs . . . all of enormous interest. . . . More important, I discovered enormous skeletons of gigantic ruminants (bisons perhaps; they are said to have existed in Mexico) . . . . Among the tiles . . . and water-pipes, I found . . . fragments of porcelain, enamels, and, most singular, a neck of glass with the iridescence of Roman ware. Are these Asiatic "souvenirs" or original products?' (Díaz y de

Ovando, 1990, p. 16). A proposal submitted to the Mexican Congress by the Secretaría de Justicia e Instrucción, *ibid.* p. 89).

23 Montezuma's breakfast See, for example, Gibson 1947. Maudslay acknowledges 'a matter of dispute whether Montezuma was a great hereditary emperor or merely the elected head of a communal household' (Maudslay 1889–1902, text vol. I, pp. 1, 2). Morgan's theory was not easily abandoned: Professor R. B. Dixon, of Harvard, still supported it in 1919.

CHAPTER 10

1 Squier and Davis See Squier and Davis 1848.

2 Bureau of American Ethnology The Division of Mound Exploration was formed in 1882, with a budget for the year of $5000 (3rd Annual Report, p. 24), about two-thirds of what Maudslay spent in one season on his expeditions.

3 Copán expedition Sources: A. C. and A. P. Maudslay 1899, pp. 127–42; Maudslay 1889–1902, text vol. I, pp. 5–32.

4 John Coles Maudslay later repaid him by contributing to his useful handbook, *Hints to Travellers* (see Coles 1889 and other editions).

5 'When first I came across a ruin' Comments following a paper by F. W. Christian (Maudslay 1891).

6 Comment by Cyrus Thomas Thomas 1899, p. 554.

7 President Bográn's telegram The author found this precious document loosely inserted in one of Maudslay's large notebooks in the library of the Royal Geographical Society. It came in response to this telegram from Maudslay: 'En pocos dias salgo de las ruinas de Copan para Inglaterra. Mis trabajos han producido muchas cosas nuevas, los cerros, asi llamados, probando de ser ruinas de templos los mas de que estan ahora excavados, saliendo de luz mucha escultura muy interesante y ya inconocida. A mi salida pondré esta escultura en la cuidada del Alcalde, pero me gustaria un permiso de U a llever conmigo unas pocas pedacitas a poner en el museo al lado de las copias en yeso que he hecho de los monumentos grandes' (draft of this telegram in Maudslay's 1885 large-format diary, Archives of the Royal Geographical Society).

CHAPTER 11

1 Narrative on Utatlán and Iximché See Maudslay 1889–1902, text vol. 2, pp. 25–38.

2 Conquest of Utatlán and Iximché Alvarado's account of his actions, and Fuentes y Guzman's description of Utatlán, quoted in A. C. and A. P. Maudslay 1899, pp. 62–70.

3 Chuitinamit A. L. Smith 1955, fig. 109.

4 Excellent plan The only significant fault is in the orientation.

5 Later work near Rabinal abandoned A. C. and A. P. Maudslay 1899, p. 101.

6 Pepita Jiménez An ironical novel by Juan Valera, and his masterpiece (1874 and later editions). What Luis, a sanctimonious young seminarian with pretensions to mysticism, was 'just going to do' was to kiss Pepita, an experience he regarded as bringing him close to union with the good, if not with God. The jolly Dutch Padre, who seems unlikely to have aspired to asceticism or mysticism, probably enjoyed to the full this tale of a young man's false mysticism being subverted by sensuality.

7 Narrative from Cahabón to Pine Ridge A. C. and A. P. Maudslay 1899, pp. 157–87.

8 Tikal stelae Numbers 5, 6, and 10 (Maudslay 1889–1902, vol. 5, pp. 47, 48).

9 Pine Ridge survey Maudslay's plot of his track from Cobán to El Cayo and through the Pine Ridge, and another entitled 'Compass traverse in the interior of British Honduras, with positions fixed in latitude and longitude shown [as] "O"' are in the Map Room, Royal Geographical Society: these are maps M11–17 and M13–9 respectively). It appears from the latter that he turned back about 9 miles north of Caracol, a great city that remained undiscovered for another fifty years.

10 Maudslay's memorandum Clegern 1962, pp. 82–94. On the general topic of development in the colony at that time see also Clegern 1967.

CHAPTER 12

1 First days at Chichén Itzá '6 Feb. Valladolid to Piste. Left in volan with Pablo [a man engaged as overseer. A *volan* is an unsprung two-wheeled cart usually drawn by three mules abreast]. 15 Feb. Cleared Casa Colorada to live in. 16 Slept alone at ruins. . . . 1 March Pablo's request to leave because of mother "Quaere? Carnival?" Gave Pablo $5 in cash.' From 'Rough Diary for 1889', Archives of the Royal Geographical Society.

2 Chichén unsafe for Godman Godman 1915, p. 21.

3 Journey and conditions at Chichén Source: Maudslay 1889–1902, text vol. 3, pp. 1–5.

4 Le Plongeon The ambitious scope of one of his books (Le Plongeon 1886) and his astonishing success in recovering prehistory are so well summarized in the full title that potential readers may consider reading it unnecessary.

Charnay (1880 part I, p. 196) reported: 'The Secretary of the Interior has written on the subject of Le Plongeon. He tells [us that] the pair were at Chichén Itzá, and one day certain distinguished persons from Merida paid a visit. On seeing the archaeologist, they feared his reason was soon to be dethroned, so intent was he on his meditation. Suddenly, like a flash, he started and ran straight for a certain point, and there, stamping the ground with his foot, he exclaimed with the air of one inspired, "Here it is!" and there was the statue!'

It was in a later work (Le Plongeon 1896, pp. 151–3) that he demonstrated to his own satisfaction that the Greek alphabet arose as a corruption, in the course of millennia, of an ancient Maya hymn beginning: 'Al-páa-ha, Be-ta, Kamma, Tel-ta', which, translated, reads 'Heavily break the waters extending over the plains. They cover the land in low places where (etc.)' – thus providing a graphic account of the cataclysm that destroyed Atlantis.

Many of Le Plongeon's stereograms of Chichén Itzá are reproduced in a modern biography of him (Desmond 1988). They were printed from the original negatives – and well reproduced, but unfortunately in none of them were the two halves of the print cut apart and transposed, as is always necessary to produce a three-dimensional illusion.

5 Putnam: 'Mr Thompson must understand' F. W. Putnam to C. P. Bowditch 25 Oct. 1888. C. P. Bowditch Papers, 1880–9, Archives of the Peabody Museum, Harvard University.

6 Atlantis not a Myth Thompson saw 'plausible evidence' for Atlantis. *Popular Science Monthly*, vol. 15, no. 6, pp. 759–64.

7 Sweet impressed by Maudslay H. N. Sweet to C. P. Bowditch, Mérida, 15 July 1889. C. P. Bowditch Papers, Peabody Museum Archives, Harvard University.

8 Thompson: 'It is not very pleasant' E. H. Thompson to C. P. Bowditch, Mérida, 6 July 1888. Archives of the Peabody Museum, Harvard University.

9 Henry Sweet See Charles G. Washburn 1928, *passim*, and obituary in the *New York Times*, 30 July 1933.

10 Serpent columns Maudslay 1896.

11 Food stores Lists survive in Maudslay's notebooks of the stores he took to Chichén Itzá; Box no. 7, for example: 18 Beef-tea, 2 Irish stew, 2 Ham soup, 5 Mock turtle, 5 Oxtail, 3 Marmalade, 3 Keating's [flea powder], 1 14-pound [tin of] Biscuits, etc.

CHAPTER 13

1 Wilbour's diary entries Wilbour 1936, pp. 553, 558, 558, 560.

2 Scarab A description of it, with request for information concerning its whereabouts, reached me from Geoffrey T. Martin, Christ's College, Cambridge, in a letter dated 30 May 1970. Unfortunately I was unable to help him.

3 Alarm in Secretaría de Justicia over Maudslay's work at Palenque In his copy of *A Glimpse at Guatemala*, now preserved in the library of the Museum of Mankind, London, Eric Thompson pasted a note he had received from the archaeologist Henry Berlin, dated 22 April 1969, in which the latter reported having discovered in the Archivo General de la Nación, Mexico City, a file pertaining to the Secretaría de Justicia y Bellas Artes, dated 1891, in which someone is reported as having learnt from a report in a San Cristóbal de las Casas newspaper that Maudslay was working at Palenque without a permit. In fact, as we have seen, Maudslay had taken unusual trouble to obtain a permit in Mexico City, and to enlist the aid of the governor of Chiapas. There seems, however, to have been a failure at some level to communicate this intelligence to other branches of federal and state authorities.

The scare was provoked by an article in the newspaper *El Ferrocarril*, of San Cristóbal Las Casas (strangely named organ for a town so far from any railway!). 'With the authorisation of the government', it said,' an English commission is now in Palenque equipped with all the instruments necessary for exploring the portentous ruins of that Department. It seems that the hour has come for the resurrection of the American Babylon. The English squad are going to uncover the tombs of the Palenquian Pharaohs. . . . It would be better if a commission from our government accompanied them. When the English are mentioned, Belize comes to mind . . . Belize!'

This item was telegraphed by Batres to the Secretaría de Justicia y Bellas Artes. On 31 March, the Secretario wired back that he had already ordered the work to be suspended, but somehow this order was not implemented, for a certain M. Fernández, an official of the Secretaría de Fomento, Colonización, Industria y Comercio, informed the Secretario de Justicia that, happening to be in Chiapas on other business, 'I visited the historic ruins of Palenque. . . . There I found the learned traveller Alfred P. Maudslay, the surveyor H. W. Price, and the estimable brothers Gorgonio and José Domingo López . . . who were engaged in making moulds of the sculptures.' In August, the scholar Francisco del Paso y Troncoso delivered a very favourable opinion of Maudslay to the Secretario, quoting also the opinion of Señor Becerra Fabre (evidently an official of some importance) who stated that 'unlike others who have come to Chiapas to dedicate themselves to similar studies, these gentlemen, far from destroying or damaging the ruins, are carrying out their studies with scrupulous care'. Four days later, J. M. García, deputy Secretary of Justice, ordered that no obstacle be put in the way of these studies, but of course Maudslay and his men had long gone home by then (Archivo General de la Nación, Mexico: Justicia y Bellas Artes, C:165, Exp:76, F:9).

4 Louis Chambon His book was published in Paris (Chambon 1893). It is an amusing and unpretentious work, enlivened with occasional salty items (such as the proverb cited on page 73). Having heard tell in Tenosique of ruins

Notes

three days' walk upstream from there, near the *montería* or logging camp of Piedras Negras, he went to see them on his way back from Yaxchilán. His brief description (which pays particular attention to Altar 4 and its supports) was the first printed reference to a site that would become famous. I am grateful to a tireless bibliographer, Miguel Antochiw, of Mérida, Yucatán, for bringing this book to light.

5 Chambon's account of the dawn *zapateado* 'Luckily, Ash Wednesday was dawning. We were performing our morning ablutions when suddenly the door burst open, and a numerous and merry crowd rushed in, the leader of which said firmly "Don't be afraid, this is to bid adieu to Carnaval!" The youths carried flowers in their hands, and the young girls wore large hats with loose ribbons falling on their shoulders. Their dresses were red, rose, monkey's rump, thigh of aroused nymph, in short, all the colours of the rainbow, and others, you know! The director and organizer of the dance, she herself (La Capitana!) came up with some of her friends to invite us to do the *zapateo*. At the sight of her lovely dark eyes, still more langourous after this exhausting night, one no longer notices the poor taste of the dresses. "But how, Capitana? We'll make ourselves ridiculous! Look, Capitana, you know quite well we don't know how to *zapatear!*" "But yes! But yes! You would offend us. . . ." So willy-nilly (and more willing than not) we decided to stamp the dance of the country to the sound of that confounded clarinettist, who had perched, for lack of a barrel, on a little folding work-table. I was afraid it would crash at any moment. But the invasion of our room, the invitation to the *zapateado*, etc. – everything had happened with such rapidity that we, stupefied, surprised, dumbfounded, came face-to-face with our dancers, M. Maudslay holding a towel in his hands, and I my toothbrush. After having cried several times "Viva don Alfredo! Viva don Ludovico!" the motley troop left us to continue our interrupted toilette.' (Chambon 1893, p. 164, translated by author).

6 Expenditures on this expedition A summary of these (excluding shipping charges and Maudslay's own passenger fare) exists:

Giuntini	Wages	72
	Travelling	60
	Expenses	40
Gorgonio, Caralampio & Mingo	Wages	160
	Travelling	50
	Expenses	60
Price	Wages	72
	Travelling	30
	Expenses	30
	Labour	400
	Material	150
	[Total] £	1124

(Museum of Mankind Archives, London, Maudslay Notebook no. 8).

CHAPTER 14

1 Maudslay's birthday He did note the passage of his thirty-third birthday while at Quiriguá in 1883 (Graham 1982, p. 438).

2 Occasional correspondence A few entries in Maudslay's field journals mention 'a letter from Miss Morris'.

3 Passed through New York On the first opportunity that arose (during his return to England from Tikal in 1881), Maudslay would have had time only for a hurried greeting.

4 Many rough and wintry passages A. C. and A. P. Maudslay 1899, p. 4.

5 Sporting So described by Christine, one of Zelia Nuttall's daughters, who married Arthur Laughton, Maudslay's mine manager. Their daughter Nadine was born at Zavaleta.

6 Pince-nez Edith Wharton, a fellow New Yorker, would not have approved, since she regarded their use as inappropriate for older ladies, but Annie may not have cared about such petty conventions – and in the matter of social class, Annie clearly outranked Wharton!

7 Loss of leg, and its consolations Sparks 1832, vol. 1, p. 224.

8 Wooden leg For a time, at least, during his early days in Paris, Morris did choose to wear a more elegant copper leg, made for him in England in 1790 (Thompson, 1943 p. 197). (It is worth noting a blemish on this historian's otherwise excellent work, for, after citing Morris's description of Talleyrand as 'a sly, cunning and malicious man', he adds parenthetically '[this] is the malicious judgment of another cripple, the American, Gouverneur Morris'. It is hard to understand how anyone who has read Morris's letters, as Thompson must have, could reach such a conclusion. There's no sign that the loss of a leg embittered him, made him malicious or diminished his hearty enjoyment of life; as a man of the world, however, Morris tended to call a spade a spade.

9 Wording of the Constitution The initial text of the Preamble was produced by the Committee of Detail; Morris rewrote it as a member of the Committee of Style, backed by fellow-members Madison and Hamilton; they concentrated 23 articles into seven (Mee 1987, pp. 269, 270).

10 Ann Cary Randolph's woes Principal sources: Swiggett 1952; Walz, J. and A, 1950; Cullen and Johnson 1977, vol. 2, pp. 161–78.

11 Will of G. Morris Sparks 1832, vol. 1, p. 504 *n*.

12 Conn. men too 'cute! Scharf 1886, vol. 2, p. 281.

13 G. Morris II, farmer Beach 1845, p. 23.

14 Gouverneur the fourth From his pen there flowed at least twenty popular novels, one of which was set in the Pacific and has the title *Yellow Men and Gold* (Morris c. 1911). On opening this book the reader is startled by the exotic, brilliantly lit photographs that illustrate it – until it becomes apparent that before publication the story had been used for a 'Photoplay, a

Goldwyn Production'. So it was a very early example of 'The Book of the Film'.

CHAPTER 15

1 Peabody Museum's permit 'The said Peabody Museum shall have the right for the term of ten years from February 1st, 1891, under the oversight of the Government, to explore and excavate the ruins at Copan and elsewhere in the Republic, provided that if, in any year, the said Peabody Museum shall fail to conduct any such exploration, then the concession shall hereafter be revoked. [Signed] Bográn.' Indeed, a generous concession.

By way of contrast, George Byron Gordon's attempt to obtain a concession in 1900 provoked a fierce debate in the Congress before being rejected. One firebrand representative, Oquelí Bustillo by name, having declared that no country gives over its ruins, etc. etc., asked rhetorically 'Ahora os pregunto: porqué Byron Gordon no ha solicitado las ruinas de Méjico, las ruinas de Chile, las ruinas de la Argentina, y las ruinas del Ecuador, por ejemplo?' (Honduras, Boletín Legislativo, Año V, no. 49).

2 Notes from Mr. Maudslay in relation to work in Copan 'In regard to the hieroglyphic stairway we should endeavor to photograph the stones that remain in situ so as to keep connection between the glyphs. Before any stones are removed we should endeavor to number the whole series (with red paint) and to make moulds of all that have any indication of glyphs. Some time these glyphs will doubtless be read and it is of the utmost importance that nothing should be lost. Special attention must be given to this stairway, and the important work of this year will be done here. Mr. Gordon is of the opinion that this upper stairway with the hieroglyphs was formerly on top and has fallen down, but Mr. Maudslay does not express the same opinion although holding himself open to change of theory. [In fact, Gordon's opinion was correct.]

'Some sort of cement should be taken down by the next expedition to repair broken monuments. Also moulding paper must be taken.

'The man who owns all the land around the same side of the river as the ruins is Don Ignacio, who is very anxious to part with his estate and who asks for it $10,000 in currency. Half the ruins are on this estate which contains thirteen caballería [a caballería, not a standardized unit, is equivalent to about 100 acres, or 40 ha]. Mr. Maudslay thinks it well worth while to purchase this land, but suggests that much care be taken in dealing with the owner who thinks the museum is made of gold, and whose price is too high. Land can be purchased from the Government for almost nothing in this region, but when in private hands is not so easily secured. Mr. Maudslay thinks we could get the land for $3,000 or $4,000. He suggests if we purchase the land that we keep some reliable man there all the time to take charge, who by leasing out to the Indians or natives of Copan plots of land could save money to the expedition, could have food on hand and possibly could get rental

by way of labor. If we want to keep the place clear inside the fence, goats would probably be the best way of doing it; but at present we must do this by letting the natives plant their milpas. Mr. Maudslay left instructions that Don Juan should allow some of the Copan villagers to make their milpas inside the fence, but he left strict injunctions that no brush fires should be built so as to do any injury to the stone monuments.

'Mr. Maudslay suggests that all the earth and vegetation be removed from the hieroglyphic stairway as he fears it may do damage. He also advises that no trees be cut down except where actually necessary for exploration. If this advice is not followed the place will become a very uncomfortable one to work in, from lack of shade. It would be a good thing to plant trees (either seed or young trees) on the Plaza. Mangoes would be the best, particularly as the natives will not cut down a fruit tree.'

Next, he offers advice about building a project house. 'In building or clearing the site it would be well to have wheelbarrows or carts so that workmen can empty their baskets into the cart and not have to carry each basketful.' (This undated typewritten document was evidently compiled by someone present at discussions between Maudslay and Bowditch and/or Putnam at the Peabody Museum. Putnam and Bowditch files, Archives of the Peabody Museum, Harvard University.) Mention of Gordon's opinion concerning the stairway surely dates this as following their first season's work.

In hindsight, it is now clear that Maudslay was mistaken in advising the clearance of soil from the stairs, for the soil had protected the inscription from erosion.

3 Hieroglyphic Stairway The anonymous author of the *British Museum Guide to the Maudslay Collection of Maya Sculpture*, (T. A. Joyce, presumably) charges the excavators of the stairway with failure to record the original sequence of the steps, thereby overstepping the 'line which divides excavation from destruction' ([Joyce] 1923, p. 76 note). But there seems to be no evidence of this having happened, for the component blocks of the steps were numbered in situ with red paint, as suggested by Maudslay.

4 Pigment prints On arrival in Guatemala Maudslay received a letter from Putnam telling him that, when the exhibition closed, he had sold the prints to the new Columbian Museum, predecessor of the Field Museum of Natural History, for the price ($500) that Maudslay had put on them, and enclosed the bank draft (F. W. Putnam to A. P. Maudslay, 16 Jan. 1894. Archives of the Peabody Museum, Harvard University).

5 Guatemalan Pavilion at Chicago See Graham 1981.

6 Morrisania of the West Later, a Morrisania of the south was to be created by Annie's nephew Gouverneur IV at Aiken, South Carolina.

7 Running the ranch The land had been part of

a reservation for Northern Utes until they were forcibly removed to Utah in 1880. This ranch, of 894 acres, lay four-and-a-half miles from Grand Valley, Colorado. Morris sold it to the St Joseph fruit-growing company. According to Maudslay's second wife, Alice, Maudslay took over running the farm from his brother-in-law, but, on finding it in a bad condition and too large, had it sold (Alice Maudslay to Hinks, 23 Apr. 1931, Archives of the Royal Geographical Society).

8 Visit to Lick Observatory A. C. and A. P. Maudslay 1899, p. 2.

9 Travel to Guatemala Source: A. C. and A. P. Maudslay 1899, chapter 1.

10 Travel within Guatemala Sources: A. C. and A. P. Maudslay 1899, chapters 5, 6, 7 to Atitlán; chapters 9 and 10 to Cobán; chapters 13 and 14 to Copán; chapter 17 to Quiriguá; chapter 18 to the coast.

11 Treating the sick A. C. and A. P. Maudslay 1899, pp. 134–6.

12 Hugh W. Price He was to carry out some excavations of his own in British Honduras along the Sittee River and at Kendal (Price 1899). He eventually settled in New Zealand.

CHAPTER 16

1 Zavaleta The name carries a strange echo of *Zavalla*, the title of a series of romantic stories by Henry (or Harry) Maudslay, a third cousin of Alfred's. On returning from a visit to Texas he told a tale of having been captured on the Río Grande by an Indian chief named Zavalla, and then escaping on the chief's marvellous horse. He worked this up into a serial *Zavalla; A New Tale of Western Life. By Harry Maudslay, son of the late Mr Amos Maudslay, of Barnsley* (the series commenced in the *The Barnsley Chronicle* on 10 Jan. 1878). His brother Robert also visited Texas, and settled there; his life story, written for a daughter, was published posthumously (R. Maudslay 1951). Their father, Amos, born in 1817, was a cobbler and chartist who wrote several books, such as *Workshop Musings* (1851), *Roland, a Masque* (1856), and *Poetry of a Day* (1853). The British Library's copy of this last contains a press review of *Workshop Musings*: 'It speaks well for the rising intelligence of the lower classes, when we see them eschewing the haunts of intemperance and the arenas of infidelity to pursue the peaceful paths of literature.'

2 Zavaleta mine and hacienda By March 1903 Maudslay had become the owner of three other gold and silver mines in the vicinity (El Carmen, La Esperanza, and Anexa a Dolores), the operation being registered as the Zapotec Mining Company. To manage the mines, and hold power of attorney during his absences, Maudslay engaged Arthur Laughton, son of the naval historian Sir John Knox Laughton. When Zelia Nuttall and her daughter Christine came to Zavaleta as guests in 1902, Laughton and

Christine fell in love, and two years later were married – against Nuttall's wishes, for she was hoping to have Alfred Tozzer as son-in-law (this information from the late Ross Parmenter). Their daughter Nadine was born at Zavaleta in September 1905. In his obituary of Maudslay, Tozzer states that he had inherited the mine (1931, p. 410), having been told this by Nadine Laughton, to whom he had written asking for information (N. Laughton to A. M. Tozzer, Cambridge, England, 23 Feb. 1931). Prima facie, this does seem unlikely. Nine years after his marriage Arthur Laughton was killed by bandits in Colima (see *The New York Times*, 25 Aug. 1913). For Nuttall see Parmenter 1971.

3 Andrew Carnegie's gifts In 1907 he added $2 million, and in 1911 a further $11.5 million.

4 British Minister's letter This was passed on by Mariscal, Secretario de Relaciones Exteriores, to the Secretario de Justicia e Bellas Artes, 18 Nov. 1902. México, Archivo General de la Nación, Secretaría de Justicia é Instrucción Pública, 1902, C:150, Exp:7, F:6.

5 Elected by members of ICA to explore Monte Albán Such a vote seems unlikely, and there is no record of anything like it in the published *Proceedings*. Such matters, however, are seldom if ever put into print.

6 Maudslay at New York International Congress of Americanists On his way back to Mexico, Maudslay attended this congress, held in October 1902, simply as an observer. On the fifth day, when each of the five vice-presidents of the congress had conducted sessions from the chair, F. W. Putnam honoured Maudslay by conducting him to take the chair, in spite of his lack of status as a vice-president.

7 Nuttall and Maudslay 'involved in plot against Batres' Zelia Nuttall had good reason for resentment. While visiting the Isla de Sacrificios, off the coast of Veracruz, she discovered a mural painting depicting the Aztec feathered serpent, and, on return, reported it to the Secretary of Public Instruction, and to Batres, with a request for permission to make some excavations – whereupon Batres quickly visited the island and claimed the discovery as his.

A grudging permission was granted her, but she was informed that her work must be supervised by Batres's son Salvador, who was still young and wild. (Three years earlier, while director of works at Teotihuacan, Salvador Batres had 'burst into the nearby town of San Juan Teotihuacan at 11 p.m., accompanied by two *rurales*, and coming to the house of Doña Delfina Ortíz, in the centre of town, made a tremendous racket with gunfire, alarming the neighbours who had been asleep, until at 1 a.m. they departed for their camp shouting blasphemies at the tops of their voices' (Mexico, Archivo General de la Nación, Instrucción Pública y Bellas Artes, C:152, Exp: n).

Nuttall's indignation at what she called the Batres–Justo Sierra coalition impelled her to resign from the Organizing Committee of the 17th International Congress of Americanists, about to be held in Mexico City in 1910, and to renounce her title of Honorary Professor of Archaeology at the Museo Nacional. She charged Batres with having obstructed not only Maudslay but eminent Mexican scholars too, such as Nicolas León, Fidel del Paso y Troncoso, and even Manuel Gamio. She showed, too, that Batres had arbitrarily changed the provenance and cultural affiliation of many well-known pieces in the Museum, undoing the work Eduard Seler had done in 1907. To these accusations she might have added his prevention of Marshall Saville from working at Yaxchilán.

8 Maler's comment on Maudslay's application T. Maler, Mérida, 3 Oct. 1903 to C. P. Bowditch. Archives of the Peabody Museum, Harvard University.

9 Se concede al Señor Maudslay 'México, Secretaría de Justicia é Instrucción Pública, 28 de noviembre de 1902. Acuerdo: Se concede al Sr. Alfred Maudslay la autorización que pide en nombre del Instituto Carnegie para explorar los monumentos de Monte Albán en el concepto de que inspeccionará constantemente la persona que designe el gobierno y que suspenderá toda exploración si de cualquiera manera atenta á la integridad de las ruinas descubiertas ó se quebranta de cualquiera modo la ley de materia ó las bases por el mismo Sr. Maudslay formuladas. Comuníquese concediendole también un ejemplar de cada una de las piezas duplicadas que se encuentren ó de las que se descubran en número mayor de dos ejemplares' (Mexico, Archivo General de la Nación: Secretaría de Justicia é Instrucción Pública, 1902, C:150, Exp:7, F:6).

10 Pumpelly 'The amount recommended for archaeological researches under Professor Raphael Pumpelly was increased in accordance with the resolution of the Board of Trustees' (Carnegie Institution of Washington, Minutes of the Executive Committee, 20 Dec. 1904).

An Advisory Committee in Prehistoric Archaeology was set up in 1902. At its meeting on 9 January 1903 the three-man committee (Holmes, Dorsey, Boas) made these recommendations: 1. Tribes of the Caddoan family (Dorsey); 2. Prehistoric archaeology (caves) (Holmes); 3. Excavations on the site of the ancient city of Monte Albán (Maudslay); 4. Exploration in Costa Rica (Hartmann). Boas's own application was turned down by his two colleagues.

11 Surgical operation Henry Lewis Morris to A. C. Maudslay, Brown Palace Hotel, Denver, Jan 1905, and same to same, 8 June 1905, mentions the operation. Maudslay seems to have then been running the ranch for a time, while recuperating (letters in author's collection).

12 Investigations by Batres at Monte Albán The report published by Batres illustrates the carved panels he removed; it also includes many photographs, but plans and text are minimal (Batres 1902a). As the great Mexican archaeologist Ignacio Bernal commented about late nineteenth- and early twentieth-century archae-

ologists, they 'only looked for "interesting" objects. Of course, we can't generalize, but there is an abyss between the immense care taken by Maudslay in copying or making casts of Mayan stelae, and the presumptuous carelessness of Batres, slicing up the Pyramid of the Sun [at Teotihuacan], or of Saville, destroying the splendid façade of a Zapotec tomb in order to obtain some urns with which it was decorated' (Bernal 1980, p. 156).

13 Saville's expedition to Yaxchilán ruined When, in 1897, the Duc de Loubat financed an expedition to Yaxchilán to be led by Saville, Batres was appointed government representative. Vast amounts of equipment, including several tons of special paper for making moulds, were shipped to Chiapas – according to Saville (1928 p. 156), although Frontera, Tabasco, seems a more likely destination. On arrival, however, Batres refused to go to Yaxchilán, claiming, as he had once before and would do again, that the site was within the Republic of Guatemala.

Saville therefore had to divert the expedition to Palenque. And then, he says, 'Batres refused to take up his abode at the ruins, and remained at the village, making only one or two trips to the ruins during the six weeks the expeditions remained in Chiapas. Owing to the fact that Batres did not like the climate, he placed every obstacle in the way of the investigators, even using his influence to prevent the hire of laborers. . . . After remaining practically alone at Palenque for several weeks, with only a handful of men to clear the forest and to carry on excavations, all hope of working there was abandoned.'

Saville's summary account (1928, pp. 155, 156) quotes from the report made by Batres to the Secretario de Instrucción Pública, in which we read that he visited the ruins repeatedly, but after a month 'Mr. Saville [became] convinced that he would meet with no success in his explorations, owing to a variety of adverse circumstances, the chief of which was his conviction that the antiquities of which he was in search have been completely destroyed by moisture.'

After spending some years at the American Museum of Natural History, Saville became Loubat Professor of American Archaeology at Columbia University. He died in 1935.

In 1909, Batres returned to Palenque to bring out the remaining tablet of the Temple of the Cross, and James Cooper Clark sent Maudslay a description of that expedition. 'The party consisted of Justo Sierra (Secretario de Instrucción Pública y Bellas Artes), his son, Don Justo, jr., Batres, a doctor, two geologists, two artists, two photographers, a man to make plaster casts, and myself. With us we took a French chef & a Spanish mayordomo (a cut-throat looking gentleman he was too) besides numerous servants. In this list, not one, with the exception of Don Leopoldo (?) may lay claim to being an archaeologist.'

Having described the work of bringing the tablet down from the Temple, not without breaking off both top corners, Clark describes (and illustrates with a sketch) the discovery of a floor slab in the Temple of the Inscriptions with eight holes drilled in it, all fitted with stone pegs. The slab was lifted, and revealed nothing but rubble and moist lime. (Decades later, this slab was found to cover the stairway leading down to the celebrated tomb of Pacal.)

'One rather amusing morning was spent in setting half-a-dozen workmen to dig in the SW corner of the Eastern Court of the Palace. While this was going on our party was marched along the Western side of this court and the photographer took cinematograph pictures of us watching the excavations! As soon as the picture was taken the work was stopped and they carefully filled in all the holes they had made so that the place would be nice and smooth again!!!' (J. Cooper Clark to A. P. Maudslay, Mexico, 26 Mar. 1909. Archives of the Museum of Mankind, London).

14 Maudslay's vandalic character L. Batres to Secretario de Instrucción Pública y Bellas Artes, C:169, Exp:8, F:10. This diatribe was provoked by the British Minister's application for a permit to export to the British Museum a collection assembled by Weetman Pearson, the contractor who drained the Valley of Mexico, built the railway across the Isthmus of Tehuantepec, and owned the largest Mexican oil company. (Batres might have been pleased to know that a very high proportion of Pearson's collection were grotesque fakes.)

15 Batres's archaeological map of the Mexican Republic See Batres 1910.

16 Maudslay's gifts to the Museo Nacional, Mexico Mexico, Archivo General de la Nación, Instrucción Pública y Bellas Artes, C:153, Exp:35, F:8. This file includes the appointment of Maudslay as Professor Honorario; his reply to E. A. Chávez from London; and a letter from the director of the museum to Chávez, 17 May 1907: 'el eminente arqueólogo inglés dosequió a este Museo una pieza arqueológica de gran valor, que es un gran vaso de barro con una deidad al frente, de procedencia mixteco-zapoteca.' Then on 5 June 1907 'Mr. Alfred Maudslay . . . donó a este museo dos deidades indígenas, hechas en cerámica y bastante interesantes, ambas de Cuilapan, distrito de Hidalgo del Estado de Guerrero.' Their source, though, was clearly Cuilapan de Guerrero, an important Zapotec site near Monte Albán, where Saville carried out excavations in 1902.

CHAPTER 17

1 Maudslay's letter to the V&A A. P. Maudslay, Armadale Castle, Isle of Skye, 31 Aug. 1885, to The Secretary, Science and Art Department, South Kensington (Victoria & Albert Museum, File no. S.F. 108. 'Bequest: Maudslay, A. P., 1885').

2 Edwin J. Lambert Like the Hunter sisters, Lambert exhibited paintings at the Royal Academy. Four watercolours by him of the tombs of John de Sheppey are in the Victoria and Albert Museum. He lived in Hampstead, and died in 1932.

3 Annie Hunter's letter A. Hunter to C. P. Bowditch, London, 3 Mar. 1916 (Archives of Peabody Museum, Harvard University).

4 Pottery illustrations See Gordon 1925.

5 Frederick DuCane Godman For his life see H. J. E[lwes] 1919. Godman's estate was valued at over £300,000, equivalent to more than £22 million today (and that may not have been the actual figure, but instead the lower limit of a category for rates of death-duties – that is, inheritance-tax). His father's partnership with Samuel Whitbread in his famous brewery would account for part of his fortune, but he seems to have been much richer than his brothers. An entirely conjectural explanation may lie in his middle name: perhaps, for some reason impossible to divine, he was made the heir of a fortune left by his maternal grandfather, Peter Du Cane, who had been a director of both the Bank of England and the East India Company.

6 Osbert Salvin For his life see A. N[ewton] 1898; also Godman 1917, pp. 2ff.

7 Spencer F. Baird's advice Baird was Secretary of the Smithsonian Institution. His letter to Salvin, dated Washington, 29 Nov. 1863: 'You ask me what I would do in your place. I would publish as soon as possible a list of all additional species with descriptions of new ones in the Ibis . . . and then begin a Manual of the Ornithology of central America. . . . You have all: free access to the collections you own the most important of all. . . . Publish by dated signatures, distributing these to fellow workers. . . . Do let me hear you have determined to do this and I shall be happy' (letter in the collection of Sybil Rampen, Oakville, Ontario). His suggestion of publishing by dated signatures was followed.

8 Salvin's Copán photos Salvin 1863. I know of two complete editions, both in private collections; apart from these, thirteen single prints (that is, not stereopairs) and the accompanying text are in the author's collection. A notice of the publication, accompanied by engravings done from four of the photographs, appeared in the *Illustrated London News* (Anon. 1863).

9 John Sibthorp's *Flora Graeca* Ten folio vols, 1806–40 (only twenty-eight copies issued). This was the first of a great flowering in the nineteenth century of encyclopedias, taxonomic treatises, bibliographies, great dictionaries of language (e.g. the *Oxford English Dictionary*) and national biographies (the *Dictionary of National Biography*), corpora, compendia, concordances, etc. Sibthorp's was a private venture, overshadowed in scale only by the *Biologia Centrali-Americana*.

10 *Biologia Centrali-Americana*, prices In 1918 Godman turned over the entire stock of *Biologia* volumes to Bernard Quaritch, the rare book dealer, for him to sell. This was a year after the work's completion, and the year before his death. For the entire work (Introduction 1 vol., Zoology 51 vols, Botany 5 vols, Archaeology 6 vols; in all 63 vols, but Fauna lacks Crustacea,

Malacostraca and one or two groups of Hymenoptera and Neuroptera) the subscription price had been £287 14s 0d; Quaritch sold them for £180. For just the archaeology volumes the price was £21, equivalent to about £1500 ($2400) today (from Quaritch's Prospectus, 1918). By another criterion, the price of a 1-ton Ford van in 1923 was £140, so the cost of seven sets of *Archaeology* volumes was about that of a mechanically rather simple van.

11 Photographs The printers discreetly introduced clouds into the skies of many views, such as those taken at Chichén Itzá, because the orthochromatic emulsions of the original plates seldom registered blue skies as less bright than clouds.

12 Gustav Eisen Eisen had been summoned to California in 1873 in the hope that he could find out why the new fig-plantations in California were proving fruitless. He was able to show that a certain wasp, not found in the area, was necessary as pollinator. Its subsequent introduction by the Department of Agriculture produced the desired result.

13 Eisen's drawings See Eisen 1888.

14 Glyph for 20 See Maudslay 1889 (the 'completion' glyph is illustrated).

15 Letter to Bowditch A. P. Maudslay to C. P. Bowditch, Guatemala, 19 Dec. 1892 (Archives of the Peabody Museum, Harvard University).

16 Goodman manuscripts Archives of the Peabody Museum, Harvard University.

17 Head-variant numerals Maudslay must have been aware of these numerals by 1888, at the latest, since they are described on p. 40 of volume 1 of his *Archaeology*, the first fascicle of which was issued in February 1889.

18 Thompson's quotation from Goodman Goodman 1897, p. 21, and his comment: Thompson 1950, p. 30.

19 The merits of Goodman's work Maudslay 1889–1902, vol. 5, p. *v*.

20 Maudslay's field notes Unfortunately he tended to write these on loose sheets of paper, which he would usually tie together later through a hole stabbed in the top left-hand corner (the same discipline he had applied to Sir Arthur Gordon's disordered papers). Naturally, in the course of travel and time these often tore loose, with consequent loss of many pages – and sometimes, apparently, of whole gatherings. As for his notes on the 1883 Quiriguá expedition, they were overlooked when his other papers were collected for deposit in the British Museum, remaining instead in his nephew Cyril's house, where the author found them forty-five years later (Graham 1982).

In some years, however, Maudslay took into the field large desk-type diaries, and these, for some reason, ended up in the Royal Geographical Society instead of in the British Museum.

CHAPTER 18

1 Walter Maudslay Following the liquidation of Maudslay, Sons and Field, Walter founded Birmingham Aluminium Castings, also known as Birmetals and Birmid, manufacturers of products ranging from aluminium cylinder blocks to tennis racket frames.

2 Northern and southern metaphors Horne 1969, pp. 22–3.

3 Maudslay, Sons and Field mortgage debentures Prospectus, *The Morning Post*, London, 13 Apr. 1889.

4 Belleville boilers See Maudslay, Sons and Field n.d. (this presumably was largely the work of Walter Maudslay).

5 Opposition to Bellevilles Remarks by William Allen, MP for Gateshead, in *The Times*, 12 Mar. 1895; Walter Maudslay's reply, 13 Mar.; Report of debate on Supply, Navy Estimates, *The Times*, 30 Apr. 1895.

6 Alfred Maudslay and debenture holders 'High Court of Justice, Chancery Division, in re Maudslay, Sons and Field (Ltd.). Alfred Maudslay (on behalf of himself and all the other holders of mortgage debenture stock issued by the defendant company. . .) v. Maudslay, Sons and Field.' *The Times*, 12 Oct. 1899, p. 2.

7 Standard Cars The name Dick chose, Standard, was meant to represent a policy of using standardized, interchangeable parts for engines and chassis of different sizes, and also as a kind of pun: the radiator emblem was the Union Jack, also a 'standard'. The company was perennially hampered by shortage of capital, as the banks, echoing the British public's lack of appreciation for industry, were always niggardly in lending to manufacturers. But even so, the company lasted for sixty years as an independent car manufacturer. The blood-line of Standard is represented also in Jaguar cars, which stem from the SS Jaguar of the late 1930s, the first SS having come into being as a Standard chassis fitted with a sports body made by the Swallow Coachbuilding Company – hence Standard Swallow, or SS.

8 Cyril Maudslay Born 11 June 1875. Married Dorothy Fleming 11 November 1921. She was a granddaughter of Alfred's sister Clara Rose, who married (21 May 1843) Telford, son of Joshua Field, Henry Maudslay's partner. One legacy of Cyril is Rosemullion Head at Mawnan, near Falmouth, which he gave to the National Trust in 1939. Walter had owned land in the district, all of which was sold by Cyril after his father's death, except the headland.

9 Eustace in debt He left debts of over £2500 (Garrard, Wolfe, solicitors, of London, to A. P. Maudslay, 20 March 1916; letter in author's collection).

10 Sale of Morrisania The Port Morris Land Company was formed to manage or dispose of the remaining land, and the trustees negotiated with the city for the estate to be bought for a park; large areas of it had already been acquired for such a purpose (Van Cortland Park and the land occupied by the Zoo and the Botanical Gardens). The Board of Social Improvement voted for it; but the eventual buyer was the New Haven Railroad, for $400,000. Annie's portion of this and some Port Morris stock from her mother's trust fund was $68,900. It was from her father's estate that she inherited the $10,000 in cash. (Letter from Henry Lewis Morris, the estate's attorney, to A. C. Morris at Zavaleta, 24 Feb. 1905 and others of this period; collection of the author.)

The subsequent decline of this area, especially Mott Haven, is notorious. Today the only real haven there for its unfortunate inhabitants is St Ann's church, the builder of which, Ann Cary Morris, was herself well enough acquainted with social and economic distress.

CHAPTER 19

1 Dolly a blood-relative As already mentioned, her mother was daughter of Alfred's sister Clara Rose. Only four years before this trip Dolly's mother had died from injuries sustained in an early motor accident: she was run over by a motorist heedlessly reversing.

2 Sweeter air See obituary notice, Anon. 1931.

3 *Relación de la Villa de Valladolid* See Marimón 1883.

4 Bernal Díaz translation After serving with Francisco Hernández de Cordoba's exploratory expedition in 1517, and then accompanying Cortés to Honduras in 1524, Bernal Díaz went to live as an *encomendero* in Guatemala – that is, a holder of land with a grant of labour and tribute from the Indians. In the 1560s he read *La Conquista de México* by López de Gómara, an author who never went to New Spain but served as chaplain to Cortés in his last years. Naturally, in his account, Gómara glorified the role of Cortés and slighted that of the common soldiers.

5 C. L. Fleischmann During the First World War, British subjects with German surnames, finding them a source of embarrassment, often discarded them. Fleischmann changed his to Fenton; thus the collection of Maya antiquities bequeathed by him to the British Museum is known as the Fenton Collection.

6 Maudslay 'much too modest' A. C. Breton to C. P. Bowditch, 31 July 1912. Papers of C. P. Bowditch, Archives of the Peabody Museum, Harvard University.

7 Location of the Great Temple according to Batres See Batres 1902, following pp. 54 and 60.

8 Other opinions on the Great Temple's position See Boone 1987, pp. 41–4.

9 Abstract of Great Temple Enclosure paper Maudslay 1913c.

10 Adela Breton, 1849–1923. A tireless and delightfully eccentric traveller and student of antiquity who is best remembered for the faithful copies in watercolours that she made of ancient paintings, such as the murals at Chichén Itzá. (These she did while camping in one of the ruined structures, in order to avoid any obligation for her lodging to the owner of the hacienda, E. H. Thompson.) For obituary see Fallaize 1923.

11 Regret at small edition A. C. Breton to C. P. Bowditch, 25 May 1914. Papers of C. P. Bowditch, Archives of the Peabody Museum, Harvard University.

12 Maudslay's opening address to ICA Maudslay 1913b.

13 Mexican delegation to ICA This is described in a report of thirty-two foolscap typewritten pages, written by Alfonso Pruneda, including also the paper he presented at the Congress, 'La legislación mexicana sobre monumentos arqueológicos'. The delegates originally named were Nicolás León, Francisco del Paso y Troncoso, Juan Martínez Hernández, and A. Carneiro de Fantoura. The Yucatec Juan Martínez Hernández made valuable contributions to Maya scholarship, and is remembered today principally for his part in arriving at the Goodman–Martínez-Thompson correlation between the Maya and Christian calendars.

Alfonso Pruneda's description of the delegates' excursion to Oxford mentions, delightfully, their visit to 'Brassnoise College'! Mexico, Archivo General de la Nación, Instrucción Pública y Bellas Artes, C:287, Exp:22, F:98.

14 Maler's relations with Maudslay For his accusations see Maler 1901–3, p. 189; for mention of his meeting Maudslay, and his retraction see Maler 1908, p. 27.

15 Failure of V&A to lend casts for ICA A. C. Breton to C. P. Bowditch 31 July 1912 (Archives of the Peabody Museum, Harvard University).

16 'Maudslay so disgusted at treatment of casts' Two extracts from copious documentation of this matter:

1. Undated memo by W. G. Johnson: 'the Collection is of the highest importance. The Americans are quite willing to buy what is now offered as a gift to the Department, which has cost £5,000, but the Grant at Washington [the Smithsonian Institution] must not be spent by their staff on any reproduction the original of which is not in the United States . . . but [Maudslay's] chief reason for hoping for a favourable reply is that he may not be compelled to keep [allow?] the Authorities of Berlin, Paris or New York to take the Collection away from England.'

2. Minute from Cecil Smith to the Secretary of the Science and Art Department of the Board of Trade, 15 Nov. 1909: 'Mr Maudslay in his conversations with me gave me to understand that he considers himself to have been badly treated both by the BM [British Museum] & by the authorities of the South Kensington Museum [V&A]. . . . It is clear that Mr Maudslay has no

right whatever to dictate to the Board what action should or should not be taken. . . . Mr. M. has been allowed exceptional latitude in this respect in the past' (File 'Maudslay, A. P. Bequest from 1885' at V&A Depository, Blythe House, London).

17 RAI addresses The first was a somewhat personal and informal review of progress in Mesoamerican archaeology (Maudslay 1912a); in the second (Maudslay 1913a), he briefly reviewed some of the papers delivered at the ICA Congress.

18 Escuela Internacional La Escuela Internacional de Arqueología y Etnología Americanas (International School of American Archaeology and Ethnology) had recently been established in Mexico City under the aegis of Boas, Seler, Gordon, and others. Nine years later, politically motivated attacks on it in the Congress led to its closure.

19 W. H. Holmes's stratigraphy See Mark 1980.

20 A big 'onion' and a smaller one If only Batres had studied Gordon's report on his excavations in the Ulua Valley, Honduras, he would have seen a diagrammatic cross-section of a mound resembling his own of the Temple of the Sun, but consisting of only two layers. These Gordon correctly assigned to different periods – perhaps the first demonstration of a building sequence (Gordon 1898, p. 12).

21 Opinions aired by Batres at an earlier congress in Mexico A blunder by Batres at the 11th International Congress may be recalled: 'Mr. Batres, by means of images reproduced by Magic Lantern, began by demonstrating that in his view [the Tablet of] the Cross at Palenque was none other than the tree under which Buddha sat to inspire himself to go and preach the gospel' – an idea he may have picked up from Orozco y Berra (see Bernal 1980, p. 111). At this, Eduard Seler jumped up to refute any such interpretation, indicating the Maya hieroglyphs on the panel, among them calendrical signs already deciphered. Congreso Internacional de Americanistas, Actas de la Undécima Reunión, 1895 (Mexico, 1897), pp. 271–4.

22 Valley of Mexico lecture Maudslay 1916.

23 Migrations of the Maya Maudslay 1908–16, vol. 1, pp. xlix–lii.

24 Maudslay's new interest in those islands In a letter to C. P. Bowditch dated Algiers, 6 Nov. 1895 (Putnam papers, Archives of the Peabody Museum, Harvard University), a Mr Herbert J. Pratt reported that 'Maudslay said, the short half-hour I saw him, that what he wanted to see was the ruins on the Caroline Islands, which I then heard of for the first time. And somebody else, I forget who, has spoken to me of the remarkable similarity of other ruins in Cambodia with the Central American ruins (the C. Island ruins being likewise similar) which added to the C. Island ruins makes three links in a chain. . . . They are undescribed and unphotographed.'

25 Caroline Islands For a lecture to the RGS by a naval officer of long experience in the Pacific see Bridge 1886. Concerning the ruins on Ponapé in the Carolines he had little to say, and Maudslay, in comments following the lecture, merely expressed interest in hearing more about them.

26 A second lecture on the Carolines (Christian 1899). Maudslay's comments on the lecture are included. In the archives of the RGS there's a hasty note from Maudslay to Keltie, scrawled in red chalk and dated 21 Nov. 1898: 'I think you can safely give notice of the Caroline Islands paper for December, but you will have to vote me a special Gold Medal. A.P.M.' Apparently, Maudslay had agreed very reluctantly to offer comments following the presentation of this lecture.

CHAPTER 20

1 Nurses Maudslay to Arthur Hinks, Morney Cross, 21 Feb. 1919 (Archives of the Royal Geographical Society).

2 Aasleagh salmon Maudslay to Hinks, Morney Cross, 25 July 1919 (Archives of the Royal Geographical Society). Aasleagh (or Ashleagh) Lodge was a large house built for salmon and trout fishing. Walter Maudslay held a long lease on it from about 1890 until it was burnt during the political troubles of 1922. It was restored, but later reduced in size by demolition of one wing. It serves now as headquarters of the Erriff Fishery.

A report entitled 'Western Fishing Industry: Inquiries at Leenane and Clifden' (*The Galway Express*, 14 Feb. 1914) includes the evidence of 'Mr. W. Maudslay, Cadogan Gardens, London, [who] deposed that he was the lessee of the Ashleagh fisheries'.

3 Thomas Atholl Joyce (1878–1942) Archaeologist and author of works on Mexican, Central American, and South American archaeology, and President of the Royal Anthropological Institute, 1931–3.

4 Letter about V&A Museum A. P. Maudslay to President, Board of Trade, Morney Cross, 6 Dec. 1921 (Archives of the Victoria and Albert Museum).

5 Moulds eaten by rats Cooper Clark 1931, p. 345.

6 Catalogue of Maudslay collection See Joyce 1923.

7 Keltie Sir John Keltie, geographer (1840–1927). Librarian, and later Secretary, of the Royal Geographical Society.

8 Annie Maudslay, obituary *The Hereford Times*, 18 Sept. 1926.

9 Annie's appearance Fifty years later Maudslay's former cowman, John Newman, told me he remembered her as disfigured by sores on her face, and keeping her head hooded.

10 Sir Grafton Elliot Smith Born New South Wales 1875. Reply to Tozzer and Spinden: *Nature* no. 2413, vol. 96, p. 593. Waldeck article: *Illustrated London News*, 15 Jan. 1927. Maudslay letter to *The Times*, 14 Feb. 1927. Maudslay's personal letter: British Museum, Dept of Ethnography archives, 'Waldeck and Elliot Smith controversy'.

11 Barmy ideas in another field Fell 1977.

12 Elliot Smith's ethnological 'Monroe Doctrine' Smith 1938.

13 Elliot Smith and elephants Smith 1927.

14 Elliot Smith attacking Maudslay H. J. Braunholtz to A. M. Tozzer, London, 6 Mar. 1931 (Archives of the Peabody Museum, Harvard University).

15 'Broadway Travellers' edition reviewed When the editor of the *Times Literary Supplement* decided, no doubt with the best of intentions, to commission reviews of two editions in English (Maudslay's and Maurice Keating's) of Bernal Díaz's *True History*, he had the misfortune to assign the task to an incompetent, for here is a sample of his work: 'Whoever can lay hands on [Genaro García's] Spanish edition and can read the language at all will do well to take it in preference to either of the English translations. He need not be deterred by trifling difficulties put in his way by Bernal Díaz's reckless punctuation.' (*TLS*, 10 May 1928)

The translator of a later edition in English (Idell 1956) confidently claimed to be rendering a service by rescuing the work from 'the fusty Victorianism of the earlier English edition', 'meaning Maudslay's (p. 12). Among other bloomers, he ends his less fusty version by having Bernal Díaz commend himself 'to God and his Blessed Mother' – a divinity seldom heard of, I think.

16 Book ready in typescript H. F. Wilson to A. P. Maudslay, Ross-on-Wye, 15 Oct. 1928 (author's collection). Wilson had been sent the text for his opinion.

17 Critical comments removed Matthew Waltham, a neighbour of Cyril Maudslay's in Somerset who had also been sent the typescript, suggested that his critical references to Sir Alexander MacAlister and Sir Arthur Palmer 'might trouble some old Queenslanders', so they were removed. As to Maudslay's picture of Cairns he wrote: 'Certainly you have depicted Cairns as, what I have no doubt he was, a mean, disagreeable and nearly disgusting man. I am doubtful, however, whether any purpose is served by putting in details that would be painful reading to his living connections, and I have put in red brackets in a few places where it seems to me omissions would not detract from the force of the character painting.' His advice seems to have been taken (Waltham letter in author's collection).

18 Sir Charles L. Wyke Born 1815; 'twin fellow-pupil of the late King of Hanover to whom his father was tutor' (*Vanity Fair*, 9 Feb. 1884, p. 77,

with caricature by 'Ape'); Vice-Consul, Port-au-Prince 1845; Vice-Consul, Guatemala 1852, and Chargé d'Affaires, 1854; Minister Plenipotentiary, Mexico, 1860; then to Hanover, Denmark, and Portugal. Retired 1884, died 1897.

19 Death of Catherwood von Hagen 1950, pp. 116, 117.

20 Honorary degree from Cambridge In presenting Maudslay to the Chancellor, the Public Orator spoke as follows (ingeniously adapting a dead language to express 'photography' and 'plaster casts'): 'Sunt quos delectant res Europae antiquiores, sunt quos Asianae, non nullos (confitebor enim) Americanae. Quis nescit Mexicanos et Incas ab Hispanis devictos? Inter quos olim gens tertia quaedam Mayana scripta palatia templa monumenta reliquit mirae quidem artis et aenigmatum plena. Hujus populi annales cremaverunt sacerdotes Hispanici; aedificia deserta in silvis invenit Johannes Lloyd Stephens; deorum vel regum imagines adjuvante Phoebo depinxit alumnus noster, et denique gypso quodam ita accurate imitatus est ut in Museo Britannico, in Museo nostro, paene ipsas effigies credamus nos videre. Interea omnem naturam animantum illis repertam in regionibus descripsit, iterum reversus. Si tandem historiarum omnium Americanarum velitis eam quae rerum gestarum magnitudine, vistorum virtute, hostium novitate ceteras antecellit, librum exquiratis illum simplicem festivum verum quem scripsit Bernal Diaz, quem reddidit Alfredus Maudslay' (from the *Cambridge Reporter*).

21 Landa translation The typescript with Ms. emendations is in the possession of Fenton's nephew, Ronald Raymond-Cox, of London, who kindly made a photocopy of it for me.

22 Charles Fenton (Formerly Fleischmann). Born in Altendorf, near Frankfurt am Main, in 1867. His mother was a Sichel, of the well-known wine-growing and wine-shipping family. He and his brother Hugo came to England before 1890, then went to Guatemala in 1893 and bought three coffee *fincas*. Hugo was British Consul in Cobán for fifty years, but Charles returned to England in 1910 (information from his grandson, Ronald Raymond-Cox). The fine collection of Maya ceramics that he had amassed in Guatemala (the Fenton Collection) was bequeathed to the British Museum.

23 The Tozzer edition of Landa Tozzer 1941.

24 Pagden's edition Pagden 1975. Some mistakes of his: on p. 162 'an animal called a *chu* which is remarkably mischievous' should be a *chic*; and three lines later he has Landa tell how tame these animals become, and how fond of 'playing with the Indian women who delouse them' – instead of how fond the animals are of 'playing with the women, and how they rid them [the women] of lice'.

25 Cramped old RGS premises At the corner of Saville Row and Burlington Gardens, now occupied by Gieves and Hawkes, tailors.

CHAPTER 21

1 Obituaries The principal notices were in *The Times*, 24 Jan. 1931; *Nature*, see J.C.C. 1931; *American Anthropologist*, see Tozzer 1931; *The Geographical Journal*, see Anon. 1931; and *Man*, see Joyce 1932. (Note that the second paragraph of Tozzer's tribute contains some errors.) Spanish-language versions of Tozzer's tribute were published in Mexico (Tozzer 1933) and in Guatemala (Tozzer 1936). The tribute by Paul Rivet (1931) closes with his opinion that 'the name of this perfect gentleman, discreet and modest, will always remain attached to the history of Americanist studies, side by side with Charnay and Seler'. Well, perhaps . . .

2 'Knighted' by colleagues Morley, for example, (1937–8, vol. 1, p. 78) called him 'Sir Alfred Maudslay, the English Traveler' (only a *traveler*?). Another, presumably following Morley, was Clegern (1967, p. 75). More recently the Getty Trust has elevated him to the rank enjoyed by younger sons of dukes and marquesses, for in its catalogue of an exhibition of photographs, *Mexico from Empire to Revolution* (2000–2001), he is styled 'Lord Alfred Maudslay'!

3 Gorgeous French furniture Schreider 1971.

4 Hearsay Often unreliable, to be sure, but so also may be the evidence of an eyewitness. Here is witness from the eye and pen of Graham Greene as he describes a sight that appears to have been deeply etched into his memory: 'The face of Lord Haig whom I saw as a pall-bearer at the funeral of Rudyard Kipling – a face flushed probably with indigestion but it looked like make-up, a look of savage stupidity and deep lines as cruel as the trenches of the Somme' (Greene 1969). A convincing picture, but it can only have been Haig's ghost that he saw, since he expired eight years before Kipling.

5 Beatrix Davenport's letter B. Davenport to C. Maudslay, 8 Ovington Square, London S.W.3, 3 Feb. 1931 (author's collection).

6 Eros excised Just two examples: (1) Directly after mentioning a discussion with Jefferson on the political situation in Pennsylvania, Morris continues: 'Return Home and dine. After Dinner take a turn in the Palais royal. A Lady invites me from her Window to pay a visit and I accordingly go up Stairs, but a nearer approach convinces me that her Health has been injured by her Attention to the phisical Necessities of her fellow Creatures. I lament to her this Misfortune, which she denies but offers at the same Time the usual Securities. I decline to avail myself of her Goodness. It is just therefore that I should present her with something to buy Ribands. It happens that I am as unjust as I am ungallant. To convince me of her Tenderness and render me more sensible to her attractive Graces she locks the Door and puts the key in her Pocket. Her Reasons are excellent but not convincing and her Tone and Manner are rather vehement than perswasive. I am very gentle but a little obstinate and ask her out of Curiosity

whether she is acquainted with such a Thing as the Police. Her Knowledge I find is equal to her Elocution. She has already the Honor of being registered in the sublime Archives of that misterious Office, and with a Candour rare in more elevated Stations, the Means by which she obtains her daily Bread are there noted by her own Avowal. Doubtless Monsieur will not expose himself to the Scandale of an Affair of this sort. . . .' (Davenport 1939, vol. 1. pp. 104, 105).

And (2) 'Go to bed a little after seven and rise a little after ten. Dress and visit Madame de Flahaut who keeps me some time. We celebrate together but St-Louis [perhaps her major-domo] comes in so abruptly as to damage our closing moment' (*ibid.*, vol. 2, p. 101).

CHAPTER 22

1 Weighty tomes The whole work (with Whatman paper edition of the text volumes) weighs in at 50.5 lb.

2 Historical necessity Was Maudslay wafted into this field by the hidden and impersonal forces of historical necessity, as cultural historians of social-determinist stripe would have us believe; or was he, as the philosopher Isaiah Berlin might have maintained, simply 'a great man'? There may be truth in both suppositions. Undoubtedly a 'job-opportunity' opened up in Mesoamerica in the 1880s, however badly advertised it was; none the less two significant applicants did go to work – these being, of course, Maudslay and Maler. (History shows us other pairs of pioneers who worked almost simultaneously along similar lines, Newton and Leibnitz for example, and Darwin and Wallace.) But had Maudslay not answered the call, it would be mystical to assume that another person would necessarily have filled his place in every respect, as Maler, for all his good work, could never have done.

3 Errors noted by Adela Breton A note pasted opposite Plate 51 of vol. 3, in that copy: 'Fig. c (ml) parts *f* and *e* are wrong. *f* should be at *c*, but reversed, the fish facing the figure. The stone taking the place of *f* is gone. *e* perhaps never existed, but was expected to match the piece 1(c)? of the corresponding sculpture.' (Errors in this transcription, too, are possible, since in Breton's manuscript *f*, *c*, and *e* are hard to distinguish.)

4 Maler's corrections 'Vol. II, Plate 97. The sculpture at right (of the spectator) is not the third Lintel of House 16 (i.e. Dintel Numero 46) [but] Stela V (divinity side) of the Edificio 20 (de Maler). The third lintel of the House M (Ed. 44) is the Lintel 46 (de Maler) entirely calcined (The Editors of the PM have omitted my representation of the divinity side of Stela V (the humanity side is destroyed!).'

5 Morley's critique of Hunter's drawings See Morley 1920, p. 22.

6 Faults in *Biologia*: purported deliberate omissions For the sake of completeness, it is necessary to mention a quite different charge that was made against Maudslay some years ago. He was accused by two art historians of deliberately omitting from his *Archaeology* certain drawings of sculptured scenes on the grounds that they would undermine his romantic view of the Maya as a peaceable people, and that in order to sustain this illusion he had deliberately withheld from publication in the *Biologia* certain portions of the image on a sculptured lintel portraying a painful blood-letting practice.

The accusation was baseless. For one thing, Maudslay never did promote any such romantic view of the Maya; and, for another, prudery was unlikely in a man who declared in his Presidential Address to the Royal Anthropological Institute: 'The Aztecs were civilized in so far as they made use of written records, were good builders and craftsmen, and possessed a rather elaborate social organization, but they were undoubtedly blood-thirsty cannibals, and so in common terms might be classed as savages – but then I have myself had personal friends in other parts of the world who had been notorious cannibals whom I found in other respects to be courtly gentlemen.' Furthermore, Maudslay did publish a complete drawing of a lintel similar to the allegedly censored one, but showing an even more painful-looking act of blood-letting. (See, if you must, Graham 1993, pp. 72, 73.)

7 Harry Pollock's tribute Pollock 1940, p. 189.

8 Morley's opinion of the likely content of the inscriptions Morley 1946, p. 262.

9 Eroding monuments One can sketch a credible graph showing the loss of legibility through time due to weathering of inscriptions carved on stone. The line would remain at zero for a period dependent on the type of stone; the curve would then trend upwards as lightly incised details within the glyphs disappeared – but these tend to be more decorative than significant; and then, after running less steeply for a time, the curve would rise again as the more deeply carved and more significant inner details and outlines of the glyphs became blurred. Thus, standing monuments from which Maudslay made casts a century ago (when they were 8–10 per cent younger) may have lost as much as twice that percentage of their legibility since then. Stelae or panels, on the other hand, that were found lying on the ground face-up as the result of collapse at a more recent date – and have remained there since moulds were taken, under continual attack from the acid decomposition-products of leaf-mould – these are likely to have lost a much greater percentage of legibility. Hence the great value of old casts.

References

A.N. [Alfred Newton]
1898 'Osbert Salvin'. *Proceedings of the Royal Society, Series B*, vol. 64, pp. xiii–xvii. London.

Anon.
1832 Review of 'The Antiquities of Mexico'. *Foreign Quarterly Review*, vol. 9, pp. 90–124.

1863 'The Ruins of Copan'. *Illustrated London News*, 16 January.

1874 *The Student's Guide to the University of Cambridge*. Cambridge.

1879a 'Our Public Schools, II, Harrow'. *The New Quarterly Magazine*, n.s., vol. 1, pp. 273–96. London.

1879b *Letters and Notes Written during the Disturbances in the Highlands of Viti Levu, Fiji, 1876.* [compiled by Sir A. H. Gordon]. Privately printed, Edinburgh.

1895 *Cuestiones entre Guatemala y México* (articles reprinted from *El Mensajero*). Reprinted in *Límites entre Guatemala y México*, Guatemala 1964.

1897 *Congreso Internacional de Americanistas, Actas de la Undécima Reunión, 1895*. Mexico.

1928 'Interviews with Famous Men'. *Trinity Magazine*, June, pp. 74–6. Cambridge.

1931 *The Geographical Journal*, vol. 78, no. 1, pp. 1–12. Royal Geographical Society, London.

1982 *Atlas Histórico de Tabasco*. Consejo Editorial del Gobierno de Tabasco.

n.d. *Résumé of Enquiry in re Tonga Mission Affairs, October, 1879. Mr. A. P. Maudslay, H.B.M. Vice-Consul, vs. Rev. S. W. Baker*, 47 pp. Wilson and Horton, Auckland.

Arens, W.
1979 *The Man-eating Myth: Anthropology and Anthropophagy*. Oxford.

Au, Hermann
1875 *Mapa de la República de Guatemala, levantado y publicado por orden del Smo. Gobierno, por H. Au*. Hamburg.

Baker, Thomas
1857 *The Steam Engine; or, the Powers of Flame. An Original Poem in Ten Cantos*. London.

Bancroft, Hubert H.
1874–5 *Native races of the Pacific States*. 5 vols, London.

Barry, F., ed.
1931 *Maria Edgeworth, Chosen Letters*. London.

Barty-King, Hugh
1979 *Girdle round the Earth*. London.

Batres, Leopoldo
1889 *Teotihuacan ó la Ciudad Sagrada de los Toltecas*. Monografías de Arqueología Mexicana. Mexico.

1902a *Exploraciones Arqueológicas en la Calle de Escalerillas, Año de 1900*. Mexico City.

1902b *Exploraciones de Monte Albán, por Leopoldo Batres, Año de 1902*. Mexico City.

1906 *Teotihuacan. Memoria que presenta Leopoldo Batres. . . relativa á las Exploraciones que por orden del Gobierno Mexicano y á sus expensas está llevando a cabo la Inspección de Monumentos Arqueológicos en las Pirámides de Teotihuacan*. Mexico City.

1910 *Carta Arqueológica de los Estados Unidos de México, formada por Leopoldo Batres*. Mexico.

Beach, Moses Yale
1845 *Wealth and Biography of the Wealthy Citizens of New York*. New York.

Bernal, Ignacio
1962 *Bibliografía de Arqueología y Etnografía Mesoamericana y Norte de México*. Mexico.

1980 *A History of Mexican Archaeology*. London.

Bernoulli, Gustav
1875 'Reise in der Republik Guatemala'. *Petermanns Geographische Mittheilungen*, vol. 21, pp. 324–40. Gotha.

Boddam-Whetham, John W.
1877 *Across Central America*. London.

Boone, Elizabeth H.
1987 'Templo Mayor Research, 1521–1978'. In Elizabeth H. Boone, ed. *The Aztec Templo Mayor, a Symposium at Dumbarton Oaks, 8th and 9th October, 1983*. Dumbarton Oaks, Washington, D.C.

Bridge, Cyprian
1886 'Cruises in Melanesia, Micronesia and Western Polynesia in 1882, 1883 and 1884, and Visits to New Guinea and the Louisiades'. *Proceedings of the Royal Geographical Society*, vol. VIII, no. 9, pp. 568–95.

Bullock, William
1824 *Six Months' Residence and Travels in Mexico Containing Remarks on the Present State of New Spain*. London.

Cal, Angel E.
1995 'Confrontación Anglo-Icaiche en Belice, 1856–1872: "La Guerra de Castas" de Belice'. *Investigadores de la Cultura Maya*, vol. 3, no. 1, pp. 6–25. Universidad Autónoma de Campeche, Mexico.

Chambon, Louis
1893 *Un Gascon au Mexique*. Paris.

Chapman, J. K.
1964 *The Career of Arthur Hamilton Gordon*. Toronto University Press.

References

Charnay, Désiré
1880–1 'The Ruins of Central America'. *The North American Review*, New York (11 parts scattered through vols 131–5).

1885 *Les Anciennes Villes du Nouveau Monde: Voyages d'explorations au Mexique et dans l'Amerique Central, 1857–1882*. Paris.

1887 *Ancient Cities of the New World, being Voyages and Explorations in Mexico and Central America, from 1857–1882*, translated and abridged by J. Gonino and H. S. Conant. New York. (Reprinted, with Introduction by I. Graham, New York, 1973.)

Chinchilla Mazariegos, Oswaldo
1996 'Peor es Nada'. *Baessler-Archiv, Beitrage für Völkerkunde*, Neue folge, Band 64, pp. 295–357. Berlin.

Christian, F. W.
1899 'Exploration in the Caroline Islands'. *The Geographical Journal*, vol. 13, no. 2, pp. 106–36. London.

Clegern, Wayne M.
1962 'Maudslay's Central America: A Strategic View in 1887'. In *Studies in Middle American Economics* no. 2. Publication no. 29, Middle American Research Institute, Tulane University.

1967 *British Honduras, Colonial Dead End, 1859–1900*. Baton Rouge, Louisiana.

Cline, Howard F.
1973 'Hubert Howe Bancroft, 1832–1918'. In Howard Cline, ed., *Handbook of Middle American Indians*, vol. 13, part 2, pp. 326–47. Austin, Texas.

Coe, William R. and Edwin M. Shook
1961 'The Carved Wooden Lintels of Tikal'. *Tikal Reports*, no. 6. The University Museum, University of Pennsylvania.

Coles, John, ed.
1889 *Hints to Travellers, Scientific and General*, 6th edition. Royal Geographical Society, London.

Conder, Claude E.
1875 'The Rock Scarp of Zion'. *Quarterly Statement*, The Palestine Exploration Fund, pp. 81–9. London.

Cooper Clark, James
1912 *The Story of Eight Deer in Codex Colombino*. London.

1931 [J.C.C.] 'Dr. Alfred P. Maudslay'. *Nature*, no. 3201, 7 Mar., pp. 345–6.

Cubas, Antonio García
1873 *México, Carta Geográfica y Administrativa de los Estados Unidos Mexicanos*. Mexico City.

1886 *Album Pintoresco de la República de México*. Mexico.

Cullen, Charles C., and Herbert A. Johnson, eds
1977 'The Commonwealth v. Randolph', in *The Papers of John Marshall*. Chapel Hill.

Davenport, Beatrix Cary, ed.
1939 *A Diary of the French Revolution by Gouverneur Morris*. 2 vols. Boston (Reprinted, Freeport, NY, 1971.)

Davidson, Caroline
1985 *The World of Mary Ellen Best*. London.

Degusta, David
1999 'Fijian Cannibalism: Osteological Evidence from Navatu'. *American Journal of Physical Anthropology*, vol. 110, pp. 215–41. New York.

2000 'Fijian Cannibalism and Mortuary Ritual: Bioarchaeological Evidence from Vunda'. *International Journal of Osteoarchaeology*, vol. 10, pp. 79–92. Chichester.

Del Río, Antonio
1822 *Description of the Ruins of an Ancient City discovered near Palenque*. London.

Derrick, R. A.
1946 *A History of Fiji*. Printing and Stationery Department, Fiji.

Desmond, Lawrence G.
1988 *A Dream of Maya: Augustus and Alice Le Plongeon in Nineteenth Century Yucatan*. Albuquerque.

Díaz y de Ovando, Clementina
1990 *Memoria de un Debate (1880): La postura de México frente al patrimonio arqueológico nacional*. UNAM, Mexico.

Dupaix, Guillaume
1831 'The Monuments of New Spain', in *The Antiquities of Mexico*, vol. IV, part 1, edited by Viscount Kingsborough. London.

Ebin, V. and D. A. Swallow
1984 'The Proper Study of Mankind . . . – Great Anthropological Collections in Cambridge*. University Museum of Archaeology and Anthropology, Cambridge.

Eisen, Gustav
1888 'On some Ancient Sculptures from the Pacific Slope of Guatemala'. *Memoirs of the California Academy of Sciences*, vol. II. San Francisco.

Elliot Smith, Sir Grafton
1924 *Elephants and Ethnologists*. London.

1927 'Elephants in Maya Art: Links between America and Asia'. *Illustrated London News*, 15 Jan., pp. 85–7.

1938 Letter to *Nature*, no. 2413, vol. 96, p. 593 (in reply to letters from A. M. Tozzer and H. J. Spinden).

Erskine, John Elphinstone
1853 *Journal of a Cruise among the Islands of the Western Pacific*. London.

Estrada Monroy, Agustin
1972 'Un viaje fascinante al Lacandón del Siglo XIX de Edwin Rockstroh'. *El Imparcial*, Guatemala (serialized during July).

Fallaize, E. M.
1923 'Adela Breton'. *Man*, no. 76.

Fell, Barry
1977 *America B.C.* New York.

Förstemann, Ernst W.
1886 *Erläuterungen zur Mayahandschrift der Königlichen Oeffentlichen Bibliothek zu Dresden.* Dresden.

Formwalt, Lee W.
1980 *The Virginia Journals of Benjamin Henry Latrobe.* New Haven.

France, Peter
1969 *The Charter of Land.* London.

Fuentes y Guzman, Francisco Antonio de
1882 *Historia de Guatemala, o Recordación Florida,* 2 vols. Madrid.

Geyl, Pieter
1961 *Encounters in History.* Cleveland, Ohio.

Gibson, Charles
1947 'Lewis Henry Morgan and the Aztec "Monarch"'. *Southwestern Journal of Anthropology*, vol. 3, pp. 78–84. Albuquerque.

Gilbert, K. R.
1965 *The Portsmouth Block-making Machinery: A Pioneering Enterprise in Mass-production.* London.

Godman, Frederick DuCane
1915 *Biologia Centrali-Americana, Introductory Volume.* London.

Gonzalez Aparicio, Luis
1973 *Plano reconstructivo de la región de Tenochtitlán.* INAH, Mexico.

Goodenough, (Mrs) J., ed.
1878 *Memoir of Commodore Goodenough, R.N., C.B., C.M.G., with Extracts from his Letters and Journals, Edited by his Widow.* 3rd edition, London.

Goodman, Joseph T.
1897 *The Archaic Maya Inscriptions.* Appendix to Maudslay 1889–1902.

1898 *The Maya Graphic System: Reasons for Believing it to be Nothing but a Cipher Code.* London.

1905 'Maya Dates', *American Anthropologist*, n.s. vol. 7, pp. 642–7.

Gordon, George B.
1898 *Researches in the Ulua Valley, Honduras.* Memoirs of the Peabody Museum, vol. 1, no. 4. Cambridge, Massachusetts.

Gordon, George B., ed.
1925 *Examples of Maya Pottery in the Museum and other Collections.* The University Museum, University of Pennsylvania, Philadelphia.

Gordon Cumming, Constance F.
1881 *At Home in Fiji,* 2 vols. Edinburgh.

Gosling, Cecil
1926 *Travel and Adventure in Many Lands.* London.

Graham, Ian J. A.
1977 'Alfred Maudslay and the discovery of the Maya'. *British Museum Yearbook*, no. 2, pp. 136–55. London.

1982 'Alfred P. Maudslay's Notes from Quiriguá, 1883'. *Mesoamérica*, Año 3, Cuaderno 4, pp. 430–42. Antigua Guatemala.

1991 'Federico Arthés y la presencia de Guatemala en la Exposición Mundial Colombina de Chicago'. *Anales de la Academia de Geografía e Historia*, vol. 51, pp. 71–7. Guatemala.

1993 'Three Early Collectors in Mesoamerica'. In *Collecting the Pre-Columbian Past, a Symposium at Dumbarton Oaks*, pp. 49–80. Dumbarton Oaks Research Library and Collection, Washington, D.C.

Grattan, C. Hartley
1963 *The Southwest Pacific to 1900.* Ann Arbor.

Gray, John A. C.
1960 *Amerika Samoa: A History of American Samoa and its U.S. Naval Administration.* Annapolis.

Greene, Graham
1969 'Terror in Trinidad', review of *The Loss of El Dorado* by V. S. Naipaul. *The Observer*, 26 Oct., p. 34. London.

H.J.E. [H. J. Elwes]
1919 'F. D. Godman'. *Proceedings of the Royal Society*, Series B, vol. 91, pp. i–vi, with portrait. London.

Haddon, A. C. and A. P. Maudslay
1928 'Baron Anatole von Hügel'. *Man*, vol. 28, pp. 169–71. London.

Hays, Terence E., volume editor
1991 *Encyclopedia of World Culture*, vol. II. Boston.

Heath, Ian
1974 'Toward a Reassessment of Gordon in Fiji'. *Journal of Pacific History*, vol. 9, pp. 81–92. Melbourne.

Holmes, William H.
1885 'Evidences of the Antiquity of Man on the Site of the City of Mexico'. *Transactions, Anthropological Society of Washington*, vol. 3, pp. 68–81.

Holtzapffel, Charles and J. J.
1847–84 *Turning and Mechanical Manipulation,* 5 vols. London.

Horne, Donald
1969 *God is an Englishman.* Sydney.

Idell, Albert
1956 *The Bernal Díaz Chronicles: The True Story of the Conquest of Mexico.* New York.

References

J.C.C.
1931 See Cooper Clark, James 1931.

Jones, J. Christopher
1970 *Design Methods*. London.

Joyce, Thomas A.
1920 *Mexican Archaeology, an Introduction*. London.

1932 'Alfred Percival Maudslay', *Man*, no. 149, May 1932.

[Joyce, Thomas A.]
1923 *Guide to the Collections of Maya Sculptures (Casts and Originals) from Central America*. British Museum, London.

King, Arden
1972 'The Journey of the Tikal Lintels to Basel'. *Verhandlungen*, Naturforschende Gesellschaft Basel, vol. 82, no. 2, p. 229. Basel.

Knight, Edward F.
1907 *The Cruise of the Alerte*. London.

Landa, Diego de
1914 *Landa's Relación de las Cosas de Yucatán, a Translation*. Edited, with introduction by Alfred M. Tozzer. Papers of the Peabody Museum, no. 18. Cambridge, Massachusetts.

Le Plongeon, Augustus
1886 *Sacred Mysteries among the Mayas and Quiches 11,500 Years Ago. Their Relation to the Sacred Mysteries of Egypt, Greece, Chaldea and India. Free Masonry in Times anterior to the Temple of Solomon*. New York.

1896 *Queen Móo and the Egyptian Sphinx*. New York.

Maine, H. S.
1877 *Lectures on the Early History of Institutions*. London.

Maler, Teobert
1901 *Researches in the Central Portion of the Usumatsintla Valley*. Memoirs of the Peabody Museum, vol. II. Peabody Museum, Harvard University, Cambridge, Massachusetts.

1908 *Explorations of the Upper Usumatsintla and Adjacent Region*. Memoirs of the Peabody Museum, vol. IV. Peabody Museum, Harvard University, Cambridge, Massachusetts.

Mark, Joan
1980 *4 Anthropologists: An American Science in its Early Years*. New York.

Marimón, Sebastian, ed.
1883 'Relación de la Villa de Valladolid escrita por el Cabildo de aquella Ciudad . . . Abril de 1579', *Proceedings of the 4th International Congress of Americanists*, vol. 2, pp. 167–95. Madrid.

Mathew, H. G. C., ed.
1986 *The Gladstone Diaries with Cabinet Minutes and Ministerial Correspondence*, vol. 9. Oxford.

Maudslay, Alfred P.
1878 Unpublished report on the Line Islands. Document CO 83/18, Public Record Office, London.

1883 'Explorations in Guatemala and Examination of the Newly Discovered Indian Ruins of Quirigua, Tikal, and the Usumacinta'. *Proceedings of the Royal Geographical Society* n.s. vol. 5, pp. 185–204. London.

1886a 'Exploration of the Ruins and Site of Copan, Central America', *Proceedings of the Royal Geographical Society* n.s. vol. 8, no. 9, pp. 568–95. London.

1886b Untitled report on recent explorations in Central America, read to the Cambridge Antiquarian Society, 3 Dec. 1883. *Cambridge Antiquarian Communications*, vol. 5, pp. cxviii–cxxi. Cambridge.

1886c Remarks following paper on Melanesia, etc. (Bridge 1886)

1889–1902 *Biologia Centrali-Americana, or, Contributions to the Knowledge of the Fauna and Flora of Mexico and Central America*, vols 55–9, *Archaeology*, with Appendix by J. T. Goodman. Edited by F. DuCane Godman and Osbert Salvin. R. H. Porter and Dulau, London.

1889a Letter from Yucatan. *Proceedings of the Royal Geographical Society* n.s. vol. 11, pp. 239–40. London.

1889b 'Paper Moulding of Monuments, or "Squeezes"'. In Coles 1889, pp. 406–10 (also in 7th and 8th editions of the same work).

1892 'The Ancient Civilisation of Central America'. *Nature*, vol. 45, pp. 617–22.

1894 'Brief Note on a Paper Read at British Association Meeting (Anthropology Section)'. *Nature*, vol. 50, 30 Aug., p. 440.

1896 'Archaeological Studies in Mexico'. *Nature*, vol. 54, 23 July, pp. 274–6.

1897a 'Archaic Maya Inscriptions', *Nature*, vol. 56, 8 July, pp. 224–6.

1897b 'A Maya Calendar Inscription Interpreted by Goodman's Tables'. *Proceedings of the Royal Society*, vol. 62, pp. 67–80. London.

1898 'Prehistoric Ruins of Honduras and Yucatan'. *Nature*, vol. 57, 14 April, pp. 569–71.

1899 'Remarks Following a Paper on the Caroline Islands', see Christian 1899, pp. 133–4.

1904 'Brief note on a Swamp Cypress at Santa María del Tule, Mexico'. *Nature*, vol. 70, 6 Oct.

1908–16 *The True History of the Conquest of New Spain by Bernal Diaz del Castillo, one of its Conquerors. From the only exact copy made of the original ms. Translated into English, with Introduction and Notes by Alfred Percival Maudslay*. M.A. Hakluyt Society, 5 vols, London.

1909 'Plano hecho en papel de Maguey, que se conserva en el Museo Nacional de México. Appendix by Antonio García Cubas'. *Anales del Museo Nacional de México*, Epoca 3, vol. 1, pp. 48–58. Mexico.

1911 'Exploration in the Department of Peten, Guatemala' (a review). *Nature*, vol. 88, pp. 247–9.

1912a 'Some American Problems' (Presidential Address). *Journal of the Royal Anthropological Institute*, vol. 42, pp. 9–22. London.

1912b *A Note on the Position and Extent of the Great Temple Enclosure of Tenochtitlan, and the Position, Structure and Orientation of the Teocalli of Huitzilopochtli*. Privately printed, London.

1913a 'Recent Archaeological Discoveries in Mexico' (Presidential Address). *Journal of the Royal Anthropological Institute*, vol. 43, pp. 10–18. London.

1913b 'Remarks as Chairman of the Organizing Committee'. *Proceedings of the XVIII International Congress of Americanists* [1912], pp. xxix–xxx. London.

1913c 'A Note on the Position and Extent of the Great Temple Enclosure (abstract)'. *Proceedings of the XVIII International Congress of Americanists* [1912], pp. 173–5. London.

1916 'The Valley of Mexico'. *The Geographical Journal*, vol. 48, pp. 11–26. London.

1921 'The Lake of Atitlan'. *Panamerican*, vol. 33, pp. 276–80. (London?).

1922 'A Note on the Teocalli of Huitzilopochtli and Tlaloc'. *Man*, vol. 22, pp. 27–9.

1927 'The Maya Sculptures'. *The Times*, 14 Feb., p. 8. London.

1928a *The Discovery and Conquest of Mexico 1517–1521, by Bernal Díaz del Castillo*, translated by Alfred P. Maudslay. Abridged and edited by Eudora Garrett. London.

1928b Addendum to obituary of von Hügel; see Haddon 1928.

1930 *Life in the Pacific Fifty Years Ago*. London.

1974 *Biologia Centrali-Americana: Archaeology*. Facsimile in reduced format, in 4 vols, with introduction by Francis Robicsek. New York.

1996 *The Discovery and Conquest of Mexico, by Bernal Díaz del Castillo*, translated by Alfred P. Maudslay, with a new introduction by Hugh Thomas. New York.

Maudslay, Alfred P. and T. A. Joyce
1913 Review of *A study of Maya Art*, by Herbert J. Spinden. *Current Anthropological Literature*, vol. II, no. 4, pp. 238–47.

Maudslay, Amos
1853 *Poetry of a Day*. London.

Maudslay, Anne Cary and Alfred Percival
1899 *A Glimpse at Guatemala*. London. (Reprinted 1979, B. Etheridge Books, Detroit.)

1958 'Un Vistazo sobre Guatemala' [a translation of Chapters 7, 10 and 17 of A. C. and A. P. Maudslay 1899]. *Antropología e Historia de Guatemala*, vol. 10, no. 1, pp. 44–71. Guatemala.

Maudslay, Athol
1891 *Nature's Weather Warnings, and Natural Phenomena*. London.

1892 See 'Yalsduam, Lohta.'

Maudslay, Robert
1951 *Texas Sheepman*, ed. Winifred Kupper. Austin.

Maudslay, Sons and Field
n.d. *Some Remarks on a Subject of Interest: A Short Treatise upon the Belleville Water-tube Boiler, its Uses and Advantages*, 94 pp. London.

Mee, Charles L.
1987 *The Genius of the People*. New York.

Morelet, Arthur
1857 *Voyage dans l'Amérique Centrale, L'Ile de Cuba et le Yucatan*. 2 vols, Paris.

1871 *Travels in Central America, including accounts of some regions unexplored since the Conquest*. New York.

Morley, Sylvanus G.
1920 *The Inscriptions at Copan*. Carnegie Institution of Washington, Publication 219. Washington, D.C.

1946 *The Ancient Maya*. Stanford.

Morrell, W. P.
1960 *Britain in the Pacific Islands*. Oxford.

Morris, Anne Cary, ed.
1888 *The Diaries and Letters of Gouverneur Morris*, 2 vols. New York.

Morris, Gouverneur (the fourth)
c. 1911 *Yellow Men and Gold. With Scenes from the Photoplay, Goldwyn Pictures*. New York.

Nuttall, Zelia M.
1910 'The Island of Sacrificios', *American Anthropologist*, n.s. vol. 12, pp. 277–82.

Pagden, Anthony R. (translator and editor)
1975 *The Maya: Diego de Landa's Account of Affairs of Yucatan*. Chicago.

Parmenter, Ross
1971 'Nuttall, Zelia Maria Magdalena'. In T. James, ed., *Notable American Women, 1607–1950, a Biographical Dictionary*, vol. 2, pp. 640–2. Cambridge, Massachusetts.

[Pembroke, 13th Earl of, and George Kingsley]
1872 *South Sea Bubbles*, 'by the Earl and the Doctor'. New York.

Philips, W. T.
1912 *Norwood in Days of Old*. London.

Pollock, Harry E. D.
1940 'Sources and Methods in the Study of
Maya Architecture'. In *The Maya and their
Neighbours*, essays dedicated to Alfred M.
Tozzer, New York.

Prescott, William H.
1843 *History of the Conquest of Mexico, with a
Preliminary View of the Ancient Mexican
Civilization, and the Life of the Conqueror,
Hernando Cortéz*, 3 vols, London.

Price, Hugh W.
1899 A communication on excavations on the
Sittee River, British Honduras. *Proceedings of the
Society of Antiquaries of London*, n.s. 17,
pp. 339–44.

Rivet, Paul
1931 'A. P. Maudslay'. *Journal de la Société des
Américanistes*, n.s., vol. 23, pp. 242–4.

Robertson, (Sir) William
1777 *History of America*. London.

Rock, Miles
1895 *Mapa de la República de Guatemala y los
adyacentes Estados Mexicanos*. Guatemala.

Rockstroh, Edwin
1881 Untitled note to editor. *Petermanns
Geographische Mittheilungen*, vol. 27, pp. 396,
397. Gotha.

1882 Untitled note to editor. *Petermanns
Geographische Mittheilungen*, vol. 28, p. 435.
Gotha.

Roe, Joseph W.
1926 *English and American Tool Builders*. New
York.

Rosny, Léon de
1869 *Archives Paléographiques de l'Orient et de
l'Amérique*, tome 1. Paris.

Roth, Jane and Steven Hooper, eds
1990 *The Fiji Journals of Baron Anatole von Hügel,
1875–77*. Fiji Museum, Suva.

Rutherford, Noel
1971 *Shirley Baker and the King of Tonga*.
Melbourne.

'S' [Stanmore, Arthur Hamilton Gordon, 1st
Baron]
1897–1912 *Fiji: Records of Private and Public Life,
1875–80*, 4 vols. Edinburgh.

Salvin, Caroline
2000 *A Pocket Eden: Guatemalan Journals
1873–1874*. Plumsock Mesoamerican Studies,
South Woodstock, Vermont.

Salvin, Osbert
1863 *A Description of a Series of Photographic
Views of the Ruins of Copan, Central America,
taken by Osbert Salvin, M.A.* London.

Sandoval, Lisandro
1945 *Un Guatemalteco sabio y altruista . . . y el
docto Edwin Rockstroh*. Guatemala.

Sarg, Francis Charles
1911 'Die Australischen Bumerangs im

Städtische Völkermuseum', *Veröffentlichungen
aus dem Städtlischen Völkermuseum
Frankfurt-am-Main*, no. 3. Frankfurt.

1938 'Alte Erinnerungen an der Alta Verapaz'
[written in 1917]. In *Deutschtum in der Alta
Verapaz, 50 jährigen Bestehens des Deutschen
Vereins zu Coban, Guatemala*. Privately printed,
Guatemala.

Saville, Marshall H.
1928 'Bibliographic Notes on Palenque,
Chiapas'. *Indian Notes and Monographs*, vol. 6,
no. 5. Museum of the American Indian, Heye
Foundation, New York.

Scarr, Deryck
1967 *Fragments of Empire: A History of the
Western Pacific Commission*. Canberra.

Scharf, J. Thomas
1886 *History of Westchester County, New York*,
2 vols. Philadelphia.

Scherzer, Karl
1855 'Ein Besuch bei der Ruinen von Quirigua'.
*Sitzungsberichte der K. Akademie der
Wissenschaften*, vol. 16. Vienna.

1937 'Una visita a Quiriguá despues de 1852'
(translation into Spanish by Roberto
Morgadanes from Frans Blom's English
translation of Scherzer 1855). *Anales de la
Sociedad de Geografía e Historia de Guatemala*,
vol. 13, pp. 447–57. Guatemala.

Schreider III, Louis
1971 'Gouverneur Morris, Connoisseur of
French Art'. *Apollo* (June), pp. 470–83. London.

Searby, Peter
1997 *A History of the University of Cambridge*,
vol. 3, 1750–1870. (General Editor, C. N. L.
Brooke). Cambridge.

Seemann, Berthold
1862 *Viti: An Account of a Government Mission to
the Vitian or Fijian Islands, in the Years 1860–61*.
Cambridge.

Sensabaugh, Leon F.
1940 'American Interest in the
Mexican–Guatemalan Boundary Dispute'.
Birmingham-Southern College Bulletin, vol. 33,
no. 4. Birmingham, Alabama.

Shipley, Sir Arthur E.
1913 *'J': A Memoir of John Willis Clark*. London.

Simpson, St John
2000 'Rediscovering Past Splendours from Iran:
19th-century Plaster Casts of Sculptures from
Persepolis'. *British Museum Magazine*, Spring,
pp. 28–9.

Smith, A. Ledyard
1955 *Archaeological Reconnaissance in Central
Guatemala*. Publication 608, Carnegie Institution
of Washington. Washington, D.C.

Smith, Hobart M.
1987 'A Brief History of the *Biologia Centrali-
Americana* with Biographical Notes on its
Editors'. In *Biologia Centrali-Americana, Reptilia
and Batrachia, by Albert C. L. G. Günther*, a

reprint by the Society for the Study of Amphibians and Reptiles. Oxford, Ohio.

Sparks, Jared
1832 *The Life of Gouverneur Morris, with Selections from His Correspondence*, 3 vols. Boston.

Spennemann, Dirk H. R.
1987 'Cannibalism in Fiji: The Analysis of Butchering Marks on Human Bones and the Historical Record'. *Domodomo*, vol. 5, part 2, pp. 29–49. Fiji.

Spinden, Herbert J.
1912 *A Study of Maya Art, Its Subject Matter & Historical Development*. Memoirs of the Peabody Museum, vol. 6, Cambridge, Massachusetts. (Reprinted by Dover Press, New York, 1975.)

Spoehr, Florence Mann
1963 *White falcon: The House of Godeffroy*. Palo Alto.

Squier, Ephraim G.
1858 *The States of Central America*. New York.

Squier, Ephraim G. and E. H. Davis
1848 *Ancient Monuments of the Mississippi Valley*, Smithsonian Institution Contributions to Knowledge, vol. 1. Washington, D.C.

Stephens, John Lloyd
1841 *Incidents of Travel in Central America, Chiapas, and Yucatan*. New York and London. (Various reprints issued.)

1843 *Incidents of Travel in Yucatan*. New York and London. (Various reprints issued.)

Stoll, Otto
1886 *Guatemala, Reisen und Schilderungen aus den Jahren 1878–83*. Leipzig.

1938 *Etnografía de la República de Guatemala* [1884], translated from German, with notes, pp. v–xxviii, by Antonio Goubaud. Guatemala City.

Swayne, Sir Eric
1917 'British Honduras'. *Geographical Journal*, vol. 50, no. 3, pp. 161–78. London.

Swiggett, Howard
1952 *The Extraordinary Mr. Morris*. Garden City, New York.

Tedlock, Denis
1985 *Popol Vuh: The Definitive Edition of the Maya Book of the Dawn of Life. . . .* New York.

Thomas, Cyrus
1885 'Who Were the Moundbuilders?' *American Antiquarian and Oriental Journal*, no. 2, pp. 65–74. Chicago.

1894 *Report on the Mound Explorations of the Bureau of Ethnology*. Bureau of Ethnology, Twelfth Annual Report. Washington, D.C.

1896 'Maudslay's Archaeological Work in Central America'. *American Anthropologist*, n.s. vol. 1, pp. 552–61. New York City.

Thompson, J. Eric S.
1950 *Maya Hieroglyphic Writing: Introduction*. Publication 589, Carnegie Institution of Washington. Washington, D.C.

Thompson, James M.
1943 *The French Revolution*. London.

Tozzer, Alfred M.
1931 'Alfred Percival Maudslay', *American Anthropologist*, n.s. vol. 33, pp. 403–13.

1933 'Alfred P. Maudslay'. *Boletín del Museo Nacional de Arqueología, Historia y Etnografía*, Ep. V, Tomo 2, pp. 63–9. Mexico.

1936 'Alfred P. Maudslay'. *Anales de la Sociedad de Geografía e Historia*, vol. XII, no. 3, pp. 340–7. Guatemala.

1941 *Landa's Relación de las Cosas de Yucatan: A Translation*. Papers of the Peabody Museum, vol. 18. Cambridge, Massachusetts.

Thompson, M. W.
1977 *General Pitt-Rivers*. Bradford-on-Avon, Wiltshire.

Valera, Juan
1874 *Pepita Jiménez*. Madrid.

Vincent, W. T.
1889–90 *The Records of the Woolwich District*, 2 vols. London.

Vivarez, H
1906 *Un Précurseur de la photographie dans l'art du portrait à bon marché: le Physionotrace*. Lille.

Von Hagen, Victor W.
1968 *Frederick Catherwood, Architect-explorer of Two Worlds*. Barre, Massachusetts.

Walz, Jay and Audrey
1950 *The Bizarre Sisters*. New York.

Washburn, Charles G.
1928 *The Life of John W. Weeks*. Boston.

Wauchope, Robert, general editor
1973 *Handbook of Middle American Indians*. Austin, Texas.

Wilbour, Charles E.
1936 *Travels in Egypt (Dec. 1880–1891)*, ed. Jean Capart. New York.

Yalsduam, Lohta [pseud.]
1892 *An Order to View*. London.

Zorrilla, Luis G.
1984 *Relaciones de México con la República de Centro América y con Guatemala*. Mexico, D.F.

Maudslay's donations and bequests

DONATIONS

To The British Museum (now in Department of Ethnography), London

Oceania: 1885 (4 or more items, with A. W.
                Franks and A. von Hügel)
          1920 (13 items)
          1927 (2 items)
Americas: 1898 (32 items)
          1902 (1 item, purchased)
          1908 (39 items, with Reginald
                Tower)
          1914 (5 items)
          1920 (12 items)
          1921 (1 item)
          1926 (8 items)
          1927 (3 items)

To the Cambridge University Museum of Archaeology

1883 Quiriguá casts

To the Victoria and Albert Museum (now in the British Museum), London

1885–97 21 stone sculptures from Copán
         Plaster casts (c. 400 flat casts
         and many in the round)

To The Royal Geographical Society, London

1897 9 photographs, Central America
      ('1 destroyed 1950 – faded')
n.d. 113 negatives of Mexico, 1900–7
1915 4 Platinotypes made from photos
      taken in Guatemala, 1883
1915 Panoramic photo of Valley of
      Mexico, taken 1883
n.d. 2 prints, with negatives, of
      Guatemala, 1883–91

To the Museo Nacional de México, Mexico City

1907 Un gran vaso de barro con una
      deidad al frente, de procedencia
      mixteco–zapoteca

BEQUESTS

To The British Museum, London

1931, per Cyril Maudslay, 8 items
(presumably these include all his
negatives of archaeological interest,
and his small-format field notes)

To The Royal Geographical Society, London

£500
Half-plate camera, roller-blind shutter,
  Ross lens, dark-slides, etc.
5 × 4 reflex camera
No. 4 Kodak panoramic camera
Various tripods, cases
  (apparently, these were lent by RGS for
  use during various later expeditions,
  but none survive)
5 sketches of Mexico in oils by L. de Forest
4 watercolours by F. Gordon Cumming
  (3 apparently lost, but one never
  delivered, and now in author's
  collection, *pro tem.*)
Large-format field notebooks (not
  mentioned in will)

To The Victoria and Albert Museum, London

'Choice of embroideries and Mexican
  textiles. All Mexican (Cholula) pottery,
  vases and tiles' (about 28 Guatemalan
  huipiles, also Oaxacan *huipiles*, and some
  Spanish and possibly Levantine textiles
  retained)

To The Royal Anthropological Institute, London

£500
Lantern slides

To Cambridge University Museum of Archaeology

£500
All Fijian and South Sea bowls, clubs,
  whales' teeth, ornaments and pottery,
  framed photographs of Central
  American monuments

To Thomas Athol Joyce (for him to allocate to other institutions, perhaps?)

'All photo-prints, maps and papers
  regarding Mexico and Central America
  . . . 4 ornamented gourds from
  Guatemala'

To The Library of Congress, Washington, D.C.

All journals, diaries and correspondence
  of Gouverneur Morris

ALFRED MAUDSLAY'S FAMILY TREE

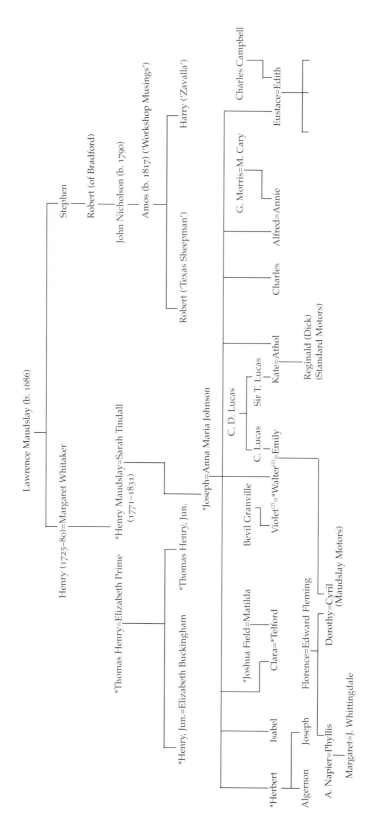

Lawrence Maudslay (b. 1686)

Henry (1725–80)=Margaret Whitaker

Stephen

Robert (of Bradford)

*Henry Maudslay=Sarah Tindall
(1771–1831)

John Nicholson (b. 1790)

Amos (b. 1817) ('Workshop Musings')

Harry ('Zavalla')

Robert ('Texas Sheepman')

*Thomas Henry=Elizabeth Prime

*Thomas Henry, Jun.

*Joseph=Anna Maria Johnson

*Henry, Jun.=Elizabeth Buckingham

C. D. Lucas

C. Lucas   Sir T. Lucas

Bevil Granville

Violet[(2)]=*Walter[(1)]=Emily

Kate=Athol

Reginald (Dick)
(Standard Motors)

Charles

G. Morris=M. Cary

Alfred=Annie

Charles Campbell

Eustace=Edith

*Joshua Field=Matilda

Clara=*Telford

Florence=Edward Fleming

Dorothy=Cyril
(Maudslay Motors)

*Herbert

Isabel

Joseph

A. Napier=Phyllis

Margaret=J. Whittingdale

Algernon

*Partners in Maudslay, Sons & Field

ANNIE MAUDSLAY'S FAMILY TREE

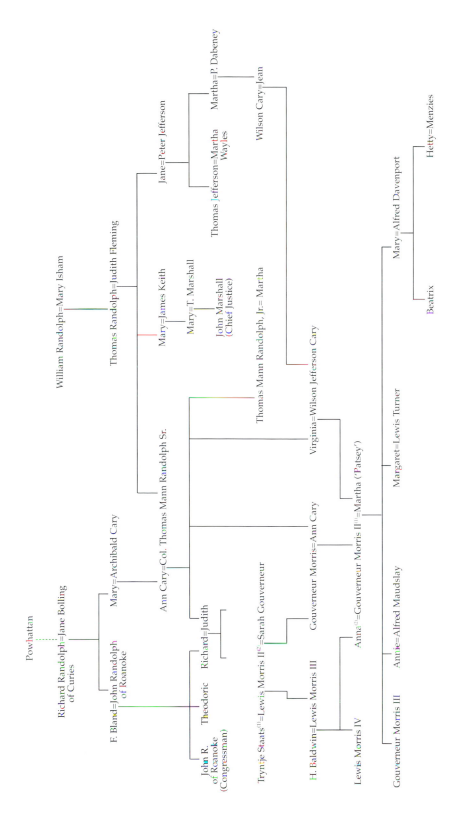

Index

INDEX

INDEX

women in Maudslay's life, 180
he marries Annie Morris, 180
appointed by Peabody Museum to do a
  short season at Copán, 194
large prints of his photographs made for
  Chicago exhibition, 195
buys gold mine in Oaxaca, builds house,
  'Zavaleta', nearby, 214
applies to Carnegie Institution for funding
  work at Monte Albán, 214
receives Mexican authorization, but
  Carnegie doesn't fund, 214–5
bad work already done at Monte Albán by
  L. Batres, 216
is denounced by Batres for his 'vandalic
  character', 217
sells Zavaleta and moves to San Angel, 219
rough estimate of his finances in the 1880s
  and 1890s, 240–1
translation of Bernal Díaz's *Historia
  Verdadera*, 214, 245–7, 253–5
president of Royal Anthropological Institute
  for 1911–12, 247–8
chairman, committee for 18th International
  Congress of Americanists, 248
writes 'Note on . . . Great Temple Enclosure
  of Tenochtitlan', 248–9
receives honorary doctorate from Oxford
  University, 251
sees last volume of *Bernal Díaz* published,
  253
literary style adopted for *Bernal Díaz*, and
  comments on it, 254–5
attempts outline of Mesoamerican
  prehistory, 255–6
tries again to have casts and originals shown
  at V&A or BM, 259–60
spends winter in Egypt, 261
diffusionist views of Sir G. Elliot Smith
  countered by APM, 261–3
prepares abridged version of *Bernal Díaz*,
  263
writes memoir, *Life in the Pacific*, 263
recorded reminiscence of Sir Charles Wyke,
  264–6
receives honorary doctorate from
  Cambridge University, 266–7
awarded Rivers medal by the Royal
  Anthropological Institute, 267
marries Alice Purdon, 267
undertakes translation of Diego de Landa's
  Relación, 267–8
makes last visit to Royal Geographical
  Society, 268
dies, 269
Will, 272–3
Will, discontent with, and Dolly Maudslay's
  revelation, 273–5
Obituaries
  Nature (James Cooper Clark), 270
  Geographical Journal (Anon.), 270
  American Anthropologist (A. M.
    Tozzer), 271
  Man (T. A. Joyce), 272
See also Maudslays, Alfred and Annie
Maudslay, Amos, 299 (ch. 16, note 1)
Maudslay, Anna Maria, 20

Maudslay, Athol
  inventor, 19
  author, 239
Maudslay, Charles, 19
  visit to Guatemala in 1872, 9
Maudslay, Clara, 20
Maudslay, Cyril
  establishes the Maudslay Motor Company,
    240
  marries Dorothy Fleming, 243
Maudslay, Dorothy ('Dolly') Fleming
  author meets her, 7
  she reveals that APM had out-of-wedlock
    child, 273
Maudslay, Eustace, 19
Maudslay, Henry junior
  excavations in Jerusalem, 77
Maudslay, Henry senior
  apprentice, 13
  slide-rest, 14
  screw-cutting lathe, 14
  'table engine', 17
Maudslay, Herbert Charles
  partner in the company, and sportsman, 19
Maudslay, Isabel, 19
Maudslay, Joseph
  inventions, 18–9
Maudslay, Reginald
  establishes the Standard Motor Company,
    239
  prolific inventor, 239
Maudslay, Robert, 299 (ch. 16, note 1)
Maudslay, Thomas Henry, 19
Maudslay, Walter
  senior partner of Maudslay, Sons and Field,
    235
  obtains British rights to Belleville boilers,
    238
Maudslay monument, 18
Maudslay, Sons and Field
  established, 17
  converted into a limited liability company,
    237
  failure of, 238
  APM applies for Receiver for stockholders,
    238
Maudslays, Alfred and Annie
  first meeting, 28
  married, 180
  purchase house in Knightsbridge, 181
  sail to New York; to Chicago for Columbian
    Exhibition, 195–6
  travel to San Francisco, meet J. Goodman,
    196
  sea voyage to San José, Guatemala, 197
  set out from Guatemala with Gorgonio to
    Antigua, 198
  Volcán de Agua, go on to Lake Atitlán and
    Chichicastenango, 200
  difficult ride, reach San Andrés Sajcabajá,
    examine ruins, 201–4
  reach San Miguel Uspantán, examine ruins
    nearby, 205
  after difficult passage of Río Chixoy, reach
    Cobán, 206
  leave with pack-train, reach Copán, greeted
    by Niña Chica, 207

321